THE SKIN OF OUR TEETH
Thornton Wilder's Pulitzer Prize-winning comedy looks at mankind throughout the ages—a groundbreaking view on civilization that brought a daring, unconventional drama to the American stage.

HOME OF THE BRAVE
Arthur Laurents's moving portrayal of a returning Jewish soldier who must deal with the emotional scars of his war experience and the racial intolerance of his society.

ALL MY SONS
Arthur Miller's first dramatic success—a taut, compassionate wartime drama that portrays a factory owner torn between devotion to his family and responsibility to society.

LOST IN THE STARS
Written with Kurt Weill, perhaps Maxwell Anderson's finest work—a musical based on *Cry, the Beloved Country*, Alan Paton's novel about the tragedy of South African racism.

THE MEMBER OF THE WEDDING
Now a theater classic, the original performances by Ethel Waters playing the cook Berenice and Julie Harris as the twelve-year-old Frankie made this work by Carson McCullers one of the greatest plays of the decade.

Selected and introduced by

HENRY HEWES

FAMOUS
AMERICAN PLAYS
OF THE

1940s

Foreword by Gordon Davidson

A LAUREL BOOK
Published by
Dell Publishing
a division of
Bantam Doubleday Dell Publishing Group, Inc.
1540 Broadway
New York, New York 10036

The trademark Laurel® is registered in the U.S. Patent and
Trademark Office.

The trademark Dell® is registered in the U.S. Patent and
Trademark Office.

ISBN: 0-440-32490-4

Printed in Canada

New Dell Edition

September 1988

30 29 28

UNI

Contents

Foreword

When I first scanned the Famous American Plays series, I felt somewhat awed by the task of composing a foreword to all the volumes. The idiosyncratic nature of the series—an attribute I find quite appealing—dictates that each volume not only embody the temperament of a decade but also reflect the spirit of the editor selecting the plays. These editors, an assortment of distinguished critics and theater practitioners including Kenneth Macgowan, Harold Clurman, Henry Hewes, Lee Strasberg, Ted Hoffman, and Robert Marx, define "the best" differently with each decade, each volume, even from play to play.

Yet somehow, despite the bent of the individual editor and with all the regrettable omissions—many choices shaped by the limitation of plays available for publication at the time (where, for example, is arguably the most famous and continuously developing twentieth-century American playwright Neil Simon?)—I still believe that the series comprises a living document to a crucial aspect of this century's American theater: the evolution and shifting emphasis in theme, approach, and even location. American theater has been on the move from Broadway to off-Broadway, from off-Broadway to off-off-Broadway, and finally from the singular concentration in and among the streets of New York to what has become the most exciting transformation of this century—the decentralization of American professional theater to include virtually every state in the union. The plays in these volumes reveal this journey and reflect the incredible changes not only in the theater but in our culture. The process of decentralization has affected and will continue to affect the very nature of the plays being written and the audiences attending them.

In the volumes covering the 1920s through the 1950s, all the plays—except for Eugene O'Neill's *The Moon of the Caribbees*—were Broadway plays. In the 1960s, only two plays included made it to Broadway from off-Broadway and from a regional theater. In the 1970s, only one did, although two others later moved to or reappeared briefly on Broadway. In the 1980s, *all* the plays started either off-Broadway, off-off-Broadway, or in regional theaters around the country, and three of them subsequently have appeared on Broadway.

The shifting emphasis in theme can be seen through the eyes of those who introduce each volume. In the 1920s the theater was considered a scene of "curious conflict" between realism and a freer form of theatricality. In the next decade, attention to the socioeconomic details of an individual's psychological condition became what Harold Clurman called "the most significant difference" between the theater of the twenties and the thirties. What informs many of the plays in that collection is a sense of political alertness married to an almost naive inexperience with actual events. Many of these plays, from *Idiot's Delight* to *End of Summer*, show what Clurman described as *interest* in subject matter rather than any authentic familiarity with it.

In the forties, we find a drama that reveals a new sense of history and a new relationship to it. As the editor of that volume reflects, "History is no longer regarded as a clear and orderly process of cause and effect, but rather as a series of traffic snarls and collisions of many people and forces moving in different directions." Plays written prior to the tragedy at Pearl Harbor give none-too-buried warnings of the imminence of danger, yet all the while they continued to reassure audiences that all would be well as long as everybody maintained faith in American hope and glory. But the theater, like the country, was trying to learn some very hard lessons by sidestepping the mistakes of past generations, on and offstage. *Home of the Brave* and *All My Sons* were both cautionary tales as much as they were realistic studies of the cost and consequences of war. The end of the conflict overseas brought renewed optimism on the boards, a response to victory that led to enthusiastic, if slightly ill-informed, ideas about theatrical innovation. But the audience for early ex-

perimental theater turned out to be far smaller than antici-
pated, although directors like Elia Kazan were making great
and subtle strides in discerning authorial personality—what
editor Henry Hewes calls "subconscious searchings"—in the
work of newly discovered playwrights like Tennessee
Williams.

Lee Strasberg found "numerous important playwrights
[but] fewer important plays in the 1950s." Yet Strasberg,
himself an innovator in modern acting technique, discerns a
uniquely modern thematic perspective in these plays in the
fusing of present, past, and future time and in the revelation
of psychological insight. Strasberg anticipates the founding
of a "new theater" that would "broaden the vision of man on
the stage" by its "awareness and perception of drama in
characters to which drama had never been previously at-
tributed, more subtle and more varied sense of relationship
between people, and a deeper penetration of their motiva-
tion." It was an exciting time for the actor, the first genera-
tion to be influenced by Strasberg's ideas. Unfortunately, too
few of the plays chosen for that volume proved of lasting
importance. Even Strasberg seems to have suspected this—
he ends his introduction, written in 1962, with a poignantly
optimistic look to the impending creation of a repertory
theater at Lincoln Center, under the guiding spirit of then-
President and Mrs. Kennedy.

Thus, as illustrated by the impressive list of plays collected
in these volumes, the plays of the twenties, thirties, forties,
and fifties embody the evolution of the theater on many
levels. In the sixties, however, was *revolution*. A remarkable
transformation had its true beginning in the early 1960s.

With the help of the Ford Foundation and the vision of W.
MacNeill Lowry, Vice President for the Arts, the theater and
theater professionals began to venture out from New York
City—not as they used to, tied to a rubber band that snapped
them back at the end of a tour or summer stock engagement
in time for the "new season on Broadway"—but as pioneers
and adventurers to new lands, eager to set down roots and
create some sense of permanence in cities all across the
United States, and to explore and reflect those communities
onstage. In 1963 the Tyrone Guthrie Theater opened its

doors in Minneapolis, in 1965 the Long Wharf in New Haven, Connecticut. In 1965 ACT traveled from Pittsburgh to Chicago and finally set up a permanent home in San Francisco. In 1964 the Actors Theatre of Louisville opened its doors. In 1963 the Seattle Repertory Theatre began, and in April 1967 the Mark Taper Forum in Los Angeles welcomed audiences for the first time. All in all, since that time 309 theaters have been established in 43 states and 150 cities. They were founded by individual artists, by partners, and by collectives. Some have inherited the structure of not-for-profit corporate entities with boards of directors, some have built buildings, some have established local, regional, and national profiles, and all have together produced an enormous body of work in less than thirty years. The Theatre Communications Group was formed in New York City as a service organization to bind this far-flung community together through meetings, publications, and advocacy.

I felt the excitement of this revolution firsthand; in fact, my career echoes the movement of the times. While when I first began looking for work in the theater in 1958 (I was still in the army), I thought about the possibility of finding work outside of New York, it was *in* New York that my life in theater had really begun: seeing Laurence Olivier in that famous double bill *Oedipus the Critic* (that memorable offstage howl); seeing the Lunts, Laurette Taylor, Gertrude Lawrence, Lee J. Cobb, Ray Bolger, John Gielgud, Judith Anderson, Melvyn Douglas, Paul Muni, Ralph Richardson. What performers! But, at that time, my options outside New York were limited. There was summer stock; there was college theater (my dad taught and directed at Brooklyn College). There was Nina Vance and the Alley Theatre in Houston; Margo Jones in Dallas; Zelda Fichandler at the Arena Stage in Washington, D.C.; the Cleveland Playhouse under K. Elmo Lowe; and a couple of theaters in San Francisco, including The Theatre of the Golden Hind and Herbert Blau and Jules Irving's Actors Workshop. And that was about it.

I felt compelled to start in New York. I chose a position as an apprentice stage manager at the American Shakespeare Festival. I worked with and under the mentorship of John Houseman, Jack Landau, Jean Rosenthal, Bernard Gersten,

Marc Blitzstein, David Hays, Dorothy Jeakins. It was as an assistant to Houseman that, finally, in 1964, I made my way to Los Angeles, where John was directing a production of *King Lear* starring Morris Carnovsky for The Theatre Group, a professional theater on the campus of UCLA. Three years later I opened the Mark Taper Forum, a 750-seat thrust stage in the Los Angeles Music Center. In April 1987 we celebrated the twentieth anniversary of our continuous production of plays: world and American premieres, classic revivals, young people's theater, and a host of developmental programs. The Taper is one of a network of theaters, a *family* of theaters that, though situated differently, still have many similarities: in structure, in attempts at creating subscription audiences, in nurturing artists, in revealing the life of the community they serve.

The regional theater movement began as an alternative to the commercial pressures of Broadway and as an alternative to living in New York City. It therefore initially concerned itself with the presentation of classics, modern and ancient, that were done commercially only sporadically. Dedicated to the development of companies of actors, designers, directors, these theaters preserved and reinterpreted the living library: Shakespeare, Shaw, Molière, Ibsen, Pirandello, the Greeks, as well as the American giants of the thirties, forties, and fifties. In fact, many of the plays reproduced in this series were and are the staples of regional theater programming. Audiences were willing to go to a theater with a recognizable, and to some extent familiar, list of plays performed and produced well. Actors and directors and designers searched for ways to make these plays come alive for contemporary audiences. These same audiences tended to shy away from new plays or unknown authors, unless they had the imprimatur, the stamp of approval, of a Broadway success (or at least a decent enough run on Broadway). Work on the "great plays" gave actors and directors a chance to stretch themselves and refine their skills (voice, movement, diction).

Then, to borrow from a book popular in the sixties, something happened. Concurrent with the social and cultural revolution with which we are all so familiar, Broadway really began to decline. (The "fabulous invalid," as it was known, began to look terminal.) Simultaneously, New York became a less hospitable or even challenging environment for artistic creativity. The reasons for this have been documented; they include soaring production costs, escalating ticket prices, urban blight, urban flight, expense account theatergoing and the loss of the regular audience; competition for attention and talent from TV and movies; and, to varying degrees, the usurpation by other media (including popular music) of the content, subject matter, and even form that was previously the territory and province of the theater.

And in the sixties the artists took to the streets, lofts, basements, churches, and parks to write the plays that began to speak of their horror, outrage, and pain over war, assassination, and the gradual corruption of the spirit exemplified by Saran Wrap and defense budgets. As Edward Parone wrote in his introduction to a collection of plays entitled *Collision Course*, these plays were "written on impulse in short bursts that seem to want to impinge directly upon their audiences without the barrier of intellect or manners or preconceptions." And in turn the regional theater began to turn its attention to the presentation of new plays (note: some, like the Mark Taper Forum and the New York Public Theater, did this from the beginning), and with this came the creation of a system for developing new theater pieces through commissions, readings, laboratories, workshops, festivals, conferences, and the use of small venues (second spaces) as homes for venturesome work.

Like many revolutions, these changes grew of necessity; only in retrospect do we see their far-reaching effects. Not only did these developments allow audiences throughout the United States to participate in the adventure and excitement of creating and discovering new works of art, but they changed or reversed the flow of material and talent (plays, playwrights, actors, directors, and designers) both out of New York and back. Broadway is no longer the generator of material and the source of personnel for the theater. It is a grand and heady as well as pain-inducing receiver of the fruits of theater from elsewhere—traditionally London and now more and more the rest of the United States.

The decentralization of the American theater is the most

challenging and enduring transformation of the last three decades. It's both the best and worst thing that could have happened, because it also makes it that much more difficult to see, taste, judge, be influenced by, and know one another's work, and it puts an extra pressure on the need to share and find some ground upon which artists and audience have common experiences. The lack of a center or single pulse makes the gift of a collection like this one, a compilation of all our work, that much more valuable.

The decentralization also has brought to the surface a whole new set of problems, questions, esthetics, and challenges for the theater of the future. First and foremost is the need for a belief in the theater as an art form rather than as a business that produces a product which is either a success (a hit that makes money) or a failure (a flop and a financial disaster). The theater searches for survival as an institution, with all of the responsibilities an institution has to itself and its community. It serves a community and must be aware of the cultural, ethnic, and social diversity of its artists and its audience. It can speak to the specifics of a city, state, region, and to a nation. It can give voice to the needs of the community as well as reflect the hopes and aspirations of a wide cross-section of its population. It can be a place that nurtures, trains, and develops talent. It can nurture the soul.

Some challenges are immediate, even practical. These resident regional theaters are housed in buildings as diverse in size and shape as their location. We have birthed in this same time period thrust stages, arena stages, small theaters, black boxes, *and very few* conventional proscenium theaters. Our writers are therefore exploring ways to create new forms of realism, naturalism, expressionism, and theatricality that let us know we are in a theater and not in front of a movie or television screen.

Other challenges are intellectual or spiritual. The "death of Freud" and the journey through the Jungian jungle may lead us to a more mythic search to satisfy our spiritual hunger and needs. The desire to better come to grips with our political and social realities can lead writers to explorations and insights unattainable on *Nightline*, but possible also because of the new access to information that even Johnny

Carson's nightly monologue provides.

Language and metaphor, technology in the service of (revealing, not dehumanizing) the individual, and acting that examines both the truth of human behavior and the extraordinary capacity of humans to perform with style, skill, and bravery—these are the possibilities that challenge the leadership of this network of theaters today in the United States.

Finally, the theater has to face its relationship and responsibility to the changing multicultural essence of this country. The challenges of nontraditional casting, of cross-cultural writing and nonhomogeneous audiences are the big questions for the future. These volumes of famous American plays, impressive and important as they are, still reflect a harsh reality: in over seven decades, the collection contains only two black playwrights, no Hispanic or Asian-American writers, and only three women. These plays therefore reflect a theater in desperate need to get in touch with its own heart and the heartbeat of the society in which it dwells. One can only imagine what future volumes will contain and what extraordinary leaps of imagination, heart, and mind they will reveal. One hopes the series will continue long into the twenty-first century as a tribute to a theater that reflects a diversity of ideas, a wealth of voices, and a fervent belief in the centrality of the art to all our lives.

—Gordon Davidson

Introduction

"If anybody tries to tell you the past, they're charlatans!" writes Thornton Wilder in *The Skin of Our Teeth*, all of which, I suppose, eminently qualifies me for the job of making some sense of our theatre in the forties. But in his play, Mr. Wilder himself attempts to tell the past by confusing it with the present, which method seems to have more merit now than it did in 1942 when that play opened to bewildered audiences. For history is no longer regarded as a clear and orderly procession of cause and effect, but rather as a series of traffic snarls and collisions of many people and forces moving in different directions. There may be an element of truth in almost any generalization one may make about the past, but there is also an element of untruth and deceit about it too.

Perhaps the way to avoid as much untruth as possible is to look back in disorder at the period that began after the thirties and is cut off arbitrarily before the fifties. There was for some of us around the beginning of the forties a mood best caught by Lorenz Hart and William Saroyan. In 1937 the great lyricist had written that since you could not be sure about any of the big things in life the thing to do was "just be sure someone loves you; be sure you love with all your might; that's the way I'd rather be right." But in the next three years he qualified this philosophy, first in 1938 by recognizing it as "such a juvenile fancy," then in 1940 by treating love as a sexual sport indulged in by

friends as long as the magic lasted. The latter came in
Pal Joey, which brought a new degree of tough-minded
humor to the musical comedy stage. If John O'Hara's
characters were slightly unsavory, they were also truer
than those we had been getting in the conventional
musical-comedy fairy tale. It was still a fairy tale, as
all good musical comedies should be, but the characters
were as they are in life, instead of being those pretty
and virtuous people theatregoers like to pretend they
are.

It was a sort of realism that had never been popular
with musical comedy audiences, who had spurned *The
Threepenny Opera* when it was first presented in 1932,
and while *Pal Joey* was hailed by many, it caused
Brooks Atkinson to ask, "Can you draw sweet water
from a foul well?" This reaction, shared by the majority of the public, indicated perhaps that 1940 theatregoers resented anything that disturbed their idealized
picture of life.

In the drama, too, Americans wanted more comforting than disturbance. Any dream, if sincere and well
intentioned, was all we needed. In 1939, Saroyan's *The
Time of Your Life* had presented us with Joe, a semi-
paralyzed character who sat in a bar and asked a prosti-
tute, "What's the dream, Kitty Duval?" And then when
the dream turned out to be a kind husband, he inter-
vened with the help of a braggart character named Kit
Carson to make the dream come true. It was suspected
by some that the bountiful Joe was Roosevelt, that
Kitty Duval was the abused spirit of liberty, and that
Kit Carson was the old pioneer spirit. And in an amus-
ing article Clare Boothe asked prophetically if the gun
that didn't work when Joe needed it was not perhaps
a criticism of F.D.R.'s armament program. While
Saroyan refused to confirm the suggestion that his play
was allegorical, another playwright, Philip Barry, sat
down and wrote an out-and-out allegory titled *Liberty
Jones.* In this play, produced in 1941, Liberty Jones is
a sick girl threatened by the Three Shirts (fascism,

nazism, and communism). During the course of the play she regains her health with the aid of Tom, an American boy who goes overseas and dies for her. While *Liberty Jones* was too mystifying to be successful, its pattern was a synthesis of the thinking employed by almost all the playwrights writing in the early forties. Recognize the threat of the militant invaders and be prepared to die for the preservation of the democratic ideal.

But in 1940 it was no longer possible to pretend that war was glorious or that it could permanently settle anything. It was a measure taken reluctantly, and glory had to be found in the courage with which we accepted an unpleasant task and in the vague hope for a better future. In 1941 Helen Hayes, appearing in Maxwell Anderson's *Candle in the Wind* had the comforting line, "Through all the history of the world there have been many wars between men and beasts. But the beasts have always lost, and the men have always won." On the other hand the prize play of the 1940-41 season was Lillian Hellman's *Watch on the Rhine*, in which she gently "shook us out of the magnolias" to urge our awareness of the danger of fascism.

And this is the way it was with the more sober plays before Pearl Harbor—warnings of danger, the reawakening of the ideals of our American heritage, and the reassuring conviction that all would be well if the good people trusted the goodness in their hearts.

After Pearl Harbor, in the years when the war became for many people a series of communiqués read with the same sort of interest and satisfaction we had hitherto received from the ball scores, the theatrical journalists from time to time called the public's attention to the fact that some people were dying and suffering, not for the rest of us, but simply because they had been picked for the job. The playwrights suggested that men in this position found a new kind of ennobling responsibility toward their comrades in arms.

The most memorable play of the war years was *The Skin of Our Teeth*. It is only obliquely a war play as it treats in general the problem of the survival of the race after any world catastrophe. Furthermore it avoids false heroics and uses a seemingly facetious approach to both the theatre and the subject matter. It begins with a newsreel which kids us into thrusting the A & P world of the present back through the history of man, and Sabina's first words ridicule the conventional nineteenth-century play form, which she immediately leaves to tell us what she really thinks about things. We are then made conscious of both the old-fashioned world of living up to external appearances and the more modern subconscious world of recognizing disreputable realities. ("We're all just as wicked as we can be" is Mr. Wilder's one-sentence summary of Freud.) Throughout the play one world keeps challenging the other, just as Wilder's content challenges the form he is obliged to put it in. Everything in the play is seen in duality—art and materialistic living, pessimism and optimism, marriage and adultery, the incredibly great progress of mankind and the pitifully small number of lessons we have learned. Mr. Wilder loves literature and philosophy, but he kids them too by arranging them in a ridiculous procession and putting words in the mouth of Aristotle he never said at all.

In performance, the whole business went off like a frantic relay race, with Tallulah Bankhead running the anchor leg. Audiences never got comfortable. They kept trying to figure out the whole crazy business. The antic disposition was so heavily laid on that the author's sarcasm was lost. The most effective moments were the fortune-teller's speech, spoken by Florence Reed, who had the advantage of being allowed to stand still, and the moment in the last act where the incurably selfish Sabina quietly agrees to share her bouillon cubes.

While *The Skin of Our Teeth* registered 359 performances on Broadway, in a *succès de curiosité,* it failed to win the Drama Critics Circle award, which went to Sidney Kingsley's *The Patriots.* However, it did win the Pulitzer Prize and in 1955 was sent to Europe as a sample of American theatre at its best. In my opinion it still awaits an ideal production.

The most memorable performance of the war years came from Laurette Taylor in an autobiographical play by a new young writer named Tennessee Williams. Titled *The Glass Menagerie,** it seemed less a play than a character sketch, but that fact constitutes old-fashioned criticism, now that we have had such similar structure in *The Member of the Wedding,* and *I Am a Camera.* If ever a performance could make the listing of reservations captious, it was Miss Taylor's. She caught the pitiful pretenses of a once elegant Southern lady whose husband had left her to bring up her two children in poverty. But she mixed this with the stubborn determination of a woman who insisted upon dreaming better things for herself and her own even though she and everyone else could see the evidence of their impracticality. Her eye was undaunted as she joked that her missing husband "worked for the telephone company and fell in love with long distance." Her obsessive concentration on pushing her children ahead was so complete that there was nothing left for self-pity. It also made each speech an act of desperation.

The character Miss Taylor caught was not quite the character the author wrote (for that, listen to his own reading on the Caedmon record). It was so true to *her* vision of the woman that she even altered some of the lines. To this day I can never see a performance of *The Glass Menagerie* without dying twice when two of her alterations (not in the printed version) fail to materialize. The first came at the end of Act II, when in

---

*Available in *Six Great Modern Plays,* a Dell Laurel Edition.

reply to her daughter's question, "What shall I wish for, Mother?" Miss Taylor replied, "Wish for . . . happiness and . . . good fortune. Happiness and . . . just a little bit of good fortune." The second alteration came in the last act, when Miss Taylor futilely tried to impress the gentleman caller that her daughter was "domesticated."

The greatness of that performance somewhat obscured our realization that we now had a new playwright of first rank, a man who wrote out of his innermost anxieties, who could treat sordid truths with elegant euphemisms that made the truth all the more ironic.

During this same period, the theatre of entertainment flourished, and one comedy, *Arsenic and Old Lace* by Joseph Kesselring, which turned horror into absurdity, is probably a classic. Who will ever forget the moment when the kindly old ladies look into the window box at a substituted corpse, and instead of being shocked at the murder, exclaim, "Why, that man is an impostor!" At a time when half the world was engaged in legalized killing, this comedy which pitted vicious murder against benign murder was just the thing.

That other form of theatre entertainment, the musical comedy, underwent quite a change in form from 1940 to 1945. The aforementioned *Pal Joey* was not the only innovation. *Lady in the Dark* built its show around psychoanalysis and took it seriously. And *Cabin in the Sky* was a Negro musical in which the Negroes were primitive but not Uncle Toms. I can still hear Dooley Wilson serenading Ethel Waters with "My Old Virginia Home on the River Nile." John Latouche's lyrics had a fine, humorous bite in this one, and his "Taking a Chance on Love" furnished Ethel Waters with the material for a showstopper.

Then in 1942 the ballet choreographer moved into the theatre with a vengeance. His presence created a need for bigger stories that would justify big artistic dances. This led to a musical version of Lynn Riggs's folk play, *Green Grow the Lilacs. Oklahoma!* as Rodgers and Hammerstein called it, became the prototype for a series of heavily laden musicals which combined psychological ballet sequences, soliloquies in song, and a folk-art background. While some complained that the fun of the old-fashioned musical comedy was disappearing, no one could help but admire the improved dancing and be engrossed with the more substantial plots.

Most musicals tried to take our minds off the war, but Irving Berlin's sentimental *This Is the Army* gave us two or three of the best war songs, including "I Left My Heart at the Stage Door Canteen." Oscar Hammerstein, III, changed the cigar factory of Bizet's *Carmen* to a contemporary war plant background and stunningly demonstrated that understandable lyrics and Negro vitality could make opera into first class theatre. And in *Early to Bed,* George Marion, Jr., and Fats Waller toasted the wartime civilian with "I'll Be Happy When the Nylons Bloom Again."

When the tide of war had turned, playwrights began looking ahead to the problem of the returning service man and to the post-war world. As far back as 1943 Lillian Hellman's *The Searching Wind* had presented a stirring final minute in which a diplomat's son returns and finds that the frivolity of his parents and people like them permitted the war to happen. He tells them, "I love this place. And I don't want any more fancy fooling around with it. I don't want any more of Father's mistakes for any reason, good or bad, or yours, Mother, because I think they do it harm. . . . I'm ashamed of both of you, and that's the truth. . . . I don't like losing my leg. . . . But everybody's welcome to it as long as it means a little something and helps to bring us out some place. All right. I've said enough. I love you both. Let's have a drink."

This attitude of "let's not repeat the mistakes of the past" became increasingly common in the theatre from

1945 to 1947. It is a part of two of the plays in this book.

In the first, Arthur Laurents's *Home of the Brave*, we have a play about the soldier's coming readjustment to an unsatisfactory civilian world and, more important still, his facing up to the truth about his war experience. In form it is the sort of play that has become an increasingly popular stereotype for American drama. Someone in trouble reviews the reasons for his trouble to find something he has not been facing up to. And at the end of the play he simply resolves to face up to his problem. Because Mr. Laurents introduced the psychiatrist himself and had the answer up his sleeve all the time, some critics found the play too clinical. However, *Home of the Brave* contains the driving theme which seems to motivate most of this young writer's work. It is the acceptance of our imperfections in a society where everyone expects the ideal. The doctor understands this but Coney does not. Thus in his second scene the playwright puts the soldiers in a serious situation which they resolve childishly and in accordance with the perfection expected from them by an imaginary ideal society.

Mr. Laurents also treats the question of anti-semitism in an interesting way. Coney is too sensitive about being insulted for his religion, just as the average unthinking American is too insensitive about it. Mr. Laurents implies that it is a two-way disease and that Coney must cure himself before he can cure his persecutors. By making this problem a lesser one than Coney's guilt about being a coward, Mr. Laurents puts things in proportion. And he suggests that the returning soldier should be more realistic in his post-war expectations from his country.

All My Sons was the second-produced play by another young playwright, Arthur Miller. In it a returning soldier refuses to take an understanding view of his own father's imperfection, with the result that the father shoots himself. The play has the virtue of pinpointing and challenging many of the attitudes that have become part of the American way—our fairy tale approach to the blackest realities, the pressure on everyone to be a success by making money, and the putting of self-interest ahead of responsibility to society. On the latter point, Mr. Miller makes it clear that the horror of Joe Keller's causing someone more innocent than himself to suffer for his crime is insignificant compared to his irresponsibility to "a universe of people."

The play is constructed with terrifying efficiency, with all of Act I and half of Act II devoted to preparation. Then, when Joe Keller hears that the son of the man who knows the truth about him is arriving in town, a tragic disintegration begins, in which Joe's true disassociation from society reveals itself. His suicide comes only after he learns that his second son had killed himself when he heard of his father's crime. Until this revelation Joe had felt that his dead second son would have forgiven him on the grounds that lying, fraud, and war profiteering are an essential part of American big business.

All My Sons won the Drama Critics Circle Prize and later started a hot controversy when it was sent abroad to spread an "unfavorable" view of American life. Oddly enough the Soviet Union removed the play from their stages because the sons' disapproval of their father's violation of ethics carried as its corollary the non-Marxist assumption that the norm of capitalist behavior is ethical. Like Tennessee Williams, the second new playwright of first rank to appear in the forties had to wait for another success before his stature was fully recognized.

From 1945 to 1948 there was a burst of creative enthusiasm for a new and better kind of theatre. No one seemed to have much of an idea of what this new theatre should be, but the words "experimental" and "repertory" were tossed around with innocent reverence.

However, the world's two foremost directors of epic theatre, Germany's Bertolt Brecht and Erwin Piscator, were unable to attract any large audience or much critical approval for their offerings here. For me, however, Brecht's *Galileo,* with Charles Laughton, constituted the most exciting use of the stage we had in the forties, with the possible exception of the modern dance theatre productions of Martha Graham and José Limon. The latter's *Moor's Pavanne* told the Othello story with a subtlety, economy, and beauty that no production of the Shakespeare play ever seems to match.

Since the audience for such "experimental" theatre turned out to be a small one, the creative enthusiasts tried the other half of their campaign slogan, repertory. In 1947 we had a visit by an Old Vic all-star repertory company, which offered us a thrilling performance by Laurence Olivier as Oedipus. In this role the great actor seemed agonizedly to hold his soul out in front of him, and his shriek when he discovered his fate shook the rafters of our universe.

The impact of this company's many fine productions spurred interest in an American Repertory Theatre, which was formed the next season and whose presentation of the classics was worthily but unexcitingly done. It was clear that for repertory to compete with the regular Broadway shows, it would have to at least equal their impact.

Again, in the spring of 1948, a superior company of English actors, headed by John Gielgud, paid us a visit. Their perfectly styled performance of *The Importance of Being Earnest* was so brilliant that we all realized that an American repertory theatre would never be able to make the grade if it tried to imitate a style that was not native to its own way of living.

Then in one twelve-month period along came the

two most famous plays of the forties. The first was Tennessee Williams's *A Streetcar Named Desire,* in which the bestial but burningly alive Stanley Kowalski destroys the civilized but nymphomaniacal Blanche DuBois. It caught poetically the brutal and yet natural forces under the fragile façade of Southern life.

The second was Arthur Miller's *Death of a Salesman,* a more manufactured play, which attempted to be "a tragedy seen not through the portals of Delphi but in the blue flame of a hot-water heater." While audiences were impressed by the drama of a man destroyed by society, Mr. Miller himself had intended that his protagonist, Willy Loman, kill himself exultantly. It was to be a death caused not by his blindness to his own situation but by his awareness of separation from values that will endure. Mr. Miller writes,

"Willy's sin was to have committed himself so completely to the counterfeits of dignity and the false coinage embodied in his idea of success that he can prove his existence only by bestowing 'power' on his posterity, a power deriving from the sale of his last asset, himself, for the price of his insurance policy."

But almost as important as what Mr. Miller had to say, was his method of saying it. *Death of a Salesman* brought in the past as it is alive in the present (not to be confused with the already familiar flashback technique, which merely helps explain the present). In this, Mr. Miller owes a considerable debt to his scene designer, Jo Mielziner, who ingeniously and daringly devised methods whereby these scenes between Willy and his own recall could occur without interrupting the flow of the "real" action.

Both of these plays were directed by Elia Kazan, whose method of direction is to get into the final result more of what he believes the author's personality to be than the author has put into the original script. In Kazan's productions the impact of a play's action tends to gain in extroverted force, but the author's intent tends to be somewhat obscured.

During the last half of the forties it became increasingly clear that the old "front proscenium arch" type of stage was in conflict with the needs of our playwrights. The neatly shaped artificial play was losing its effectiveness and the authors were concerned with subconscious searchings. It was now desirable for the audience to feel closer to the events onstage. Eugene O'Neill's *The Iceman Cometh,* as produced in 1947 on a conventional stage, seemed tedious with the actors laboring to blow up each scene with "acting." It was not until it was revived in the round eleven years later that the play really succeeded.

The same applies to Tennessee Williams's *Summer and Smoke,* which began in the round at Margo Jones's theatre in Dallas but then was transferred to a conventional Broadway playhouse. It disappointed the majority of the critics and it was not even included as one of the ten to be published in abridged form in *The Best Plays of 1948-1949.* Yet *Summer and Smoke* is a beautiful story, better constructed than any of Mr. Williams's other plays, and it finally came into its own when revived in the round in 1952.

The Member of the Wedding was adapted by Carson McCullers from her own novel in the summer of 1948 as she sat across a kitchen table from Tennessee Williams, who was writing *Summer and Smoke.* It, too, requires an intimacy most Broadway playhouses lack, and it was fortunate that it was able to play at the Empire Theatre, which despite its old-fashioned stage, was, before it gave way to an office building, the most intimate of the New York theatres. For in this play the audience must feel right in the kitchen with Berenice and the children. While the story seems to be about Frankie and her growth from childhood into adolescence, it is really held together by Berenice, the cook, who experiences the play's sadness more deeply than the children. The intense performance of Julie Harris as Frankie elevated her to overnight stardom

and brought public attention to an organization called
Actors Studio in which she had developed. (In the
fifties, under the direction of three old Group Theatre
members, Cheryl Crawford, Elia Kazan, and Lee
Strasberg, Actors Studio was to become the single most
important factor in revitalizing our theatre.) But it
was Ethel Waters's great portrayal as the cook that
remains most memorable—first at the end of the second
act as she took John Henry on her lap to sing a hymn
she herself had brought to the play, "His Eye Is on
the Sparrow." And then at the final curtain as she sits
alone wearing some handed-down, moth-eaten furs and
sings the hymn to comfort herself at the loss of her
husband, John Henry, and the childhood companion-
ship of Frankie.

In the period of post-war idealism, the theatre of
entertainment was affected too. More and more, audiences were demanding that even their comedies be
spiked with some underlying seriousness. *Anna Lu-
casta, Born Yesterday,* and *Mr. Roberts* all used gags
and farcical situations, but their characters were rec-
ognizably real and there was a lesson to be learned
from each story.

The musical comedy, which had already changed
from chorus cuties to intense-visaged ballet dancers,
and from flatly romantic boys and girls to more so-
phisticated and complex leading characters, now acquired a social consciousness. There was *South Pacific,* with Rodgers and Hammerstein's "You've Got
to Be Taught" attacking anti-miscegenation; *Finian's
Rainbow,* whose plot involved metamorphosing a vicious Dixiecrat senator into a Negro so that he could
see how it felt to be discriminated against; and there
was *Love Life,* which attempted to examine marriage
in the light of the entire social and political history of
America. Of course not all musicals were that ambi-
tious. Irving Berlin, Cole Porter, and Frank Loesser
contented themselves with such fun-musicals as *Annie*

Get Your Gun, which featured Ethel Merman singing what was to become Broadway's permanent theme song, "There's No Business Like Show Business"; *Kiss Me, Kate,* with its melody-rich score; and *Where's Charley?* which gave Ray Bolger the showstopper of all showstoppers, "Once in Love with Amy." But some composers yearned to write musicals that would be serious both in form and in content. Kurt Weill and Langston Hughes transformed Elmer Rice's *Street Scene* into something that resembled opera, with arias and quartets. However, they also included rhythm numbers such as "Wrapped in a Ribbon and Tied with a Bow." While the latter was strictly a musical-comedy number, it fitted the situation perfectly. Marc Blitzstein went a step further in *Regina,* based on Lillian Hellman's *The Little Foxes,* where he included partially sung dialogue, and for the most part succeeded in his objective of keeping the audience from being conscious of where speech left off and singing began. And composer-dramatist Gian-Carlo Menotti invaded Broadway with *The Medium,* a very dramatic sort of contemporary opera. The idea behind these three projects was to make serious musical works exciting and immediate enough to interest a lively theatre audience wider than just the opera house aficionados.

A fourth example of this trend was the musical *Lost in the Stars.* Beyond its beauty as a piece of work (to appreciate its full effect, listen to the recording of the score, which composer Kurt Weill's widow, Lotte Lenya, considers to have been his finest work after *The Threepenny Opera* and *Mahoganny*), it amalgamates the organic wholeness of opera and the dramatic focus of a play.

Unfortunately, the Broadway production was not ideal. It suffered from a pictorial staging and the "singer's diction" used by the performers. The need was for singers with the technique that comes from musical study but with the acting ability to sing in character. Thus it is that the best recording of the title song was made by Walter Huston, who could hardly sing at all.

Nevertheless, *Lost in the Stars* is, in my opinion, Maxwell Anderson's finest work. Mr. Anderson in his plays often overwhelmed them with rhetoric. Yet, here, because he was adapting someone else's story (Alan Paton's *Cry, the Beloved Country*) he suppressed his own effusiveness and poured his sentiment into the lyrics. And in lyrics the very talents that tended to defeat some of his plays became virtues.

Lost in the Stars is a musical that will not really come into its own until it is produced on the open stage, which is the stage of the future. Why is that stage not prevalent now, ten years after the appearance of so many works that cry out for it? The reasons are probably economic. First of all, in a time when office buildings can produce so much more income than a theatre, which is used only two and a half hours a day, no one has been able to afford to build a new theatre in New York. And secondly, our theatre owners lack vision and prefer to renovate theatres backward to the nostalgic past.

In the forties the stifling effect of faulty economics and unimaginative theatre owners was felt in another way. The increased pressure upon the producer, the playwright, and the performer for a smash hit, even at the cost of the artistic integrity of a production, had by the end of the forties transformed the theatre into a much more neurotic place than it had been at the beginning of the decade. One symptom of this was the already mentioned tendency of plays to be less conclusive and formal. Another was the growth to an absurd degree of out-of-town revision of plays, made to meet the objections of dozens of people who cared less about what the play meant to the author than what the play meant to them. And finally, unsure audiences now cautiously waited for the critics' verdict before deciding that they had or had not experienced a satisfactory evening. We had certainly moved forward in our ability to express complexity and to face reality, but we had lost much of the gaiety and magic that attended our earlier plays. We had gone, perhaps, from too carefree to too careful.

HENRY HEWES

THE SKIN
OF OUR TEETH

A Play in Three Acts

by Thornton Wilder

First production, November 18, 1942, at the
Plymouth Theatre, New York, with the following cast:

ANNOUNCER, *Morton DaCosta*
SABINA, *Tallulah Bankhead*
MR. FITZPATRICK, *E. G. Marshall*
MRS. ANTROBUS, *Florence Eldridge*
DINOSAUR, *Remo Buffano*
MAMMOTH, *Andrew Ratousheff*
TELEGRAPH BOY, *Dickie Van Patten*
GLADYS, *Frances Heflin*
HENRY, *Montgomery Clift*
MR. ANTROBUS, *Fredric March*
DOCTOR, *Blair Davies*
PROFESSOR, *Ralph Kellard*
JUDGE, *Joseph Smiley*
HOMER, *Ralph Cullinan*
MISS E. MUSE, *Edith Faversham*
MISS T. MUSE, *Emily Lorraine*
MISS M. MUSE, *Eva Mudge Nelson*
USHER, *Stanley Prager*
USHER, *Harry Clark*
GIRL ⎫
GIRL ⎭ *Drum Majorettes* ⎰ *Elizabeth Scott*
⎱ *Patricia Riordan*
FORTUNE TELLER, *Florence Reed*
CHAIR PUSHER, *Earl Sydnor*
CHAIR PUSHER, *Carroll Clark*

CONVEENER, *Stanley Weede*
CONVEENER, *Seumas Flynn*
CONVEENER, *Aubrey Fassett*
CONVEENER, *Stanley Prager*
CONVEENER, *Harry Clark*
BROADCAST OFFICIAL, *Morton DaCosta*
DEFEATED CANDIDATE, *Joseph Smiley*
MR. TREMAYNE, *Ralph Kellard*
HESTER, *Eulabelle Moore*
IVY, *Viole Dean*
FRED BAILEY, *Stanley Prager*

ACT ONE *Home, Excelsior, New Jersey.*
ACT TWO *Atlantic City Boardwalk.*
ACT THREE *Home, Excelsior, New Jersey.*

Act one

A projection screen in the middle of the curtain. The first lantern slide: the name of the theatre, and the words: NEWS EVENTS OF THE WORLD. An ANNOUNCER'S *voice is heard.*

ANNOUNCER. The management takes pleasure in bringing to you—The News Events of the World:
[*Slide of the sun appearing above the horizon.*]
Freeport, Long Island.
The sun rose this morning at 6:32 a.m. This gratifying event was first reported by Mrs. Dorothy Stetson of Freeport, Long Island, who promptly telephoned the Mayor.
The Society for Affirming the End of the World at once went into a special session and postponed the arrival of that event for TWENTY-FOUR HOURS. All honor to Mrs. Stetson for her public spirit.
New York City:
[*Slide of the front doors of the theatre in which this play is playing; three cleaning* WOMEN *with mops and pails.*]
The X Theatre. During the daily cleaning of this theatre a number of lost objects were collected as usual by Mesdames Simpson, Pateslewski, and Moriarty.
Among these objects found today was a wedding

ring, inscribed: To Eva from Adam. Genesis II:18.
The ring will be restored to the owner or owners,
if their credentials are satisfactory.

Tippehatchee, Vermont:

[*Slide representing a glacier.*]

The unprecedented cold weather of this summer
has produced a condition that has not yet been satis-
factorily explained. There is a report that a wall of
ice is moving southward across these counties. The
disruption of communications by the cold wave now
crossing the country has rendered exact information
difficult, but little credence is given to the rumor
that the ice had pushed the Cathedral of Montreal
as far as St. Albans, Vermont.

For further information see your daily papers.

Excelsior, New Jersey:

[*Slide of a modest suburban home.*]

The home of Mr. George Antrobus, the inventor
of the wheel. The discovery of the wheel, following
so closely on the discovery of the lever, has centered
the attention of the country on Mr. Antrobus of this
attractive suburban residence district. This is his
home, a commodious seven-room house, conveniently
situated near a public school, a Methodist church,
and a firehouse; it is right handy to an A. and P.

[*Slide of* MR. ANTROBUS *on his front steps, smiling and
lifting his straw hat. He holds a wheel.*]

Mr. Antrobus, himself. He comes of very old stock
and has made his way up from next to nothing.

It is reported that he was once a gardener, but left
that situation under circumstances that have been
variously reported.

Mr. Antrobus is a veteran of foreign wars, and bears
a number of scars, front and back.

[*Slide of* MRS. ANTROBUS, *holding some roses.*]

This is Mrs. Antrobus, the charming and gracious

president of the Excelsior Mothers' Club.

Mrs. Antrobus is an excellent needlewoman; it is she who invented the apron on which so many interesting changes have been rung since.

[*Slide of the* FAMILY *and* SABINA.]

Here we see the Antrobuses with their two children, Henry and Gladys, and friend. The friend in the rear, is Lily Sabina, the maid.

I know we all want to congratulate this typical American family on its enterprise. We all wish Mr. Antrobus a successful future. Now the management takes you to the interior of this home for a brief visit.

Curtain rises. Living room of a commuter's home. SABINA—*straw-blonde, over-rouged—is standing by the window back center, a feather duster under her elbow.*

SABINA. Oh, oh, oh! Six o'clock and the master not home yet.

Pray God nothing serious has happened to him crossing the Hudson River. If anything happened to him, we would certainly be inconsolable and have to move into a less desirable residence district.

The fact is I don't know what'll become of us. Here it is the middle of August and the coldest day of the year. It's simply freezing; the dogs are sticking to the sidewalks; can anybody explain that? No.

But I'm not surprised. The whole world's at sixes and sevens, and why the house hasn't fallen down about our ears long ago is a miracle to me.

[*A fragment of the right wall leans precariously over the stage.* SABINA *looks at it nervously and it slowly rights itself.*]

Every night this same anxiety as to whether the master will get home safely: whether he'll bring home anything to eat. In the midst of life we are in the midst of death, a truer word was never said.

[*The fragment of scenery flies up into the lofts.* SABINA *is struck dumb with surprise, shrugs her shoulders and starts dusting* MR. ANTROBUS' *chair, including the under side.*]

Of course, Mr. Antrobus is a very fine man, an excellent husband and father, a pillar of the church, and has all the best interests of the community at heart. Of course, every muscle goes tight every time he passes a policeman; but what I think is that there are certain charges that ought not to be made, and I think I may add, ought not to be allowed to be made; we're all human; who isn't?

[*She dusts* MRS. ANTROBUS' *rocking chair.*]

Mrs. Antrobus is as fine a woman as you could hope to see. She lives only for her children; and if it would be any benefit to her children she'd see the rest of us stretched out dead at her feet without turning a hair—that's the truth. If you want to know anything more about Mrs. Antrobus, just go and look at a tigress, and look hard.

As to the children—

Well, Henry Antrobus is a real, clean-cut American boy. He'll graduate from High School one of these days, if they make the alphabet any easier.—Henry, when he has a stone in his hand, has a perfect aim; he can hit anything from a bird to an older brother —Oh! I didn't mean to say that!—but it certainly was an unfortunate accident, and it was very hard getting the police out of the house.

Mr. and Mrs. Antrobus' daughter is named Gladys. She'll make some good man a good wife some day, if he'll just come down off the movie screen and ask her.

So here we are!

We've managed to survive for some time now, catch

as catch can, the fat and the lean, and if the dinosaurs don't trample us to death, and if the grasshoppers don't eat up our garden, we'll all live to see better days, knock on wood.

Each new child that's born to the Antrobuses seems to them to be sufficient reason for the whole universe's being set in motion; and each new child that dies seems to them to have been spared a whole world of sorrow, and what the end of it will be is still very much an open question.

We've rattled along, hot and cold, for some time now—

[*A portion of the wall above the door, right, flies up into the air and disappears.*]

—and my advice to you is not to inquire into why or whither, but just enjoy your ice cream while it's on your plate—that's my philosophy.

Don't forget that a few years ago we came through the depression by the skin of our teeth! One more tight squeeze like that and where will we be?

[*This is a cue line.* SABINA *looks angrily at the kitchen door and repeats:*]

. . . we came through the depression by the skin of our teeth; one more tight squeeze like that and where will we be?

[*Flustered, she looks through the opening in the right wall; then goes to the window and reopens the Act.*] Oh, oh, oh! Six o'clock and the master not home yet. Pray God nothing has happened to him crossing the Hudson. Here it is the middle of August and the coldest day of the year. It's simply freezing; the dogs are sticking. One more tight squeeze like that and where will we be?

VOICE [*off-stage*]. Make up something! Invent something!

SABINA. Well . . . uh . . . this certainly is a fine American home . . . and—uh . . . everybody's very happy . . . and—uh . . .

[*Suddenly flings pretense to the winds and coming downstage says with indignation:*]

I can't invent any words for this play, and I'm glad I can't. I hate this play and every word in it.

As for me, I don't understand a single word of it, anyway—all about the troubles the human race has gone through, there's a subject for you.

Besides, the author hasn't made up his silly mind as to whether we're all living back in caves or in New Jersey today, and that's the way it is all the way through.

Oh—why can't we have plays like we used to have— *Peg o' My Heart,* and *Smilin' Thru,* and *The Bat*— good entertainment with a message you can take home with you?

I took this hateful job because I had to. For two years I've sat up in my room living on a sandwich and a cup of tea a day, waiting for better times in the theatre. And look at me now: I—I who've played *Rain* and *The Barretts of Wimpole Street* and *First Lady*—God in Heaven!

[*The* STAGE MANAGER *puts his head out from the hole in the scenery.*]

MR. FITZPATRICK. Miss Somerset! ! Miss Somerset!

SABINA. Oh! Anyway!—nothing matters! It'll all be the same in a hundred years.

[*Loudly.*]

We came through the depression by the skin of our teeth,—that's true!—one more tight squeeze like that and where will we be?

[*Enter* MRS. ANTROBUS, *a mother.*]

MRS. ANTROBUS. Sabina, you've let the fire go out.

SABINA [*in a lather*]. One-thing-and-another; don't-know-whether-my-wits-are-upside-or-down; might-as-well-be-dead-as-alive-in-a-house-all-sixes-and-sevens.

MRS. ANTROBUS. You've let the fire go out. Here it is the coldest day of the year right in the middle of August and you've let the fire go out.

SABINA. Mrs. Antrobus, I'd like to give my two weeks' notice, Mrs. Antrobus. A girl like I can get a situation in a home where they're rich enough to have a fire in every room, Mrs. Antrobus, and a girl don't have to carry the responsibility of the whole house on her two shoulders. And a home without children, Mrs. Antrobus, because children are a thing only a parent can stand, and a truer word was never said; and a home, Mrs. Antrobus, where the master of the house don't pinch decent, self-respecting girls when he meets them in a dark corridor. I mention no names and make no charges. So you have my notice, Mrs. Antrobus. I hope that's perfectly clear.

MRS. ANTROBUS. You've let the fire go out!—Have you milked the mammoth?

SABINA. I don't understand a word of this play.—Yes, I've milked the mammoth.

MRS. ANTROBUS. Until Mr. Antrobus comes home we have no food and we have no fire. You'd better go over to the neighbors and borrow some fire.

SABINA. Mrs. Antrobus! I can't! I'd die on the way, you know I would. It's worse than January. The dogs are sticking to the sidewalks. I'd die.

MRS. ANTROBUS. Very well, I'll go.

SABINA [*even more distraught, coming forward and sinking on her knees*]. You'd never come back alive; we'd all perish; if you weren't here, we'd just perish. How do we know Mr. Antrobus'll be back? We don't know. If you go out, I'll just kill myself.

MRS. ANTROBUS. Get up, Sabina.

SABINA. Every night it's the same thing. Will he come back safe, or won't he? Will we starve to death, or freeze to death, or boil to death or will we be killed by burglars? I don't know why we go on living. I don't know why we go on living at all. It's easier being dead.

[*She flings her arms on the table and buries her head in them. In each of the succeeding speeches she flings her head up—and sometimes her hands—then quickly buries her head again.*]

MRS. ANTROBUS. The same thing! Always throwing up the sponge, Sabina. Always announcing your own death. But give you a new hat—or a plate of ice cream—or a ticket to the movies, and you want to live forever.

SABINA. You don't care whether we live or die; all you care about is those children. If it would be any benefit to them you'd be glad to see us all stretched out dead.

MRS. ANTROBUS. Well, maybe I would.

SABINA. And what do they care about? Themselves— that's all they care about.

[*Shrilly.*]

They make fun of you behind your back. Don't tell me: they're ashamed of you. Half the time, they pretend they're someone else's children. Little thanks you get from them.

MRS. ANTROBUS. I'm not asking for any thanks.

SABINA. And Mr. Antrobus—you don't understand *him*. All that work he does—trying to discover the alphabet and the multiplication table. Whenever he tries to learn anything you fight against it.

MRS. ANTROBUS. Oh, Sabina, I know you.

When Mr. Antrobus raped you home from your Sabine hills, he did it to insult me.

He did it for your pretty face, and to insult me.

You were the new wife, weren't you?

For a year or two you lay on your bed all day and polished the nails on your hands and feet:

You made puff-balls of the combings of your hair and you blew them up to the ceiling.

And I washed your underclothes and I made you chicken broths.

I bore children and between my very groans I stirred the cream that you'd put on your face.

But I knew you wouldn't last.

You didn't last.

SABINA. But it was I who encouraged Mr. Antrobus to make the alphabet. I'm sorry to say it, Mrs. Antrobus, but you're not a beautiful woman, and you can never know what a man could do if he tried. It's girls like I who inspire the multiplication table.

I'm sorry to say it, but you're not a beautiful woman, Mrs. Antrobus, and that's the God's truth.

MRS. ANTROBUS. And you didn't last—you sank to the kitchen. And what do you do there? *You let the fire go out!*

No wonder to you it seems easier being dead.

Reading and writing and counting on your fingers is all very well in their way—but I keep the home going.

MRS. ANTROBUS. —There's that dinosaur on the front lawn again.—Shoo! Go away. Go away.

[*The baby* DINOSAUR *puts his head in the window.*]

DINOSAUR. It's cold.

MRS. ANTROBUS. You go around to the back of the house where you belong.

DINOSAUR. It's cold.

[*The* DINOSAUR *disappears.* MRS. ANTROBUS *goes calmly out.* SABINA *slowly raises her head and speaks to the audience. The central portion of the center wall rises, pauses, and disappears into the loft.*]

SABINA. Now that you audience are listening to this, too, I understand it a little better.

I wish eleven o'clock were here; I don't want to be dragged through this whole play again.

[*The* TELEGRAPH BOY *is seen entering along the back wall of the stage from the right. She catches sight of him and calls:*]

Mrs. Antrobus! Mrs. Antrobus! Help! There's a strange man coming to the house. He's coming up the walk, help!

[*Enter* MRS. ANTROBUS *in alarm, but efficient.*]

MRS. ANTROBUS. Help me quick!

[*They barricade the door by piling the furniture against it.*]

Who is it? What do you want?

TELEGRAPH BOY. A telegram for Mrs. Antrobus from Mr. Antrobus in the city.

SABINA. Are you sure, are you sure? Maybe it's just a trap!

MRS. ANTROBUS. I know his voice, Sabina. We can open the door.

[*Enter the* TELEGRAPH BOY, *12 years old, in uniform. The* DINOSAUR *and* MAMMOTH *slip by him into the room and settle down front right.*]

I'm sorry we kept you waiting. We have to be careful, you know.

[*To the* ANIMALS.]

H'm . . . Will you be quiet?

[*They nod.*]

Have you had your supper?

[*They nod.*]

Are you *ready* to come in?

[*They nod.*]

Young man, have you any fire with you? Then light the grate, will you?

[*He nods, produces something like a briquet; and kneels by the imagined fireplace, footlights center. Pause.*]

What are people saying about this cold weather?

[*He makes a doubtful shrug with his shoulders.*]

Sabina, take this stick and go and light the stove.

SABINA. Like I told you, Mrs. Antrobus; two weeks. That's the law. I hope that's perfectly clear. [*Exit.*]

MRS. ANTROBUS. What about this cold weather?

TELEGRAPH BOY [*lowered eyes*]. Of course, I don't know anything . . . but they say there's a wall of ice moving down from the North, that's what they say. We can't get Boston by telegraph, and they're burning pianos in Hartford.

. . . It moves everything in front of it, churches and post offices and city halls.

I live in Brooklyn myself.

MRS. ANTROBUS. What are people doing about it?

TELEGRAPH BOY. Well . . . uh . . . Talking, mostly.

Or just what you'd do a day in February.

There are some that are trying to go South and the roads are crowded; but you can't take old people and children very far in a cold like this.

MRS. ANTROBUS. —What's this telegram you have for me?

TELEGRAPH BOY [*fingertips to his forehead*]. If you wait just a minute; I've got to remember it.

[*The* ANIMALS *have left their corner and are nosing him. Presently they take places on either side of him, leaning against his hips, like heraldic beasts. This telegram was flashed from Murray Hill to University Heights! And then by puffs of smoke from*

University Heights to Staten Island.

And then by lantern from Staten Island to Plain-
field, New Jersey. What hath God wrought!

[*He clears his throat.*]

"To Mrs. Antrobus, Excelsior, New Jersey:

"My dear wife, will be an hour late. Busy day at
the office. Don't worry the children about the cold
just keep them warm burn everything except Shakespeare."

[*Pause.*]

MRS. ANTROBUS. Men! —He knows I'd burn ten Shake-
speares to prevent a child of mine from having one
cold in the head. What does it say next?

[*Enter* SABINA.]

TELEGRAPH BOY. "Have made great discoveries today
have separated em from en."

SABINA. I know what that is, that's the alphabet, yes
it is. Mr. Antrobus is just the cleverest man. Why,
when the alphabet's finished, we'll be able to tell
the future and everything.

TELEGRAPH BOY. Then listen to this: "Ten tens make
a hundred semi-colon consequences far-reaching."
[*Watches for effect.*]

MRS. ANTROBUS. The earth's turning to ice, and all he
can do is to make up new numbers.

TELEGRAPH BOY. Well, Mrs. Antrobus, like the head
man at our office said: a few more discoveries like
that and we'll be worth freezing.

MRS. ANTROBUS. What does he say next?

TELEGRAPH BOY. I . . . I can't do this last part very
well.

[*He clears his throat and sings.*]

"Happy w'dding ann'vers'ry to you, Happy ann'-
vers'ry to you—"

[*The* ANIMALS *begin to howl soulfully;* SABINA *screams
with pleasure.*]

MRS. ANTROBUS. Dolly! Frederick! Be quiet.

TELEGRAPH BOY [*above the din*]. "Happy w'dding ann'-vers'ry, dear Eva; happy w'dding ann'vers'ry to you."

MRS. ANTROBUS. Is that in the telegram? Are they singing telegrams now?

[*He nods.*]

The earth's getting so silly no wonder the sun turns cold.

SABINA. Mrs. Antrobus, I want to take back the notice I gave you. Mrs. Antrobus, I don't want to leave a house that gets such interesting telegrams and I'm sorry for anything I said. I really am.

MRS. ANTROBUS. Young man, I'd like to give you something for all this trouble; Mr. Antrobus isn't home yet and I have no money and no food in the house—

TELEGRAPH BOY. Mrs. Antrobus . . . I don't like to . . . appear to . . . ask for anything, but . . .

MRS. ANTROBUS. What is it you'd like?

TELEGRAPH BOY. Do you happen to have an old needle you could spare? My wife just sits home all day thinking about needles.

SABINA [*shrilly*]. We only got two in the house. Mrs. Antrobus, you know we only got two in the house.

MRS. ANTROBUS [*after a look at* SABINA *taking a needle from her collar*]. Why yes, I can spare this.

TELEGRAPH BOY [*lowered eyes*]. Thank you, Mrs. Antrobus. Mrs. Antrobus, can I ask you something else? I have two sons of my own; if the cold gets worse, what should I do?

SABINA. I think we'll all perish, that's what I think. Cold like this in August is just the end of the whole world.

[*Silence.*]

MRS. ANTROBUS. I don't know. After all, what does one do about anything? Just keep as warm as you can.

And don't let your wife and children see that you're worried.

TELEGRAPH BOY. Yes. . . . Thank you, Mrs. Antrobus. Well, I'd better be going.—Oh, I forgot! There's one more sentence in the telegram. "Three cheers have invented the wheel."

MRS. ANTROBUS. A wheel? What's a wheel?

TELEGRAPH BOY. I don't know. That's what it said. The sign for it is like this. Well, goodbye.

[*The* WOMEN *see him to the door, with goodbyes and injunctions to keep warm.*]

SABINA [*apron to her eyes, wailing*]. Mrs. Antrobus, it looks to me like all the nice men in the world are already married; I don't know why that is. [*Exit.*]

MRS. ANTROBUS [*thoughtful; to the* ANIMALS]. Do you remember hearing tell of any cold like this in August?

[*The* ANIMALS *shake their heads.*]

From your grandmothers or anyone?

[*They shake their heads.*]

Have you any suggestions?

[*They shake their heads. She pulls her shawl around, goes to the front door and opening it an inch calls:*]

HENRY. GLADYS. CHILDREN. Come right in and get warm. No, no, when mama says a thing she means it.

Henry! HENRY. Put down that stone. You know what happened last time.

[*Shriek.*]

HENRY! Put down that stone!

Gladys! Put down your dress! ! Try and be a lady.

[*The* CHILDREN *bound in and dash to the fire. They take off their winter things and leave them in heaps on the floor.*]

GLADYS. Mama, I'm hungry. Mama, why is it so cold?

HENRY [*at the same time*]. Mama, why doesn't it snow? Mama, when's supper ready? Maybe it'll snow and we can make snowballs.

GLADYS. Mama, it's so cold that in one more minute I just couldn't of stood it.

MRS. ANTROBUS. Settle down, both of you, I want to talk to you.

[*She draws up a hassock and sits front center over the orchestra pit before the imaginary fire. The* CHILDREN *stretch out on the floor, leaning against her lap. Tableau by Raphael. The* ANIMALS *edge up and complete the triangle.*]

It's just a cold spell of some kind. Now listen to what I'm saying:

When your father comes home I want you to be extra quiet.

He's had a hard day at the office and I don't know but what he may have one of his moods.

I just got a telegram from him very happy and excited, and you know what that means. Your father's temper's uneven; I guess you know that.

[*Shriek.*]

Henry! Henry!

Why—why can't you remember to keep your hair down over your forehead? You must keep that scar covered up. Don't you know that when your father sees it he loses all control over himself? He goes crazy. He wants to die.

[*After a moment's despair she collects herself decisively, wets the hem of her apron in her mouth and starts polishing his forehead vigorously.*]

Lift your head up. Stop squirming. Blessed me, sometimes I think that it's going away—and then there it is: just as red as ever.

HENRY. Mama, today at school two teachers forgot and

called me by my old name. They forgot, Mama. You'd better write another letter to the principal, so that he'll tell them I've changed my name. Right out in class they called me: Cain.

MRS. ANTROBUS [*putting her hand on his mouth, too late; hoarsely*]. Don't say it.

[*Polishing feverishly.*]

If you're good they'll forget it. Henry, you didn't hit anyone . . . today, did you?

HENRY. Oh . . . no-o-o!

MRS. ANTROBUS [*still working, not looking at Gladys*]. And, Gladys, I want you to be especially nice to your father tonight. You know what he calls you when you're good—his little angel, his little star. Keep your dress down like a little lady. And keep your voice nice and low. Gladys Antrobus!! What's that red stuff you have on your face?

[*Slaps her.*]

You're a filthy detestable child!

[*Rises in real, though temporary, repudiation and despair.*]

Get away from me, both of you! I wish I'd never seen sight or sound of you. Let the cold come! I can't stand it. I don't want to go on. [*She walks away.*]

GLADYS [*weeping*]. All the girls at school do, Mama.

MRS. ANTROBUS [*shrieking*]. I'm through with you, that's all!—Sabina! Sabina!—Don't you know your father'd go crazy if he saw that paint on your face? Don't you know your father thinks you're perfect? Don't you know he couldn't live if he didn't think you were perfect?—Sabina!

[*Enter* SABINA.]

SABINA. Yes, Mrs. Antrobus!

MRS. ANTROBUS. Take this girl out into the kitchen and wash her face with the scrubbing brush.

MR. ANTROBUS [*outside, roaring*]. "I've been working on the railroad, all the livelong day . . . etc."

[*The* ANIMALS *start running around in circles, bellowing.* SABINA *rushes to the window.*]

MRS. ANTROBUS. Sabina, what's that noise outside?

SABINA. Oh, it's a drunken tramp. It's a giant, Mrs. Antrobus. We'll all be killed in our beds, I know it!

MRS. ANTROBUS. Help me quick. Quick. Everybody.

[*Again they stack all the furniture against the door.* MR. ANTROBUS *pounds and bellows.*]

Who is it? What do you want?—Sabina, have you any boiling water ready?—Who is it?

MR. ANTROBUS. Broken-down camel of a pig's snout, open this door.

MRS. ANTROBUS. God be praised! It's your father.—Just a minute, George!—Sabina, clear the door, quick. Gladys, come here while I clean your nasty face!

MR. ANTROBUS. She-bitch of a goat's gizzard, I'll break every bone in your body. Let me in or I'll tear the whole house down.

MRS. ANTROBUS. Just a minute, George, something's the matter with the lock.

MR. ANTROBUS. Open the door or I'll tear your livers out. I'll smash your brains on the ceiling, and Devil take the hindmost.

MRS. ANTROBUS. Now, you can open the door, Sabina. I'm ready.

[*The door is flung open. Silence.* MR. ANTROBUS—*face of a Keystone Comedy Cop—stands there in fur cap and blanket. His arms are full of parcels, including a large stone wheel with a center in it. One hand carries a railroad man's lantern. Suddenly he bursts into joyous roar.*]

MR. ANTROBUS. Well, how's the whole crooked family?

[*Relief. Laughter. Tears. Jumping up and down.* ANI-

MALS *cavorting.* ANTROBUS *throws the parcels on the ground. Hurls his cap and blanket after them. Heroic embraces. Melee of* HUMANS *and* ANIMALS, SABINA *included.*]

I'll be scalded and tarred if a man can't get a little welcome when he comes home. Well, Maggie, you old gunny-sack, how's the broken down old weather hen?—Sabina, old fishbait, old skunkpot.—And the children—how've the little smellers been?

GLADYS. Papa, Papa, Papa, Papa, Papa.

MR. ANTROBUS. How've they been, Maggie?

MRS. ANTROBUS. Well, I must say, they've been as good as gold. I haven't had to raise my voice once. I don't know what's the matter with them.

ANTROBUS [*kneeling before* GLADYS]. Papa's little weasel, eh?—Sabina, there's some food for you.—Papa's little gopher?

GLADYS [*her arm around his neck*]. Papa, you're always teasing me.

ANTROBUS. And Henry? Nothing rash today, I hope. Nothing rash?

HENRY. No, Papa.

ANTROBUS [*roaring*]. Well that's good, that's good— I'll bet Sabina let the fire go out.

SABINA. Mr. Antrobus, I've given my notice. I'm leaving two weeks from today. I'm sorry, but I'm leaving.

ANTROBUS [*roar*]. Well, if you leave now you'll freeze to death, so go and cook the dinner.

SABINA. Two weeks, that's the law. [*Exit.*]

ANTROBUS. Did you get my telegram?

MRS. ANTROBUS. Yes.—What's a wheel?

[*He indicates the wheel with a glance.* HENRY *is rolling it around the floor. Rapid, hoarse interchange:* MRS. ANTROBUS: *What does this cold weather mean? It's below freezing.* ANTROBUS: *Not before the children!* MRS. ANTROBUS: *Shouldn't we do something about it*

—start off, move? ANTROBUS: *Not before the children!!! He gives* HENRY *a sharp slap.*]

HENRY. Papa, you hit me!

ANTROBUS. Well, remember it. That's to make you remember today. Today. The day the alphabet's finished; and the day that we *saw* the hundred—the hundred, the hundred, the hundred, the hundred, the hundred—there's no end to 'em.

I've had a day at the office!

Take a look at that wheel, Maggie—when I've got that to rights: you'll see a sight.

There's a reward there for all the walking you've done.

MRS. ANTROBUS. How do you mean?

ANTROBUS [*on the hassock looking into the fire; with awe*]. Maggie, we've reached the top of the wave. There's not much more to be done. We're there!

MRS. ANTROBUS [*cutting across his mood sharply*]. And the ice?

ANTROBUS. The ice!

HENRY [*playing with the wheel*]. Papa, you could put a chair on this.

ANTROBUS [*broodingly*]. Ye-e-s, any booby can fool with it now—but I thought of it first.

MRS. ANTROBUS. Children, go out in the kitchen. I want to talk to your father alone.

[*The* CHILDREN *go out.* ANTROBUS *has moved to his chair up left. He takes the goldfish bowl on his lap; pulls the canary cage down to the level of his face. Both the* ANIMALS *put their paws up on the arm of his chair.* MRS. ANTROBUS *faces him across the room, like a judge.*]

MRS. ANTROBUS. Well?

ANTROBUS [*shortly*]. It's cold.—How things been, eh? Keck, keck, keck.—And you, Millicent?

MRS. ANTROBUS. I know it's cold.

ANTROBUS [*to the canary*]. No spilling of sunflower seed, eh? No singing after lights-out, y'know what I mean?

MRS. ANTROBUS. You can try and prevent us freezing to death, can't you? You can do something? We can start moving. Or we can go on the animals' backs?

ANTROBUS. The best thing about animals is that they don't talk much.

MAMMOTH. It's cold.

ANTROBUS. Eh, eh, eh! Watch that!—
—By midnight we'd turn to ice. The roads are full of people now who can scarcely lift a foot from the ground. The grass out in front is like iron—which reminds me, I have another needle for you.—The people up north—where are they?
Frozen . . . crushed. . . .

MRS. ANTROBUS. Is that what's going to happen to us?— Will you answer me?

ANTROBUS. I don't know. I don't know anything. Some say that the ice is going slower. Some say that it's stopped. The sun's growing cold. What can I do about that? Nothing we can do but burn everything in the house, and the fenceposts and the barn. Keep the fire going. When we have no more fire, we die.

MRS. ANTROBUS. Well, why didn't you say so in the first place?

[MRS. ANTROBUS *is about to march off when she catches sight of two* REFUGEES, *men, who have appeared against the back wall of the theatre and who are soon joined by others.*]

REFUGEES. Mr. Antrobus! Mr. Antrobus! Mr. An-nn-tro-bus!

MRS. ANTROBUS. Who's that? Who's that calling you?

ANTROBUS [*clearing his throat guiltily*]. H'm—let me see.

[*Two* REFUGEES *come up to the window.*]

REFUGEE. Could we warm our hands for a moment, Mr. Antrobus. It's very cold, Mr. Antrobus.

ANOTHER REFUGEE. Mr. Antrobus, I wonder if you have a piece of bread or something that you could spare.

[*Silence. They wait humbly.* MRS. ANTROBUS *stands rooted to the spot. Suddenly a knock at the door, then another hand knocking in short rapid blows.*]

MRS. ANTROBUS. Who are these people? Why, they're all over the front yard. What have they come *here* for?

[*Enter* SABINA.]

SABINA. Mrs. Antrobus! There are some tramps knocking at the back door.

MRS. ANTROBUS. George, tell these people to go away. Tell them to move right along. I'll go and send them away from the back door. Sabina, come with me. [*She goes out energetically.*]

ANTROBUS. Sabina! Stay here! I have something to say to you.

[*He goes to the door and opens it a crack and talks through it.*]

Ladies and gentlemen! I'll have to ask you to wait a few minutes longer. It'll be all right . . . while you're waiting you might each one pull up a stake of the fence. We'll need them all for the fireplace. There'll be coffee and sandwiches in a moment.

[SABINA *looks out door over his shoulder and suddenly extends her arm pointing, with a scream.*]

SABINA. Mr. Antrobus, what's that??—that big white thing? Mr. Antrobus, it's ICE. It's ICE!!

ANTROBUS. Sabina, I want you to go in the kitchen and make a lot of coffee. Make a whole pail full.

SABINA. Pail full!!

ANTROBUS [*with gesture*]. And sandwiches . . . piles of them . . . like this.

SABINA. Mr. An . . . !!

[*Suddenly she drops the play, and says in her own person as* MISS SOMERSET, *with surprise.*]

Oh, *I* see what this part of the play means now! This means refugees.

[*She starts to cross to the proscenium.*]

Oh, I don't like it. I don't like it.

[*She leans against the proscenium and bursts into tears.*]

ANTROBUS. Miss Somerset!

STAGE MANAGER [*off-stage*]. Miss Somerset!

SABINA [*energetically, to the audience*]. Ladies and gentlemen! Don't take this play serious. The world's not coming to an end. You know it's not. People exaggerate! Most people really have enough to eat and a roof over their heads. Nobody actually starves—you can always eat grass or something. That ice-business—why it was a long, long time ago. Besides they were only savages. Savages don't love their families—not like we do.

ANTROBUS *and* STAGE MANAGER. Miss Somerset!!

[*There is renewed knocking at the door.*]

SABINA. All right. I'll say the lines, but I won't think about the play.

[*Enter* MRS. ANTROBUS.]

SABINA [*parting thrust at the audience*]. And I advise *you* not to think about the play, either. [*Exit* SABINA.]

MRS. ANTROBUS. George, these tramps say that you asked them to come to the house. What does this mean?

[*Knocking at the door.*]

ANTROBUS. Just . . . uh. . . . There are a few friends, Maggie, I met on the road. Real nice, real useful people. . . .

MRS. ANTROBUS [*back to the door*]. Now, don't you ask them in!

George Antrobus, not another soul comes in here over my dead body.

ANTROBUS. Maggie, there's a doctor there. Never hurts to have a good doctor in the house. We've lost a peck of children, one way and another. You can never tell when a child's throat will get stopped up. What you and I have seen—! ! ! [*He puts his fingers on his throat, and imitates diphtheria.*]

MRS. ANTROBUS. Well, just one person then, the Doctor. The others can go right along the road.

ANTROBUS. Maggie, there's an old man, particular friend of mine—

MRS. ANTROBUS. I won't listen to you—

ANTROBUS. It was he that really started off the A.B.C.'s.

MRS. ANTROBUS. I don't care if he perishes. We can do without reading or writing. We can't do without food.

ANTROBUS. Then let the ice come!! Drink your coffee!! I don't want any coffee if I can't drink it with some good people.

MRS. ANTROBUS. Stop shouting. Who else is there trying to push us off the cliff?

ANTROBUS. Well, there's the man . . . who makes all the laws. Judge Moses!

MRS. ANTROBUS. Judges can't help us now.

ANTROBUS. And if the ice melts? . . . and if we pull through? Have you and I been able to bring up Henry? What have we done?

MRS. ANTROBUS. Who are those old women?

ANTROBUS [*coughs*]. Up in town there are nine sisters. There are three or four of them here. They're sort of music teachers . . . and one of them recites and one of them—

MRS. ANTROBUS. That's the end. A singing troupe! Well, take your choice, live or die. Starve your own children before your face.

ANTROBUS [*gently*]. These people don't take much.
They're used to starving.

They'll sleep on the floor.

Besides, Maggie, listen: no, listen:

Who've we got in the house, but Sabina? Sabina's
always afraid the worst will happen. Whose spirits
can she keep up?

Maggie, these people never give up. They think
they'll live and work forever.

MRS. ANTROBUS [*walks slowly to the middle of the
room*]. All right, let them in. Let them in. You're
master here.

[*Softly.*]

—But these animals must go. Enough's enough.
They'll soon be big enough to push the walls down,
anyway. Take them away.

ANTROBUS [*sadly*]. All right. The dinosaur and mammoth—! Come on, baby, come on, Frederick. Come
for a walk. That's a good little fellow.

DINOSAUR. It's cold.

ANTROBUS. Yes, nice cold fresh air. Bracing.

[*He holds the door open and the* ANIMALS *go out. He
beckons to his friends. The* REFUGEES *are typical el-
derly out-of-works from the streets of New York today.* JUDGE MOSES *wears a skull cap.* HOMER *is a blind
beggar with a guitar. The seedy crowd shuffles in
and waits humbly and expectantly.* ANTROBUS *intro-
duces them to his wife who bows to each with a
stately bend of her head.*]

Make yourself at home. Maggie, this is the doctor
. . . m . . . Coffee'll be here in a minute. . . . Professor, this is my wife. . . . And . . . Judge . . . Maggie,
you know the Judge.

[*An old blind man with a guitar.*]

Maggie, you know . . . you know Homer?—Come
right in, Judge.—

Miss Muse—are some of your sisters here? Come
right in. . . .

Miss E. Muse; Miss T. Muse, Miss M. Muse.

MRS. ANTROBUS. Pleased to meet you.

Just . . . make yourself comfortable. Supper'll be
ready in a minute. [*She goes out, abruptly.*]

ANTROBUS. Make yourself at home, friends. I'll be right
back.

[*He goes out. The* REFUGEES *stare about them in awe.
Presently several voices start whispering "Homer!
Homer!" All take it up.* HOMER *strikes a chord or
two on his guitar, then starts to speak:*]

HOMER.

> Μῆνιν ἄειδε, θεά, Πηληϊάδεω Ἀχιλῆος,
> οὐλομένην, ἣ μυρί᾽ Ἀχαιοῖς ἄλγε᾽ ἔθηκεν,
> πολλὰς δ᾽ ἰφθίμους ψυχὰς—

[HOMER'S *face shows he is lost in thought and memory
and the words die away on his lips. The* REFUGEES
*likewise nod in dreamy recollection. Soon the whis-
per "Moses, Moses!" goes around. An aged Jew parts
his beard and recites dramatically:*]

MOSES.

> בְּרֵאשִׁית בָּרָא אֱלֹהִים אֵת הַשָּׁמַיִם וְאֵת הָאָרֶץ: וְהָאָרֶץ הָיְתָה תֹהוּ
> וָבֹהוּ וְחֹשֶׁךְ עַל־פְּנֵי תְהוֹם וְרוּחַ אֱלֹהִים מְרַחֶפֶת עַל־פְּנֵי הַמָּיִם:

[*The same dying away of the words take place, and on
the part of the* REFUGEES *the same retreat into recollection. Some of them murmur, "Yes, yes." The
mood is broken by the abrupt entrance of* MR. *and*
MRS. ANTROBUS *and* SABINA *bearing platters of sandwiches and a pail of coffee.* SABINA *stops and stares
at the guests.*]

MR. ANTROBUS. Sabina, pass the sandwiches.

SABINA. I thought I was working in a respectable house

that had respectable guests. I'm giving my notice,
Mr. Antrobus: two weeks, that's the law.

MR. ANTROBUS. Sabina! Pass the sandwiches.

SABINA. Two weeks, that's the law.

MR. ANTROBUS. There's the law. That's Moses.

SABINA [*stares*]. The Ten Commandments—FAUGH!!
— [*To audience.*] That's the worst line I've ever had
to say on any stage.

ANTROBUS. I think the best thing to do is just not to
stand on ceremony, but pass the sandwiches around
from left to right.—Judge, help yourself to one of
these.

MRS. ANTROBUS. The roads are crowded, I hear?

THE GUESTS [*all talking at once*]. Oh, ma'am, you can't
imagine. . . . You can hardly put one foot before
you . . . people are trampling one another.

[*Sudden silence.*]

MRS. ANTROBUS. Well, you know what I think it is—I
think it's sun-spots!

THE GUESTS [*discreet hubbub*]. Oh, you're right, Mrs.
Antrobus . . . that's what it is. . . . That's what I was
saying the other day.

[*Sudden silence.*]

ANTROBUS. Well, I don't believe the whole world's going to turn to ice.

[*All eyes are fixed on him, waiting.*]

I can't believe it. Judge! Have we worked for nothing? Professor! Have we just failed in the whole
thing?

MRS. ANTROBUS. It is certainly very strange—well, fortunately on both sides of the family we come of
very hearty stock.—Doctor, I want you to meet my
children. They're eating their supper now. And of
course I want them to meet you.

MISS M. MUSE. How many children have you, Mrs. Antrobus?

MRS. ANTROBUS. I have two—a boy and a girl.

MOSES [*softly*]. I understood you had two sons, Mrs. Antrobus.

[MRS. ANTROBUS *in blind suffering; she walks toward the footlights.*]

MRS. ANTROBUS [*in a low voice*]. Abel, Abel, my son, my son, Abel, my son, Abel, Abel, my son.

[*The* REFUGEES *move with few steps toward her as though in comfort murmuring words in Greek, Hebrew, German, et cetera. A piercing shriek from the kitchen—*SABINA'S *voice. All heads turn.*]

ANTROBUS. What's that?

[SABINA *enters, bursting with indignation, pulling on her gloves.*]

SABINA. Mr. Antrobus—that son of yours, that boy Henry Antrobus—I don't stay in this house another moment!—He's not fit to live among respectable folks and that's a fact.

MRS. ANTROBUS. Don't say another word, Sabina. I'll be right back.

[*Without waiting for an answer she goes past her into the kitchen.*]

SABINA. Mr. Antrobus, Henry has thrown a stone again and if he hasn't killed the boy that lives next door, I'm very much mistaken. He finished his supper and went out to play; and I heard such a fight; and then I saw it. I saw it with my own eyes. And it looked to me like stark murder.

[MRS. ANTROBUS *appears at the kitchen door, shielding* HENRY *who follows her. When she steps aside, we see on* HENRY'S *forehead a large ochre and scarlet scar in the shape of a C.* MR. ANTROBUS *starts toward him. A pause.* HENRY *is heard saying under his breath:*]

HENRY. He was going to take the wheel away from me. He started to throw a stone at me first.

MRS. ANTROBUS. George, it was just a boyish impulse. Remember how young he is.

[*Louder, in an urgent wail.*]

George, he's only four thousand years old.

SABINA. And everything was going along so nicely!

[*Silence.* ANTROBUS *goes back to the fireplace.*]

ANTROBUS. Put out the fire! Put out all the fires.

[*Violently.*]

No wonder the sun grows cold.

[*He starts stamping on the fireplace.*]

MRS. ANTROBUS. Doctor! Judge! Help me!—George, have you lost your mind?

ANTROBUS. There is no mind. We'll not try to live.

[*To the guests.*]

Give it up. Give up trying.

[MRS. ANTROBUS *seizes him.*]

SABINA. Mr. Antrobus! I'm downright ashamed of you.

MRS. ANTROBUS. George, have some more coffee.— Gladys! Where's Gladys gone?

[GLADYS *steps in, frightened.*]

GLADYS. Here I am, mama.

MRS. ANTROBUS. Go upstairs and bring your father's slippers. How could you forget a thing like that, when you know how tired he is?

[ANTROBUS *sits in his chair. He covers his face with his hands.* MRS. ANTROBUS *turns to the* REFUGEES:]

Can't some of you sing? It's your business in life to sing, isn't it? Sabina!

[*Several of the women clear their throats tentatively, and with frightened faces gather around* HOMER's *guitar. He establishes a few chords. Almost inaudibly they start singing, led by* SABINA: "Jingle Bells." MRS. ANTROBUS *continues to* ANTROBUS *in a low voice, while taking off his shoes:*]

George, remember all the other times. When the volcanoes came right up in the front yard.

And the time the grasshoppers ate every single leaf and blade of grass, and all the grain and spinach you'd grown with your own hands. And the summer there were earthquakes every night.

ANTROBUS. Henry! Henry!

[*Puts his hand on his forehead.*]

Myself. All of us, we're covered with blood.

MRS. ANTROBUS. Then remember all the times you were pleased with him and when you were proud of yourself.—Henry! Henry! Come here and recite to your father the multiplication table that you do so nicely.

[HENRY *kneels on one knee beside his father and starts whispering the multiplication table.*]

HENRY [*finally*]. Two times six is twelve; three times six is eighteen—I don't think I know the sixes.

[*Enter* GLADYS *with the slippers.* MRS. ANTROBUS *makes stern gestures to her: Go in there and do your best. The* GUESTS *are now singing "Tenting Tonight."*]

GLADYS [*putting slippers on his feet*]. Papa . . . papa . . . I was very good in school today. Miss Conover said right out in class that if all the girls had as good manners as Gladys Antrobus, that the world would be a very different place to live in.

MRS. ANTROBUS. You recited a piece at assembly, didn't you? Recite it to your father.

GLADYS. Papa, do you want to hear what I recited in class?

[*Fierce directorial glance from her mother.*]

"THE STAR" by Henry Wadsworth LONGFELLOW.

MRS. ANTROBUS. Wait!!! The fire's going out. There isn't enough wood! Henry, go upstairs and bring down the chairs and start breaking up the beds.

[*Exit* HENRY. *The singers return to "Jingle Bells," still very softly.*]

GLADYS. Look, Papa, here's my report card. Lookit.
Conduct A! Look, Papa. Papa, do you want to hear
the Star, by Henry Wadsworth Longfellow? Papa,
you're not mad at me, are you?—I know it'll get
warmer. Soon it'll be just like spring, and we can
go to a picnic at the Hibernian Picnic Grounds like
you always like to do, don't you remember? Papa,
just look at me once.

[*Enter* HENRY *with some chairs.*]

ANTROBUS. You recited in assembly, did you?

[*She nods eagerly.*]

You didn't forget it?

GLADYS. No! ! ! I was perfect.

[*Pause. Then* ANTROBUS *rises, goes to the front door
and opens it. The* REFUGEES *draw back timidly; the
song stops; he peers out of the door, then closes it.*]

ANTROBUS [*with decision, suddenly*]. Build up the fire.
It's cold. Build up the fire. We'll do what we can.
Sabina, get some more wood. Come around the fire,
everybody. At least the young ones may pull
through. Henry, have you eaten something?

HENRY. Yes, papa.

ANTROBUS. Gladys, have you had some supper?

GLADYS. I ate in the kitchen, papa.

ANTROBUS. If you do come through this—what'll you be
able to do? What do you know? Henry, did you take
a good look at that wheel?

HENRY. Yes, papa.

ANTROBUS [*sitting down in his chair*]. Six times two
are—

HENRY. —twelve; six times three are eighteen; six times
four are—Papa, it's hot and cold. It makes my head
all funny. It makes me sleepy.

ANTROBUS [*gives him a cuff*]. Wake up. I don't care if
your head is sleepy. Six times four are twenty-four.
Six times five are—

HENRY. Thirty. Papa!

ANTROBUS. Maggie, put something into Gladys's head on the chance she can use it.

MRS. ANTROBUS. What do you mean, George?

ANTROBUS. Six times six are thirty-six.

Teach her the beginning of the Bible.

GLADYS. But, Mama, it's so cold and close.

[HENRY *has all but drowsed off. His father slaps him sharply and the lesson goes on.*]

MRS. ANTROBUS. "In the beginning God created the heavens and the earth; and the earth was waste and void; and the darkness was upon the face of the deep—"

[*The singing starts up again louder.* SABINA *has returned with wood.*]

SABINA [*after placing wood on the fireplace comes down to the footlights and addresses the audience*]. Will you please start handing up your chairs? We'll need everything for this fire. Save the human race. —Ushers, will you pass the chairs up here? Thank you.

HENRY. Six times nine are fifty-four; six times ten are sixty.

[*In the back of the auditorium the sound of chairs being ripped up can be heard.* USHERS *rush down the aisles with chairs and hand them over.*]

GLADYS. "And God called the light Day and the darkness he called Night."

SABINA. Pass up your chairs, everybody. Save the human race.

CURTAIN

Act two

Toward the end of the intermission, though with the house lights still up, lantern slide projections begin to appear on the curtain. Timetables for trains leaving Pennsylvania Station for Atlantic City. Advertisements of Atlantic City hotels, drugstores, churches, rug merchants; fortune tellers, Bingo parlors.

When the house lights go down, the voice of an ANNOUNCER *is heard.*

ANNOUNCER. The Management now brings you the News Events of the World. Atlantic City, New Jersey:

[*Projection of a chrome postcard of the waterfront, trimmed in mica with the legend: FUN AT THE BEACH.*]

This great convention city is playing host this week to the anniversary convocation of that great fraternal order—the Ancient and Honorable Order of Mammals, Subdivision Humans. This great fraternal, militant and burial society is celebrating on the Boardwalk, ladies and gentlemen, its six hundred thousandth Annual Convention.

It has just elected its president for the ensuing term—

[*Projection of* MR. *and* MRS. ANTROBUS *posed as they will be shown a few moments later.*]

Mr. George Antrobus of Excelsior, New Jersey. We show you President Antrobus and his gracious and charming wife, every inch a mammal. Mr. Antrobus has had a long and chequered career. Credit has been paid to him for many useful enterprises including the introduction of the lever, of the wheel and the brewing of beer. Credit has been also extended to President Antrobus's gracious and charming wife for many practical suggestions, including the hem, the gore, and the gusset; and the novelty of the year—frying in oil. Before we show you Mr. Antrobus accepting the nomination, we have an important announcement to make. As many of you know, this great celebration of the Order of the Mammals has received delegations from the other rival Orders —or shall we say: esteemed concurrent Orders: the WINGS, the FINS, the SHELLS, and so on. These Orders are holding their conventions also, in various parts of the world, and have sent representatives to our own, two of a kind.

Later in the day we will show you President Antrobus broadcasting his words of greeting and congratulation to the collected assemblies of the whole natural world.

Ladies and Gentlemen! We give you President Antrobus!

[*The screen becomes a Transparency.* MR. ANTROBUS *stands beside a pedestal;* MRS. ANTROBUS *is seated wearing a corsage of orchids.* ANTROBUS *wears an untidy Prince Albert; spats; from a red rosette in his buttonhole hangs a fine long purple ribbon of honor. He wears a gay lodge hat—something between a fez and a legionnaire's cap.*]

ANTROBUS. Fellow-mammals, fellow-vertebrates, fellow-humans, I thank you. Little did my dear parents think—when they told me to stand on my own two feet—that I'd arrive at this place.

My friends, we have come a long way.

During this week of happy celebration it is perhaps not fitting that we dwell on some of the difficult times we have been through. The dinosaur is extinct—

[*Applause.*]

—the ice has retreated; and the common cold is being pursued by every means within our power.

[MRS. ANTROBUS *sneezes, laughs prettily, and murmurs: "I beg your pardon."*]

In our memorial service yesterday we did honor to all our friends and relatives who are no longer with us, by reason of cold, earthquakes, plagues and ... and ... [*Coughs.*] differences of opinion.

As our Bishop so ably said ... uh ... so ably said. ...

MRS. ANTROBUS [*closed lips*]. Gone, but not forgotten.

ANTROBUS. "They are gone, but not forgotten."

I think I can say, I think I can prophesy with complete ... uh ... with complete ...

MRS. ANTROBUS. Confidence.

ANTROBUS. Thank you, my dear— With complete lack of confidence, that a new day of security is about to dawn.

The watchword of the closing year was: Work. I give you the watchword for the future: Enjoy Yourselves.

MRS. ANTROBUS. George, sit down!

ANTROBUS. Before I close, however, I wish to answer one of those unjust and malicious accusations that were brought against me during this last electoral campaign.

Ladies and gentlemen, the charge was made that at various points in my career I leaned toward joining some of the rival orders—that's a lie.

As I told reporters of the *Atlantic City Herald*, I do not deny that a few months before my birth I hesitated between ... uh ... between pinfeathers and gill-breathing—and so did many of us here—but for the last million years I have been viviparous, hairy and diaphragmatic.

[*Applause. Cries of "Good old Antrobus," "The Prince chap!" "Georgie," etc.*]

ANNOUNCER. Thank you. Thank you very much, Mr. Antrobus.

Now I know that our visitors will wish to hear a word from that gracious and charming mammal, Mrs. Antrobus, wife and mother—Mrs. Antrobus!

[MRS. ANTROBUS *rises, lays her program on her chair, bows and says:*]

MRS. ANTROBUS. Dear friends, I don't really think I should say anything. After all, it was my husband who was elected and not I.

Perhaps, as president of the Women's Auxiliary Bed and Board Society—I had some notes here, oh, yes, here they are—I should give a short report from some of our committees that have been meeting in this beautiful city.

Perhaps it may interest you to know that it has at last been decided that the tomato is edible. Can you all hear me? The tomato *is* edible.

A delegate from across the sea reports that the thread woven by the silkworm gives a cloth . . . I have a sample of it here . . . can you see it? smooth, elastic. I should say that it's rather attractive—though personally I prefer less shiny surfaces. Should the windows of a sleeping apartment be open or shut? I know all mothers will follow our debates on this matter with close interest. I am sorry to say that the most expert authorities have not yet decided. It does seem to me that the night air would be bound to be unhealthy for our children, but there are many distinguished authorities on both sides. Well, I could go on talking forever—as Shakespeare says: a woman's work is seldom done; but I think I'd better join my husband in saying thank you, and sit down. Thank you. [*She sits down.*]

ANNOUNCER. Oh, Mrs. Antrobus!

MRS. ANTROBUS. Yes?

ANNOUNCER. We understand that you are about to celebrate a wedding anniversary. I know our listeners would like to extend their felicitations and hear a few words from you on that subject.

MRS. ANTROBUS. I have been asked by this kind gentleman . . . yes, my friends, this spring Mr. Antrobus and I will be celebrating our five thousandth wedding anniversary.

I don't know if I speak for my husband, but I can say that, as for me, I regret every moment of it.

[*Laughter of confusion.*]

I beg your pardon. What I *mean* to say is that I do not regret one moment of it. I hope none of you catch my cold. We have two children. We've always had two children, though it hasn't always been the same two. But as I say, we have two fine children, and we're very grateful for that. Yes, Mr. Antrobus and I have been married five thousand years. Each wedding anniversary reminds me of the times when there were no weddings. We had to crusade for marriage. Perhaps there are some women within the sound of my voice who remember that crusade and those struggles; we fought for it, didn't we? We chained ourselves to lampposts and we made disturbances in the Senate—anyway, at last we women got the ring.

A few men helped us, but I must say that most men blocked our way at every step: they said we were unfeminine.

I only bring up these unpleasant memories, because I see some signs of backsliding from that great victory.

Oh, my fellow mammals, keep hold of that.

My husband says that the watchword for the year is Enjoy Yourselves. I think that's very open to misunderstanding. My watchword for the year is: Save the Family. It's held together for over five thousand years: Save it! Thank you.

ANNOUNCER. Thank you, Mrs. Antrobus.

[*The transparency disappears.*]

We had hoped to show you the Beauty Contest that took place here today.

President Antrobus, an experienced judge of pretty girls, gave the title of Miss Atlantic City 1942, to Miss Lily-Sabina Fairweather, charming hostess of our Boardwalk Bingo Parlor.

Unfortunately, however, our time is up, and I must take you to some views of the Convention City and conveeners— enjoying themselves.

A burst of music; the curtain rises.

The Boardwalk. The audience is sitting in the ocean. A handrail of scarlet cord stretches across the front of the stage. A ramp—also with scarlet handrail—descends to the right corner of the orchestra pit where a great scarlet beach umbrella or a cabana stands. Front and right stage left are benches facing the sea; attached to each bench is a street-lamp.

The only scenery is two cardboard cut-outs six feet high, representing shops at the back of the stage. Reading from left to right they are: SALT WATER TAFFY; FORTUNE TELLER; then the blank space; BINGO PARLOR; TURKISH BATH. They have practical doors, that of the Fortune Teller's being hung with bright gypsy curtains.

By the left proscenium and rising from the orchestra pit is the weather signal; it is like the mast of a ship with cross bars. From time to time black discs are hung on it to indicate the storm and hurricane warnings. Three roller chairs, pushed by melancholy NEGROES *file by empty. Throughout the act they traverse the stage in both directions.*

From time to time, CONVEENERS, *dressed like* MR. ANTROBUS, *cross the stage. Some walk sedately by; others engage in inane horseplay. The old gypsy* FORTUNE TELLER *is seated at the door of her shop, smoking a corncob pipe.*

From the Bingo Parlor comes the voice of the CALLER.

BINGO CALLER. A—Nine; A—Nine. C—Twenty-six; C— Twenty-six.

A—Four; A—Four. B—Twelve.

CHORUS [*back-stage*]. Bingo!!!

[*The front of the Bingo Parlor shudders, rises a few feet in the air and returns to the ground trembling.*]

FORTUNE TELLER [*mechanically, to the unconscious back of a passerby, pointing with her pipe*]. Bright's disease! Your partner's deceiving you in that Kansas City deal. You'll have six grandchildren. Avoid high places.

[*She rises and shouts after another:*]

Cirrhosis of the liver!

[SABINA *appears at the door of the Bingo Parlor. She hugs about her a blue raincoat that almost conceals her red bathing suit. She tries to catch the* FORTUNE TELLER's *attention.*]

SABINA. Ssssst! Esmeralda! Ssssst!

FORTUNE TELLER. Keck!

SABINA. Has President Antrobus come along yet?

FORTUNE TELLER. No, no, no. Get back there. Hide yourself.

SABINA. I'm afraid I'll miss him. Oh, Esmeralda, if I fail in this, I'll die; I know I'll die. President Antrobus!!! And I'll be his wife! If it's the last thing I'll do, I'll be Mrs. George Antrobus.—Esmeralda, tell me my future.

FORTUNE TELLER. Keck!

SABINA. All right, I'll tell *you* my future.

[*Laughing dreamily and tracing it out with one finger on the palm of her hand.*]

I've won the Beauty Contest in Atlantic City—well, I'll win the Beauty Contest of the whole world. I'll take President Antrobus away from that wife of his. Then I'll take every man away from his wife. I'll turn the whole earth upside down.

FORTUNE TELLER. Keck!

SABINA. When all those husbands just think about me they'll get dizzy. They'll faint in the streets. They'll have to lean against lampposts.—Esmeralda, who was Helen of Troy?

FORTUNE TELLER [*furiously*]. Shut your foolish mouth. When Mr. Antrobus comes along you can see what you can do. Until then—go away.

[SABINA *laughs. As she returns to the door of her Bingo Parlor a group of* CONVEENERS *rush over and smother her with attentions:* "Oh, Miss Lily, you know me. You've known me for years."]

SABINA. Go away, boys, go away. I'm after bigger fry than you are.—Why, Mr. Simpson!! How *dare* you!! I expect that even you nobodies must have girls to amuse you; but where you find them and what you do with them, is of absolutely no interest to me.

[*Exit. The* CONVEENERS *squeal with pleasure and stumble in after her. The* FORTUNE TELLER *rises, puts her pipe down on the stool, unfurls her voluminous skirts, gives a sharp wrench to her bodice and strolls towards the audience, swinging her hips like a young woman.*]

FORTUNE TELLER. I tell the future. Keck. Nothing easier. Everybody's future is in their face. Nothing easier.

But who can tell your past—eh? Nobody!

Your youth—where did it go? It slipped away while you weren't looking. While you were asleep. While you were drunk? Puh! You're like our friends, Mr. and Mrs. Antrobus; you lie awake nights trying to know your past. What did it mean? What was it trying to say to you?

Think! Think! Split your heads. I can't tell the past and neither can you. If anybody tries to tell you the past, take my word for it, they're charlatans! Charlatans! But I can tell the future.

[*She suddenly barks at a passing chair-pusher.*]

Apoplexy!

[*She returns to the audience.*]

Nobody listens.—Keck! I see a face among you now —I won't embarrass him by pointing him out, but, listen, it may be you: Next year the watchsprings inside you will crumple up. Death by regret—Type Y. It's in the corners of your mouth. You'll decide that you should have lived for pleasure, but that you missed it. Death by regret—Type Y. . . . Avoid mirrors. You'll try to be angry—but no!—no anger.

[*Far forward, confidentially.*]

And now what's the immediate future of our friends, the Antrobuses? Oh, you've seen it as well as I have, keck—that dizziness of the head; that Great Man dizziness? The inventor of beer and gunpowder. The sudden fits of temper and then the long stretches of

inertia? "I'm a sultan; let my slave-girls fan me"?
You know as well as I what's coming. Rain. Rain.
Rain in floods. The deluge. But first you'll see shameful things—shameful things. Some of you will be saying: "Let him drown. He's not worth saving. Give the whole thing up." I can see it in your faces. But you're wrong. Keep your doubts and despairs to yourselves.

Again there'll be the narrow escape. The survival of a handful. From destruction—total destruction.

[*She points, sweeping with her hand, to the stage.*]
Even of the animals, a few will be saved: two of a kind, male and female, two of a kind.

[*The heads of* CONVEENERS *appear about the stage and in the orchestra pit, jeering at her.*]

CONVEENERS. Charlatan! Madam Kill-joy! Mrs. Jeremiah! Charlatan!

FORTUNE TELLER. And *you*! Mark my words before it's too late. Where'll *you* be?

CONVEENERS. The croaking raven. Old dust and ashes. Rags, bottles, sacks.

FORTUNE TELLER. Yes, stick out your tongues. You can't stick your tongues out far enough to lick the death-sweat from your foreheads. It's too late to work now —bail out the flood with your soup spoons. You've had your chance and you've lost.

CONVEENERS. Enjoy yourselves!!!

[*They disappear. The* FORTUNE TELLER *looks off left and puts her finger on her lip.*]

FORTUNE TELLER. They're coming—the Antrobuses. Keck. Your hope. Your despair. Your selves.

[*Enter from the left,* MR. *and* MRS. ANTROBUS *and* GLADYS.]

MRS. ANTROBUS. Gladys Antrobus, stick your stummick in.

GLADYS. But it's easier this way.

MRS. ANTROBUS. Well, it's too bad the new president has such a clumsy daughter, that's all I can say. Try and be a lady.

FORTUNE TELLER. Aijah! That's been said a hundred billion times.

MRS. ANTROBUS. Goodness! Where's Henry? He was here just a minute ago. Henry!

[*Sudden violent stir. A roller-chair appears from the left. About it are dancing in great excitement* HENRY *and a* NEGRO CHAIR-PUSHER.]

HENRY [*slingshot in hand*]. I'll put your eye out. I'll make you yell, like you never yelled before.

NEGRO [*at the same time*]. Now, I warns you. I warns you. If you make me mad, you'll get hurt.

ANTROBUS. Henry! What is this? Put down that slingshot.

MRS. ANTROBUS [*at the same time*]. Henry! HENRY! Behave yourself.

FORTUNE TELLER. That's right, young man. There are too many people in the world as it is. Everybody's in the way, except one's self.

HENRY. All I wanted to do was—have some fun.

NEGRO. Nobody can't touch my chair, nobody, without I allow 'em to. You get clean away from me and you get away fast. [*He pushes his chair off, muttering.*]

ANTROBUS. What were you doing, Henry?

HENRY. Everybody's always getting mad. Everybody's always trying to push you around. I'll make him sorry for this; I'll make him sorry.

ANTROBUS. Give me that slingshot.

HENRY. I won't. I'm sorry I came to this place. I wish I weren't here. I wish I weren't anywhere.

MRS. ANTROBUS. Now, Henry, don't get so excited about nothing. I declare I don't know what we're going to do with you. Put your slingshot in your pocket, and don't try to take hold of things that don't belong to you.

ANTROBUS. After this you can stay home. I wash my hands of you.

MRS. ANTROBUS. Come now, let's forget all about it. Everybody take a good breath of that sea air and calm down.

[*A passing* CONVEENER *bows to* ANTROBUS *who nods to him.*]

Who was that you spoke to, George?

ANTROBUS. Nobody, Maggie. Just the candidate who ran against me in the election.

MRS. ANTROBUS. The man who ran against you in the election!!

[*She turns and waves her umbrella after the disappearing* CONVEENER.]

My husband didn't speak to you and he never will speak to you.

ANTROBUS. Now, Maggie.

MRS. ANTROBUS. After those lies you told about him in your speeches! Lies, that's what they were.

GLADYS *and* HENRY. Mama, everybody's looking at you. Everybody's laughing at you.

MRS. ANTROBUS. If you must know, my husband's a SAINT, a downright SAINT, and you're not fit to speak to him on the street.

ANTROBUS. Now, Maggie, now, Maggie, that's enough of that.

MRS. ANTROBUS. George Antrobus, you're a perfect worm. If you won't stand up for yourself, I will.

GLADYS. Mama, you just act awful in public.

MRS. ANTROBUS [*laughing*]. Well, I must say I enjoyed it. I feel better. Wish his wife had been there to hear it. Children, what do you want to do?

GLADYS. Papa, can we ride in one of those chairs? Mama, I want to ride in one of those chairs.

MRS. ANTROBUS. No, sir. If you're tired you just sit where you are. We have no money to spend on foolishness.

ANTROBUS. I guess we have money enough for a thing like that. It's one of the things you do at Atlantic City.

MRS. ANTROBUS. Oh, we have? I tell you it's a miracle my children have shoes to stand up in. I didn't think I'd ever live to see them pushed around in chairs.

ANTROBUS. We're on a vacation, aren't we? We have a right to some treats, I guess. Maggie, some day you're going to drive me crazy.

MRS. ANTROBUS. All right, go. I'll just sit here and laugh at you. And you can give me my dollar right in my hand. Mark my words, a rainy day is coming. There's a rainy day ahead of us. I feel it in my bones. Go on, throw your money around. I can starve. I've starved before. I know how.

[*A* CONVEENER *puts his head through Turkish Bath window, and says with raised eyebrows:*]

CONVEENER. Hello, George. How are ya? I see where you brought the WHOLE family along.

MRS. ANTROBUS. And what do you mean by that?

[CONVEENER *withdraws head and closes window.*]

ANTROBUS. Maggie, I tell you there's a limit to what I can stand. God's Heaven, haven't I worked *enough*? Don't I get *any* vacation? Can't I even give my children so much as a ride in a roller-chair?

MRS. ANTROBUS [*putting out her hand for raindrops*]. Anyway, it's going to rain very soon and you have your broadcast to make.

ANTROBUS. Now, Maggie, I warn you. A man can stand a family only just so long. I'm warning you.

[*Enter* SABINA *from the Bingo Parlor. She wears a*

flounced red silk bathing suit, 1905. Red stockings, shoes, parasol. She bows demurely to ANTROBUS and starts down the ramp. ANTROBUS and the CHILDREN stare at her. ANTROBUS bows gallantly.]

MRS. ANTROBUS. Why, George Antrobus, how can you say such a thing! You have the best family in the world.

ANTROBUS. Good morning, Miss Fairweather.

[SABINA *finally disappears behind the beach umbrella or in a cabana in the orchestra pit.*]

MRS. ANTROBUS. Who on earth was that you spoke to, George?

ANTROBUS [*complacent; mock-modest*]. Hm . . . m . . . just a . . . solambaka keray.

MRS. ANTROBUS. What? I can't understand you.

GLADYS. Mama, wasn't she beautiful?

HENRY. Papa, introduce her to me.

MRS. ANTROBUS. Children, will you be quiet while I ask your father a simple question?—Who did you say it was, George?

ANTROBUS. Why—uh . . . a friend of mine. Very nice refined girl.

MRS. ANTROBUS. I'm waiting.

ANTROBUS. Maggie, that's the girl I gave the prize to in the beauty contest—that's Miss Atlantic City 1942.

MRS. ANTROBUS. Hm! She looked like Sabina to me.

HENRY [*at the railing*]. Mama, the life-guard knows her, too. Mama, he knows her well.

ANTROBUS. Henry, come here.—She's a very nice girl in every way and the sole support of her aged mother.

MRS. ANTROBUS. So was Sabina, so was Sabina; and it took a wall of ice to open your eyes about Sabina.— Henry, come over and sit down on this bench.

ANTROBUS. She's a very different matter from Sabina. Miss Fairweather is a college graduate, Phi Beta Kappa.

MRS. ANTROBUS. Henry, you sit here by mama. Gladys—

ANTROBUS [*sitting*]. Reduced circumstances have required her taking a position as hostess in a Bingo Parlor; but there isn't a girl with higher principles in the country.

MRS. ANTROBUS. Well, let's not talk about it.—Henry, I haven't seen a whale yet.

ANTROBUS. She speaks seven languages and has more culture in her little finger than you've acquired in a lifetime.

MRS. ANTROBUS [*assumed amiability*]. All right, all right, George. I'm glad to know there are such superior girls in the Bingo Parlors.—Henry, what's that? [*Pointing at the storm signal, which has one black disk.*]

HENRY. What is it, Papa?

ANTROBUS. What? Oh, that's the storm signal. One of those black disks means bad weather; two means storm; three means hurricane; and four means the end of the world.

[*As they watch it a second black disk rolls into place.*]

MRS. ANTROBUS. Goodness! I'm going this very minute to buy you all some raincoats.

GLADYS [*putting her cheek against her father's shoulder*]. Mama, don't go yet. I like sitting this way. And the ocean coming in and coming in. Papa, don't you like it?

MRS. ANTROBUS. Well, there's only one thing I lack to make me a perfectly happy woman: I'd like to see a whale.

HENRY. Mama, we saw two. Right out there. They're delegates to the convention. I'll find you one.

GLADYS. Papa, ask me something. Ask me a question.

ANTROBUS. Well . . . how big's the ocean?

GLADYS. Papa, you're teasing me. It's—three-hundred

and sixty million square miles—and—it—covers—
three-fourths—of—the—earth's—surface—and—its—
—deepest-place—is—five—and—a—half—miles—deep—
and—its—average—depth—is—twelve-thousand—feet.
No, Papa, ask me something hard, real hard.

MRS. ANTROBUS [*rising*]. Now I'm going off to buy those
raincoats. I think that bad weather's going to get
worse and worse. I hope it doesn't come before your
broadcast. I should think we have about an hour or
so.

HENRY. I hope it comes and zzzzzz everything before it.
I hope it—

MRS. ANTROBUS. Henry!—George, I think . . . maybe,
it's one of those storms that are just as bad on land
as on the sea. When you're just as safe and safer
in a good stout boat.

HENRY. There's a boat out at the end of the pier.

MRS. ANTROBUS. Well, keep your eye on it. George, you
shut your eyes and get a good rest before the broadcast.

ANTROBUS. Thundering Judas, do I have to be told
when to open and shut my eyes? Go and buy your
raincoats.

MRS. ANTROBUS. Now, children, you have ten minutes
to walk around. Ten minutes. And, Henry: control
yourself. Gladys, stick by your brother and don't
get lost.

[*They run off.*]

MRS. ANTROBUS. Will you be all right, George?

[CONVEENERS *suddenly stick their heads out of the
Bingo Parlor and Salt Water Taffy store, and voices
rise from the orchestra pit.*]

CONVEENERS. George. Geo-r-r-rge! George! Leave the
old hen-coop at home, George. Do-mes-ticated
Georgie!

MRS. ANTROBUS [*shaking her umbrella*]. Low common
 oafs! That's what they are. Guess a man has a right
 to bring his wife to a convention, if he wants to.
[*She starts off.*]
 What's the matter with a family, I'd like to know.
 What else have they got to offer?
[*Exit.* ANTROBUS *has closed his eyes. The* FORTUNE TEL-
 LER *comes out of her shop and goes over to the left
 proscenium. She leans against it, watching* SABINA
 quizzically.]
FORTUNE TELLER. Heh! Here she comes!
SABINA [*loud whisper*]. What's he doing?
FORTUNE TELLER. Oh, he's ready for you. Bite your lips,
 dear, take a long breath and come on up.
SABINA. I'm nervous. My whole future depends on this.
 I'm nervous.
FORTUNE TELLER. Don't be a fool. What more could
 you want? He's forty-five. His head's a little dizzy.
 He's just been elected president. He's never known
 any other woman than his wife. Whenever he looks
 at her he realizes that she knows every foolish thing
 he's ever done.
SABINA [*still whispering*]. I don't know why it is, but
 every time I start one of these I'm nervous.
[*The* FORTUNE TELLER *stands in the center of the stage
 watching the following:*]
FORTUNE TELLER. You make me tired.
SABINA. First tell me my fortune.
[*The* FORTUNE TELLER *laughs drily and makes the ges-
 ture of brushing away a nonsensical question.* SA-
 BINA *coughs and says:*]
 Oh, Mr. Antrobus—dare I speak to you for a mo-
 ment?
ANTROBUS. What?—Oh, certainly, certainly, Miss Fair-
 weather.

SABINA. Mr. Antrobus . . . I've been so unhappy. I've wanted . . . I've wanted to make sure that you don't think that I'm the kind of girl who goes out for beauty contests.

FORTUNE TELLER. That's the way!

ANTROBUS. Oh, I understand. I understand perfectly.

FORTUNE TELLER. Give it a little more. Lean on it.

SABINA. I knew you would. My mother said to me this morning: Lily, she said, that fine Mr. Antrobus gave you the prize because he saw at once that you weren't the kind of girl who'd go in for a thing like that. But, honestly, Mr. Antrobus, in this world, honestly, a good girl doesn't know where to turn.

FORTUNE TELLER. Now you've gone too far.

ANTROBUS. My dear Miss Fairweather!

SABINA. You wouldn't know how hard it is. With that lovely wife and daughter you have. Oh, I think Mrs. Antrobus is the finest woman I ever saw. I wish I were like her.

ANTROBUS. There, there. There's . . . uh . . . room for all kinds of people in the world, Miss Fairweather.

SABINA. How wonderful of you to say that. How generous!—Mr. Antrobus, have you a moment free? . . . I'm afraid I may be a little conspicuous here . . . could you come down, for just a moment, to my beach cabana . . . ?

ANTROBUS. Why—uh . . . yes, certainly . . . for a moment . . . just for a moment.

SABINA. There's a deck chair there. Because: you know you *do* look tired. Just this morning my mother said to me: Lily, she said, I hope Mr. Antrobus is getting a good rest. His fine strong face has deep deep lines in it. Now isn't it true, Mr. Antrobus: you work too hard?

FORTUNE TELLER. Bingo! [*She goes into her shop.*]

SABINA. Now you will just stretch out. No, I shan't say a word, not a word. I shall just sit there—privileged. That's what I am.

ANTROBUS [*taking her hand*]. Miss Fairweather . . . you'll . . . spoil me.

SABINA. Just a moment. I have something I wish to say to the audience.—Ladies and gentlemen. I'm not going to play this particular scene tonight. It's just a short scene and we're going to skip it. But I'll tell you what takes place and then we can continue the play from there on. Now in this scene—

ANTROBUS [*between his teeth*]. But, Miss Somerset!

SABINA. I'm sorry. I'm sorry. But I have to skip it. In this scene, I talk to Mr. Antrobus, and at the end of it he decides to leaves his wife, get a divorce at Reno and marry me. That's all.

ANTROBUS. Fitz!—Fitz!

SABINA. So that now I've told you we can jump to the end of it—where you say—

[*Enter in fury* MR. FITZPATRICK, *the stage manager.*]

MR. FITZPATRICK. Miss Somerset, we insist on your playing this scene.

SABINA. I'm sorry, Mr. Fitzpatrick, but I can't and I won't. I've told the audience all they need to know and now we can go on.

[*Other* ACTORS *begin to appear on the stage, listening.*]

MR. FITZPATRICK. And *why* can't you play it?

SABINA. Because there are some lines in that scene that would hurt some people's feelings and I don't think the theatre is a place where people's feelings ought to be hurt.

MR. FITZPATRICK. Miss Somerset, you can pack up your things and go home. I shall call the understudy and I shall report you to Equity.

SABINA. I sent the understudy up to the corner for a cup of coffee and if Equity tries to penalize me I'll drag the case right up to the Supreme Court. Now listen, everybody, there's no need to get excited.

MR. FITZPATRICK *and* ANTROBUS. Why can't you play it . . . what's the matter with the scene?

SABINA. Well, if you must know, I have a personal guest in the audience tonight. Her life hasn't been exactly a happy one. I wouldn't have my friend hear some of these lines for the whole world. I don't suppose it occurred to the author that some other women might have gone through the experience of losing their husbands like this. Wild horses wouldn't drag from me the details of my friend's life, but . . . well, they'd been married twenty years, and before he got rich, why, she'd done the washing and everything.

MR. FITZPATRICK. Miss Somerset, your friend will forgive you. We must play this scene.

SABINA. Nothing, nothing will make me say some of those lines . . . about "a man outgrows a wife every seven years" and . . . and that one about "the Mohammedans being the only people who looked the subject square in the face." Nothing.

MR. FITZPATRICK. Miss Somerset! Go to your dressing room. I'll *read* your lines.

SABINA. Now everybody's nerves are on edge.

MR. ANTROBUS. Skip the scene.

[MR. FITZPATRICK *and the other* ACTORS *go off.*]

SABINA. Thank you. I knew you'd understand. We'll do just what I said. So Mr. Antrobus is going to divorce his wife and marry me. Mr. Antrobus, you say: "It won't be easy to lay all this before my wife."

[*The* ACTORS *withdraw.* ANTROBUS *walks about, his hand to his forehead muttering:*]

ANTROBUS. Wait a minute. I can't get back into it as easily as all that. "My wife is a very obstinate woman." Hm . . . then you say . . . hm . . . Miss

Fairweather, I mean Lily, it won't be easy to lay all this before my wife. It'll hurt her feelings a little.

SABINA. Listen, George: *other* people haven't got feelings. Not in the same way that we have—we who are presidents like you and prize-winners like me. Listen, other people haven't got feelings; they just imagine they have. Within two weeks they go back to playing bridge and going to the movies.

Listen, dear: everybody in the world except a few people like you and me are just people of straw. Most people have no insides at all. Now that you're president you'll see that. Listen, darling, there's a kind of secret society at the top of the world—like you and me—that know this. The world was made for us. What's life anyway? Except for two things, pleasure and power, what is life? Boredom! Foolishness. You know it is. Except for those two things, life's nau-se-at-ing. So—come here!

[*She moves close. They kiss.*]

So.

Now when your wife comes, it's really very simple; just tell her.

ANTROBUS. Lily, Lily: you're a wonderful woman.

SABINA. Of course I am.

[*They enter the cabana and it hides them from view. Distant roll of thunder. A third black disk appears on the weather signal. Distant thunder is heard. MRS. ANTROBUS appears carrying parcels. She looks about, seats herself on the bench left, and fans herself with her handkerchief. Enter GLADYS right, followed by two CONVEENERS. She is wearing red stockings.*]

MRS. ANTROBUS. Gladys!

GLADYS. Mama, here I am.

MRS. ANTROBUS. Gladys Antrobus!!! Where did **you** get those dreadful things?

GLADYS. Wha-a-t? Papa liked the color.

MRS. ANTROBUS. You go back to the hotel this minute!

GLADYS. I won't. I won't. Papa liked the color.

MRS. ANTROBUS. All right. All right. You stay here. I've a good mind to let your father see you that way. You stay right here.

GLADYS. I . . . I don't want to stay if . . . if you don't think he'd like it.

MRS. ANTROBUS. Oh . . . it's all one to me. I don't care what happens. I don't care if the biggest storm in the whole world comes. Let it come.

[*She folds her hands.*]

Where's your brother?

GLADYS [*in a small voice*]. He'll be here.

MRS. ANTROBUS. Will he? Well, let him get into trouble. I don't care. I don't know where your father is, I'm sure.

[*Laughter from the cabana.*]

GLADYS [*leaning over the rail*]. I think he's . . . Mama, he's talking to the lady in the red dress.

MRS. ANTROBUS. Is that so?

[*Pause.*]

We'll wait till he's through. Sit down here beside me and stop fidgeting . . . what are you crying about?

[*Distant thunder. She covers* GLADYS's *stockings with a raincoat.*]

GLADYS. You don't like my stockings.

[*Two* CONVEENERS *rush in with a microphone on a standard and various paraphernalia. The* FORTUNE TELLER *appears at the door of her shop. Other characters gradually gather.*]

BROADCAST OFFICIAL. Mrs. Antrobus! Thank God we've found you at last. Where's Mr. Antrobus? We've been hunting everywhere for him. It's about time for the broadcast to the conventions of the world.

MRS. ANTROBUS [*calm*]. I expect he'll be here in a minute.

BROADCAST OFFICIAL. Mrs. Antrobus, if he doesn't show up in time, I hope you will consent to broadcast in his place. It's the most important broadcast of the year.

[SABINA *enters from cabana followed by* ANTROBUS.]

MRS. ANTROBUS. No, I shan't. I haven't one single thing to say.

BROADCAST OFFICIAL. Then won't you help us find him, Mrs. Antrobus? A storm's coming up. A hurricane. A deluge!

SECOND CONVEENER [*who has sighted* ANTROBUS *over the rail*]. Joe! Joe! Here he is.

BROADCAST OFFICIAL. In the name of God, Mr. Antrobus, you're on the air in five minutes. Will you kindly please come and test the instrument? That's all we ask. If you just please begin the alphabet slowly.

[ANTROBUS, *with set face, comes ponderously up the ramp. He stops at the point where his waist is level with the stage and speaks authoritatively to the* OFFICIALS.]

ANTROBUS. I'll be ready when the time comes. Until then, move away. Go away. I have something I wish to say to my wife.

BROADCAST OFFICIAL [*whimpering*]. Mr. Antrobus! This is the most important broadcast of the year.

[*The* OFFICIALS *withdraw to the edge of the stage.* SABINA *glides up the ramp behind* ANTROBUS.]

SABINA [*whispering*]. Don't let her argue. Remember arguments have nothing to do with it.

ANTROBUS. Maggie, I'm moving out of the hotel. In fact, I'm moving out of everything. For good. I'm going to marry Miss Fairweather. I shall provide generously for you and the children. In a few years you'll be able to see that it's all for the best. That's all I have to say.

BROADCAST OFFICIAL. Mr. Antrobus! I hope you'll be ready. This is the most important broadcast of the year.

BINGO ANNOUNCER. A—Nine; A—Nine. D—Forty-two; D—Forty-two. C—Thirty; C—Thirty. B—Seventeen; B—Seventeen. C—Forty; C—Forty.

GLADYS. What did Papa say, Mama? I didn't hear what Papa said.

CHORUS. Bingo!!

BROADCAST OFFICIAL. Mr. Antrobus. All we want to do is test your voice with the alphabet.

ANTROBUS. Go away. Clear out.

MRS. ANTROBUS [*composedly with lowered eyes*]. George, I can't talk to you until you wipe those silly red marks off your face.

ANTROBUS. I think there's nothing to talk about. I've said what I have to say.

SABINA. Splendid!!

ANTROBUS. You're a fine woman, Maggie, but . . . but a man has his own life to lead in the world.

MRS. ANTROBUS. Well, after living with you for five thousand years I guess I have a right to a word or two, haven't I?

ANTROBUS [*to* SABINA]. What can I answer to that?

SABINA. Tell her that conversation would only hurt her feelings. It's-kinder-in-the-long-run-to-do-it-short-and-quick.

ANTROBUS. I want to spare your feelings in every way I can, Maggie.

BROADCAST OFFICIAL. Mr. Antrobus, the hurricane signal's gone up. We could begin right now.

MRS. ANTROBUS [*calmly, almost dreamily*]. I didn't

marry you because you were perfect. I didn't even marry you because I loved you. I married you because you gave me a promise.

[*She takes off her ring and looks at it.*]

That promise made up for your faults. And the promise I gave you made up for mine. Two imperfect people got married and it was the promise that made the marriage.

ANTROBUS. Maggie . . . I was only nineteen.

MRS. ANTROBUS [*she puts her ring back on her finger*]. And when our children were growing up, it wasn't a house that protected them; and it wasn't our love, that protected them—it was that promise.

And when that promise is broken—this can happen!

[*With a sweep of the hand she removes the raincoat from* GLADYS's *stockings.*]

ANTROBUS [*stretches out his arm, apoplectic*]. Gladys!! Have you gone crazy? Has everyone gone crazy?

[*Turning on* SABINA.]

You did this. You gave them to her.

SABINA. I never said a word to her.

ANTROBUS [*to* GLADYS]. You go back to the hotel and take those horrible things off.

GLADYS [*pert*]. Before I go, I've got something to tell you—it's about Henry.

MRS. ANTROBUS [*claps her hands peremptorily*]. Stop your noise—I'm taking her back to the hotel, George. Before I go I have a letter. . . . I have a message to throw into the ocean.

[*Fumbling in her handbag.*]

Where is the plagued thing? Here it is.

[*She flings something—invisible to us—far over the heads of the audience to the back of the auditorium.*]

It's a bottle. And in the bottle's a letter. And in the letter is written all the things that a woman knows.

It's never been told to any man and it's never been told to any woman, and if it finds its destination, a new time will come. We're not what books and plays say we are. We're not what advertisements say we are. We're not in the movies and we're not on the radio.

We're not what you're all told and what you think we are:

We're ourselves. And if any man can find one of us he'll learn why the whole universe was set in motion. And if any man harm any one of us, his soul—the only soul he's got—had better be at the bottom of that ocean—and that's the only way to put it. Gladys, come here. We're going back to the hotel.

[*She drags* GLADYS *firmly off by the hand, but* GLADYS *breaks away and comes down to speak to her father.*]

SABINA. Such goings-on. Don't give it a minute's thought.

GLADYS. Anyway, I think you ought to know that Henry hit a man with a stone. He hit one of those colored men that push the chairs and the man's very sick. Henry ran away and hid and some policemen are looking for him very hard. And I don't care a bit if you don't want to have anything to do with Mama and me, because I'll never like you again and I hope nobody ever likes you again—so there!

[*She runs off.* ANTROBUS *starts after her.*]

ANTROBUS. I . . . I have to go and see what I can do about this.

SABINA. You stay right here. Don't you go now while you're excited. Gracious sakes, all these things will be forgotten in a hundred years. Come, now, you're on the air. Just say anything—it doesn't matter what. Just a lot of birds and fishes and things.

BROADCAST OFFICIAL. Thank you, Miss Fairweather.

Thank you very much. Ready, Mr. Antrobus.

ANTROBUS [*touching the microphone*]. What is it, what is it? Who am I talking to?

BROADCAST OFFICIAL. Why, Mr. Antrobus! To our order and to all the other orders.

ANTROBUS [*raising his head*]. What are all those birds doing?

BROADCAST OFFICIAL. Those are just a few of the birds. Those are the delegates to our convention—two of a kind.

ANTROBUS [*pointing into the audience*]. Look at the water. Look at them all. Those fishes jumping. The children should see this!—There's Maggie's whales!! Here are your whales, Maggie!!

BROADCAST OFFICIAL. I hope you're ready, Mr. Antrobus.

ANTROBUS. And look on the beach! You didn't tell me these would be here!

SABINA. Yes, George. Those are the animals.

BROADCAST OFFICIAL [*busy with the apparatus*]. Yes, Mr. Antrobus, those are the vertebrates. We hope the lion will have a word to say when you're through. Step right up, Mr. Antrobus, we're ready. We'll just have time before the storm.

[*Pause. In a hoarse whisper:*]

They're wait-ing.

[*It has grown dark. Soon after he speaks a high whistling noise begins. Strange veering lights start whirling about the stage. The other characters disappear from the stage.*]

ANTROBUS. Friends. Cousins. Four score and ten billion years ago our forefather brought forth upon this planet the spark of life,—

[*He is drowned out by thunder. When the thunder stops the* FORTUNE TELLER *is seen standing beside him.*]

FORTUNE TELLER. Antrobus, there's not a minute to be lost. Don't you see the four disks on the weather signal? Take your family into that boat at the end of the pier.

ANTROBUS. My family? I have no family. Maggie! Maggie! They won't come.

FORTUNE TELLER. They'll come.—Antrobus! Take these animals into that boat with you. All of them—two of each kind.

SABINA. George, what's the matter with you? This is just a storm like any other storm.

ANTROBUS. Maggie!

SABINA. Stay with me, we'll go . . .

[*Losing conviction.*] This is just another thunderstorm—isn't it? Isn't it?

ANTROBUS. Maggie!!!

[MRS. ANTROBUS *appears beside him with Gladys.*]

MRS. ANTROBUS [*matter-of-fact*]. Here I am and here's Gladys.

ANTROBUS. Where've you been? Where have you been? Quick, we're going into that boat out there.

MRS. ANTROBUS. I know we are. But I haven't found Henry.

[*She wanders off into the darkness calling "Henry!"*]

SABINA [*low urgent babbling, only occasionally raising her voice*]. I don't believe it. I don't believe it's anything at all. I've seen hundreds of storms like this.

FORTUNE TELLER. There's no time to lose. Go. Push the animals along before you. Start a new world. Begin again.

SABINA. Esmeralda! George! Tell me—is it really serious?

ANTROBUS [*suddenly very busy*]. Elephants first. Gently, gently.—Look where you're going.

GLADYS [*leaning over the ramp and striking an animal on the back*]. Stop it or you'll be left behind!

ANTROBUS. Is the Kangaroo there? *There* you are! Take those turtles in your pouch, will you?

[*To some other animals, pointing to his shoulder.*] Here! You jump up here. You'll be trampled on.

GLADYS [*to her father, pointing below*]. Papa, look—the snakes!

MRS. ANTROBUS. I can't find Henry. Hen-ry!

ANTROBUS. Go along. Go along. Climb on their backs. —Wolves! Jackals—whatever you are—tend to your own business!

GLADYS [*pointing, tenderly*]. Papa—look.

SABINA. Mr. Antrobus—take me with you. Don't leave me here. I'll work. I'll help. I'll do anything.

[*Three* CONVEENERS *cross the stage, marching with a banner.*]

CONVEENERS. George! What are you scared of?—George! Fellas, it looks like rain.—"Maggie, where's my umbrella?"—George, setting up for Barnum and Bailey.

ANTROBUS [*again catching his wife's hand*]. Come on now, Maggie—the pier's going to break any minute.

MRS. ANTROBUS. I'm not going a step without Henry. Henry!

GLADYS [*on the ramp*]. Mama! Papa! Hurry. The pier's cracking, Mama. It's going to break.

MRS. ANTROBUS. Henry! Cain! CAIN!

[HENRY *dashes onto the stage and joins his mother.*]

HENRY. Here I am, Mama.

MRS. ANTROBUS. Thank God!—now come quick.

HENRY. I didn't think you wanted me.

MRS. ANTROBUS. Quick! [*She pushes him down before her into the aisle.*]

SABINA [*All the* ANTROBUSES *are now in the theatre aisle.* SABINA *stands at the top of the ramp*]. Mrs. Antrobus, take me. Don't you remember me? I'll work. I'll help. Don't leave me here!

MRS. ANTROBUS [*impatiently, but as though it were of*

no importance]. Yes, yes. There's a lot of work to be done. Only hurry.

FORTUNE TELLER [*now dominating the stage. To* SABINA *with a grim smile*]. Yes, go—back to the kitchen with you.

SABINA [*half-down the ramp. To* FORTUNE TELLER]. I don't know why my life's always being interrupted —just when everything's going fine!!

[*She dashes up the aisle. Now the* CONVEENERS *emerge doing a serpentine dance on the stage. They jeer at the* FORTUNE TELLER.]

CONVEENERS. Get a canoe—there's not a minute to be lost! Tell me my future, Mrs. Croaker.

FORTUNE TELLER. Paddle in the water, boys—enjoy yourselves.

VOICE *from the Bingo Parlor.* A—Nine; A—Nine. C— Twenty-four. C—Twenty-four.

CONVEENERS. Rags, bottles, and sacks.

FORTUNE TELLER. Go back and climb on your roofs. Put rags in the cracks under your doors.—Nothing will keep out the flood. You've had your chance. You've had your day. You've failed. You've lost.

VOICE *from the Bingo Parlor.* B—Fifteen. B—Fifteen.

FORTUNE TELLER [*shading her eyes and looking out to sea*]. They're safe. George Antrobus! Think it over! A new world to make.—Think it over!

CURTAIN

Act three

Just before the curtain rises, two sounds are heard from the stage: a cracked bugle call.

The curtain rises on almost total darkness. Almost all the flats composing the walls of MR. ANTROBUS'S *house, as of Act I, are up, but they lean helter-skelter against one another, leaving irregular gaps. Among the flats missing are two in the back wall, leaving the frames of the window and door crazily out of line.*

Off-stage, back right, some red Roman fire is burning. The bugle call is repeated. Enter SABINA *through the tilted door. She is dressed as a Napoleonic camp follower, "la fille du regiment," in begrimed reds and blues.*

SABINA. Mrs. Antrobus! Gladys! Where are you?

The war's over. The war's over. You can come out. The peace treaty's been signed.

Where are they?—Hmpf! Are they dead, too? Mrs. Annnntrobus! Glaaaadus! Mr. Antrobus'll be here this afternoon. I just saw him downtown. Huuuurry and put things in order. He says that now that the war's over we'll all have to settle down and be perfect.

[*Enter* MR. FITZPATRICK, *the stage manager, followed by the whole company, who stand waiting at the edges of the stage.* MR. FITZPATRICK *tries to interrupt* SABINA.]

MR. FITZPATRICK. Miss Somerset, we have to stop a moment.

SABINA. They may be hiding out in the back—

MR. FITZPATRICK. Miss Somerset! We have to stop a moment.

SABINA. What's the matter?

MR. FITZPATRICK. There's an explanation we have to make to the audience.—Lights, please.

[*To the actor who plays* MR. ANTROBUS.]

Will you explain the matter to the audience?

[*The lights go up. We now see that a balcony or elevated runway has been erected at the back of the stage, back of the wall of the Antrobus house. From its extreme right and left ends ladder-like steps descend to the floor of the stage.*]

ANTROBUS. Ladies and gentlemen, an unfortunate accident has taken place back stage. Perhaps I should say *another* unfortunate accident.

SABINA. I'm sorry. I'm sorry.

ANTROBUS. The management feels, in fact, we all feel that you are due an apology. And now we have to ask your indulgence for the most serious mishap of all. Seven of our actors have . . . have been taken ill. Apparently, it was something they ate. I'm not exactly clear what happened.

[*All the* ACTORS *start to talk at once.* ANTROBUS *raises his hand.*]

Now, now—not all at once. Fitz, do you know what it was?

MR. FITZPATRICK. Why, it's perfectly clear. These seven actors had dinner together, and they ate something that disagreed with them.

SABINA. Disagreed with them!!! They have ptomaine poisoning. They're in Bellevue Hospital this very minute in agony. They're having their stomachs pumped out this very minute, in perfect agony.

ANTROBUS. Fortunately, we've just heard they'll all recover.

SABINA. It'll be a miracle if they do, a downright miracle. It was the lemon meringue pie.

ACTORS. It was the fish . . . it was the canned tomatoes . . . it was the fish.

SABINA. It was the lemon meringue pie. I saw it with my own eyes; it had blue mold all over the bottom of it.

ANTROBUS. Whatever it was, they're in no condition to take part in this performance. Naturally, we haven't enough understudies to fill all those roles; but we do have a number of splendid volunteers who have kindly consented to help us out. These friends have watched our rehearsals, and they assure me that they know the lines and the business very well. Let me introduce them to you—my dresser, Mr. Tremayne— himself a distinguished Shakespearean actor for many years; our wardrobe mistress, Hester; Miss Somerset's maid, Ivy; and Fred Bailey, captain of the ushers in this theatre.

[*These persons bow modestly.* IVY *and* HESTER *are colored girls.*]

Now this scene takes place near the end of the act. And I'm sorry to say we'll need a short rehearsal, just a short run-through. And as some of it takes place in the auditorium, we'll have to keep the curtain up. Those of you who wish can go out in the lobby and smoke some more. The rest of you can listen to us, or . . . or just talk quietly among yourselves, as you choose. Thank you. Now will you take it over, Mr. Fitzpatrick?

MR. FITZPATRICK. Thank you.—Now for those of you who are listening perhaps I should explain that at the end of this act, the men have come back from the war and the family's settled down in the house. And the author wants to show the hours of the night passing by over their heads, and the planets crossing the sky . . . uh . . . over their heads. And he says—this is hard to explain—that each of the hours of the night is a philosopher, or a great thinker. Eleven o'clock, for instance, is Aristotle. And nine o'clock is Spinoza. Like that. I don't suppose it means anything. It's just a kind of poetic effect.

SABINA. Not mean anything! Why, it certainly does. Twelve o'clock goes by saying those wonderful things. I think it means that when people are asleep they have all those lovely thoughts, much better than when they're awake.

IVY. Excuse me, I think it means—excuse me, Mr. Fitzpatrick—

SABINA. What were you going to say, Ivy?

IVY. Mr. Fitzpatrick, you let my father come to a rehearsal; and my father's a Baptist minister, and he said that the author meant that—just like the hours and stars go by over our heads at night, in the same way the ideas and thoughts of the great men are in the air around us all the time and they're working on us, even when we don't know it.

MR. FITZPATRICK. Well, well, maybe that's it. Thank you, Ivy. Anyway—the hours of the night are philosophers. My friends, are you ready? Ivy, can you be eleven o'clock? "This good estate of the mind possessing its object in energy we call divine." Aristotle.

IVY. Yes, sir. I know that and I know twelve o'clock and I know nine o'clock.

MR. FITZPATRICK. Twelve o'clock? Mr. Tremayne, the Bible.

TREMAYNE. Yes.

MR. FITZPATRICK. Ten o'clock? Hester—Plato?

[*She nods eagerly.*]

Nine o'clock, Spinoza—Fred?

BAILEY. Yes, Sir.

[FRED BAILEY *picks up a great gilded cardboard numeral IX and starts up the steps to the platform.* MR. FITZPATRICK *strikes his forehead.*]

MR. FITZPATRICK. The planets!! We forgot all about the planets.

SABINA. O my God! The planets! Are they sick too?

[ACTORS *nod.*]

MR. FITZPATRICK. Ladies and gentlemen, the planets are singers. Of course, we can't replace them, so you'll have to imagine them singing in this scene. Saturn sings from the orchestra pit down here. The Moon is way up there. And Mars with a red lantern in his hand, stands in the aisle over there— Tz-tz-tz. It's too bad; it all makes a very fine effect. However! Ready—nine o'clock: Spinoza.

BAILEY [*walking slowly across the balcony, left to right*]. "After experience had taught me that the common occurrences of daily life are vain and futile—"

FITZPATRICK. Louder, Fred. "And I saw that all the objects of my desire and fear—"

BAILEY. "And I saw that all the objects of my desire and fear were in themselves nothing good nor bad save insofar as the mind was affected by them—"

FITZPATRICK. Do you know the rest? All right. Ten o'clock. Hester. Plato.

HESTER. "Then tell me, O Critias, how will a man choose the ruler that shall rule over him? Will he not—"

FITZPATRICK. Thank you. Skip to the end, Hester.

HESTER. ". . . can be multiplied a thousand fold in its effects among the citizens."

FITZPATRICK. Thank you.—Aristotle, Ivy?

IVY. "This good estate of the mind possessing its object in energy we call divine. This we mortals have occasionally and it is this energy which is pleasantest and best. But God has it always. It is wonderful in us; but in Him how much more wonderful."

FITZPATRICK. Midnight. Midnight, Mr. Tremayne. That's right—you've done it before.—All right, everybody. You know what you have to do.—Lower the curtain. House lights up. Act Three of THE SKIN OF OUR TEETH.

[*As the curtain descends he is heard saying:*]

You volunteers, just wear what you have on. Don't try to put on the costumes today.

[*House lights go down. The Act begins again. The Bugle call. Curtain rises. Enter* SABINA.]

SABINA. Mrs. Antrobus! Gladys! Where are you? The war's over.—You've heard all this—

[*She gabbles the main points.*]

Where—are—they? Are—they—dead, too, et cetera.
I—just—saw—Mr.—Antrobus—downtown, et cetera.

[*Slowing up:*]

He says that now that the war's over we'll all have to settle down and be perfect. They may be hiding out in the back somewhere. Mrs. An-tro-bus.

[*She wanders off. It has grown lighter. A trapdoor is cautiously raised and* MRS. ANTROBUS *emerges waist-high and listens. She is disheveled and worn; she wears a tattered dress and a shawl half covers her head. She talks down through the trapdoor.*]

MRS. ANTROBUS. It's getting light. There's still something burning over there—Newark, or Jersey City. What? Yes, I could swear I heard someone moving about up here. But I can't see anybody. I say: I can't see anybody.

[*She starts to move about the stage.* GLADYS'S *head appears at the trapdoor. She is holding a* BABY.]

GLADYS. Oh, Mama. Be careful.

MRS. ANTROBUS. Now, Gladys, you stay out of sight.

GLADYS. Well, let me stay here just a minute. I want the baby to get some of this fresh air.

MRS. ANTROBUS. All right, but keep your eyes open. I'll see what I can find. I'll have a good hot plate of soup for you before you can say Jack Robinson. Gladys Antrobus! Do you know what I think I see? There's old Mr. Hawkins sweeping the sidewalk in front of his A. and P. store. Sweeping it with a broom. Why, he must have gone crazy, like the others! I see some other people moving about, too.

GLADYS. Mama, come back, come back.

[MRS. ANTROBUS *returns to the trapdoor and listens.*]

MRS. ANTROBUS. Gladys, there's something in the air. Everybody's movement's sort of different. I see some women walking right out in the middle of the street.

SABINA'S VOICE. Mrs. An-tro-bus!

MRS. ANTROBUS *and* GLADYS. What's that?!!

SABINA'S VOICE. Glaaaadys! Mrs. An-tro-bus!

[*Enter* SABINA.]

MRS. ANTROBUS. Gladys, that's Sabina's voice as sure as I live.—Sabina! Sabina!—Are you *alive*?!!

SABINA. Of course, I'm alive. How've you girls been? —*Don't* try and kiss me. I never want to kiss another human being as long as I live. Sh-sh, there's nothing to get emotional about. Pull yourself together, the war's over. Take a deep breath—the war's over.

MRS. ANTROBUS. The war's over!! I don't believe you. I don't believe you. I can't believe you.

GLADYS. Mama!

SABINA. Who's that?

MRS. ANTROBUS. That's Gladys and her baby. I don't believe you. Gladys, Sabina says the war's over. Oh, Sabina.

SABINA [*leaning over the* BABY]. Goodness! Are there

any babies left in the world! Can it *see?* And can it cry and everything?

GLADYS. Yes, he can. He notices everything very well.

SABINA. Where on earth did you get it? Oh, I won't ask.—Lord, I've lived all these seven years around camp and I've forgotten how to behave.—Now we've got to think about the men coming home.—Mrs. Antrobus, go and wash your face, I'm ashamed of you. Put your best clothes on. Mr. Antrobus'll be here this afternoon. I just saw him downtown.

MRS. ANTROBUS *and* GLADYS. He's alive!! He'll be here!! Sabina, you're not joking?

MRS. ANTROBUS. And Henry?

SABINA [*dryly*]. Yes, Henry's alive, too, that's what they say. Now don't stop to talk. Get yourselves fixed up. Gladys, you look terrible. Have you any decent clothes?

[SABINA *has pushed them toward the trapdoor.*]

MRS. ANTROBUS [*half down*]. Yes, I've something to wear just for this very day. But, Sabina—who won the war?

SABINA. Don't stop now—just wash your face.

[*A whistle sounds in the distance.*]

Oh, my God, what's that silly little noise?

MRS. ANTROBUS. Why, it sounds like . . . it sounds like what used to be the noon whistle at the shoe-polish factory. [*Exit.*]

SABINA. That's what it is. Seems to me like peacetime's coming along pretty fast—shoe polish!

GLADYS [*half down*]. Sabina, how soon after peacetime begins does the milkman start coming to the door?

SABINA. As soon as he catches a cow. Give him time to catch a cow, dear.

[*Exit* GLADYS. SABINA *walks about a moment, thinking.*]

Shoe polish! My, I'd forgotten what peacetime was like.

[*She shakes her head, then sits down by the trapdoor and starts talking down the hole.*]

Mrs. Antrobus, guess what I saw Mr. Antrobus doing this morning at dawn. He was tacking up a piece of paper on the door of the Town Hall. You'll die when you hear: it was a recipe for grass soup, for a grass soup that doesn't give you the diarrhea. Mr. Antrobus is still thinking up new things.—He told me to give you his love. He's got all sorts of ideas for peacetime, he says. No more laziness and idiocy, he says. And oh, yes! Where are his books? What? Well, pass them up. The first thing he wants to see are his books. He says if you've burnt those books, or if the rats have eaten them, he says it isn't worthwhile starting over again. Everybody's going to be beautiful, he says, and diligent, and very intelligent.

[*A hand reaches up with two volumes.*]

What language is that? Pu-u-gh—mold! And he's got such plans for you, Mrs. Antrobus. You're going to study history and algebra—and so are Gladys and I—and philosophy. You should hear him talk:

[*Taking two more volumes.*]

Well, these are in English, anyway.—To hear him talk, seems like he expects you to be a combination, Mrs. Antrobus, of a saint and a college professor, and a dancehall hostess, if you know what I mean.

[*Two more volumes.*]

Ugh. German!

[*She is lying on the floor; one elbow bent, her cheek on her hand, meditatively.*]

Yes, peace will be here before we know it. In a week or two we'll be asking the Perkinses in for a quiet evening of bridge. We'll turn on the radio and hear how to be big successes with a new toothpaste. We'll trot down to the movies and see how girls with wax faces live—all *that* will begin again. Oh, Mrs. Antrobus, God forgive me but I enjoyed the war. Everybody's at their best in wartime. I'm sorry it's over. And, oh, I forgot! Mr. Antrobus sent you another message—can you hear me?—

[*Enter* HENRY, *blackened and sullen. He is wearing torn overalls, but has one gaudy admiral's epaulette hanging by a thread from his right shoulder, and there are vestiges of gold and scarlet braid running down his left trouser leg. He stands listening.*]

Listen! Henry's never to put foot in this house again, he says. He'll kill Henry on sight, if he sees him.

You don't know about Henry??? Well, where have you been? What? Well, Henry rose right to the top. Top of *what?* Listen, I'm telling you. Henry rose from corporal to captain, to major, to general.—I don't know how to say it, but the enemy is *Henry; Henry is* the enemy. Everybody knows that.

HENRY. He'll kill me, will he?

SABINA. Who are *you?* I'm not afraid of you. The war's over.

HENRY. I'll kill him so fast. I've spent seven years trying to find him; the others I killed were just substitutes.

SABINA. Goodness! It's Henry!—

[*He makes an angry gesture.*]

Oh, I'm not afraid of you. The war's over, Henry Antrobus, and you're not any more important than any other unemployed. You go away and hide yourself, until we calm your father down.

HENRY. The first thing to do is to burn up those old books; it's the ideas he gets out of those old books that . . . that makes the whole world so you can't live in it.

[*He reels forward and starts kicking the books about, but suddenly falls down in a sitting position.*]

SABINA. You leave those books alone!! Mr. Antrobus is looking forward to them a-special.—Gracious sakes, Henry, you're so tired you can't stand up. Your mother and sister'll be here in a minute and we'll think what to do about you.

HENRY. What did they ever care about me?

SABINA. There's that old whine again. All you people think you're not loved enough, nobody loves you. Well, you start being lovable and we'll love you.

HENRY [*outraged*]. I don't want anybody to love me.

SABINA. Then stop talking about it all the time.

HENRY. I *never* talk about it. The last thing I want is anybody to pay any attention to me.

SABINA. I can hear it behind every word you say.

HENRY. I want everybody to hate me.

SABINA. Yes, you've decided that's second best, but it's still the same thing.—Mrs. Antrobus! Henry's here. He's so tired he can't stand up.

MRS. ANTROBUS *and* GLADYS, *with her* BABY, *emerge. They are dressed as in Act I.* MRS. ANTROBUS *carries some objects in her apron, and* GLADYS *has a blanket over her shoulder.*]

MRS. ANTROBUS *and* GLADYS. Henry! Henry! Henry!

HENRY [*glaring at them*]. Have you anything to eat?

MRS. ANTROBUS. Yes, I have, Henry. I've been saving it for this very day—two good baked potatoes. No! Henry! one of them's for your father. Henry!! Give me that other potato back this minute.

[SABINA *sidles up behind him and snatches the other potato away.*]

SABINA. He's so dog-tired he doesn't know what he's doing.

MRS. ANTROBUS. Now you just rest there, Henry, until I can get your room ready. Eat that potato good and slow, so you can get all the nourishment out of it.

HENRY. You all might as well know right now that I haven't come back here to live.

MRS. ANTROBUS. Sh. . . . I'll put this coat over you. Your room's hardly damaged at all. Your football trophies are a little tarnished, but Sabina and I will polish them up tomorrow.

HENRY. Did you hear me? I don't live here. I don't belong to anybody.

MRS. ANTROBUS. Why, how can you say a thing like that! You certainly do belong right here. Where else would you want to go? Your forehead's feverish, Henry, seems to me. You'd better give me that gun, Henry. You won't need that any more.

GLADYS [*whispering*]. Look, he's fallen asleep already, with his potato half-chewed.

SABINA. Puh! The terror of the world.

MRS. ANTROBUS. Sabina, you mind your own business, and start putting the room to rights.

[HENRY *has turned his face to the back of the sofa.* MRS. ANTROBUS *gingerly puts the revolver in her apron pocket, then helps* SABINA. SABINA *has found a rope hanging from the ceiling. Grunting, she hangs all her weight on it, and as she pulls the walls begin to move into their right places.* MRS. ANTROBUS *brings the overturned tables, chairs and hassock into the positions of Act I.*]

SABINA. That's all we do—always beginning again! Over and over again. Always beginning again.

[*She pulls on the rope and a part of the wall moves into place. She stops. Meditatively:*]

How do we know that it'll be any better than before? Why do we go on pretending? Some day the whole earth's going to have to turn cold anyway, and until that time all these other things'll be happening again: it will be more wars and more walls of ice and floods and earthquakes.

MRS. ANTROBUS. Sabina! Stop arguing and go on with your work.

SABINA. All right. I'll go on just out of *habit,* but I won't believe in it.

MRS. ANTROBUS [*aroused*]. Now, Sabina. I've let you talk long enough. I don't want to hear any more of it. Do I have to explain to you what everybody knows —everybody who keeps a home going? Do I have to say to you what nobody should ever *have* to say, because they can read it in each other's eyes?
Now listen to me:

[MRS. ANTROBUS *takes hold of the rope.*]

I could live for seventy years in a cellar and make soup out of grass and bark, without ever doubting that this world has a work to do and will do it.
Do you hear me?

SABINA [*frightened*]. Yes, Mrs. Antrobus.

MRS. ANTROBUS. Sabina, do you see this house—216 Cedar Street—do you see it?

SABINA. Yes, Mrs. Antrobus.

MRS. ANTROBUS. Well, just to have known this house is to have seen the idea of what we can do someday if we keep our wits about us. Too many people have suffered and died for my children for us to start reneging now. So we'll start putting this house to rights. Now, Sabina, go and see what you can do in the kitchen.

SABINA. Kitchen! Why is it that however far I go away, I always find myself back in the kitchen? [*Exit.*]

MRS. ANTROBUS [*still thinking over her last speech, relaxes and says with a reminiscent smile*]: Goodness gracious, wouldn't you know that my father was a parson? It was just like I heard his own voice speaking and he's been dead five thousand years. There! I've gone and almost waked Henry up.

HENRY [*talking in his sleep, indistinctly*]. Fellows . . .

what have they done for us? . . . Blocked our way at every step. Kept everything in their own hands. And you've stood it. When are you going to wake up?

MRS. ANTROBUS. Sh, Henry. Go to sleep. Go to sleep. Go to sleep.—Well, that looks better. Now let's go and help Sabina.

GLADYS. Mama, I'm going out into the backyard and hold the baby right up in the air. And show him that we don't have to be afraid any more.

[*Exit* GLADYS *to the kitchen.* MRS. ANTROBUS *glances at* HENRY, *exits into kitchen.* HENRY *thrashes about in his sleep. Enter* ANTROBUS, *his arms full of bundles, chewing the end of a carrot. He has a slight limp. Over the suit of Act I he is wearing an overcoat too long for him, its skirts trailing on the ground. He lets his bundles fall and stands looking about. Presently his attention is fixed on* HENRY, *whose words grow clearer.*]

HENRY. All right! What have you got to lose? What have they done for us? That's right—nothing. Tear everything down. I don't care what you smash. We'll begin again and we'll show 'em.

[ANTROBUS *takes out his revolver and holds it pointing downwards. With his back toward the audience he moves toward the footlights.* HENRY'S *voice grows louder and he wakes with a start. They stare at one another. Then* HENRY *sits up quickly. Throughout the following scene* HENRY *is played, not as a misunderstood or misguided young man, but as a representation of strong unreconciled evil.*]

All right! Do something.

[*Pause.*]

Don't think I'm afraid of you, either. All right, do what you were going to do. Do it.

[*Furiously.*]

Shoot me, I tell you. You don't have to think I'm

any relation of yours. I haven't got any father or any mother, or brothers or sisters. And I don't want any. And what's more I haven't got anybody over me; and I never will have. I'm alone, and that's all I want to be: alone. So you can shoot me.

ANTROBUS. You're the last person I wanted to see. The sight of you dries up all my plans and hopes. I wish I were back at war still, because it's easier to fight you than to live with you. War's a pleasure—do you hear me?—War's a pleasure compared to what faces us now: trying to build up a peacetime with you in the middle of it.

[ANTROBUS *walks up to the window*.]

HENRY. I'm not going to be a part of any peacetime of yours. I'm going a long way from here and make my own world that's fit for a man to live in. Where a man can be free, and have a chance, and do what he wants to do in his own way.

ANTROBUS [*his attention arrested; thoughtfully. He throws the gun out of the window and turns with hope*]. . . . Henry, let's try again.

HENRY. Try what? Living *here*?—Speaking polite downtown to all the old men like you? Standing like a sheep at the street corner until the red light turns to green? Being a good boy and a good sheep, like all the stinking ideas you get out of your books? Oh, no. I'll make a world, and I'll show you.

ANTROBUS [*hard*]. How can you make a world for people to live in, unless you've first put order in yourself? Mark my words: I shall continue fighting you until my last breath as long as you mix up your idea of liberty with your idea of hogging everything for yourself. I shall have no pity on you. I shall pursue you to the far corners of the earth. You and I want the same thing; but until you think of it as something that everyone has a right to, you are my deadly enemy and I will destroy you.—I hear your mother's voice in the kitchen. Have you seen her?

HENRY. I have no mother. Get it into your head. I don't belong here. I have nothing to do here. I have no home.

ANTROBUS. Then why did you come here? With the whole world to choose from, why did you come to this one place: 216 Cedar Street, Excelsior, New Jersey. . . . Well?

HENRY. What if I did? What if I wanted to look at it once more, to see if—

ANTROBUS. Oh, you're related, all right—When your mother comes in you must behave yourself. Do you hear me?

HENRY [*wildly*]. What is this?—*must behave* yourself. Don't you say *must* to me.

ANTROBUS. Quiet!

[*Enter* MRS. ANTROBUS *and* SABINA.]

HENRY. Nobody can say *must* to me. All my life everybody's been crossing me—everybody, everything, all of you. I'm going to be free, even if I have to kill half the world for it. Right now, too. Let me get my hands on his throat. I'll show him.

[*He advances toward* ANTROBUS. *Suddenly,* SABINA *jumps between them and calls out in her own person:*]

SABINA. Stop! Stop! Don't play this scene. You know what happened last night. Stop the play.

[*The men fall back, panting.* HENRY *covers his face with his hands.*]

Last night you almost strangled him. You became a regular savage. Stop it!

HENRY. It's true. I'm sorry. I don't know what comes over me. I have nothing against him personally. I respect him very much . . . I . . . I admire him. But something comes over me. It's like I become fifteen years old again. I . . . I . . . listen: my own father used to whip me and lock me up every Saturday night. I never had enough to eat. He never let me have enough money to buy decent clothes. I was ashamed to go downtown. I never could go to the dances. My father and my uncle put rules in the way of everything I wanted to do. They tried to prevent my living at all.—I'm sorry. I'm sorry.

MRS. ANTROBUS [*quickly*]. No, go on. Finish what you were saying. Say it all.

HENRY. In this scene it's as though I were back in High School again. It's like I had some big emptiness inside me—the emptiness of being hated and blocked at every turn. And the emptiness fills up with the one thought that you have to strike and fight and kill. Listen, it's as though you have to kill somebody else so as not to end up killing yourself.

SABINA. That's not true. I knew your father and your uncle and your mother. You imagined all that. Why, they did everything they could for you. How can you say things like that? They didn't lock you up.

HENRY. They did. They did. They wished I hadn't been born.

SABINA. That's not true.

ANTROBUS [*in his own person, with self-condemnation, but cold and proud*]. Wait a minute. I have something to say, too. It's not wholly his fault that he wants to strangle me in this scene. It's my fault, too. He wouldn't feel that way unless there were something in me that reminded him of all that. He talks about an emptiness. Well, there's an emptiness in me, too. Yes—work, work, work—that's all I do. I've ceased to *live*. No wonder he feels that anger coming over him.

MRS. ANTROBUS. There! At least you've said it.

SABINA. We're all just as wicked as we can be, and that's the God's truth.

MRS. ANTROBUS [*nods a moment, then comes forward; quietly*]. Come. Come and put your head under some cold water.

SABINA [*in a whisper*]. I'll go with him. I've known him a long while. You have to go on with the play. Come with me.

[HENRY *starts out with* SABINA, *but turns at the exit and says to* ANTROBUS:]

HENRY. Thanks. Thanks for what you said. I'll be all right tomorrow. I won't lose control in that place. I promise.

[*Exeunt* HENRY *and* SABINA. ANTROBUS *starts toward the front door, fastens it.* MRS. ANTROBUS *goes up stage and places the chair close to table.*]

MRS. ANTROBUS. George, do I see you limping?

ANTROBUS. Yes, a little. My old wound from the other war started smarting again. I can manage.

MRS. ANTROBUS [*looking out of the window*]. Some lights are coming on—the first in seven years. People are walking up and down looking at them. Over in Hawkins' open lot they've built a bonfire to celebrate the peace. They're dancing around it like scarecrows.

ANTROBUS. A bonfire! As though they hadn't seen enough things burning.—Maggie—the dog died?

MRS. ANTROBUS. Oh, yes. Long ago. There are no dogs left in Excelsior.—You're back again! All these years. I gave up counting on letters. The few that arrived were anywhere from six months to a year late.

ANTROBUS. Yes, the ocean's full of letters, along with the other things.

MRS. ANTROBUS. George, sit down, you're tired.

ANTROBUS. No, you sit down. I'm tired but I'm restless. [*Suddenly, as she comes forward.*]
Maggie! I've lost it. I've lost it.

MRS. ANTROBUS. What, George? What have you lost?

ANTROBUS. The most important thing of all: The desire to begin again, to start building.

MRS. ANTROBUS [*sitting in the chair right of the table*]. Well, it will come back.

ANTROBUS [*at the window*]. I've lost it. This minute I feel like all those people dancing around the bonfire—just relief. Just the desire to settle down; to slip into the old grooves and keep the neighbors from walking over my lawn.—Hm. But during the war—in the middle of all that blood and dirt and hot and cold—every day and night, I'd have moments, Maggie, when I *saw* the things that we could do when it was over. When you're at war you think about a better life; when you're at peace you think about a more comfortable one. I've lost it. I feel sick and tired.

MRS. ANTROBUS. Listen! The baby's crying.
I hear Gladys talking. Probably she's quieting Henry again. George, while Gladys and I were living here —like moles, like rats, and when we were at our wits' end to save the baby's life—the only thought we clung to was that you were going to bring something good out of this suffering. In the night, in the dark, we'd whisper about it, starving and sick.—Oh, George, you'll have to get it back again. Think! What else kept us alive all these years? Even now, it's not comfort we want. We can suffer whatever's necessary; only give us back that promise.

[*Enter* SABINA *with a lighted lamp. She is dressed as in Act I.*]

SABINA. Mrs. Antrobus . . .

MRS. ANTROBUS. Yes, Sabina?

SABINA. Will you need me?

MRS. ANTROBUS. No, Sabina, you can go to bed.

SABINA. Mrs. Antrobus, if it's all right with you, I'd like to go to the bonfire and celebrate seeing the war's over. And, Mrs. Antrobus, they've opened the Gem Movie Theatre and they're giving away a hand-painted soup tureen to every lady, and I thought one of us ought to go.

ANTROBUS. Well, Sabina, I haven't any money. I haven't seen any money for quite a while.

SABINA. Oh, you don't need money. They're taking anything you can give them. And I have some . . . some . . . Mrs. Antrobus, promise you won't tell anyone. It's a little against the law. But I'll give you some, too.

ANTROBUS. What is it?

SABINA. I'll give you some, too. Yesterday I picked up a lot of . . . of beef cubes!

[MRS. ANTROBUS *turns and says calmly:*]

MRS. ANTROBUS. But, Sabina, you know you ought to give that in to the Center downtown. They know who needs them most.

SABINA [*outburst*]. Mrs. Antrobus, I didn't make this war. I didn't ask for it. And, in my opinion, after anybody's gone through what we've gone through, they have a right to grab what they can find. You're a very nice man, Mr. Antrobus, but you'd have got on better in the world if you'd realized that dog-eat-dog was the rule in the beginning and always will be. And most of all now.

[*In tears.*]

Oh, the world's an awful place, and you know it is. I used to think something could be done about it; but I know better now. I hate it. I hate it.

[*She comes forward slowly and brings six cubes from the bag.*]

All right. All right. You can have them.

ANTROBUS. Thank you, Sabina.

SABINA. Can I have . . . can I have one to go to the movies?

[ANTROBUS *in silence gives her one.*]

Thank you.

ANTROBUS. Good night, Sabina.

SABINA. Mr. Antrobus, don't mind what I say. I'm just an ordinary girl, you know what I mean, I'm just an ordinary girl. But you're a bright man, you're a very bright man, and of course you invented the alphabet and the wheel, and, my God, a lot of things . . . and if you've got any other plans, my God, don't let me upset them. Only every now and then I've got to go to the movies. I mean my nerves can't stand it. But if you have any ideas about improving the crazy old world, I'm really with you. I really am. Because it's . . . it's . . . Good night.

[*She goes out.* ANTROBUS *starts laughing softly with exhilaration.*]

ANTROBUS. Now I remember what three things always went together when I was able to see things most clearly: three things. Three things:

[*He points to where* SABINA *has gone out.*]

The voice of the people in their confusion and their need. And the thought of you and the children and this house . . . And . . . Maggie! I didn't dare ask you: my books! They haven't been lost, have they?

MRS. ANTROBUS. No. There are some of them right here. Kind of tattered.

ANTROBUS. Yes.—Remember, Maggie, we almost lost them once before? And when we finally did collect a few torn copies out of old cellars they ran in everyone's head like a fever. They as good as rebuilt the world.

[*Pauses, book in hand, and looks up.*]

Oh, I've never forgotten for long at a time that living is struggle. I know that every good and excellent thing in the world stands moment by moment on the razor-edge of danger and must be fought for—whether it's a field, or a home, or a country. All I ask is the chance to build new worlds and God has always given us that. And has given us [*Opening the book.*] voices to guide us; and the memory of our mistakes to warn us. Maggie, you and I will remember in peacetime all the resolves that were so clear to us in the days of war. We've come a long ways. We've learned. We're learning. And the steps of our journey are marked for us here.

[*He stands by the table turning the leaves of a book.*]

Sometimes out there in the war—standing all night on a hill—I'd try and remember some of the words in these books. Parts of them and phrases would come back to me. And after a while I used to give names to the hours of the night.

[*He sits, hunting for a passage in the book.*]

Nine o'clock I used to call Spinoza. Where is it: "After experience had taught me—"

[*The back wall has disappeared, revealing the platform.* FRED BAILEY *carrying his numeral has started from left to right.* MRS. ANTROBUS *sits by the table sewing.*]

BAILEY. "After experience had taught me that the common occurrences of daily life are vain and futile; and I saw that all the objects of my desire and fear were in themselves nothing good nor bad save insofar as the mind was affected by them; I at length determined to search out whether there was something truly good and communicable to man."

[*Almost without break* HESTER, *carrying a large Roman*

numeral ten, starts crossing the platform. GLADYS *appears at the kitchen door and moves toward her mother's chair.*]

HESTER. "Then tell me, O Critias, how will a man choose the ruler that shall rule over him? Will he not choose a man who has first established order in himself, knowing that any decision that has its spring from anger or pride or vanity can be multiplied a thousandfold in its effects upon the citizens?"

[HESTER *disappears and* IVY, *as eleven o'clock starts speaking.*]

IVY. "This good estate of the mind possessing its object in energy we call divine. This we mortals have occasionally and it is this energy which is pleasantest and best. But God has it always. It is wonderful in us; but in Him how much more wonderful."

[*As* MR. TREMAYNE *starts to speak,* HENRY *appears at the edge of the scene, brooding and unreconciled, but present.*]

TREMAYNE. "In the beginning, God created the Heavens and the earth; And the Earth was waste and void; And the darkness was upon the face of the deep. And the Lord said let there be light and there was light."

[*Sudden black-out and silence, except for the last strokes of the midnight bell. Then just as suddenly the lights go up, and* SABINA *is standing at the window, as at the opening of the play.*]

SABINA. Oh, oh, oh. Six o'clock and the master not home yet. Pray God nothing serious has happened to him crossing the Hudson River. But I wouldn't be surprised. The whole world's at sixes and sevens, and why the house hasn't fallen down about our ears long ago is a miracle to me.

[*She comes down to the footlights.*]

This is where you came in. We have to go on for ages and ages yet.

You go home.

The end of this play isn't written yet.

Mr. and Mrs. Antrobus! Their heads are full of plans and they're as confident as the first day they began—and they told me to tell you: good night.

HOME OF THE BRAVE

by Arthur Laurents

First production, December 27, 1945,
at the Belasco Theatre, New York City,
with the following cast:

CAPT. HAROLD BITTERGER, *Eduard Franz*
MAJOR DENNIS ROBINSON, JR., *Kendall Clark*
T. J., *Russell Hardie*
CONEY, *Joseph Pevney*
FINCH, *Henry Barnard*
MINGO, *Alan Baxter*

SCENES

ACT ONE

Scene I *Hospital Room. A Pacific Base.*
Scene II *Office. The Pacific Base.*
Scene III *A Clearing. A Pacific Island.*

ACT TWO

Scene I *Hospital Room.*
Scene II *Another Clearing. The Island.*
Scene III *Hospital Room.*

ACT THREE

Scene I *Hospital Room. Two weeks later.*
Scene II *The Office. A few days later.*

Act one

SCENE I

SCENE—*Hospital Room. A Pacific Base.*

This is a small room, the office, really, of CAPTAIN
HAROLD BITTERGER, *a doctor. There is a window, rear,
through which we can see tropical foliage and bright
sunlight. Up right is a door; downstage of this, a desk
heavy with papers and a chair behind the desk. Across
the room, near the left wall, is an army cot. Near this
a small table. There are two chairs near the desk.*

Seated in one of these chairs is MAJOR DENNIS E.
ROBINSON, JR. *He is about twenty-six, a cigarette ad
with a blond crew-cut. He is self-conscious about his
rank and position (and his shortcomings) and attempts
to hide his natural boyishness by a stalwart military
manner.*

In the other chair is CORPORAL T. J. EVERITT, *a rather
pompously good-looking Rotarian.* T.J. *is about thirty-
five. He resents the Army, his position, almost everything. He has found it difficult to adjust himself to
this new life and, therefore, seems and acts more pet-
tish and mean than he actually is.*

*Standing in front of the desk with a sheaf of papers
in his hand is the* DOCTOR, CAPTAIN BITTERGER: *a stocky
man with graying hair, about forty-three. He knows a*

*good deal about men, particularly soldiers, is anxious
to learn more, to have the world learn more.*

When the curtain rises, there is silence. The DOCTOR
has apparently just asked a question. The MAJOR *and*
T.J. *look at him uncomfortably for a second, then turn
away.*

DOCTOR [*impatiently*]. Well?

MAJOR [*a slight wait*]. I don't know, Doctor.

DOCTOR [*holding up the sheaf of papers*]. This is the
whole story.

MAJOR. All that we know.

DOCTOR. All the events, at any rate.

MAJOR. Yes, sir.

T.J. Captain, maybe Sergeant Mingo—

DOCTOR [*brusquely*]. I've spoken to Sergeant Mingo.
You *all* agree on the facts. Wonderful things: facts.
Wonderful word. Doesn't mean a goddam thing.

MAJOR. Doctor, if there's—

DOCTOR. They help. Facts help, Major. And I thank
you for them. But they're not quite enough.

MAJOR. I hope you don't think, sir—

DOCTOR. Major, forgive me. I'm sorry about your feelings. And yours, Corporal. And Sergeant Mingo's.
And the whole world's. But at this point, I'm only
interested in one man. A patient. A Private First
Class Peter Coen.

[*Slight pause.*]

T.J. Doctor—

DOCTOR. Yes?

T.J. I just happened to remember. There was something else. There was a fight.

MAJOR. A fight? When?

DOCTOR. The last day you were on the island, wasn't it?

T.J. Yes, sir.

MAJOR. I didn't know! Who had a fight?

DOCTOR [*to* T.J.]. You see, I did speak to Sergeant Mingo, Corporal.

T.J. Well, I just happened to remember it now.

DOCTOR. Really?

T.J. It didn't seem so important. I just forgot it.

DOCTOR. Everything's important with a case like this.

MAJOR. Coney's going to be all right, isn't he?

DOCTOR. I'm a psychiatrist, Major, not a clairvoyant. The boy suffered a traumatic shock. Now he has paralysis. Amnesia. Physical manifestations. They're curable—sometimes. And sometimes—

MAJOR. Can we see him?

DOCTOR. He won't recognize you.

MAJOR. I'd like to see him, though.

DOCTOR. He's due for a treatment now.

MAJOR. Just for a second, Captain.

DOCTOR [*after a moment's hesitation—to* T.J.]. Corporal, he's in the first ward to your left. Do you want to bring him in?

T.J. Well—yes, sir. [*He goes out.*]

DOCTOR [*during following, he prepares for the amytal injection to follow*]. Fine day. God's in His heaven and all's wrong with the world.

MAJOR. How are you treating him, Captain?

DOCTOR. Narcosynthesis, Major. [*Turns and looks at the* MAJOR *who obviously doesn't understand.*] Narcosynthesis. You administer a drug that acts as a release for the patient. Usually, he will relive the experiences immediately preceding shock if the doctor leads him. Usually one or two injections are enough for him to recover physically. . . . I'm starting the treatment today.

MAJOR. You mean Coney'll be able to walk? He'll get his memory back?

DOCTOR. Maybe. I don't know. But suppose he can

walk, suppose he can remember—that's only half the battle. There'll still be something in him—deep in him—that caused all this.

MAJOR. But can't this narcosynthesis—

DOCTOR. It's not perfect. It was started about fifteen years ago. We're still learning. But we've learned a great deal using it in this war. See? War has its uses.

MAJOR. I hope to God it works for Coney.

DOCTOR. His collapse wasn't your fault.

MAJOR. Well—he was my responsibility.

DOCTOR. The job was.

MAJOR. That's what I thought but—

DOCTOR. Major, how old are you? Twenty-five?

MAJOR. Twenty-six.

DOCTOR. Well, twenty-six. What do you know? Your job. Period. Let me tell you something, Major—Robinson?

MAJOR. That's right, sir.

DOCTOR. Look, Robinson. You were right. The job comes first. The men count. But they count second. How many were there on that mission? Five. But you were doing that job for hundreds, for thousands, for the whole goddam war. That's a little more important—

MAJOR. I know. But Coney's important, too.

DOCTOR. Sure. And maybe if you were smarter—but you're twenty-six. And hell! I'm not so smart. How the devil do I know that if you were smarter, you could have prevented this? Matter of fact, I doubt it. Maybe you're wrong, maybe I'm wrong—and God knows that's possible—too goddam possible—but that kid's crack-up goes back to a thousand million people being wrong.

MAJOR. What do you mean?

DOCTOR. They don't take a man for himself . . . for what he is.

MAJOR. I don't get it.

DOCTOR [*smiling*]. I didn't think you would. You probably never came face to face—

[*The door opens and* T.J. *brings in* CONEY *who is in a wheel chair.* CONEY *is dressed in the dark-red hospital robe. He is slumped in the chair with a melancholic, frightened look on his face.*]

MAJOR. Hello, Coney!

T.J. He didn't know me.

MAJOR. Coney . . . how do you feel, fellow?

CONEY. All right, sir.

DOCTOR. Coney . . . do you remember Major Robinson?

CONEY [*looks at the* MAJOR *slowly, then back to the* DOCTOR]. No, sir.

MAJOR. Coney, you remember. Don't you remember me? Don't you remember Mingo?

CONEY. Mingo? Mingo?

MAJOR [*to* DOCTOR]. Does he remember about—Finch?

DOCTOR. Ask him.

CONEY. What? Who?

MAJOR. Coney . . . Coney . . . remember Finch?

CONEY. No, sir. No, sir. [*His voice cracks.*] Doctor—

DOCTOR. All right, son. All right . . .

CONEY. Doctor—

DOCTOR [*to* T.J.]. Help me lift him on the bed, please. [*They do.*] Thanks. Chair. [T.J. *quickly brings him a chair. He sits in it and holds* CONEY's *hand.*] I'm sorry.

MAJOR. Will you let us know?

DOCTOR. Yes.

MAJOR. Let's go. So long, Coney. Be seeing you. [*He waits a moment for an answer. But there is none. They walk out, closing the door behind them.*]

DOCTOR [*his manner changes now. He is soft, gentle, kind—a father to this boy*]. Don't be frightened, son. There's nothing to be frightened of. Nothing in the world. [*He gets up, as he continues, and pulls down the shade. The room is in half light. As he talks, he moves the small table with his instruments near the bed.*] You know who I am, don't you, Coney?

CONEY. Doctor . . .

DOCTOR. Sure. I'm your doctor. And you know what doctors do, don't you? They make you well. And that's what I'm going to do. I'm going to make you well, Coney. I'm going to fix you up so you'll remember everything and be able to walk again. [*He is now rolling up* CONEY's *sleeve and putting on a tourniquet.*] You'd like to walk again, wouldn't you?

CONEY. Yes, sir.

DOCTOR. Well, you will. You'll be fine. [*He begins to swab* CONEY's *arm.*] Now, you mustn't be afraid. This isn't going to hurt. I'm your doctor. Doctors don't hurt, son. They make you better. [*Takes out hypo.*] All you'll feel will be a little prick with a needle. Just like when you stick yourself with a pin. That's all this is. Just a long pin. Do you understand?

CONEY. Yes, sir.

DOCTOR. All right. Now when I put the needle in, I want you to start counting backwards from one hundred. Backwards. 99, 98, 97. Like that. Is that clear?

CONEY. Yes, sir. [*A frightened cry.*] Doctor, I—

DOCTOR. This is going to make you feel fine, son. This is going to make you sleep without all those bad dreams. . . . Now then. Just a little— [*He removes the tourniquet and injects the needle.*] Sting—there. Now you start counting. 100, 99 . . .

CONEY [*as he gets along in this counting, his speech gets slightly thicker and there is an occasional cough*]. 100—99—98—97—96—95—94—93—92—91—90—89—87—86—85—84—8—

DOCTOR. 83.

CONEY. 83—82—81—82—1—

[*The* DOCTOR *has been watching the needle in* CONEY'S *arm. Now he looks up and leans forward deliberately.*]

DOCTOR. Who do you work for, Coney?

CONEY. Major Robinson.

[*A brief second's pause. The* DOCTOR *sits up and smiles.*]

DOCTOR. Is he a good C.O.?

CONEY. Oh, the Major's an all right guy. Darn decent. And he knows his stuff. He's decent only . . .

DOCTOR. Only what?

CONEY. He's an all right guy. He's O.K.

DOCTOR. Not as smart as Mingo, though, is he?

CONEY. Oh, he knows more about engineering but Mingo's a sharp boy. He knows. He knows plenty. You know his wife writes poetry?

DOCTOR. She does?

CONEY. Yep. Real poetry. Sometimes, he's kind of touchy, though.

DOCTOR. Touchy? Like you?

CONEY. No . . . No, not like me. None of them are like me. I—I—

DOCTOR. You what, Coney?

CONEY. Mingo's sensitive about—well, about his wife. About how they treat him—us. Once . . . once I heard a poem. A poem Mingo's wife wrote. I heard that.

DOCTOR. Did he recite it to you?

CONEY. Once . . . Just once . . .

DOCTOR. Why shouldn't he recite it to you? You're his buddy.

CONEY. Oh, no. I'm not his buddy. He doesn't have a buddy. You can't get real close to Mingo.

DOCTOR. Who's your buddy, Coney? [*Pause.*] Who's

your buddy? [*No answer.*] Finch? Finch is your
buddy, isn't he? [*He withdraws the needle.*]

CONEY. Yes.

DOCTOR. He's been your buddy almost since you came
in the Army.

CONEY [*low*]. Yes.

DOCTOR. Finch is an all right guy. He likes you. And
you like him, don't you?

CONEY. Yes, I— [*Suddenly, loudly.*] No. No, I don't. He
doesn't really like me! He's like all of them. He
doesn't like me and I hate him! I hate him!

DOCTOR. You really hate Finch?

CONEY. Yes! [*A long pause. Then, very quietly.*] No.
Finch is a sweet kid. He's my buddy, the dumb Arizona hayseed. Didn't know from nothing when he
came into the outfit. But he's learning. He's a sweet
kid. He doesn't seem like the others only—only I
wonder if he is.

DOCTOR. If Finch is what?

CONEY. Like the others.

DOCTOR. What others?

CONEY. The ones who make the cracks.

DOCTOR. Who, Coney? Who makes the cracks?

CONEY. T.J. [*Venomously.*] Corporal T.J. Everitt.
[*With slow fury.*] I hate his guts.

DOCTOR. What cracks does he make, Coney?

CONEY. Finch doesn't let him get away with them,
though. Finch— [*He suddenly springs up to a sitting
position. He is frightened.*] Finch! Where's Finch?

DOCTOR. He's all right.

CONEY. Where is he? Where's Finch?

DOCTOR. He's all right.

CONEY. Where is he?

DOCTOR. Don't worry about him.

CONEY [*calling*]. Finch? [*Frightened.*] Finch? [*He looks
around frantically.*]

DOCTOR [*hesitates—and then throws an arm around* CONEY]. Hi, Coney.

CONEY [*cheerfully*]. Finch! Where the hell have you been? The Major wants us in his office.

[*The lights start to dim down.*]

DOCTOR. What for?

CONEY. How the hell would I know what for? Do they ever tell you anything in the Army? All I know is we got to get to the Major's office on the double. So come on. Let's take off!

[*By now, the stage is blacked out. Through the darkness, we hear the distant sound of a field telephone ringing. The sound gets louder and louder gradually.*]

SCENE II

SCENE—*An office. A Pacific Base.*

This fairly wide but shallow room is a section of a quonset hut. The hut serves as an army office building; wooden partitions separate one "room" from another. This one is an outer office. The spotted walls, the littered desks, the equipment in the corners, the four or five posters—none of this really belies the temporary air that this room and the thousands like it invariably have.

In the center of the rear wall is a door marked plainly with a wooden plaque: MAJOR ROBINSON. *Up right are a desk and a chair. Down left is another door which leads to the street outside. Upstage of this are another desk and a chair. There are one or two other chairs or crates serving as chairs in the room. Each side wall has a small window through which the morning sun is boiling despite the tropical trees.*

AT RISE: *As the lights come up the telephone is ringing and through the screened street door we see two soldiers running up. First is* PFC. PETER COEN—"CONEY" *—and we now see that he is of medium height with a strong, solid body. His face is fairly nondescript until he smiles. Then his hard, tough manner washes away in warmth and good humor. He is about twenty-three and wears faded green coveralls.*

The second soldier looks a little younger and a little neater. He is a tall, bony kid named FINCH—*a private. He is immediately likable. He is rather simple, rather gentle and, at the moment, a little worried.*

It is apparent that neither of the boys knows what they are here for. They look about the empty room for a moment and then CONEY *moves center with a shrug.*

CONEY. Nobody's home.

FINCH. I thought you said the Major wanted us on the double.

[*Telephone stops ringing.*]

CONEY. They always want you here two minutes ago, but they're never here when you're here.

FINCH. We could have cleaned up.

CONEY [*wandering around, snooping at the papers on the desks*]. What've you got to be clean for anyway? Short arm? The only thing we could pick up around here is mildew.

FINCH. Oh, that's charming.

CONEY. Delightful.

[*A slight pause.*]

FINCH. Who else did he send for?

CONEY [*taking out a cigarette*]. I don't know. Maybe he only wants us. Fresh young meat for the grinder.

FINCH. Oh! Great! [FINCH *refuses the cigarette and walks over to the window.*]

CONEY [*tenderly*]. Hey, jerk . . . [FINCH *turns around.*]
   Hell, I'm no pipeline. It might be a furlough.

FINCH [*denying it*]. Yep, yep.

CONEY. It might be. We've been over two years plus
   and it says in the book—

FINCH. What book, Grimm's Fairy Tales?

CONEY [*quietly*]. I guess. [*Slight pause.*] Ah, come on,
   Finch. You think every time they send for you in the
   Army, it's for something bad.

FINCH. Isn't it?

CONEY [*trying hard to pick* FINCH *up*]. You know, if it
   is a furlough, we'll have a chance to look for a spot
   for that bar we're gonna have.

FINCH. I thought we decided.

CONEY. That whistle stop in Arizona?

FINCH. It's a nice town. And it's near home.

CONEY. Your home. Listen, did you tell her?

FINCH. Tell who?

CONEY. Your mother, jerk. About us going to own a
   bar together after the war.

FINCH. I told her it was going to be a restaurant.

CONEY. A restaurant!

FINCH. Mothers don't understand about bars. But I
   wrote her about how I'm going to paint pictures on
   the walls and about how it's going to be the kind of
   place you said.

CONEY. Where a guy can bring his wife.

FINCH. She liked that.

CONEY. Sure. I know just how it should be run. Your
   mother'll like it fine. [FINCH *starts to whistle a tune
   called "Shoo, Fly."*] Finch . . .

FINCH. Huh?

CONEY. Does your mother know who I am?

FINCH. Of course.

CONEY. I mean, does she know my name?

FINCH. Well, sure she does!

CONEY. Oh.

FINCH. What did you think?

CONEY. I don't know. I just wondered.

FINCH. You can be an A-1 jerk sometimes. The whole family knows about you and Mom's so het up, I think she's got ideas about mating you and my sister.

CONEY. Yep, yep.

FINCH. What do you think she sends you all that food for? My sister cooks it.

CONEY. Ah, Finch . . .

FINCH. Ah, Finch, nothing! And all those letters telling me to be sure to bring you home when we get our furlough. . . .

CONEY. Nuts.

FINCH. There's plenty of room. It's only a ranch, of course—nothing fancy—

CONEY. Like a quonset hut.

FINCH. We'd have a helluva time.

CONEY. My mother wants to meet you but— Judas, I sleep on the couch.

FINCH. We wouldn't have enough time on a furlough to visit both— Gosh! You think it might be a furlough, Coney? You think it might be?

CONEY. Quién sabe?

FINCH. The orderly room said it was something special.

CONEY. Like a new kind of latrine duty.

FINCH. Oh, great! Make up your mind, will you? First you tell me no furlough; then you start me thinking maybe there will be one; then—

[*During this, the street door opens and, unseen by* FINCH *or* CONEY, T/SGT. CARL MINGO *comes in.* MINGO *is about twenty-seven. He has dark red hair and looks taller than he is. He gives a feeling of strength; he's someone you want to know. He stands now at the door for a moment and then knocks on the sill and says:*]

MINGO. Is this the way to the powder **room**? [*He comes in, closing the door behind him.*]

FINCH. Are you in on this, Mingo?

MINGO. In on what?

CONEY. Whatever it is.

FINCH. Don't you know?

MINGO. Gentlemen, I don't know from nothing.

CONEY. Yep, yep.

MINGO. I don't, Coney. So help me.

FINCH. We thought—well, we were kind of hoping that —well it might be for a furlough. We've been over two years. You've been over longer. You've seen more action than anybody else. Maybe . . . [*Finishing lamely.*] Well, it could be a furlough.

MINGO [*kindly*]. Sure. It could be, kid. We could all do with a couple of weeks in a rest camp.

FINCH. Rest camp?

CONEY. Cut it out. The Arizona tumbleweed's homesick.

FINCH. Blow it, will ya.

MINGO. One week back there and I'll bet you'd really be homesick—for this joint.

CONEY [*to* MINGO]. Hey, what's been eating you the last couple of days?

MINGO. Mosquitoes.

FINCH. Gee, I was sure you'd know what they wanted us for, Mingo.

MINGO. Why should I know?

CONEY. Didn't you learn anything at college?

MINGO. I only went a year. Write my wife. She's a big hot diploma girl.

CONEY. Yuk, yuk.

MINGO. Maybe we're moving out.

FINCH. Again?

MINGO. Maybe.

FINCH. Why?

MINGO. The General's restless.

FINCH. But where would we be going?

MINGO. Where the little men make with the big bullets.

CONEY. Now that's a real charming thought.

FINCH. Delightful. [*Slight pause.*] Remember that first time, Coney? When Major Robinson said: Men, you're going to have the excitement you've been itching for?

MINGO. Major Blueberry Pie.

FINCH. He was a captain then.

MINGO. Pardon me. Captain Blueberry Pie.

CONEY. Sometimes the Maj acts like war was a hot baseball game. Batter up! Sqush. Sub-stitute please!

FINCH. That's charming!

CONEY. I'm a charming fellow.

FINCH. You stink.

[*The door to the street opens and* CORPORAL T. J. EVERITT *comes in. He, like the others, wears faded coveralls. But* T.J. *is in a temper.*]

T.J. What the hell is this? They put me in charge of a detail, tell me I've got to finish that new road by noon—and then they yank me off with no explanation. What's going on around here?

MINGO. It is not for engineers to reason why.

CONEY. My ouija board's on strike.

T.J. I wasn't asking you, Coney.

MINGO. Your guess is as good as ours, T.J.

FINCH. I heard a rumor they were going to give you a commission, T.J.

CONEY. All of us.

FINCH. Only Coney and me are going to be captains.

CONEY. Majors.

FINCH. Colonels.

CONEY. What the hell—generals.

FINCH. Congratulations, General Coen.

CONEY. Gracias, Commander Finch.

T.J. Oh, blow it, will you? [*To* MINGO.] You'd think that by now they'd have somebody mature enough to run an outfit.

FINCH. The Major's all right. I don't see you doing any better.

T.J. If I couldn't do better with my eyes blindfolded, I'd resign.

CONEY. The Army's kind of touchy about resigning, T.J.

MINGO. Just what makes you such a hot blue-plate special, T.J.?

FINCH. Don't you know who he is, Mingo? Tell him, Coney.

CONEY [*exaggerated sotto voce*]. That's T. J. Everitt, former vice-president in charge of distribution for Universal Products, Inc.

FINCH. No!

CONEY. Yeah!

T.J. Oh, Christ! Do we have to go through that again?

FINCH. Say, is he the Joe who used to make fifteen thousand a year?

CONEY. Oh, that was a bad year. He usually made sixteen thousand.

FINCH. No!

CONEY. Yeah!

FINCH. Think of his taxes!

CONEY. Rugged.

MINGO. Say, what's he doing now?

CONEY. Now? Oh, now he's a corporal making sixty-two bucks a month.

FINCH. No!

CONEY. Yeah!

FINCH. Tsk! Tsk! What won't they think of next!

T.J. That's enough.

CONEY. Well, I heard just the—

T.J. All right. That's enough—Jakie!

CONEY [*quietly*]. Hold your hats, boys.

FINCH [*to* T.J.]. Can that.

T.J. [*to* FINCH]. Why don't you let your little friend—

FINCH. I said can it!

T.J. I heard you.

MINGO. Well, then, can it and can it for good!

CONEY. Drop it, fellas. It isn't worth it.

T.J. [*to* MINGO]. Oh, the firm has a new partner.

MINGO. Up your floo, Rockefeller.

[*The rear door opens and* MAJOR ROBINSON *comes out to his office.*]

MAJOR. At ease, men. I'm sorry I had to keep you waiting. . . . You'd better make yourselves comfortable. We're in for a session. Sit if you want to. Smoke. But stay put and give me your attention. [CONEY *gestures "thumbs down" to* FINCH. MAJOR, *brusquely.*] What's that for, Coen?

CONEY. Oh, we . . . we thought maybe this was about furloughs, sir.

MAJOR. No. Sit down, Finch. I realize you men have furloughs coming to you. Particularly Mingo. And you ought to know that if I could get them for you, I would. However, we've got a job to do. Right, Mingo?

MINGO [*with a wry smile*]. Yes, sir.

MAJOR [*with charm*]. Well, maybe after this you'll get those furloughs. I certainly hope so. . . . Anybody been bothered with anything lately—anything physical, I mean?

T.J. Well, Major, my back—

MAJOR. I know, T.J. Outside of that, though? [*He looks around at the men. There is no answer.*] All right. Now—before anything else, get this straight: everything you hear from now on is top secret. Whatever you do or don't do, it's secret. Running off at the mouth will get a court-martial. Understand? [*The men nod.*] O.K. . . . I'll get right to the point. You four men are the best engineers in the outfit. We need A-1 engineers for this job. [MINGO *smiles.*] What's the matter, Mingo?

MINGO. Nothing, sir.

MAJOR. I mean that. Seriously. Now—there's an island —never mind where—that we want to invade next. It's darned important that we take that island. It can shorten this whole bloody war. . . . But right now, there are fifteen thousand Japs on it. To take it and hold it—we'll need airstrips. And we'll need 'em quick. To fly supplies in and to have a base for fighters and bombers. Clear? . . . Well, I'm flying to that island tonight.

FINCH. With fifteen thousand Japs on it, sir?

MAJOR. Yes, I need a few men to go with me. One to sketch the terrain and draw maps— [CONEY *nudges* FINCH; *the others stare at* FINCH.] —and three others to help survey. I suppose two more would really be enough but—well, it's a ticklish job, all right, and— what is it, T.J.?

T.J. I was thinking about aerial photographs.

MAJOR. Leave the thinking to me and Headquarters, please. Aerial photos don't show what we want to find out. Too much foliage.

MINGO. Is there any intelligence on the Jap airstrips?

MAJOR. There's only one strip and it stinks. Besides, if we don't blow it up, they will. . . . Any other questions?

MINGO. Major . . .

MAJOR. Yes?

MINGO. Did you say you were flying to this island?

MAJOR. Yes. Natives'll pick us up offshore with canoes when we get there.

MINGO. How long do you figure the job will take?

MAJOR. Four days. Top. Then we get off the island the same way we got on.

MINGO. Canoes and then the plane.

MAJOR. Yes.

T.J. Suppose something happens?

MAJOR. The Japs are only defending the side of the island facing us. We'll be working in back of them —on the part facing Japan. Actually, it shouldn't be too bad because we shouldn't ever run into them. [*With a smile.*] I say "we." Really, it's up to you.

CONEY. To us?

MAJOR. This is purely voluntary, fellows. Whether you come or not—that's up to each of you. [*Pause.*] I know how you feel. You've all been in plenty; you've done plenty. And I'm not going to try to kid you about this job: it's no picnic. But believe me, it's worth doing. And anyway, it's got to be done. [*Another pause. He walks around a bit.*] I wouldn't have asked you—particularly you, Mingo, except that I need the best men I have. That's the kind of job it is. But it's still up to each of you individually. If you say "no," there won't be any questions asked. I mean that. . . . Talk it over. Together or by yourselves. That's up to you. I'm sorry, but I can't give you more than— [*He looks at his watch.*] —ten minutes but—it came up damn fast and—well, you men know the Army. [*He walks up to the door to his office, starts to open it and then turns.*] Just remember it's damned important. Probably the least you'll get out of this will be a furlough. I can't promise, of course, that you'll get one but—that isn't the reason for going anyway. The reason is that you're the best men for the job. [*He exits into his office. There is a slight pause.*]

MINGO [*softly—with a wry smile*]. Oh, my aching back.

CONEY. What?

MINGO. That vaseline about volunteering.

FINCH. What do you mean?

T.J. With a nice little bribe of furloughs.

CONEY. He didn't say he was promising us furloughs.

MINGO. Well—if he wanted to play fair and square with us, he would have called us in one at a time and not let us know who the others were. That's volunteering.

CONEY. Why?

MINGO. Because that way, if a man wants out, he can get out,—and no one's the wiser. But this way! Well, who's going to chicken out in front of anyone else?

T.J. What do you mean—chicken out?

MINGO. Are you going?

T.J. Are you?

MINGO. I'm not making up your mind.

T.J. I'm not asking you to!

MINGO [*lightly*]. O.K.

[*Pause.*]

FINCH. Fifteen thousand Japs. [*Whistles softly.*]

CONEY. The first day I was inducted, some Joe said: Keep your eyes open, your mouth shut and never volunteer. No matter what it's for, it stinks.

MINGO. Well, who's gonna ride the broomstick to that island? That stinks, but good.

CONEY. If it's the way you said . . .

MINGO. What way?

CONEY. You know. That this is half-assed volunteering.

MINGO. Oh . . . It is.

CONEY. Then either we all go or we all don't go.

T.J. Why?

MINGO. Because if one of us says "yes," nobody else can say: Count me out, Major. I'm sitting home on my yellow butt.

T.J. It doesn't mean you're yellow.

MINGO. Could you say "count me out"?

[FINCH *whistles "Shoo, Fly." Slight pause.*]

CONEY. I wonder what would happen if we all said it. [*Slight pause.*]

FINCH. Maybe it won't be so tough. He said the Japs are all on the other side of the island.

T.J. There's no law they have to stay there.

CONEY. The more times you go in, the less chance you have of coming out in one piece.

FINCH. That's a charming thought.

CONEY. Delightful.

[*There is a pause during which* FINCH *starts to whistle "Shoo, Fly." He sings the last two lines.*]

FINCH. Shoo, fly, don't bother me. For I'm in Company Q.

T.J. Company G.

CONEY. Anybody can make it rhyme. [*Slight pause.*]

T.J. Well, Christ! We ought to talk about it, anyway!

MINGO. About what? Japs? They have several ways of killing you. They can—

T.J. Oh, put your head in a bowl, will you? [*Slight pause.*]

FINCH. How long did he say?

CONEY. Four days.

FINCH. No. I mean to decide.

CONEY. Ten minutes.

MINGO. What's the difference? It's either too much or

too little. The dirtiest trick you can play on a man in war is to make him think.

FINCH. Well, what do you say, Coney?

CONEY. I don't know.

FINCH. Well, you say it.

T.J. Oh, great. Let's play follow the leader.

FINCH. Mind your own business, T.J.!

MINGO. This *is* his business, Finch. It's kind of all our business.

FINCH. What do you mean?

MINGO. Whatever you two decide, we're stuck with it.

CONEY. Hey! Hey!

MINGO. It's perfectly O.K. by me, Coney.

T.J. It's O.K. by you?

MINGO. Yeah.

T.J. That's great! Well, maybe it's O.K. for the three of you, but what makes you think I'll string along?

MINGO. You haven't got the guts to do anything else.

FINCH [*to* CONEY]. Come on, you jerk. What do you say?

CONEY. You know what I say? I say I think of four G.I.s going to an island crawling with fifteen thousand Japs, and I say they're crazy.

MINGO. O.K. Then we don't go. We don't have to.

CONEY. But the Major says we're the four best men. It's important and it's winning the war.

T.J. You mean you want to go?

CONEY. Nobody wants to go.

MINGO. You can say that again.

FINCH. Well, you say it, Coney. Somebody has to.

CONEY. No. I don't want to, Finch. This is tough enough for a guy to decide for himself, but to decide for three other guys—I don't want to.

MINGO. Seems like we're putting him on a big black spot marked X, Finch.

CONEY. Look, Mingo, going on a mission like this ain't kidding. When they tell you to do something, it's not so bad. You have to do it, so you do it. But this way. Well, what the hell! Let somebody else decide. [*He stops as the rear door opens and the* MAJOR *walks in.*]

MAJOR. Sorry, men. Time's up. . . . I want to say one thing again. If you've decided the job is too much for you, there'll be no questions asked. All you have to do is say "yes" or "no." . . . I—well, whatever you say, I want to thank you for your past work. [*He faces toward* MINGO *as though he were going to ask him first; changes his mind; looks at the others, and finally stops at* FINCH.] Well, Finch? Yes or no?

[FINCH *looks at the* MAJOR *and then looks directly at* CONEY. *There is a slight pause. Then the* MAJOR *looks at* CONEY, *too. They all look at him now. He looks at* FINCH, *pauses, then turns slightly more to the* MAJOR.]

CONEY. Yes, sir.

[*Blackout. After a pause, through the darkness comes the sound of crickets; then, faintly at first, the cries of jungle birds.*]

SCENE III

SCENE—*Clearing. A Pacific Island.*

Before the lights go up, we hear a jungle bird shriek. A few more birds shriek, and then we hear FINCH *whistling "Shoo, Fly." Slowly, the scene fades in.*

We are looking at part of what must be a fairly large clearing in the midst of the jungle. It ends in a vague semicircle of bushes and trees. There is another

*tree, separate from the others fairly downstage, left.
Vines drop from this and crawl over the rest of the
cleared area, which is dotted with some small bushes.
Hot, muggy sunlight slices down, but the general feeling is of some place dank and unpleasant. This is not
motion-picture jungle; it is not pretty.*

When the lights go up, FINCH *is propped up, downstage, against a pile of equipment. He is completing
a map, and has his sketching pad braced on his knees.*
CONEY *is next to him, cleaning his rifle. Both have
their guns next to them and, like all the men in this
scene, wear jungle combat uniforms.*

There is a slight wait as FINCH *works and whistles.
Then a bird screeches again.*

CONEY. This place smells.

FINCH. It's not so bad.

CONEY. I don't mean stinks. I mean smells. Really. This
kind of smells. [*He sniffs.*] Like a graveyard.

FINCH. When did you ever smell a graveyard?

CONEY. When we set foot on this trap four days ago.
[*A bird screams again.*] Shut up! They make you
jumpy, Finch?

FINCH. Some. Coyotes are worse.

CONEY. I never heard coyotes, but I'd like to. I'd like
to be where I could hear 'em this minute.

FINCH. In Arizona.

CONEY. God knows you couldn't hear 'em in Pittsburgh.

FINCH. They're kind of scary—if you wake up and hear
them in the middle of the night.

CONEY. I remember waking up in the middle of the
night and hearing something. I was ten years old.

FINCH. What'd you hear?

CONEY. A human coyote. [*Gets up.*] I've really got the jumps.

FINCH. We'll be out of here tonight. Why don't you relax? It's a fine day.

CONEY. Yep, yep.

FINCH. It is. I'd like to lie under a tree and have cocoanuts fall in my lap.

CONEY. I'd rather have a Polynesian babe fall in mine.

FINCH. Too much trouble. I'll take cocoanuts.

CONEY. You have to open cocoanuts.

FINCH *and* CONEY [*together*]. Yuk, yuk, yuk.

FINCH. Well—it may not be a good map, but it's a pretty one.

CONEY. You finished?

FINCH. Almost. They ought to be finished soon, too. They're just rechecking.

CONEY. Yeah. [*Bird screams.*] All right, sweetheart. We heard you the first time!

FINCH. Coney . . .

CONEY. Yeah?

FINCH. You think girls want it as much as fellas?

CONEY. More.

FINCH. But more girls are virgins.

CONEY. Enemy propaganda.

FINCH. I wonder if my sister is. Would you care?

CONEY. What?

FINCH. If the girl you married wasn't?

CONEY. Stop trying to cook up something between me and your sister.

FINCH. She's a good cook.

CONEY. I thought we were going to run a bar?

FINCH. A bar-restaurant.

CONEY. How's she on mixing drinks?

FINCH. She could learn.

CONEY. I wish she'd send up a stiff one now. I'm beginning to see Japs.

FINCH. They're on the other side of the island.

CONEY. It's not like Japs to stay there. [*Bird screams.*] Ah . . .

FINCH. Mingo's wife writes poetry.

CONEY. Yeah. I know.

FINCH. He ever let you read any of it?

CONEY. He never lets anybody read it. It probably stinks.

FINCH. I wonder what she's like.

CONEY. Not bad. From her picture. Did you ever see that picture of the Major's girl?

FINCH. Oh, my aching back!

CONEY. And I'll bet he's a virgin. Him and T.J.

FINCH. T.J.'s been married three times.

CONEY. He's still a virgin.

FINCH. How could he be?

CONEY. He's mean enough. [*Bird screams.*] And you too, you bitch.

FINCH. That's charming.

CONEY. Delightful.

[*There is a rustling in the bushes.* CONEY *jerks for his gun, then lies back again as* T.J. *comes out.*]

T.J. [*he is perspiring heavily*]. You're certainly working yourselves into an early grave.

FINCH. I'm finishing the map.

T.J. What's your friend doing? Posing for it?

CONEY. I'm thinking up inter-office memos.

T.J. Don't rupture yourself.

CONEY. You guys finish?

T.J. If you're so interested, go see for yourself.

CONEY. That's charming.

FINCH. Delightful.

T.J. Screw off. [*Starts to sit.*] Christ, I'm dripping. [*Bird screams and he turns violently.*]

CONEY. Watch out for the birdie.

T.J. Look, Coney, I've—

FINCH [*cutting in*]. What are they doing there anyway, T.J.?

T.J. Oh, you know the boy Major. He's got to do things his way. Which makes it twice as long.

FINCH. We'll get off tonight on schedule, though.

T.J. If I were running it, we'd have been through and left yesterday.

CONEY. Yep, yep.

T.J. Yes! [*To* FINCH.] He wants the clinometer.

FINCH. Who does?

T.J. The Major.

FINCH. You know where it is.

T.J. Why don't you get the lead out of your can and do something for once?

CONEY [*to* FINCH]. You finish your map.

FINCH. It's finished, Coney.

CONEY. Well, let T. J. Rockefeller do something besides blowing that tin horn.

T.J. Look who's talking.

FINCH [*jumping up*]. Yeah, look! He stood guard two nights out of three while you snored your fat face off. The Major told him to take it easy today and you know it.

T.J. [*to* FINCH]. The little kike lover.

FINCH. You always get around to that, don't you?

T.J. Every time I see your friend's face.

CONEY. You son of a bitch.

T.J. Watch your language or I'll ram it down your throat, Jew boy.

FINCH. You'll get yours rammed down your throat first.

T.J. Not by him.

CONEY. Listen, T.J.—

T.J. You listen to me, you lousy yellow Jew bastard! I'm going to— [*At this,* FINCH *steps forward and clips* T.J. T.J. *reels but comes back at* FINCH.] You little—

[*He swings,* FINCH *ducks and socks him again.* T.J. *hits back.* CONEY *tries to break it up but they are punching away as* MINGO *rushes in from down right.*]

MINGO. What the hell is this? Come on, break it up. [*He steps in.*] Why don't you jerks save it for the Japs?

T.J. He's more interested in saving his yellow Jew friend.

[CONEY *turns away sharply and walks a little up right by a tree. There is a brief pause.*]

MINGO [*evenly*]. The Major wants the clinometer, T.J. [T.J. *just stands, looking at him.*] Go bring it to him! [*There is a slight wait. Then* T.J. *goes to the pile of gear, fishes out the clinometer and exits down right.*] We're practically through.

[FINCH *doesn't answer.* CONEY *stands by the tree, his back to the audience.* MINGO *takes out a cigarette and lights up.*]

FINCH [*low*]. That bastard.

MINGO. We've got plenty of time to pack up and get to the beach. The plane isn't due till nightfall. . . . One thing you can say for the Major. He gets the job done.

FINCH. That bastard.

MINGO. All right.

FINCH. It's not all right.

MINGO. Well—the Major should have known, I guess, but—none of them bother to find out what a guy's like.

FINCH. What makes him such a bastard?

MINGO. Hell, the guy's thirty-five, thirty-six. He can't adjust himself to the Army so he winds up hating everything and resenting everybody. He's just a civilian in G.I. clothes.

FINCH. So am I, but he still stinks.

MINGO. Sure. He stinks from way back. The Army makes him worse. I'm not apologizing for him. I think he's a bastard, too. But you ought to try to understand him.

CONEY [*turning around sharply*]. You try to understand him! I haven't got time. [*Coming over to them.*] I'm too busy trying to understand all this crap about Jews.

FINCH. Coney . . .

CONEY. I told you I heard something in the middle of the night once. Some drunken bum across the hall from my aunt's yelling: Throw out the dirty shee-nies! . . . That was us. But I just turned over and went back to sleep. I was used to it by then. What the hell! I was ten. That's old for a Jew. When I was six, my first week in school, I stayed out for the Jew-ish New Year. The next day a bunch of kids got around me and said: "Were you in school yester-day?" I smiled and said, "No." They wiped the smile off my face. They beat the hell out of me. I had to get beat up a coupla more times before I learned that if you're a Jew, you stink. You're not like other guys. You're—you're alone. You're—you're something —strange, different. [*Suddenly furious.*] Well, god-damit, you make us different, you dirty bastards! What the hell do you want us to do?

FINCH. Coney . . .

CONEY. Let me alone.

MINGO. Coney, listen—

CONEY. Tell your wife to write a poem about it.

MINGO. Screw me *and* my wife. You know damn well Finch at least doesn't feel like that.

CONEY. I don't know anything. I'm a lousy yellow Jew bastard. [*He turns and walks back to the tree.* FINCH *hesitates and then walks to him.*]

FINCH. Coney . . .

CONEY. Drop it.

FINCH. You know that doesn't go for me.

CONEY. I said drop it, Finch.

FINCH. Maybe I'm dumb. Maybe I'm an Arizona hay-seed like you say. But I never met any Jewish boys till I got in the Army. I didn't even realize out loud that *you* were until somebody said something.

CONEY. I can imagine what.

FINCH. Yes. And I took a poke at him, too. Because I couldn't see any reason for it. And there isn't any. O.K. I'm a jerk, but to me—you like a guy or you don't. That's all there is to it. That's all there ever will be to it. . . . And you know that—don't you? [*He waits for an answer, but there is none. He takes a step back toward* MINGO *and then turns and moves swiftly to* CONEY *and puts an arm around him.*] Aw heck, aren't we buddies?

CONEY [*turning—with a smile*]. You corny bastard.

FINCH. You stubborn jerk.

[*Shot rings out from off right. The three on stage freeze.*]

CONEY. What the—

MINGO. Ssh!

[*They stand and listen. A bird screams a few times.*]

FINCH. Maybe it was T.J. He's dumb enough.

MINGO. Not that dumb. A shot could bring the Japs—

CONEY. Listen!

[*They hold for a moment, listening to the right.*]

MINGO. Take cover. Quick!

[*They pick up their guns and start for the bushes up-stage just as the* MAJOR *and* T.J. *run out from the bushes, right. From here to curtain, the men speak in hushed tones.*]

MAJOR. Sniper took a pot shot and missed.

FINCH. Judas!

MAJOR. Grab the gear and let's beat it fast.

FINCH. Right.

MAJOR [*to* MINGO]. You and Coney keep your rifles ready.

CONEY. Yes, sir.

MAJOR. Forget that sir! Japs love officers. [FINCH *and* T.J. *are hastily picking up gear. The* MAJOR *is picking up equipment.* CONEY *and* MINGO *put on their packs and helmets, always watching to the right.*] Got the maps, Finch?

FINCH. All packed.

MAJOR. Good. Would happen the last day.

MINGO. Did you finish?

MAJOR. Yes. Watch there.

[MINGO *moves closer to the bushes down right with his rifle ready.* CONEY *is also facing in that direction but is nearer center.*]

CONEY. It's so damn dark in there.

T.J. And we're out in the open.

MAJOR. Knock off, T.J. Get that talkie.

[FINCH *starts for it just as two sharp shots crack out from off right. The men flatten to the earth, except* MINGO *who grabs his right arm, dropping his rifle. Then he drops down. A moment's hesitation—then* CONEY *fires. A wait of a moment—and then the sound of a body crashing through the trees.*]

CONEY [*softly*]. Got the bastard!

MAJOR. Stay down. There may be others. Finch—see if he's dead. [FINCH *starts to crawl toward the spot where the body crashed.*] If he isn't, use your knife. There's been enough shooting to bring the whole island down on us. . . . Anybody hit?

MINGO. Yes.

MAJOR. Where?

MINGO. Right arm.

MAJOR. Bad?

MINGO. Bad enough.

MAJOR. We've got to get out of here. I'll make a tourniquet. [*He starts to crawl toward* MINGO. FINCH, *by this time, has reached the bushes and is on his knees, peering through at the body.*]

FINCH. Major, I don't think he—

[*The bushes move slightly.*]

MAJOR. *Make sure!* [FINCH *turns slightly to look at him.*] Quick—goddamit—make sure!

[FINCH *turns back and then with a sharp movement, gets up, and goes into the bushes with his knife raised. A pause. The sound of* FINCH *rustling in the bushes off right. Then he comes back.*]

FINCH. O.K.

MAJOR [*whipping out a handkerchief which he proceeds to make into a tourniquet for* MINGO]. If there was anybody else, we should have heard by now. Still— [FINCH *has walked up right and now starts to retch. The* MAJOR *turns at the sound and sees* CONEY *move toward* FINCH.] Let him alone. Pick up the gear. We've got to beat it.

[*A bird screams.*]

T.J. Well, for Chrissakes, let's go.

MAJOR. All right. [*Getting up.*] We'll make for that clearing near the beach.

MINGO [*getting up*]. Thanks.

MAJOR. I'll do better later. Forget the pack.

MINGO. I can take it.

[*The* MAJOR *puts his pack on, starts to pick up some equipment.* T.J. *stands impatiently near the bushes, left.*]

T.J. You never can tell about those slant-eyed bastards. Come on. Let's get out of here.

MAJOR. Take it easy. Who's got the maps?

CONEY. Finch.

FINCH [*coming downstage*]. I never can get used to it. I'm sorry.

MAJOR. O.K. Forget about it. You got the maps?

FINCH. Yes, sir.

MAJOR. Everybody set?

CONEY. I'll take care of Finch. [FINCH *shakes his head violently*.] What's the matter?

FINCH. I never can get used to it. I got the shakes.

MAJOR. Forget it.

FINCH. It was like killing a dead man.

MAJOR. If you didn't kill him, he would have killed us.

FINCH. I got the shakes, Coney.

CONEY. We all have, Finch.

[*Bird screams.*]

T.J. Christ!

MAJOR. Come on. Let's go. [*He plunges into the brush.*]

T.J. Come on, Mingo.

MINGO [*to* FINCH]. So it stinks. Come on, kiddo.

T.J. Mingo!

MINGO. All right. After you, feedbox.

[T.J. *goes into the brush.* CONEY *picks up* FINCH's *pack and helps him put it on.* MINGO *pauses at the end of the brush.*]

MINGO. Coney—

CONEY. We're coming. [MINGO *exits off left.* CONEY, *picking up his gear.*] Let's go, Finch. It ain't healthy around here. [FINCH *starts to wander around.*] Finch, listen—

FINCH. I'm all right, I'm all right. I just can't remember where I put the map case.

CONEY. O Judas!

FINCH. You go.

CONEY. Try to think.

FINCH. I had it just before I—

CONEY. This is a helluva time!

FINCH. I just had it.

CONEY. Maybe one of them has it.

FINCH. No.

[*A bird screams. They are both looking feverishly for the case.*]

CONEY. Listen, we'll lose them.

FINCH. We gotta have those maps.

CONEY. The maps won't do us any good if we get picked off!

FINCH. That's the only thing we came here for.

CONEY. Goddamit. Where the hell are they? [*Bird screams.*] Christ!

FINCH. Shut up.

CONEY. You'll get us both killed! You dumb Arizona bastard!

FINCH. I'm not asking you to stay, you lousy yellow— [*He cuts off. They both stand dead still, staring at each other.*] —jerk! [*He turns and begins looking again for the map case.* CONEY *waits a moment, his head bowed in hurt. Then he turns swiftly and starts for the bushes. Just as he gets there,* FINCH *spots the case.*] Here they are! I knew I— [*A shot smashes out. He clutches his belly and falls.* CONEY, *whose back is to* FINCH, *flattens out at the sound of the shot. Then he looks around.*]

CONEY. Finch!

FINCH. Okay.

CONEY [*as he scrambles to him*]. You hit?

FINCH. Coney, I didn't mean—

CONEY. Never mind. Are you hit?

FINCH. Take the maps.

CONEY. Where'd they hit you?

FINCH [*thrusting the map case at him*]. Take the maps.

CONEY. Finch—

FINCH. Take 'em!

CONEY. Give me your arm. [CONEY *tries to carry him.* FINCH *pushes* CONEY *down.*]

FINCH. I'm all right, you dumb bastard—

CONEY. You sure you—

FINCH. I'll follow. Go on. Quick! [CONEY *looks at him and then darts to the bushes, left.* FINCH *watches him and when* CONEY *looks back, he starts crawling.*] I'm coming, I tell you! Go on, go on!

[CONEY *turns and disappears into the brush. Immediately,* FINCH *stops crawling and lies flat. Then he gathers his strength and starts to crawl again. Suddenly he stops and listens. He swings his body around so that he is facing the jungle, right. The bushes, right, begin to rustle.* FINCH, *still holding his rifle, begins to inch his body downstage toward the tree. When* FINCH *is out of sight downstage left, the bushes move.*]

CONEY [*calling softly, offstage*]. Finch! Where are you, Finch? Finch! [*Coming on.*] Finch, for Christ' sake where are you? [*A shot rings out and* CONEY *hits the dirt. A pause.*] Finch? Finch? [*Looking around, he starts to back off upstage.*] Where are you, Finch?

[*The bushes rustle off.* CONEY *is still calling softly as the curtain falls.*]

Act two

SCENE I

SCENE—*Hospital Room. The Pacific Base.*

CONEY *is stretched out on the bed with his head*

buried in the pillow. The DOCTOR is sitting on the bed, patting his shoulder.

DOCTOR [*gently*]. Coney . . . Coney.

CONEY. I shouldn't have left him. I shouldn't have left him. Mingo.

DOCTOR. What?

CONEY [*turning*]. I should have stayed with him.

DOCTOR. If you'd stayed with him the maps would be lost. The maps were your job and the job comes first.

CONEY. So to hell with Finch!

DOCTOR. Finch knew he had to get those maps. He told you to take them and go, didn't he? Didn't he, Coney?

CONEY. He's dead.

DOCTOR. Didn't he say: Take the maps and get out of here?

[*Pause.*]

CONEY. I shouldn't've left him.

DOCTOR. Coney, take the maps and get out of here!

CONEY. No, Finch.

DOCTOR. Take them and beat it. Go on, will you?

CONEY. Finch— Are you sure—

DOCTOR. Go on! [*A slight pause.* CONEY *slowly raises himself up on his arms. The* DOCTOR *watches him tensely.* CONEY *moves as though to get off the bed.*] Go on!

[CONEY *starts to make the effort to get off the bed. Then slowly, he sinks back, shaking his head pitifully.*]

CONEY [*pathetically*]. I can't. I can't.

DOCTOR. Coney . . . go on!

CONEY. I can't, Doc. I'm sorry.

[*There is a slight pause. The* DOCTOR *takes a new tack now.*]

DOCTOR. Coney . . . remember when Finch was shot?

CONEY. Yeah. I remember.

DOCTOR. When you heard that shot and saw he was hit, what did you think of?

CONEY. I—I got a bad feeling.

DOCTOR. But what did you think of, Coney? At that moment, what went through your mind?

CONEY. I didn't want to leave him.

DOCTOR. What did you think of at that instant, Coney?

CONEY. He told me to leave him.

DOCTOR. Coney. Listen. A shot! You turn. [*Slaps his hands together sharply.*] You turn now. You see it's Finch.

CONEY. Finch!

DOCTOR. What are you thinking of, Coney? [*No answer.*] Coney, what just went through your mind?

CONEY. I . . . I . . .

DOCTOR. What?

CONEY. I didn't want to leave him.

DOCTOR. Coney—

CONEY. But he said to leave him! He said to take the maps and beat it. It wasn't because I was yellow. It was because he said to go. Finch said to go!

DOCTOR. You were right to go. You were right to go, Coney.

CONEY. They didn't think so.

DOCTOR. How do you know?

CONEY. I know. I could tell that T.J.—

DOCTOR. Did he say anything?

CONEY. No.

DOCTOR. Did the Major say anything? Did Mingo say anything?

CONEY. No.

DOCTOR. Of course not. Because you were right to leave. You did what you had to do: you saved the maps. That's what you had to do, Coney.

CONEY [*plaintively*]. Was it? Was it really?

DOCTOR. Of course it was, son. It was the only thing you could do.

[*Pause.*]

CONEY. We did come to get the maps.

DOCTOR. Sure.

CONEY. And I saved them.

DOCTOR. Yes.

CONEY. I saved them . . . But Finch made them and . . . and . . . now . . .

DOCTOR. Coney, you had to leave him, you know that.

CONEY. Yes.

DOCTOR. You can't blame yourself.

CONEY. No . . . Only . . .

DOCTOR. Only what?

CONEY. I still got that feeling.

DOCTOR. What feeling?

CONEY. I don't know. That—that bad feeling.

DOCTOR. Did you first get it when you heard that shot? When you saw it was Finch who was hit?

CONEY. I—I'm not sure.

DOCTOR. Did it come back stronger when you found you couldn't walk?

CONEY. I—think so.

DOCTOR. When was that, Coney? When did you find you couldn't walk?

CONEY. It was . . . It was . . . I don't know.

DOCTOR. Think.

CONEY. I'm trying to.

DOCTOR. Why did it happen? Why couldn't you walk?

CONEY. I—I can't remember.

DOCTOR. Why can't you walk now?

CONEY. I—I don't know. I just can't.

DOCTOR. Why?

CONEY. I don't know. I think it started when—when—

DOCTOR. When what, Coney?

CONEY. When—when—

DOCTOR. When what, Coney?

CONEY. Oh, gee, Doc, I'm afraid I'm gonna cry.

DOCTOR. Go on, son. Cry if you want to.

CONEY. But guys don't cry. You shouldn't cry.

DOCTOR. Let it out, son. Let it all out.

CONEY. No, no, I don't want to. I cried when Finch—

DOCTOR. When Finch what?

CONEY. When he—when . . .

DOCTOR. When you left him?

CONEY. No. No, it was after that. Long after that. I'd been waiting for him.

DOCTOR. Where?

[*The lights start to fade.*]

CONEY. In the clearing. The clearing by the beach. We were all there. Waiting. Nothing to do but wait and listen to those lousy birds. And all the time, I was wondering about Finch, waiting for Finch, hoping that . . .

[*The stage is dark now. Through the last, there have been the faint sounds of crickets and jungle birds.*]

SCENE II

SCENE—*Another clearing. The Pacific Island.*

This clearing is smaller than the other; there is more of a feeling of being hemmed in. The trees, bushes and vines at the edge are thicker, closer, darker. At the rear, just left of center, however, there is the suggestion of a path. This leads to the beach.

It is late afternoon, but the filtered sunlight is very hot.

Before the lights come up, we again hear the screech

of birds. This continues intermittently through the scene.

Although the men reach a high excitement pitch in this scene, they never yell. Their voices are tight and tense, but they remain aware of where they are and of the danger.

AT RISE: CONEY *is peering anxiously through the trees, right.* T.J. *is sitting fairly near him, drinking from his canteen.* MINGO *is down left, sitting back against some equipment while the* MAJOR, *who kneels next to him, loosens the tourniquet on his arm. All the men have removed their packs, but have their rifles ready.*

CONEY. We ought to be able to hear him coming.

T.J. If we could hear him, the Japs could hear him. Finch isn't that dumb.

[*The* MAJOR *takes out his knife and slashes* MINGO'S sleeve.]

MINGO. Bleeding pretty bad.

MAJOR. Not too bad.

T.J. [*to* CONEY]. You make me hot just standing. Why don't you sit down? [*No answer.*] Listen, if Finch is busy ducking them, it'll take him time to get here.

CONEY [*coldly*]. He was hit.

MINGO. How's it look, Major?

MAJOR. A little messy.

MINGO [*struggling to take his first-aid kit off his web belt with one hand*]. This damn first-aid kit is more—

MAJOR. Let me.

T.J. [*to* CONEY]. You don't know how bad he was hit?

CONEY. No.

T.J. Ah, come on and relax, Coney. [*Holds out his canteen.*] Have a drink.

CONEY [*reaching for his own canteen*]. I've got some. I

wouldn't want you to catch anything, T.J. [*He drinks from his own canteen. The* MAJOR *starts to sprinkle sulfa over* MINGO'S *wound.* MINGO *turns his face and looks toward* CONEY.]

MINGO [*to* CONEY]. Open mine for me, will you, kiddo?

CONEY [*holding out his own*]. Here.

MINGO. Thanks. [*He drinks.*]

MAJOR [*looking at* MINGO'S *wound*]. I think you've got two slugs in there.

CONEY. How's it feel, Mingo?

MINGO. Fine. Ready to be lopped off.

CONEY. That's charming.

T.J. Delightful. [CONEY *shoots him a look.*]

MINGO [*to* CONEY]. Quit worrying, kiddo. Finch knows the way here.

MAJOR. Sure. He drew the maps. [*The* MAJOR *starts to bandage* MINGO'S *wound.*]

CONEY. He might think we're out there on the beach.

MAJOR. The beach is too open. He knows we wouldn't wait there.

MINGO. Anyway, he'd have to come through here to— [*He gasps.*]

MAJOR. Sorry.

MINGO. That's O.K.

T.J. I was just thinking. If the Japs spot Finch, they might let him go—thinking he'd lead them to us.

CONEY. Finch wouldn't lead any Japs to us.

T.J. But if he didn't know.

CONEY. He'd know. And he'd never give us away! [*He turns and walks back to his watching position by the trees.*]

T.J. I didn't say he would deliberately. For Chrissake, you get so—

MINGO. Hang up, T.J.

MAJOR. And keep your voices down. . . . How's that, Mingo?

MINGO. Feels O.K. [*Attempt at lightness.*] It ought to do till they amputate.

MAJOR. Amputate?

MINGO. Just a bad joke, Major.

MAJOR. I'll say it is. That sulfa should prevent infection.

MINGO. Sure.

MAJOR. And if you loosen the tourniquet every twenty minutes—

MINGO. I know. I'm just building it up. [*Bird screams.*] On your way, vulture. No meat today.

MAJOR. The plane'll be here in about an hour, Mingo. You can be in the hospital tomorrow.

CONEY [*turning*]. Major—suppose Finch isn't here?

MAJOR. What?

CONEY [*coming closer*]. Suppose Finch isn't here when the plane comes?

MAJOR. He'll be here.

CONEY. But suppose he isn't?

MAJOR. We'll worry about that when the time comes.

MINGO. What would we do, though?

MAJOR. I said we'll worry about that when the time comes. [*Pause.*] Lord, it's sticky.

MINGO [*to* CONEY]. He's got over an hour yet, Coney.

CONEY. You know darn well if he's going to get here, he'll turn up in the next few minutes or not at all. [*Pause.*]

T.J. I don't need a shower. I'm giving myself one.

MINGO. That's part of the charm of the South Seas.

T.J. I once took a cruise in these waters.

MINGO. I once set up a travel booklet about them. I was a linotyper after I had to quit college. You learn a lot of crap setting up type. I learned about the balmy blue Pacific. Come to the Heavenly Isles! An orchid on every bazoom—and two bazooms on every babe. I'd like to find the gent who wrote that booklet. I'd like to find him now and make him come to his goddam Heavenly Isles!

[*Slight pause.*]

T.J. You know—if they hit Finch bad . . .

MINGO. Shut up. [*He tests his arm, trying to see how well he can move it. He winces.*]

MAJOR. It'll be all right, Mingo.

MINGO. I wonder how a one-armed linotyper would make out.

CONEY. Major . . . I gotta go look for him.

MAJOR. Finch knows the path, Coney.

CONEY. Yeah, but maybe he— [*He cuts off as T.J., who is looking off right, suddenly brings up his gun. The others grab theirs and wait tensely, watching T.J. He holds for a moment, staring into the trees, and then a bird screams. He lowers his gun.*]

T.J. Sorry.

MAJOR. What was it?

T.J. Animal, bird, something. I don't know. Since I came up with that cheerful idea of Japs following Finch—sorry.

MAJOR. Forget it. It's better to be over-alert than to be caught napping.

MINGO. I wonder if the squints know how many of us there are.

MAJOR. Not yet. And I don't think they know where we are, either. [*He walks over to CONEY.*] That's why you can't go look for him, Coney. If they've got him—well, go in there and they'll get you too. And us along with you.

CONEY. I should've stayed with him.

MAJOR. You had to get those maps back and you did. Now we've got to get off this island so we can bring those maps back. That comes first.

CONEY. So—to hell with Finch.

MINGO. Kid, the Major's right. We've got to take care of the job first.

MAJOR. Look, Coney—

CONEY. Yeah. I know. I know.

T.J. I wish we were the hell out of here. . . . All of us. [*Slight pause.*] I don't suppose there's anything we can do.

MINGO. Sure. You know what we can do. We can wait.

T.J. That's all you ever do in this man's army.

MINGO [*dryly*]. What man's army?

T.J. You wait for chow, you wait for mail, you wait for pay. And when you're not waiting for that, you wait for something to wait for.

MINGO. Yeah. We wait. And back there, in those lovely forty-eight States—

[*A scream from some distance off right.*]

CONEY. What was that?

[*Slight pause.*]

T.J. Ah, a bird.

CONEY. That was no bird.

MINGO. Coney, you're just—

CONEY. That was no bird.

T.J. A cigar to the boy with the ears.

CONEY. That was no bird! Listen! [*Slight pause. A bird.*) No. Listen!

MAJOR. Ease up, Coney. I know you—

[*The scream again. And this time it is recognizable as:*]

CONEY. It's Finch! He's yelling for me! [*He picks up his gun and starts for the bushes. The* MAJOR *grabs him.*]

MAJOR. Coney—

CONEY. You heard him!

MAJOR. Yes, but—

CONEY. Please, sir. They're killing him. They're killing Finch!

MAJOR. They're not killing him and they won't kill him.

CONEY. Not them. Not much.

MAJOR. I tell you he won't be killed. It's just a trick. They're purposely making him yell.

CONEY. Please, Major, let me—

MAJOR [*holding tight*]. Coney, you can't go in there! They're sticking him just to make him yell like that. Just to make us come after him.

CONEY. All right!

MAJOR. But when we do—they'll get us. Don't you understand?

CONEY. I don't care!

MAJOR. Coney, listen to me. They're just trying to find out where we are. They're just trying to get us. It's a trick.

CONEY. I don't care, sir. Let me go, please!

MAJOR. Coney, will you listen to me?

[FINCH *screams again.*]

CONEY. You listen to him. [*With a savage jerk, he breaks away from the* MAJOR *and starts into the bushes.*]

MINGO. Coney! Stop trying to be a goddam hero! [CONEY *stops just as he is about to go into the jungle. He doesn't turn around to face* MINGO *who stands where he is and talks very fast.*] It's just a trick. A dirty, lousy trick. Sure, they're jabbing Finch and making him yell. But if you go after him—they'll kill him. And you too. [CONEY *turns around slowly.*] There isn't a lousy thing we can do, kid.

[*A slight pause.* CONEY *walks toward* MINGO *very slowly, then suddenly hurls his rifle to the ground and sits by it.*]

CONEY. So—to hell with Finch.

MINGO [*going to him*]. No.

CONEY. Let them make hamburger out of him.

MINGO. Kid, there's nothing we can do.

CONEY. You can— [FINCH *screams again*.] O Christ!

MINGO. Don't listen. Try not to listen. You know—the way you do with guns. You don't hear them after a while.

CONEY. That isn't guns; it's Finch!

MINGO. Pretend it's just yelling. Hell, you ought to be used to yelling and noise. You're a city kid.

CONEY. What?

MINGO. You come from Pittsburgh, don't you? [FINCH *screams again*.] Don't you, Coney?

CONEY. Mingo, they're killing him.

MINGO. That bar you and he were going to have—was it going to be in Pittsburgh? [FINCH *screams*.] Was it going to be in Pittsburgh, Coney?

CONEY. Finch!

MINGO. Kid, it's not so bad if he's yelling. You've got to be alive to yell.

CONEY. Major, please—

MINGO. Don't listen. Tell me about the bar.

CONEY. Major, let me—

MINGO. Talk.

CONEY. I can't.

MINGO. Remember that Jap knife I picked up? The one you wanted to—

CONEY. Mingo—let me—

MINGO. Say, whatever happened that night when you were on guard and—

CONEY. Mingo—

MINGO. You like poetry?

CONEY. Mingo, he's being—

[FINCH *screams*.]

MINGO. My wife writes poetry, Coney. Remember you always wanted to hear some?

CONEY. Please—

MINGO. Didn't you always want to hear some? Listen.

[FINCH *screams again, weaker now.*]

CONEY. Oh dear God!

MINGO. Listen. [*Quickly.*]

> "We are only two and yet our howling
> Can encircle the world's end.
> Frightened,

[FINCH *screams—weakly.*]

> you are my only friend.

[*Slower now.*]

> And frightened, we are everyone.
> Someone must take a stand.
> Coward, take my coward's hand."

[*There is a long pause. They sit waiting. Slowly,* CONEY *stretches out, buries his face in the ground and starts to cry. A bird screams.* T.J. *looks up.*]

T.J. [*quietly*]. Lousy birds. [T.J. *begins to whistle "Shoo, Fly" very sweetly. A long pause. Then,* MINGO *gets up.*]

MAJOR. Helluva thing.

MINGO. Yeah. In the Marianas, I saw a fellow after the Japs had gotten hold of him. They'd put pieces of steel through his cheeks—here—you know. Like a bit for a horse.

T.J. You couldn't talk about something pleasant, could you?

MINGO. Sorry.

T.J. We'll all have a chance to find out what the squints do if we keep sitting here.

MAJOR. Well, the plane won't come till after it gets dark and we can't dig up the canoes till sundown.

T.J. There ought to be something we can do besides sit around here on our butts.

MAJOR. Suppose you go down the beach and see if the canoes are still where we buried them.

T.J. Go out on the beach now? It's too light! ‗

MAJOR. The canoes are right at the edge of the trees. You don't have to go out in the open.

T.J. But even if they're not there, there's nothing I can do about it.

MAJOR. You can find out! Now you heard me. Get going, T.J.! [T.J. *hesitates, then picks up his rifle and starts upstage.*] If you run into trouble, fire four quick shots.

[T.J. *doesn't answer but storms off through the path up right. During the following, the lights begin to dim as the sun goes down.*]

MINGO. I think the big executive is a little afraid.

MAJOR. I guess he doesn't like to take orders from me.

MINGO. He doesn't like much of anything, Major.

MAJOR. Does he— [*Hesitates.*] Mingo, does he make cracks about the Jews?

MINGO. Yes, Major. He does. He does indeed.

MAJOR. To Coney?

MINGO. Coney's a Jew.

MAJOR. Funny. I never think of him as a Jew.

MINGO. Yeah, it is funny. I never think of you as a Gentile.

[*A slight pause. Then the* MAJOR *speaks awkwardly— in a low voice.*]

MAJOR. Guess I said the wrong thing.

MINGO. I'm sorry, Major. I shouldn't've—

MAJOR. There are a lot of things you know, Mingo, that I guess I should but I—

MINGO. Look, sir, I didn't—

MAJOR. Wait. I'd like to get this off my chest. There are a lot of things I'd like to get off my chest. [*A pause.*] For one thing, I'd like to thank you, Mingo.

MINGO. For what?

MAJOR. For the rumpus just now with Coney . . . when you stopped him from running off half-cocked after Finch. . . .

MINGO. I just repeated what you'd said.

MAJOR. Yeah, but he—well, you stopped him. Thanks.

MINGO. Nuts.

MAJOR. I shouldn't have needed you or anybody else to—

MINGO. It's no crime to get help, Major.

MAJOR. No. But it's lousy to think you need it. I know you fellows—well, take T.J. I know he thinks I'm too young to give him orders.

MINGO. He'd think God was too young.

MAJOR. I didn't know what T.J. was like before we started. I guess I should have.

MINGO. Yes. I think you should have.

MAJOR. I know what you think, too.

MINGO. What do you mean?

MAJOR. An officer's got to have the respect of his men. He's no good otherwise, Mingo.

MINGO. Depends what you think respect is.

MAJOR. You think I care about the job and not about Finch. I care about Finch! I do now! But the job comes first. And I know my job, Mingo. I know it darn well!

MINGO. O.K., sir.

MAJOR. This isn't what I started out to say at all. [*Pause.*] Look—I'm a Major . . . but I'm twenty-six. I don't know all the answers and I don't think I know 'em. Judas, I'm not even sure what this lousy war is all about. There are fifty million things I don't know that I wish I did. But I'm a Major. I've got to have the respect of my men. And there's only one way I can get it: by knowing my job and running it.

MINGO. Nobody wants to run the show, Major. Maybe T.J.—but he's a first-class crud, anyway. We just want the same thing, too.

MAJOR. What?

MINGO. Respect. For us—as guys.

MAJOR. But an officer—

MINGO. An officer's a guy, isn't he, Major?

MAJOR. Yeah.

MINGO. O.K. All we want is for you—every once in a while to—talk to us—like this.

MAJOR [*smiling*]. O.K.

MINGO [*smiling*]. O.K.

[*The* MAJOR *takes out a pack of cigarettes and holds one out for* MINGO. *Then he lights it for him.*]

MAJOR. How's the arm?

MINGO. Lousy.

MAJOR. Want me to change the bandage?

MINGO. No. I just want to get out of here. Thanks. [*For the cigarette.*]

MAJOR. Don't worry about it so. It'll be O.K.

MINGO. I know, but I—well, I'd kinda hate to go back to the States anyway. And to go back with a—well, I guess I have too good an imagination.

MAJOR. I think you're just worried about going back to your wife with—well, a bum wing, say.

MINGO [*slightly bitter*]. Oh, my wife wouldn't care.

MAJOR. No. She sounds like a fine girl.

MINGO. How do you know?

MAJOR. From that poem. Wasn't that hers?

MINGO. What po— Oh. That. Yeah, that was hers.

MAJOR. Most people think it's sissy stuff but—I like poetry. I was trying to remember that last part. "Frightened, we are—"

MINGO [*reeling it off*]. "Everyone. Someone must make a stand. Coward, take my coward's hand."

MAJOR. I like that.

MINGO. Sure. It's great. My wife's a great little writer. Pretty, too. It's just a pity she doesn't read her own stuff once in a while.

MAJOR. What do you mean?

MINGO. She writes good letters, too. I remember the first one, the first one she wrote me in the Army. "My darling darling," it began. She likes repetition. "My darling darling, I will never again use the word love—except to say I love you."

MAJOR. That's nice.

MINGO. Oh, that's very nice. Almost as nice as her last letter. I can remember that one, too. I got that about a week ago. That began: "My darling, this is the hardest letter I've ever had to write. But it's only fair to be honest with you and tell you that—" [*He is too choked up to go on. Slight pause.*]

MAJOR [*embarrassed.*] Want another cigarette?

MINGO. No . . . thanks.

MAJOR. The sun's going down.

MINGO. They call that the G.I. letter, you know. Because there are so many of them.

MAJOR. I know.

MINGO. I can understand. Hell, I'm away and she meets another guy. But—Christ!

MAJOR. Well . . .

MINGO. It makes me want to hate all civilians. Then I remember I used to be one myself. A couple of million years ago . . . Hell, they can't all be bad.

MAJOR. Of course not.

MINGO. Then I remember that we've got stinkers here too. Like T.J. And so I try to stay on the beam. It's kind of hard though, when I think of that bitch and what— [*He cuts off as there is a rustling noise from the bushes right. They freeze. The rustling gets louder. The* MAJOR *grabs his rifle and, at the same time,* CONEY *sits up with his rifle ready.*] T.J.

MAJOR. He wouldn't be coming from there.

[*The rustling gets still louder. And then, in the fading light,* T.J. *appears, scrambling through the brush.*]

T.J. The canoes are still there. I scratched holy hell out of myself though.

[*The rifles are lowered.*]

MAJOR. Why didn't you come back by the trail?

T.J. I got lost. [*To* CONEY.] When did you wake up?

CONEY. Just now.

MAJOR. Are you hungry, Coney? Why don't you eat something?

CONEY. K ration isn't kosher.

[*A slight pause. From now on, it begins to get dark rapidly.*]

MINGO. The birds have shut up anyway.

MAJOR [*looking up*]. I think it's dark enough to dig up the canoes and get 'em ready.

MINGO. What about the gear?

MAJOR. There's no point in taking it until the canoes are ready . . . only—we need someone to watch it. In case.

MINGO. I don't mind.

T.J. How's your arm?

MINGO. My arm?

MAJOR. You couldn't use your rifle if—

CONEY [*getting up suddenly*]. I'll stay.

MAJOR. Oh, thanks, Coney, but you'd better—

CONEY [*harshly*]. What's wrong with me staying?

MAJOR [*quietly*]. O.K. Thanks.

MINGO. Maybe I'd better stay, too, Major. With this bum wing, I won't be able to—

CONEY. I'm not afraid to stay alone, Mingo!

MAJOR. You can help lift the canoes with your left arm anyway, Mingo.

MINGO. Sure.

MAJOR. Let's go. [*He starts for the path up left fol-*

lowed by T.J. and MINGO. *Just before he goes into the trees, he turns and calls to* CONEY.] Four quick shots if anything happens, Coney.

CONEY. Yes, sir.

MINGO. Nothing will, kiddo. See you. [*He disappears after the* MAJOR *and* T.J. *into the jungle. By now, the sun has gone down altogether. The jungle that rims the stage is pitch black, but there is pale light center in the clearing, dimming out to the edges.* CONEY *does not look after the others when they go. He stands still for a moment and then takes out a cigarette. He holds it, then suddenly shoves it in his mouth, holds his rifle ready and whirls around. He listens sharply for a moment, then slowly turns. His shoulders slump, the rifle comes down, and he takes the cigarette out of his mouth. He walks to the pile of equipment, looks at it and is about to sit down when suddenly he freezes. The cigarette drops to the ground, the rifle comes up. Slowly, very slowly, he starts to turn and, when he is halfway around, leaps like a cat to the dimly lighted edge of the clearing, right. He holds there for a moment, listening. Then, he leans forward a little.*]

CONEY [*softly*]. Finch? [*He moves closer to the trees. Plaintively.*] Finch? [*He listens for a moment, and then suddenly whirls so that his gun is pointed up right. He whirls again so that it is pointed up left. He darts back across the stage to the pile of equipment and stands there breathing hard, moving the rifle back and forth in a small arc. Then, suddenly, he hurls the gun down in front of him and sinks to his haunches.*] Your name is Coen and you're a— [*His voice cracks. He covers his face with his hands. He remains that way for a long moment and then sinks to the ground, bracing himself with his left hand and covering his face with his right. A second later, the bushes down right begin to rustle softly.* CONEY *doesn't hear this. The rustling gets louder; the bushes move; and then a body begins to crawl out very slowly; just the shape is discernible in the dim light by the trees, but soon it is apparent that the body is not crawling, but dragging itself. It gets closer to the lighted area and stops. A hand comes up and gestures—as though the man were trying to talk and couldn't. Finally, with a great effort, the body drags itself farther into the light. The clothes are slashed and splotched with blood and the face is battered—but it's* FINCH. *He sees* CONEY *and tries again to call to him. Again, his hand comes out in a pathetically futile gesture; he tries desperately hard to speak—but no sound comes. He tries to move farther but can't. Finally, in an outburst of impotent fury, he tries again to call and now his voice shouts out in a shrill scream.*]

FINCH. Coney! [*Like a bullet,* CONEY *drops his hands. His face is wide with terror; his body is rigid. He cannot believe he really heard anything. Then slowly, slowly, his head turns. He looks straight at* FINCH—*but does not believe he sees him.*]

CONEY [*plaintively, with a suggestion of a tear*]. Finch? . . . Is that you, Finch?

FINCH. Coney!

CONEY [*frantically, he scrambles over and puts an arm around* FINCH, *who groans in pain*]. Finch! Oh, Christ, Finch! Finch! [*He reaches for his canteen, quickly opens it and props* FINCH's *head in his lap. As he starts to give him water, he talks.*] Oh, I'm glad! I'm so glad, Finch! You all right? You're going to be all right now, Finch. You're going to be all right now— [FINCH *cannot hold the water and spews it up.*] Easy, fellow. Easy, Finch. [FINCH *begins to retch;* CONEY *holds his head.*] Oh, that's charming.

That's really charming. You go right ahead. That's
fine and charming, Finch.

[FINCH *has stopped now and tries to talk.*]

FINCH [*just getting the word out*]. Delightful.

CONEY. Oh, you bastard! You damn son of a bitch bastard! I might've known they couldn't finish you off,
you damn Arizona bastard. Let me see what they—
[*He touches* FINCH, *trying to see his wounds.* FINCH
gasps in pain.] I'm sorry. I'm sorry, kid, but I—what?
What, Finch? I can't hear you. What? [*He bends
down, his ear close to* FINCH's *mouth.*] Oh for Chrissake, sure the lousy maps are all right. We've got
to get you fixed up— [*Again he touches* FINCH *and*
FINCH *groans.*] All right. Just lie still. The guys are
getting the canoes now. The plane'll be here soon
and you'll be back to the base in no time. You can
goldbrick out the rest of the war in the hospital, you
lucky bastard! You'll probably get a slew of medals,
to say nothing of a big fat Purple Heart. And you'll
go home and leave me stuck here. Hey, did I tell
you I missed you, you jerk? O Jesus, I'm so glad,
Finch. [FINCH's *head suddenly rolls over and flops
to one side.*] I'm so glad, I'm so . . . [*He stops. He
is absolutely quiet for a moment. Then, begging.*]
Finch? Finch? Ah, Finch, please don't be dead! [*He
turns* FINCH's *body slightly and ducks his head down
so he can listen to* FINCH's *heart. There is a pause;
and then, with his head still on* FINCH's *chest, he says
softly:*] O God. O God. O God. O God. O God. [*His
voice cracks on the last and he begins to cry softly.
Slowly, he straightens up. He is whimpering very
quietly.* FINCH's *body rolls back, stomach down.*
CONEY *looks at it for a long moment and then, suddenly, stops crying and with a violent, decisive brutal
gesture, shoves the body so it rolls over on its back.
He stares at the horror he sees for a few seconds.*

Then, swiftly, he lifts the head into his lap with one hand and, with a long arc-like sweep, cradles the torso with his other arm and bends across it. An anguished groan.] Oh, no, Finch! [*He begins to rock the body as though it were a baby.*] Oh, no, Finch! Oh, no, no, no! [*Just at this moment, a voice cracks out from some distance off right. It is a Jap voice.*]

FIRST JAP. Hey, Yank! Come out and fight!

[CONEY *looks up sharply, cradling the head closer. From farther up right comes another voice.*]

SECOND JAP. Hey, Yank! Come out and fight!

[CONEY's *head turns in the direction of the second voice.*]

CONEY. Finch, they're after you again! But I won't leave you this time. I promise I won't, Finch.

THIRD JAP. Come and fight, yellow bastard.

CONEY. I won't leave you, Finch. I promise, I promise, I promise! [*He takes his bayonet out and starts to scoop up the ground furiously. At the same time, the* JAPS *continue yelling. Their shouts overlap with variations of the same cry. As he digs.*] Don't worry, Finch. I told you I wouldn't let them get you. I promised, didn't I? Didn't I? And I won't. Because I'm not a yellow bastard. I won't leave you, Finch. [*He is digging feverishly now; the yelling is coming closer; and the* MAJOR *rushes on from the path upstage, followed by* MINGO.]

MAJOR. Coney!

MINGO. He's got Finch!

MAJOR [*to* MINGO]. Get the map case. [MINGO *quickly searches through the pile of equipment for the map case. The* MAJOR *goes to* CONEY *who is digging furiously.*] Coney, come on. We've got to—God, he's dead!

CONEY. They won't get him, though, Major. They want to but they won't. I'm going to bury him!

FIRST JAP. Fight, you yellow bastard.

MAJOR. Bury— Listen, Coney, we— Coney, you can't bury him. We've got to get out of here.

THIRD JAP. Hey! Yank, come out and fight.

MINGO [*coming over with the map case*]. Got them Major.

MAJOR. Coney—

MINGO. What's the matter with him?

MAJOR. Finch is dead and he's trying to bury him.

MINGO. O God! Coney, get up.

THIRD JAP. Come out, you Yank bastard.

CONEY. I can't leave Finch.

MINGO. We'll take him. Come on. Get up.

CONEY. I can't leave Finch.

MINGO. Get up, Coney.

CONEY. Finch—

MINGO. Don't worry about him.

MAJOR. We'll take him.

MINGO. Come on, Coney.

[CONEY *tries to get up. He drags himself a few inches, but he cannot get up.*]

CONEY. I *can't.*

MAJOR. What do you mean you can't?

CONEY. I can't move, Major. I can't move!

THIRD JAP. Yank, come out and fight.

MINGO. Holy God! Try.

CONEY. I am—but I can't.

MINGO. Now stop that. You've got to get out of here.

CONEY. I can't, Mingo. I can't walk. I can't move.

SECOND JAP. Come out and fight.

MINGO. Were you shot? Were you hit?

FIRST JAP. Yank, come out and fight.

CONEY. No.

SECOND JAP. Fight, you yellow bastard.

MAJOR. Then why can't you walk?

CONEY [*building to hysteria now*]. I don't know!

MINGO. What's the matter with you?

THIRD JAP. Yank, come out and fight.

CONEY. I don't know!

MINGO. Coney—

CONEY. I don't know! I don't know! I don't know! [*He is crying wildly now;* MINGO *and the* MAJOR *are trying to lift him; and the screaming of the* JAPS *is getting louder and louder. The* JAPS *continue through the blackness and gradually fade out.*]

SCENE III

SCENE—*Hospital Room. The Pacific Base.*
Before the lights come up, we hear CONEY *counting.*

CONEY. 85—84—83—82—81—80—79—

DOCTOR. 78.

CONEY. 78—77—76—75. [*The lights are up now.* CONEY *is on the bed, the* DOCTOR *sitting by him watching the needle.*] 74—73—72—73—7—

[*The* DOCTOR *withdraws the needle and gets up.*]

DOCTOR. Coney, do you remember how you got off that island?

CONEY. I think—Mingo. Something about Mingo.

DOCTOR. Yes. Mingo picked you up and carried you out.

CONEY. I—I remember water. Being in the canoe on water. There were bullets.

DOCTOR. Some of the Japs fired machine guns when they realized what was happening.

CONEY. I think maybe I passed out because—it's all kind of dark. Then I'm in the plane.

DOCTOR. T.J. lifted you in.

CONEY. T.J.?

DOCTOR. Yes.

CONEY. But Mingo . . .

DOCTOR. Mingo couldn't lift you in alone. His right arm was no good.

CONEY. Oh, yeah . . . yeah.

DOCTOR. That's all you remember, though?

CONEY. I remember being taken off the plane.

DOCTOR. I mean on the island. That's all you remember of what happened on the island.

CONEY. Yes.

DOCTOR. Then why can't you walk, Coney?

CONEY. What?

DOCTOR. You weren't shot, were you?

CONEY. No.

DOCTOR. You didn't break your legs, did you?

CONEY. No.

DOCTOR. Then why can't you walk, Coney?

CONEY. I don't know. I don't know.

DOCTOR. But you said you remember everything that happened.

CONEY. I—yes. Yes.

DOCTOR. Do you remember waking up in the hospital? Do you remember waking up with that bad feeling?

CONEY. Yes.

[*Slight pause. The* DOCTOR *walks next to the bed.*]

DOCTOR. Coney, when did you first get that bad feeling?

CONEY. It was—I don't know.

DOCTOR. Coney— [*He sits down.*] Coney, did you first get it right after Finch was shot?

CONEY. No.

DOCTOR. What did you think of when Finch was shot?

CONEY. I don't know.

DOCTOR. You said you remember everything that happened. And you do. You remember that, too. You remember how you felt when Finch was shot, don't you, Coney? Don't you?

CONEY [*sitting bolt upright*]. Yes. [*A long pause. His hands twist his robe and then lay still. With dead, flat tones.*] When we were looking for the map case, he said—he started to say: You lousy yellow Jew bastard. He only said you lousy yellow jerk, but he started to say you lousy yellow Jew bastard. So I knew. I knew.

DOCTOR. You knew what?

CONEY. I knew he'd lied when—when he said he didn't care. When he said people were people to him. I knew he lied. I knew he hated me because I was a Jew so—I was glad when he was shot.

[*The* DOCTOR *straightens up.*]

DOCTOR. Did you leave him there because you were glad?

CONEY. Oh, no!

DOCTOR. You got over it.

CONEY. I was—I was sorry I felt glad. I was ashamed.

DOCTOR. Did you leave him because you were ashamed?

CONEY. No.

DOCTOR. Because you were afraid?

CONEY. No.

DOCTOR. No. You left him because that was what you had to do. Because you were a good soldier. [*Pause.*] You left him and you ran through the jungle, didn't you?

CONEY. Yes.

DOCTOR. And you walked around in the clearing by the beach, didn't you?

CONEY. Yes.

DOCTOR. So your legs were all right.

CONEY. Yes.

DOCTOR. Then if anything did happen to your legs, it happened when Finch crawled back. And you say nothing happened to you then.

CONEY. I don't know.

DOCTOR. Did anything happen?

CONEY. I don't know. Maybe—maybe.

DOCTOR. But if anything did happen, you'd remember?

CONEY. I don't know.

DOCTOR. You *do* remember what happened when Finch crawled back, don't you? Don't you, Coney?

CONEY [*covers his face*]. Finch . . . Finch . . .

DOCTOR. Remember that. Think back to that, Coney. You were alone in the clearing and Finch crawled in.

CONEY. O God . . . O dear God . . .

DOCTOR. Remember. [*He gets up quickly, moves across the room and in a cracked voice calls:*] Coney!

CONEY [*plaintively—he turns sharply*]. Finch? . . . Finch?

DOCTOR [*a cracked whisper*]. Coney . . .

CONEY. Oh, Finch, Finch! Is that you, Finch? [*He cradles an imaginary head in his lap and begins to rock back and forth.*] I'm so glad. I'm so glad, Finch! I'm so . . . [*He stops short, waits, then ducks his head down as though to listen to* FINCH's *heart. A moment, then he straightens up and then, with the same decisive, brutal gesture as before, shoves the imaginary body of* FINCH *so that it rolls over. He looks at it in horror and then the* DOCTOR *calls out:*]

DOCTOR. Hey, Yank! Come out and fight!

CONEY. They won't get you, Finch. I won't leave you this time, I promise! [*He begins to pantomime digging feverishly.*]

DOCTOR. Come out and fight, Yank.

CONEY. I won't leave you this time!

[*The* DOCTOR *walks over deliberately and grabs* CONEY'S *hand, stopping it in the middle of a digging motion.*]

DOCTOR [*curtly*]. What are you trying to bury him in, Coney? [CONEY *stops and stares up at him.*] This isn't earth, Coney. This is a bed. Feel it. It's a bed. Underneath is a floor, a wooden floor. Hear? [*He stamps.*] You can't bury Finch, Coney, because he isn't here. You're not on that island. You're in a hospital. You're in a hospital, Coney, and I'm your doctor. I'm your doctor!

[*Pause.*]

CONEY. Yes, sir.

DOCTOR. And you remember now, you remember that nothing happened to your legs at all, did it?

CONEY. No, sir.

DOCTOR. But you had to be carried here.

CONEY. Yes, sir.

DOCTOR. Why?

CONEY. Because I can't walk.

DOCTOR. Why can't you walk?

CONEY. I don't know.

DOCTOR. *I do.* It's because you didn't want to, isn't it, Coney? Because you knew if you couldn't walk, then you couldn't leave Finch. That's it, isn't it?

CONEY. I don't know.

DOCTOR. That must be it. Because there's nothing wrong with your legs. They're fine, healthy legs and you can walk. You can walk. You had a shock and you didn't want to walk. But you're over the shock and now you do want to walk, don't you? You do want to walk, don't you, Coney?

CONEY. Yes. Yes.

DOCTOR. Then get up and walk.

CONEY. I—can't.

DOCTOR. Yes, you can.

CONEY. No.

DOCTOR. Try.

CONEY. I can't.

DOCTOR. Try.

CONEY. I can't.

DOCTOR. Get up and walk! [*Pause.*] Coney, get up and
walk! [*Pause.*] You lousy, yellow Jew bastard, get
up and walk!

[*At that,* CONEY *straightens up in rage. He is shaking,
but he grips the edge of the bed and swings his feet
over. He is in a white fury, and out of his anger
comes this tremendous effort. Still shaking, he stands
up; holds for a moment; and glares at the* DOCTOR.
*Then, with his hands outstretched before him as
though he is going to kill the* DOCTOR, *he starts to
walk. First one foot, then the other, left, right, left—
but he begins to cry violently and as he sinks to the
floor, the* DOCTOR *moves forward swiftly and grabs
him.*]

DOCTOR [*triumphantly*]. All right, son! All right!

CURTAIN

Act three

SCENE I

SCENE—*Hospital Room. Two weeks later.*

There is a bright cheerful look about the room now.
The window is open; sunlight streams in. The bed is
pushed close against the wall and has a neat, unused
look. There is a typewriter on the desk.

CONEY, *wearing a hospital "zoot suit," is seated at the desk typing very laboriously. The door opens and* T.J. *comes in.* CONEY *stutters slightly in this scene when he is agitated.*

T.J. Oh! Hi, Coney!

[*A second's awkward pause.*]

MAJOR [*coming in*]. Coney! Gosh, it's good to see you, fellow!

CONEY. It's good to see you, Major.

T.J. You're looking fine, just fine!

MAJOR. We've sure missed you. When are you coming back to us?

CONEY. I—don't know if I am, sir. I'm—working for the Doc now.

T.J. Working?

CONEY. Yes. I type up his records and—sort of keep 'em straight for him.

MAJOR. Why, the dirty dog! Stealing my best man!

CONEY [*with a smile*]. It's really not very much work, sir.

MAJOR. I didn't know you could type.

CONEY. Oh—hunt and peck.

T.J. Well, it's great you're not a patient any more.

CONEY. I'm still a patient. In a way.

MAJOR. Do you—still get the—

CONEY. Shots? No. But the Doc—well—he and I talk.

T.J. Talk?

CONEY. Yes. Once a day.

T.J. Why?

CONEY. Well, it's—part of the treatment.

T.J. Brother, I'd like to be that kind of a patient.

CONEY. Maybe you should be.

MAJOR [*leaping in hastily*]. The Doc's quite a guy, isn't he?

CONEY. Yes, sir. He— [*Slight note of appeal.*] He says
I'm coming along fine.

MAJOR. Oh, anybody can see you are, can't they, T.J.?

T.J. Sure.

MAJOR. We've got something to tell you that ought to
put you right on top of the world. The island— [*He
stops. Cautiously.*] You remember the island, Coney?

CONEY [*wry smile*]. Yes, I remember, Major.

MAJOR. It was invaded four days ago. And everything
went off 100 per cent perfect—thanks to our maps.

CONEY. Oh, that's swell.

MAJOR. We've gotten commendations a yard long.

T.J. Wait till you get out of here! Your back's going
to be sore from all the patting it's going to get!

MAJOR. The Doc wanted to tell you about it but . . .
well . . .

T.J. We felt since we were all in it together, Coney—

CONEY. Did you, T.J.?

T.J. Sure. Weren't we?

CONEY. In a way, we were. And in a way, we weren't.

T.J. Wait a minute, kid, don't forget how I . . .

CONEY [*getting a little unstable now*]. Don't you worry
about my memory, T.J. The Doc fixed me up fine
and it's all right.

T.J. Sure, I know.

CONEY. Maybe it'd be better if I did forget a few
things. If I forgot that— [*He breaks off as the door
opens and the DOCTOR comes in.*]

DOCTOR [*kidding slightly*]. Well! Who said this was
visiting hour?

MAJOR. We were looking for you, Doc. We wanted
your permission to see Coney.

DOCTOR [*still the kidding tone*]. I'm afraid you can't
have it.

MAJOR [*following suit*]. That's too bad. I guess we'd
better run along, T.J.

DOCTOR [*no smile now*]. Yes. I think you'd better.

MAJOR. Oh. I'm sorry, sir. I—

DOCTOR. That's O.K. I'll tell you what. You're going to see Mingo this afternoon, aren't you?

MAJOR. Yes.

DOCTOR. Drop around after that.

MAJOR. Sure! Thanks, Doc. [*Turns to go.*] I'll see you later, Coney.

CONEY. Yes, sir.

T.J. Take care, Coney.

CONEY. Yeah.

MAJOR. Thanks again, Doc. [*He and* T.J. *go out.* CONEY *had edged toward the desk when the* DOCTOR *came in. Now, he goes behind it and sits down at the typewriter.*]

DOCTOR. I'm sorry I had to run them out.

CONEY [*putting a sheet of paper in the typewriter*]. That's all right, sir. I didn't care.

DOCTOR. Nice boy, the Major.

CONEY. Yes, sir. [*He starts to type slowly.*]

DOCTOR. How'd you get on with T.J.?

CONEY. All right. [*A slight pause.*] No. Not really all right. He makes me think of things and I—want to jump at him.

DOCTOR. Why not? That's a good, healthy reaction.

CONEY. Honest, Doc?

DOCTOR. Of course. [*Indicating the typing.*] Never mind that. This isn't your working period. It's mine.

CONEY. Now?

DOCTOR. Yes. Now.

CONEY. But we don't usually—

DOCTOR [*cutting him*]. I know. But we're going to work now. I'll tell you why later.

CONEY. Yes, sir. [*He gets up from behind the desk and sits in the chair center.*]

DOCTOR. How do you feel?

CONEY. All right.

DOCTOR. Did you dream last night?

CONEY. No.

DOCTOR. Good. The Major told you about the invasion?

CONEY. Yes.

DOCTOR. Well?

CONEY. I'm—afraid I didn't care very much, sir.

DOCTOR. You will. In time you'll feel that everything outside has some connection with you and everything in you has some connection with everything outside. . . . What bothers you now, Coney?

CONEY. That—feeling, sir.

DOCTOR. The bad feeling?

CONEY. Yes, sir.

DOCTOR. You still have it?

CONEY [*very low*]. Yes, sir.

DOCTOR. Yes, sir; yes, sir. Two weeks of psychotherapy and they expect—

CONEY. I'm sorry, sir. I try to get rid of it but—

DOCTOR. No, no, son. It's not your fault. I was just— Come, we're going to talk about that bad feeling.

CONEY. Yes, sir.

DOCTOR. And we're going to get rid of it.

CONEY. Yes, sir.

DOCTOR. We are, Coney.

CONEY. Yes, sir.

DOCTOR [*very gently*]. *We*. Not me. The two of us. I think we can do it, Coney.

CONEY. I wish we could, sir.

DOCTOR. I think we can. It's hard work. It's trying to cram the biggest thing in your life into a space this small. But I think we can do it. I want to try, Coney. I want to help you, Peter.

[*Slight pause.*]

CONEY. That's—the first time anybody's called me Peter

since I've been in the Army. [*Pause.*] You're a right guy, Doc.

DOCTOR. I don't want you to think about anything except what I say now.

CONEY. O.K.

DOCTOR. Are you comfortable?

CONEY. Yes, sir.

DOCTOR. You still have that bad feeling?

CONEY. Yes, sir.

DOCTOR. It's sort of a guilty feeling?

CONEY. Yes, sir.

DOCTOR. When did you feel it first, Peter? Right after Finch was shot, wasn't it?

CONEY. Yes.

DOCTOR. And what did you think later?

CONEY. I thought I—well, you know, Doc.

DOCTOR. Tell me.

CONEY. I thought I felt—like you said: guilty, because I left him. But then—then you told me what Mingo said—what they all said. That I did what I had to do. I had to leave Finch to get the maps back.

DOCTOR. And you know that's right now, don't you? You know that's what you have to do in a war.

CONEY. Yes, sir.

DOCTOR. But you still have that guilty feeling.

CONEY. Yeah.

DOCTOR. Then it can't come from what you thought at all. It can't come from leaving Finch, can it, Peter?

CONEY. No, but—what did it come from?

DOCTOR. Coney, the first time you were in this room, the first time you were under that drug, do you know what you said about Finch? You said: I hate him.

CONEY. But I don't, I don't!

DOCTOR. I know you don't. And later on, you said that when Finch was shot—maybe you can remember yourself now. How did you feel when Finch was shot, Peter?

[*Pause.*]

CONEY [*low, very ashamed*]. I was glad.

DOCTOR. Why were you glad?

CONEY. I thought—

DOCTOR. Go on, son.

CONEY. I thought he was going to call me a lousy yellow Jew bastard. So—I was glad he got shot.

DOCTOR. Peter, I want you to listen hard to what I'm going to tell you. I want you to listen harder than you ever listened to anything in your whole life. Peter, *every soldier in this world* who sees a buddy get shot has that one moment when he feels glad. Yes, Peter, every single one. Because deep underneath he thinks: I'm glad it wasn't me. I'm glad *I'm* still alive.

CONEY. But—oh, no. Because what I thought was—

DOCTOR. I know. You thought you were glad because Finch was going to make a crack about your being a Jew. Maybe later, you were glad because of that. But at that moment you were glad it wasn't *you* who was shot. You were glad *you* were still alive. A lot of fellows think a lot of things later. But every single soldier, every single one of them has that moment when he thinks: I'm glad it wasn't me! . . . And that's what you thought. . . . [*Gently.*] You see the whole point of this, Peter? You've been thinking you had some special kind of guilt. But you've got to realize something. You're the same as anybody else. You're no different, son, no different at all.

CONEY. I'm a Jew.

DOCTOR. This, Peter, this sensitivity has been like a disease in you. It was there before anything happened on that island. It started way back. I only wish to God I had time to really dig and find out where and when and why. But it's been a disease. Sure, it's been aggravated by T.J. By people at home in our own country—but if you can cure yourself, you can help cure them and you've got to, Pete, you've got to!

CONEY. O.K., if you say so.

DOCTOR. You can and you must, Pete. Believe me, you can.

CONEY. I believe you, Doc. [*He gets up and starts to the desk.*]

DOCTOR. Peter . . .

CONEY. Are we through, Doc?

DOCTOR. Peter, don't you understand?

CONEY. Yes! Sure! I understand! I understand up here! But here— [*Indicates his heart.*] deep in here, I just can't. I just can't believe it's true. I wanta believe, Doc, don't you know that? I want to believe that every guy who sees his buddy get shot feels glad. I wanta believe I'm not different but I—I— [*The life goes out of him, and he goes behind the desk to the typewriter.*] It's hard, Doc. It's just damn hard. [*There is a slight pause.* CONEY *starts to type and then the* DOCTOR *reaches across and tears the paper out of the machine.*]

DOCTOR. Coney, listen to me. I've had to try to tell you this fast, too fast. Because we haven't time, any more, Coney, we haven't time.

CONEY. What?

DOCTOR. It's like everything else in war, Coney. We live too fast, we die too fast, we have to work too fast. We've had two short weeks of this, thirty pitiful minutes a day. You've done wonderfully. Beautifully —but now—

CONEY. What are you getting at, Doc?

DOCTOR. I'm trying to tell you that we're almost through, son. You're leaving.

CONEY. What?

DOCTOR. You're being sent back to the States.

CONEY [*frightened*]. Doc!

DOCTOR. At the end of this week.

CONEY. Why? Why do I have to go, sir? Did I do something?

DOCTOR. You helped make some maps. Those maps helped make an invasion. And after every invasion, we need bed space, Coney. For cases very much like yours.

CONEY. But I—

DOCTOR. You see, you're not so different, son.

CONEY. But I can't go! I'm not better, Doc, I'm not all better!

DOCTOR. Son, sit down. Sit down. You'll get care in the States. Good care. Sure, you're leaving sooner than I'd prefer, but that's just part of war. That just means you've got to work now, every minute, every single minute you have left here, you've got to work, Pete, you've got to!

CONEY. I don't want to leave you, Doc!

DOCTOR. Peter—

CONEY. I'm scared, Doc!

DOCTOR. You won't be if you work. If you think every minute about what I told you.

CONEY. Doc, I'm scared.

DOCTOR. Every minute, Pete.

CONEY. Doc!

DOCTOR. Come on, Pete. Work!

CONEY. I—

DOCTOR. Come on!

CONEY. Every guy who sees his buddy get shot feels like I did. Feels glad it wasn't him. Feels glad he's still alive . . . So what I felt when Finch got shot had nothing to do with being a Jew. Because I'm no different. I'm just— [*Breaks off in a sudden appeal.*]

Oh, Doc, help me, will you? Get it through my dumb head? Get it through me— [*Indicates his heart.*] here? Can't you straighten me out before I go?

DOCTOR. I'll do my damnedest. But you've got to help me. Will you, Peter?

CONEY. I'll try. I'll try. [*In a burst.*] Oh God, I've got to try!

CURTAIN

SCENE II

SCENE—*The Office. Pacific Base.*

AT RISE: *The mid-morning sun fills the room. There is a great air of bustle and activity. Odds and ends of equipment, records, papers are piled on the desks, on chairs, on the floor. Three or four crates are scattered about.*

T.J. is busy packing these crates and nailing them down. Right now, he is transferring records from the cabinet upstage to one of the crates which is near the desk, down left. MINGO *is seated at this in dress uniform. He has his chair propped up against the side wall and faces into the room so that his right arm cannot be seen.*

During the following, T.J. *bustles back and forth between the crates and the cabinet.*

T.J. And if you think I'm going to shed any tears over leaving this hole, you're crazy.

MINGO. You and me both.

T.J. Yeah, but we're moving on to another base. You're going home.

MINGO. Home is where you hang your hat and your wife.

T.J. Ah, don't let that arm get you.

MINGO. Don't let it get you, bud. [*He gets up—showing an empty right sleeve.*] These O.D.'s itch like a bitch. Poem.

T.J. Whose idea were they?

MINGO. Some jerk who thought we'd catch cold when we hit the States.

T.J. When do you leave?

MINGO. Pretty soon. If the Major doesn't get here pretty soon . . .

T.J. [*going into the* MAJOR's *office*]. Oh, he'll be back in a minute. [*Brushing by* MINGO.] Excuse me.

MINGO. Well, I got a jeep coming by to take me to the airfield.

T.J. [*coming out with papers which he puts in the crate*]. Are you flying?

MINGO. On wings of steel.

T.J. Say, that's a break!

MINGO. I'm the original rabbit's foot kid.

T.J. I hear Coney's going back with you.

MINGO. Yeah.

T.J. How is he?

MINGO. He's all right.

T.J. They sending him back in your care?

MINGO. No! I said he's all right.

T.J. O.K. I was just asking. You know as well as I do that cases like Coney get discharged from the hospital and then one little thing happens—and off they go again.

MINGO. Look—you leave that kid alone.

T.J. Leave *him* alone! Why in hell don't you guys lay off me for a while?

MINGO. Huh?

T.J. The whole damn bunch of you! Everything I do is wrong!

MINGO. Everybody picks on poor T.J.

T.J. Not only on me! On anybody who made real money as a civilian.

MINGO. What?

[*Telephone starts to ring in the* MAJOR's *office.*]

T.J. Sure! That gripes the hell out of you, doesn't it? So it keeps us out of your little club. You and Coney and—

MINGO. The phone's ringing, T.J.

T.J. [*going inside*]. I hear it!

MINGO. If a man answers, don't hang up.

T.J. [*offstage*]. Corporal Everitt speaking— No, sir, he's not. [*Comes out.*] That Colonel's a constipated old maid.

MINGO. When are you pulling out?

T.J. Oh—some time tonight or tomorrow morning; I'm not sure. [*Holding up two long pipe-like metal map cases.*] Now what the hell am I going to do with these?

MINGO [*looks at* T.J., *then at the cases and shakes his head*]. No. I guess not. Where's the outfit going?

T.J. [*stacking the cases near the crates*]. Damned if I know.

MINGO. Crap.

T.J. I don't, Mingo.

MINGO. Crap.

T.J. All right. It's a military secret then.

MINGO. Just because I'm leaving, T.J.—

[*The telephone rings again.*]

T.J. [*going inside*]. If that's the Colonel again, I'm going to tell him to screw off.

MINGO. Yep, yep. [*He gets up just as the outer door opens and* CONEY *walks in. He, too, wears dress uniform and carries a barracks bag which he sets down. He looks better now, but his stance, his walk, his voice, show that he is still a little unsure.*] Hi, kiddo!

CONEY. Hi.

MINGO [*kindly*]. It sure took you long enough to get here. [*He pulls a chair over for* CONEY.]

CONEY [*sitting*]. I stopped to say good-bye to the Doc.

MINGO. He's a nice gent. How do you feel, kid?

CONEY. Fine! How are you?

MINGO. Oh— [*He pokes his empty sleeve.*] a little underweight.

CONEY. Yeah.

MINGO. It feels kind of funny to be leaving, doesn't it?

CONEY. We used to talk so much about going home. . . .

MINGO. Home? You mean back to the States.

CONEY. What do you mean?

MINGO [*snapping out of it*]. Oh! What the hell! We're going back to the land of mattresses and steaks medium rare!

[T.J. *comes out of the* MAJOR'S *office.*]

T.J. Well, Coney! How are you, fellow?

CONEY. O.K.

T.J. [*looking at him a little too curiously*]. You look fine, too, just fine. Feeling all right, eh?

MINGO. Want to see his chart, T.J.?

T.J. All set to fly back to the States. Some guys get all the breaks.

MINGO. Yep. Some guys sure do.

T.J. Well, what the hell! You fellows will be safe and sound in blue suits while we're still here winning the war for you.

MINGO. Thanks, bub.

T.J. I don't know what you're beefing about.

CONEY. Nobody's beefing, T.J. Except maybe you.

T.J. I got this whole mess to clean up single-handed.

MINGO [*to* CONEY]. They're pulling out, too, but Montgomery Ward won't say where.

T.J. You know we're not supposed to tell, Mingo.

MINGO. Yeah. Coney and I have a hot pipeline to Tojo.

T.J. That's not the point. You're not in the outfit any more. You're—well, you guys are just out of it now.

MINGO. Don't break my Purple Heart, friend. [*The outer door opens and the* MAJOR *comes in.*] Hi, Major.

CONEY. Hello, Major.

MAJOR. Gee, I was afraid I'd miss you fellows.

T.J. The Colonel called twice, Major.

MAJOR. Oh, Judas.

T.J. I told him you'd be right back.

MAJOR. O.K. [*To* MINGO *and* CONEY.] I'm glad you could come over and say good-bye. We've been together for so—

[*Telephone rings.*]

T.J. Shall I get it?

MAJOR. No, it's probably the Colonel. I cornered that half-track. You can start loading these crates, T.J. [*To* MINGO *and* CONEY, *as he starts into the office.*] This'll only take a minute, fellows.

MINGO. That's O.K.

MAJOR [*inside—on telephone*]. Major Robinson . . . Yes, Colonel. Yes, sir . . .

T.J. [*struggling to lift the crate*]. Why the devil couldn't he get a detail to do this?

MINGO. T.S.

T.J. Yuk, yuk. [*As he staggers towards the door.*] Christ, this is heavy! [CONEY *walks swiftly to the door and opens it for* T.J. *A slight pause.* T.J. *quietly.*] Thanks, Coney. [*He goes out.* CONEY *shuts the door.*]

MINGO. Suddenly, it smells better in here.

CONEY. Yeah.

[*The* MAJOR *comes out of his office.*]

MAJOR. The Colonel's a wonderful man, but he worries more than my mother. . . . Well, Coney—

CONEY. Yes, sir.

MAJOR. Ah, forget that "sir."

MINGO. We're not civilians yet.

MAJOR. I didn't mean it that way and you know it, Mingo. I sure wish you were both going with us.

MINGO. So do we— [*Trying to find out where.*] wherever it is.

MAJOR. That doesn't matter. I'm sure going to miss you, though.

MINGO. T.J.'s taken over pretty well.

MAJOR. The only reason he's taken over is that there isn't anyone else this minute. . . . Fellows, I—oh, nuts!

MINGO. You don't have to say anything, Major.

MAJOR. I wish I knew how to say it. The three of us have been together for such a long time that it's— well, like saying good-bye to your family.

MINGO. Thanks.

CONEY [*simultaneously*]. Thank you, sir.

MAJOR. I ought to be thanking you, but I just can't. I—well, wish both of you have all the—

[*The outer door opens, and* T.J. *comes in.*]

T.J. They want you over HQ, Major.

MAJOR. I was just there.

T.J. Well, they sent Maroni for you.

MAJOR. O Lord! . . . [*To* CONEY *and* MINGO.] Look, will you two stick around for a little while?

MINGO. Well . . .

MAJOR. I'll be right back. [*To* T.J.] You can pack that stuff on my desk in there, T.J. [*He has started out and now trips against a barracks bag which was next to the crate* T.J. *removed.*] What the devil is this doing here?

CONEY. I'm sorry, sir, that's mine.

MAJOR [*embarrassed*]. Oh ... O.K.—I'll be right back. [*He goes out.*]

T.J. I wish he'd make up his mind. Half an hour ago, he said not to pack the stuff on his desk. [*He starts for the inner office.*]

MINGO. You really have it tough, don't you, T.J.?

T.J. [*going in*]. Oh, blow it, will you?

MINGO [*kicking his barracks bag out of the way—to* CONEY]. Well, G.I. Joe, I think we're just a little bit in the way around here.

CONEY. Yeah.

MINGO. I wish that jeep would come and get us the hell out.

CONEY. He'd like it, too.

MINGO. T.J.?

CONEY. Yeah.

MINGO. Oh, he's very happy playing King of the Hill.

CONEY. I get a kick out of the way he looks at me.

MINGO [*taking out a cigarette*]. How?

CONEY. Like he's trying to see if I'm—still off my rocker.

MINGO. Oh! Forget it. [*He takes out a match and begins struggling to light the cigarette.* T.J. *comes back into the room and carries some papers over to the crate.*]

T.J. More crap in there.

MINGO. You're wasting your time. You can throw out half of it.

[CONEY *moves to give* MINGO *a light and then stops. He knows* MINGO *wants to do this alone.*]

CONEY. Mingo was going to throw it out but that mission came up.

T.J. Look. You fellows are finished, so just let me do this my way, will you?

MINGO. Sure.

T.J. [*striking a match broadly*]. Here.

MINGO. It's more fun this way.

T.J. O.K. [*Shrugs and starts to nail down the crate.*] Does it bother you, the arm, I mean?

MINGO. No. It makes me light as a bird. [*Lights the match finally.*]

T.J. [*to* MINGO]. I didn't mean that. I meant does it hurt?

MINGO. Some.

T.J. Well—

CONEY [*trying to change the subject*]. What'd they put us in O.D.'s for?

T.J. They'll give you a new arm back in the States, kid.

MINGO. I know.

T.J. You ought to be able to work them for a good pension, too.

MINGO. Sure.

CONEY [*quietly*]. Shut up.

T.J. What's eating you?

CONEY. Shut up.

T.J. Why? Mingo's not kidding himself about—

CONEY. Shut up.

T.J. Take it easy, Coney, or—

CONEY. Or what?

MINGO. Coney . . .

CONEY. No. [*To* T.J.] Or what?

T.J. Are you trying to start something?

CONEY. I'm trying to tell you to use your head if you got one.

T.J. If *I* got one? Look friend, it takes more than a few

days in the jungle to send me off my trolley. It's only your kind that's so goddam sensitive.

CONEY. What do you mean—my kind?

T.J. What do you think I mean?

[*There is a second's wait. Then* CONEY'S *fist lashes out and socks* T.J. *squarely on the jaw, sending him to the floor.* CONEY *stands there with fists clenched, trembling.*]

T.J. [*getting up*]. It's a good thing you just got out of the booby hatch or I'd—

MINGO. You've got to get those crates out, don't you?

T.J. Look, Mingo . . . [T.J. *looks at him, then picks up a crate and carries it out. During this,* CONEY *has just been standing, staring straight ahead. His trembling gets worse. Suddenly, his head snaps up as though he hears* FINCH *again. His hands shoot up to cover his ears. At this point,* MINGO *shuts the door after* T.J.]

MINGO. Nice going, kiddo. [*He turns, sees* CONEY, *and quickly crosses to him.*] Coney! Coney, what's the matter?

CONEY [*numbly. He is starting to lose control again*]. I'm just like anyone else.

MINGO. Take it easy, kid, sit down.

CONEY. I'm just like anyone else.

MINGO. Sure, sure. Sit down. [*He goes for a chair.*]

CONEY [*getting wilder*]. That's what the Doc said, Mingo.

MINGO [*bringing the chair over*]. And he's right. Ease up, Coney.

CONEY. That's what he said.

MINGO. Sure, sure. Take it easy.

CONEY [*sitting*]. I'm just like anyone else.

MINGO. That's right. You are.

CONEY. That's right.

MINGO. Yes.

CONEY [*jumping up in a wild outburst that knocks the chair over*]. Yes! Who're you kidding? It's not right! I'm not the same!

MINGO. Kid, you gotta get hold of yourself.

CONEY. You know I'm not!

MINGO. Kid, stop it. Listen to me!

CONEY. No!

MINGO. Listen—

CONEY. I'm tired of listening! I'm sick of being kidded! I got eyes! I got ears! I know!

MINGO. Coney, you can't—

CONEY. You heard T.J.!

MINGO. And I saw you give him what he deserved!

CONEY. What's the use? He'll just say it again. You can't shut him up!

MINGO. What do you—

CONEY. You can't shut any of them up—ever!

MINGO. All right! So he makes cracks about you. Forget it!

CONEY. Let's see you forget it!

MINGO. What the hell do you think I'm trying to do? [*A slight pause. This has caught* CONEY.]

CONEY. What?

MINGO. He makes cracks about me, too. Don't you think I know it?

CONEY. But those cracks—it's not the same, Mingo.

MINGO. To him, it's the same. To that son of a bitch and all the son of a bitches like him, it's the same; we're easy targets for him to take pot shots at.

CONEY. But we're not—

MINGO. No, we're not the same! I really *am* something special. There's nothing in this sleeve but air, kiddo.

CONEY. But everybody around here knows you.

MINGO. Around here I'm in khaki, so they call me a

hero. But back in the States, put me in a blue suit and I'm a stinking cripple!

CONEY. No. Not you, Mingo!

MINGO. Why not me?

CONEY. Because you're—you're . . .

MINGO. What? Too tough? That's what I keep trying to tell myself: Mingo, you're too tough to eat your lousy heart out about this. O.K., you lost a wing, but you're not gonna let it go down the drain for nothing.

CONEY. You couldn't.

MINGO. No? You should've seen me in the hospital. When I woke up and found it was off. All I could think of was the close shaves I'd had; all the times I'd stood right next to guys, seen 'em get shot and felt glad I was still alive. But when I woke up—

CONEY. Wait a minute—

MINGO [*continuing*]. I wasn't so sure.

CONEY [*cutting again*]. Wait a minute! Mingo wait! [MINGO *stops and looks at him.*] Say that again.

MINGO. Huh?

CONEY. Say it again.

MINGO. What?

CONEY. What you just said.

MINGO. About waking up in the hospital and . . .

CONEY. No, no. About standing next to guys when they were shot.

MINGO. Oh. Well, it was pretty rugged to see.

CONEY. But how you felt, Mingo, how you felt!

MINGO. Well, I—felt sorry for them, of course.

CONEY. No! No, that isn't it!

MINGO. I don't know what you mean, kiddo.

CONEY. When you saw them, Mingo, when you saw them get shot, you just said you felt—you felt—

MINGO. Oh. I felt glad I was still alive.

CONEY. Glad it wasn't you.

MINGO. Sure. Glad it wasn't me.

CONEY. Who told you to say that?

MINGO. Who *told* me?

CONEY. Yeah! Who told you?

MINGO. Nobody told me, kiddo. I saw it. I felt it. Hell, how did you feel when you saw Finch get it?

CONEY [*almost glowing*]. Just like you, Mingo. Just like you! *Just like you!*

MINGO. Hey, what's got into you?

CONEY. I was crazy . . . yelling I was different. [*Now the realization comes.*] I *am* different. Hell, you're different! Everybody's different— But so what? It's O.K. because underneath, we're—hell, we're all guys! We're all— O Christ! I can't say it, but am I making any sense?

MINGO. Are you!

CONEY. And like what you said about your arm? Not letting it go down the drain for nothing. Well, I'll be damned if I'm gonna let me go for nothing!

MINGO. Now we're riding, kiddo!

CONEY. It won't be easy . . .

MINGO. What is?

CONEY [*grinning*]. Yeah. What is?

MINGO. Hey!

CONEY. What?

MINGO. Maybe this is cockeyed.

CONEY. What?

MINGO. That bar you were going to have.

CONEY. Bar?

MINGO. With Finch.

CONEY. Oh. Yeah. Sure.

MINGO. You want a partner?

CONEY. A—

MINGO [*a shade timidly*]. A one-armed bartender would be kind of a novelty, Pete.

[*A great smile breaks over* CONEY'S *face. He tries to talk, to say what he feels. But all that can come out is:*]

CONEY. Ah Judas, Mingo!

[*Offstage comes the sound of a jeep horn.*]

MINGO. Hey, that sounds like our chauffeur. Soldier, the carriage waits without!

CONEY. Yes, sir! [*He goes to his barracks bag.* MINGO *goes to his, but has to struggle to lift it with his left hand.*]

MINGO [*as he walks to the bag*]. You'll have to keep an eye on me, you know. This arm's gonna—dammit.

CONEY. Hey, coward.

MINGO [*turning*]. What?

CONEY [*coming to him*]. Take my coward's hand. [*He lifts the bag up on* MINGO'S *back.*]

MINGO. Pete, my boy, you've got a charming memory.

[*A slight pause.*]

CONEY [*softly*]. Delightful! [*He lifts up his own bag and the two start out proudly as—*

THE CURTAIN FALLS

ALL MY SONS

by Arthur Miller

From *Arthur Miller's Collected Plays.*
Copyright © 1947, 1957, by Arthur Miller.
Reprinted by permission of The Viking Press, Inc.

First production, January 29, 1947,
at the Coronet Theatre, New York,
with the following cast:

JOE KELLER, *Ed Begley*
KATE KELLER, *Beth Merrill*
CHRIS KELLER, *Arthur Kennedy*
ANN DEEVER, *Lois Wheeler*
GEORGE DEEVER, *Karl Malden*
DR. JIM BAYLISS, *John McGovern*
SUE BAYLISS, *Peggy Meredith*
FRANK LUBEY, *Dudley Sadler*
LYDIA LUBEY, *Hope Cameron*
BERT, *Eugene Steiner*

ACT ONE *The back yard of the Keller home
        in the outskirts of an American town.
        August of our era.*
ACT TWO *Scene, as before.
        The same evening, as twilight falls.*
ACT THREE *Scene, as before.
        Two o'clock the following morning.*

Act one

The back yard of the Keller home in the outskirts of an American town. August of our era.

The stage is hedged on right and left by tall, closely planted poplars which lend the yard a secluded atmosphere. Upstage is filled with the back of the house and its open, unroofed porch which extends into the yard some six feet. The house is two stories high and has seven rooms. It would have cost perhaps fifteen thousand in the early twenties when it was built. Now it is nicely painted, looks tight and comfortable, and the yard is green with sod, here and there plants whose season is gone. At the right, beside the house, the entrance of the driveway can be seen, but the poplars cut off view of its continuation downstage. In the left corner, downstage, stands the four-foot high stump of a slender apple tree whose upper trunk and branches lie toppled beside it, fruit still clinging to its branches.

Downstage right is a small, trellised arbor, shaped like a sea-shell, with a decorative bulb hanging from its forward-curving roof. Garden chairs and a table are scattered about. A garbage pail on the ground next to the porch steps, a wire leaf-burner near it.

On the rise: It is early Sunday morning. JOE KELLER *is sitting in the sun reading the want ads of the Sunday paper, the other sections of which lie neatly on the ground beside him. Behind his back, inside the arbor,* DOCTOR JIM BAYLISS *is reading part of the paper at the table.*

KELLER *is nearing sixty. A heavy man of stolid mind and build, a business man these many years, but with the imprint of the machine-shop worker and boss still upon him. When he reads, when he speaks, when he listens, it is with the terrible concentration of the un-educated man for whom there is still wonder in many commonly known things, a man whose judgments must be dredged out of experience and a peasant-like com-mon sense. A man among men.*

DOCTOR BAYLISS *is nearly forty. A wry self-controlled man, an easy talker, but with a wisp of sadness that clings even to his self-effacing humor.*

At curtain, JIM *is standing at left, staring at the broken tree. He taps a pipe on it, blows through the pipe, feels in his pockets for tobacco, then speaks.*

JIM. Where's your tobacco?

KELLER. I think I left it on the table. [JIM *goes slowly to table in the arbor, finds a pouch, and sits there on the bench, filling his pipe.*] Gonna rain tonight.

JIM. Paper says so?

KELLER. Yeah, right here.

JIM. Then it can't rain.

[FRANK LUBEY *enters, through a small space between the poplars.* FRANK *is thirty-two but balding. A pleasant, opinionated man, uncertain of himself, with a tendency toward peevishness when crossed, but always wanting it pleasant and neighborly. He rather saunters in, leisurely, nothing to do. He does not notice* JIM *in the arbor. On his greeting,* JIM *does not bother looking up.*]

FRANK. Hya.

KELLER. Hello, Frank. What's doin'?

FRANK. Nothin'. Walking off my breakfast. [*Looks up at the sky.*] That beautiful? Not a cloud.

KELLER [*looks up*]. Yeah, nice.

FRANK. Every Sunday ought to be like this.

KELLER [*indicating the sections beside him*]. Want the paper?

FRANK. What's the difference, it's all bad news. What's today's calamity?

KELLER. I don't know, I don't read the news part any more. It's more interesting in the want ads.

FRANK. Why, you trying to buy something?

KELLER. No, I'm just interested. To see what people want, y'know? For instance, here's a guy is lookin' for two Newfoundland dogs. Now what's he want with two Newfoundland dogs?

FRANK. That is funny.

KELLER. Here's another one. Wanted—Old Dictionaries. High prices paid. Now what's a man going to do with an old dictionary?

FRANK. Why not? Probably a book collector.

KELLER. You mean he'll make a living out of that?

FRANK. Sure, there's a lot of them.

KELLER [*shakes his head*]. All the kind of business goin' on. In my day, either you were a lawyer, a doctor, or you worked in a shop. Now . . .

FRANK. Well, I was going to be a forester once.

KELLER. Well, that shows you; in my day, there was no such thing. [*Scanning the page, sweeping it with his hand.*] You look at a page like this you realize how ignorant you are. [*Softly, with wonder, as he scans page.*] Pssl

FRANK [*noticing tree*]. Hey, what happened to your tree?

KELLER. Ain't that awful? The wind must've got it last night. You heard the wind, didn't you?

FRANK. Yeah, I got a mess in my yard, too. [*Goes to tree.*] What a pity. [*Turns to* KELLER.] What'd Kate say?

KELLER. They're all asleep yet. I'm just waiting for her to see it.

FRANK [*struck*]. You know?—it's funny.

KELLER. What?

FRANK. Larry was born in August. He'd been twenty-seven this month. And his tree blows down.

KELLER [*touched*]. I'm surprised you remember his birthday, Frank. That's nice.

FRANK. Well, I'm working on his horoscope.

KELLER. How can you make him a horoscope? That's for the future, ain't it?

FRANK. Well, what I'm doing is this, see. Larry was reported missing on November 25th, right?

KELLER. Yeah?

FRANK. Well, then, we assume that if he was killed it was on November 25th. Now, what Kate wants . . .

KELLER. Oh, Kate asked you to make a horoscope?

FRANK. Yeah, what she wants to find out is whether November 25th was a favorable day for Larry.

KELLER. What is that, favorable day?

FRANK. Well, a favorable day for a person is a fortunate day, according to his stars. In other words it would be practically impossible for him to have died on his favorable day.

KELLER. Well, was that his favorable day?—November 25th?

FRANK. That's what I'm working on to find out. It takes time! See, the point is, if November 25th was his favorable day, then it's completely possible he's alive somewhere, because . . . I mean it's possible. [*He notices* JIM *now.* JIM *is looking at him as though at an idiot. To* JIM—*with an uncertain laugh.*] I didn't even see you.

KELLER [*to* JIM]. Is he talkin' sense?

JIM. Him? He's all right. He's just completely out of his mind, that's all.

FRANK [*peeved*]. The trouble with you is, you don't *believe* in anything.

JIM. And your trouble is that you believe in *anything*. *You* didn't see my kid this morning, did you?

FRANK. No.

KELLER. Imagine? He walked off with his thermometer. Right out of his bag.

JIM [*gets up*]. What a problem. One look at a girl and he takes her temperature. [*Goes to driveway, looks upstage toward street.*]

FRANK. That boy's going to be a real doctor; he's smart.

JIM. Over my dead body he'll be a doctor. A good beginning, too.

FRANK. Why? It's an honorable profession.

JIM [*looks at him tiredly*]. Frank, will you stop talking like a civics book?

[KELLER *laughs.*]

FRANK. Why, I saw a movie a couple of weeks ago, reminded me of you. There was a doctor in that picture . . .

KELLER. Don Ameche!

FRANK. I think it was, yeah. And he worked in his basement discovering things. That's what you ought to do; you could help humanity, instead of . . .

JIM. I would love to help humanity on a Warner Brothers salary.

KELLER [*points at him, laughing*]. That's very good, Jim.

JIM [*looks toward house*]. Well, where's the beautiful girl was supposed to be here?

FRANK [*excited*]. Annie came?

KELLER. Sure, sleepin' upstairs. We picked her up on the one o'clock train last night. Wonderful thing.

Girl leaves here, a scrawny kid. Couple of years go by, she's a regular woman. Hardly recognized her, and she was running in and out of this yard all her life. That was a very happy family used to live in your house, Jim.

JIM. Like to meet her. The block can use a pretty girl. In the whole neighborhood there's not a damned thing to look at. [*Enter* SUE, *Jim's wife. She is rounding forty, an overweight woman who fears it. On seeing her* JIM *wryly adds:*] . . . Except my wife, of course.

SUE [*in same spirit*]. Mrs. Adams is on the phone, you dog.

JIM [*to* KELLER]. Such is the condition which prevails— [*Going to his wife.*] My love, my light. . . .

SUE. Don't sniff around me. [*Points to their house.*] And give her a nasty answer. I can smell her perfume over the phone.

JIM. What's the matter with her now?

SUE. I don't know, dear. She sounds like she's in terrible pain—unless her mouth is full of candy.

JIM. Why don't you just tell her to lay down?

SUE. She enjoys it more when you tell her to lay down. And when are you going to see Mr. Hubbard?

JIM. My dear; Mr. Hubbard is not sick, and I have better things to do than to sit there and hold his hand.

SUE. It seems to me that for ten dollars you could hold his hand.

JIM [*to* KELLER]. If your son wants to play golf tell him I'm ready. Or if he'd like to take a trip around the world for about thirty years. [*He exits.*]

KELLER. Why do you needle him? He's a doctor, women are supposed to call him up.

SUE. All I said was Mrs. Adams is on the phone. Can I have some of your parsley?

KELLER. Yeah, sure. [*She goes to parsley box and pulls some parsley.*] You were a nurse too long, Susie. You're too . . . too . . . realistic.

SUE [*laughing, points at him*]. Now you said it!

[*Enter* LYDIA LUBEY. *She is a robust, laughing girl of twenty-seven.*]

LYDIA. Frank, the toaster . . . [*Sees the others.*] Hya.

KELLER. Hello!

LYDIA [*to* FRANK]. The toaster is off again.

FRANK. Well, plug it in, I just fixed it.

LYDIA [*kindly, but insistently*]. Please, dear, fix it back like it was before.

FRANK. I don't know why you can't learn to turn on a simple thing like a toaster! [FRANK *exits.*]

SUE [*laughs*]. Thomas Edison.

LYDIA [*apologetically*]. He's really very handy. [*She sees broken tree.*] Oh, did the wind get your tree?

KELLER. Yeah, last night.

LYDIA. Oh, what a pity. Annie get in?

KELLER. She'll be down soon. Wait'll you meet her, Sue, she's a knockout.

SUE. I should've been a man. People are always introducing me to beautiful women. [*To* JOE.] Tell her to come over later; I imagine she'd like to see what we did with her house. And thanks. [SUE *exits.*]

LYDIA. Is she still unhappy, Joe?

KELLER. Annie? I don't suppose she goes around dancing on her toes, but she seems to be over it.

LYDIA. She going to get married? Is there anybody . . . ?

KELLER. I suppose . . . say, it's a couple years already. She can't mourn a boy forever.

LYDIA. It's so strange . . . Annie's here and not even married. And I've got three babies. I always thought it'd be the other way around.

KELLER. Well, that's what a war does. I had two sons, now I got one. It changed all the tallies. In my day when you had sons it was an honor. Today a doctor could make a million dollars if he could figure out a way to bring a boy into the world without a trigger finger.

LYDIA. You know, I was just reading . . .

[*Enter* CHRIS KELLER *from house, stands in doorway.*]

LYDIA. Hya, Chris . . .

[FRANK *shouts from offstage.*]

FRANK. Lydia, come in here! If you want the toaster to work don't plug in the malted mixer.

LYDIA [*embarrassed, laughs*]. Did I . . . ?

FRANK. And the next time I fix something don't tell me I'm crazy! Now come in here!

LYDIA [*to* KELLER]. I'll never hear the end of this one.

KELLER [*calling to* FRANK]. So what's the difference? Instead of toast have a malted!

LYDIA. Sh! sh! [*She exits, laughing.*]

[CHRIS *watches her off. He is thirty-two; like his father, solidly built, a listener. A man capable of immense affection and loyalty. He has a cup of coffee in one hand, part of a doughnut in other.*]

KELLER. You want the paper?

CHRIS. That's all right, just the book section. [*He bends down and pulls out part of paper on porch floor.*]

KELLER. You're always reading the book section and you never buy a book.

CHRIS [*coming down to settee*]. I like to keep abreast of my ignorance. [*He sits on settee.*]

KELLER. What is that, every week a new book comes out?

CHRIS. Lot of new books.

KELLER. All different.

CHRIS. All different.

KELLER [*shakes his head, puts knife down on bench, takes oilstone up to the cabinet*]. Psss! Annie up yet?

CHRIS. Mother's giving her breakfast in the dining-room.

KELLER. [*looking at broken tree*]. See what happened to the tree?

CHRIS [*without looking up*]. Yeah.

KELLER. What's Mother going to say?

[BERT *runs on from driveway. He is about eight. He jumps on stool, then on* KELLER'S *back.*]

BERT. You're finally up.

KELLER [*swinging him around and putting him down*]. Ha! Bert's here! Where's Tommy? He's got his father's thermometer again.

BERT. He's taking a reading.

CHRIS. What!

BERT. But it's only oral.

KELLER. Oh, well, there's no harm in oral. So what's new this morning, Bert?

BERT. Nothin'. [*He goes to broken tree, walks around it.*]

KELLER. Then you couldn't've made a complete inspection of the block. In the beginning, when I first made you a policeman you used to come in every morning with something new. Now, nothin's ever new.

BERT. Except some kids from Thirtieth Street. They started kicking a can down the block, and I made them go away because you were sleeping.

KELLER. Now you're talkin', Bert. Now you're on the ball. First thing you know I'm liable to make you a detective.

BERT [*pulls him down by the lapel and whispers in his ear*]. Can I see the jail now?

KELLER. Seein' the jail ain't allowed, Bert. You know that.

BERT. Aw, I betcha there isn't even a jail. I don't see any bars on the cellar windows.

KELLER. Bert, on my word of honor there's a jail in the basement. I showed you my gun, didn't I?

BERT. But that's a hunting gun.

KELLER. That's an arresting gun!

BERT. Then why don't you ever arrest anybody? Tommy said another dirty word to Doris yesterday, and you didn't even demote him.

KELLER [*he chuckles and winks at* CHRIS, *who is enjoying all this*]. Yeah, that's a dangerous character, that Tommy. [*Beckons him closer.*] What word does he say?

BERT [*backing away quickly in great embarrassment*]. Oh, I can't say that.

KELLER [*grabs him by the shirt and pulls him back*]. Well, gimme an idea.

BERT. I can't. It's not a nice word.

KELLER. Just whisper it in my ear. I'll close my eyes. Maybe I won't even hear it.

BERT [*on tiptoe, puts his lips to* KELLER's *ear, then in unbearable embarrassment steps back*]. I can't, Mr. Keller.

CHRIS [*laughing*]. Don't make him do that.

KELLER. Okay, Bert. I take your word. Now go out, and keep both eyes peeled.

BERT [*interested*]. For what?

KELLER. For what! Bert, the whole neighborhood is depending on you. A policeman don't ask questions. Now peel them eyes!

BERT [*mystified, but willing*]. Okay. [*He runs offstage back of arbor.*]

KELLER [*calling after him*]. And mum's the word, Bert.

BERT [*stops and sticks his head through the arbor*]. About what?

KELLER. Just in general. Be v-e-r-y careful.

BERT [*nods in bewilderment*]. Okay. [BERT *exits.*]

KELLER [*laughs*]. I got all the kids crazy!

CHRIS. One of these days, they'll all come in here and beat your brains out.

KELLER. What's she going to say? Maybe we ought to tell her before she sees it.

CHRIS. She saw it.

KELLER. How could she see it? I was the first one up. She was still in bed.

CHRIS. She was out here when it broke.

KELLER. When?

CHRIS. About four this morning. [*Indicating window above them.*] I heard it cracking and I woke up and looked out. She was standing right here when it cracked.

KELLER. What was she doing out here four in the morning?

CHRIS. I don't know. When it cracked she ran back into the house and cried in the kitchen.

KELLER. Did you talk to her?

CHRIS. No, I . . . I figured the best thing was to leave her alone.

[*Pause.*]

KELLER [*deeply touched*]. She cried hard?

CHRIS. I could hear her right through the floor of my room.

KELLER [*slight pause*]. What was she doing out here at that hour? [CHRIS *silent. An undertone of anger showing.*] She's dreaming about him again. She's walking around at night.

CHRIS. I guess she is.

KELLER. She's getting just like after he died. [*Slight pause.*] What's the meaning of that?

CHRIS. I don't know the meaning of it. [*Slight pause.*] But I know one thing, Dad. We've made a terrible mistake with Mother.

KELLER. What?

CHRIS. Being dishonest with her. That kind of thing always pays off, and now its paying off.

KELLER. What do you mean, dishonest?

CHRIS. You know Larry's not coming back and I know it. Why do we allow her to go on thinking that we believe with her?

KELLER. What do you want to do, argue with her?

CHRIS. I don't want to argue with her, but it's time she realized that nobody believes Larry is alive any more. [KELLER *simply moves away, thinking, looking at the ground.*] Why shouldn't she dream of him, walk the nights waiting for him? Do we contradict her? Do we say straight out that we have no hope any more? That we haven't had any hope for years now?

KELLER [*frightened at the thought*]. You can't say that to her.

CHRIS. We've got to say it to her.

KELLER. How're you going to prove it? Can you prove it?

CHRIS. For God's sake, three years! Nobody comes back after three years. It's insane.

KELLER. To you it is, and to me. But not to her. You can talk yourself blue in the face, but there's no body and there's no grave, so where are you?

CHRIS. Sit down, Dad. I want to talk to you.

KELLER [*looks at him searchingly a moment, and sitting . . .*]. The trouble is the goddam newspapers. Every month some boy turns up from nowhere, so the next one is going to be Larry, so . . .

CHRIS. All right, all right, listen to me. [*Slight pause. KELLER sits on settee.*] You know why I asked Annie here, don't you?

KELLER [*he knows, but . . .*]. Why?

CHRIS. You know.

KELLER. Well, I got an idea, but . . . What's the story?

CHRIS. I'm going to ask her to marry me.

[*Slight pause.*]

KELLER [*nods*]. Well, that's only your business, Chris.

CHRIS. You know it's not only my business.

KELLER. What do you want me to do? You're old enough to know your own mind.

CHRIS [*asking, annoyed*]. Then it's all right, I'll go ahead with it?

KELLER. Well, you want to be sure Mother isn't going to . . .

CHRIS. Then it isn't just my business.

KELLER. I'm just sayin' . . .

CHRIS. Sometimes you infuriate me, you know that? Isn't it your business, too, if I tell this to Mother and she throws a fit about it? You have such a talent for ignoring things.

KELLER. I ignore what I gotta ignore. The girl is Larry's girl . . .

CHRIS. She's not Larry's girl.

KELLER. From Mother's point of view he is not dead and you have no right to take his girl. [*Slight pause.*] Now you can go on from there if you know where to go, but I'm tellin' you I don't know where to go. See? I don't know. Now what can I do for you?

CHRIS. I don't know why it is, but every time I reach out for something I want, I have to pull back because other people will suffer. My whole bloody life, time after time after time.

KELLER. You're a considerate fella, there's nothing wrong in that.

CHRIS. To hell with that.

KELLER. Did you ask Annie yet?

CHRIS. I wanted to get this settled first.

KELLER. How do you know she'll marry you? Maybe she feels the same way Mother does?

CHRIS. Well, if she does, then that's the end of it. From her letters I think she's forgotten him. I'll find out. And then we'll thrash it out with Mother? Right? Dad, don't avoid me.

KELLER. The trouble is, you don't see enough women. You never did.

CHRIS. So what? I'm not fast with women.

KELLER. I don't see why it has to be Annie. . . .

CHRIS. Because it is.

KELLER. That's a good answer, but it don't answer anything. You haven't seen her since you went to war. It's five years.

CHRIS. I can't help it. I know her best. I was brought up next door to her. These years when I think of someone for my wife, I think of Annie. What do you want, a diagram?

KELLER. I don't want a diagram . . . I . . . I'm . . . She thinks he's coming back, Chris. You marry that girl and you're pronouncing him dead. Now what's going to happen to Mother? Do you know? I don't!

[*Pause.*]

CHRIS. All right, then, Dad.

KELLER [*thinking* CHRIS *has retreated*]. Give it some more thought.

CHRIS. I've given it three years of thought. I'd hoped that if I waited, Mother would forget Larry and then we'd have a regular wedding and everything happy. But if that can't happen here, then I'll have to get out.

KELLER. What the hell is *this*?

CHRIS. I'll get out. I'll get married and live some place else. Maybe in New York.

KELLER. Are you crazy?

CHRIS. I've been a good son too long, a good sucker. I'm through with it.

KELLER. You've got a business here, what the hell is this?

CHRIS. The business! The business doesn't inspire me.

KELLER. Must you be inspired?

CHRIS. Yes, I like it an hour a day. If I have to grub for money all day long at least at evening I want it beautiful. I want a family, I want some kids. I want to build something I can give myself to. Annie is in the middle of that. Now . . . where do I find it?

KELLER. You mean . . . [*Goes to him.*] Tell me something, you mean you'd leave the business?

CHRIS. Yes. On this I would.

KELLER [*pause*]. Well . . . you don't want to think like that.

CHRIS. Then help me stay here.

KELLER. All right, but . . . but don't think like that. Because what the hell did I work for? That's only for you, Chris, the whole shootin' match is for you!

CHRIS. I know that, Dad. Just you help me stay here.

KELLER [*puts a fist up to* CHRIS' *jaw*]. But don't think that way, you hear me?

CHRIS. I am thinking that way.

KELLER [*lowering his hand*]. I don't understand you, do I?

CHRIS. No, you don't. I'm a pretty tough guy.

KELLER. Yeah. I can see that.

[MOTHER *appears on porch. She is in her early fifties, a woman of uncontrolled inspirations, and an overwhelming capacity for love.*]

MOTHER. Joe?

CHRIS [*going toward porch*]. Hello, Mom.

MOTHER [*indicating house behind her. To* KELLER]. Did you take a bag from under the sink?

KELLER. Yeah, I put it in the pail.

MOTHER. Well, get it out of the pail. That's my potatoes.

[CHRIS *bursts out laughing—goes up into alley.*]

KELLER [*laughing*]. I thought it was garbage.

MOTHER. Will you do me a favor, Joe? Don't be helpful.

KELLER. I can afford another bag of potatoes.

MOTHER. Minnie scoured that pail in boiling water last night. It's cleaner than your teeth.

KELLER. And I don't understand why, after I worked forty years and I got a maid, why I have to take out the garbage.

MOTHER. If you would make up your mind that every bag in the kitchen isn't full of garbage you wouldn't be throwing out my vegetables. Last time it was the onions.

[CHRIS *comes on, hands her bag.*]

KELLER. I don't like garbage in the house.

MOTHER. Then don't eat. [*She goes into the kitchen with bag.*]

CHRIS. That settles you for today.

KELLER. Yeah, I'm in last place again. I don't know, once upon a time I used to think that when I got money again I would have a maid and my wife would take it easy. Now I got money, and I got a maid, and my wife is workin' for the maid. [*He sits in one of the chairs.* MOTHER *comes out on last line. She carries a pot of stringbeans.*]

MOTHER. It's her day off, what are you crabbing about?

CHRIS [*to* MOTHER]. Isn't Annie finished eating?

MOTHER [*looking around preoccupiedly at yard*]. She'll be right out. [*Moves.*] That wind did some job on this place. [*Of the tree.*] So much for that, thank God.

KELLER [*indicating chair beside him*]. Sit down, take it easy.

MOTHER [*she presses her hand to top of her head*]. I've got such a funny pain on the top of my head.

CHRIS. Can I get you an aspirin?

MOTHER [*picks a few petals off ground, stands there smelling them in her hand, then sprinkles them over plants*]. No more roses. It's so funny . . . everything decides to happen at the same time. This month is his birthday; his tree blows down, Annie comes. Everything that happened seems to be coming back. I was just down the cellar, and what do I stumble over? His baseball glove. I haven't seen it in a century.

CHRIS. Don't you think Annie looks well?

MOTHER. Fine. There's no question about it. She's a beauty . . . I still don't know what brought her here. Not that I'm not glad to see her, but . . .

CHRIS. I just thought we'd all like to see each other again. [MOTHER *just looks at him, nodding ever so slightly—almost as though admitting something.*] And I wanted to see her myself.

MOTHER [*her nods halt. To* KELLER]. The only thing is I think her nose got longer. But I'll always love that girl. She's one that didn't jump into bed with somebody else as soon as it happened with her fella.

KELLER [*as though that were impossible for* ANNIE]. Oh, what're you . . . ?

MOTHER. Never mind. Most of them didn't wait till the telegrams were opened. I'm just glad she came, so you can see I'm not *completely* out of my mind. [*Sits, and rapidly breaks stringbeans in the pot.*]

CHRIS. Just because she isn't married doesn't mean she's been mourning Larry.

MOTHER [*with an undercurrent of observation*]. Why then isn't she?

CHRIS [*a little flustered*]. Well . . . it could've been any number of things.

MOTHER [*directly at him*]. Like what, for instance?

CHRIS [*embarrassed, but standing his ground*]. I don't know. Whatever it is. Can I get you an aspirin?

[MOTHER *puts her hand to her head.*]

MOTHER [*she gets up and goes aimlessly toward the trees on rising*]. It's not like a headache.

KELLER. You don't sleep, that's why. She's wearing out more bedroom slippers than shoes.

MOTHER. I had a terrible night. [*She stops moving.*] I never had a night like that.

CHRIS [*looks at* KELLER]. What was it, Mom? Did you dream?

MOTHER. More, more than a dream.

CHRIS [*hesitantly*]. About Larry?

MOTHER. I was fast asleep, and [*Raising her arm over the audience.*] Remember the way he used to fly low past the house when he was in training? When we used to see his face in the cockpit going by? That's the way I saw him. Only high up. Way, way up, where the clouds are. He was so real I could reach out and touch him. And suddenly he started to fall. And crying, crying to me . . . Mom, Mom! I could hear him like he was in the room. Mom! . . . it was his voice! If I could touch him I knew I could stop him, if I could only . . . [*Breaks off, allowing her outstretched hand to fall.*] I woke up and it was so funny . . . The wind . . . it was like the roaring of his engine. I came out here . . . I must've still been half asleep. I could hear that roaring like he was going by. The tree snapped right in front of me . . . and I like . . . came awake. [*She is looking at tree. She suddenly realizes something, turns with a reprimanding finger shaking slightly at* KELLER.] See? We should never have planted that tree. I said so in the first place; it was too soon to plant a tree for him.

CHRIS [*alarmed*]. Too soon!

MOTHER [*angering*]. We rushed into it. Everybody was in such a hurry to bury him. I *said* not to plant it yet. [*To* KELLER.] I *told* you to . . . !

CHRIS. Mother, Mother! [*She looks into his face.*] The wind blew it down. What significance has that got? What are you talking about? Mother, please . . . Don't go through it all again, will you? It's no good, it doesn't accomplish anything. I've been thinking, y'know?—maybe we ought to put our minds to forgetting him?

MOTHER. That's the third time you've said that this week.

CHRIS. Because it's not right; we never took up our lives again. We're like at a railroad station waiting for a train that never comes in.

MOTHER [*presses top of her head*]. Get me an aspirin, heh?

CHRIS. Sure, and let's break out of this, heh, Mom? I thought the four of us might go out to dinner a couple of nights, maybe go dancing out at the shore.

MOTHER. Fine. [*To* KELLER.] We can do it tonight.

KELLER. Swell with me!

CHRIS. Sure, let's have some fun. [*To* MOTHER.] You'll start with this aspirin. [*He goes up and into house with new spirit. Her smile vanishes.*]

MOTHER [*with an accusing undertone*]. Why did he invite her here?

KELLER. Why does that bother you?

MOTHER. She's been in New York three and a half years, why all of a sudden . . . ?

KELLER. Well, maybe . . . maybe he just wanted to see her . . .

MOTHER. Nobody comes seven hundred miles "just to see."

KELLER. What do you mean? He lived next door to the girl all his life, why shouldn't he want to see her again? [MOTHER *looks at him critically.*] Don't look at me like that, he didn't tell me any more than he told you.

MOTHER [*a warning and a question*]. He's not going to marry her.

KELLER. How do you know he's even thinking of it?

MOTHER. It's got that about it.

KELLER [*sharply watching her reaction*]. Well? So what?

MOTHER [*alarmed*]. What's going on here, Joe?

KELLER. Now listen, kid . . .

MOTHER [*avoiding contact with him*]. She's not his girl, Joe; she knows she's not.

KELLER. You can't read her mind.

MOTHER. Then why is she still single? New York is full of men, why isn't she married? [*Pause.*] Probably a hundred people told her she's foolish, but she's waited.

KELLER. How do you know why she waited?

MOTHER. She knows what I know, that's why. She's faithful as a rock. In my worst moments, I think of her waiting, and I know again that I'm right.

KELLER. Look, it's a nice day. What are we arguing for?

MOTHER [*warningly*]. Nobody in this house dast take her faith away, Joe. Strangers might. But not his father, not his brother.

KELLER [*exasperated*]. What do you want me to do? What do you want?

MOTHER. I want you to act like he's coming back. Both of you. Don't think I haven't noticed you since Chris invited her. I won't stand for any nonsense.

KELLER. But, Kate . . .

MOTHER. Because if he's not coming back, then I'll kill myself! Laugh. Laugh at me. [*She points to tree.*] But why did that happen the very night she came back? Laugh, but there are meanings in such things. She goes to sleep in his room and his memorial breaks in pieces. Look at it; look. [*She sits on bench.*] Joe . . .

KELLER. Calm yourself.

MOTHER. Believe with me, Joe. I can't stand all alone.

KELLER. Calm yourself.

MOTHER. Only last week a man turned up in Detroit, missing longer than Larry. You read it yourself.

KELLER. All right, all right, calm yourself.

MOTHER. You above all have got to believe, you . . .

KELLER [*rises*]. Why me above all?

MOTHER. . . . Just don't stop believing . . .

KELLER. What does that mean, me above all?

[BERT *comes rushing on.*]

BERT. Mr. Keller! Say, Mr. Keller . . . [*Pointing up driveway.*] Tommy just said it again!

KELLER [*not remembering any of it*]. Said what? . . . Who? . . .

BERT. The dirty word.

KELLER. Oh. Well . . .

BERT. Gee, aren't you going to arrest him? I warned him.

MOTHER [*with suddenness*]. Stop that, Bert. Go home. [BERT *backs up, as she advances.*] There's no jail here.

KELLER [*as though to say, "Oh-what-the-hell-let-him-be-lieve-there-is"*]. Kate . . .

MOTHER [*turning on* KELLER *furiously*]. There's no jail here! I want you to stop that jail business!

[*He turns, shamed, but peeved.*]

BERT [*past her to* KELLER]. He's right across the street . . .

MOTHER. Go home, Bert. [BERT *turns around and goes up driveway. She is shaken. Her speech is bitten off, extremely urgent.*] I want you to stop that, Joe. That whole jail business!

KELLER [*alarmed, therefore angered*]. Look at you, look at you shaking.

MOTHER [*trying to control herself, moving about, clasping her hands*]. I can't help it.

KELLER. What have I got to hide? What the hell is the matter with you, Kate?

MOTHER. I didn't say you had anything to hide, I'm just telling you to stop it! Now stop it! [*As* ANN *and* CHRIS *appear on porch.* ANN *is twenty-six, gentle, but despite herself capable of holding fast to what she knows.* CHRIS *opens door for her.*]

ANN. Hya, Joe!

[*She leads off a general laugh that is not self-conscious because they know one another too well.*]

CHRIS [*bringing* ANN *down, with an outstretched, chivalric arm*]. Take a breath of that air, kid. You never get air like that in New York.

MOTHER [*genuinely overcome with it*]. Annie, where did you get that dress!

ANN. I couldn't resist. I'm taking it right off before I ruin it. [*Swings around.*] How's that for three weeks' salary?

MOTHER [*to* KELLER]. Isn't she the most . . . ? [*To* ANN.] It's gorgeous, simply gor . . .

CHRIS [*to* MOTHER]. No kidding, now, isn't she the prettiest gal you ever saw?

MOTHER [*caught short by his obvious admiration, she finds herself reaching out for a glass of water and aspirin in his hand, and . . .*]. You gained a little weight, didn't you, darling? [*She gulps pill and drinks.*]

ANN. It comes and goes.

KELLER. Look how nice her legs turned out!

ANN [*she runs to fence*]. Boy, the poplars got thick, didn't they?

KELLER [*moves to settee and sits*]. Well, it's three years, Annie. We're gettin' old, kid.

MOTHER. How does Mom like New York?

[ANN *keeps looking through trees.*].

ANN [*a little hurt*]. Why'd they take our hammock away?

KELLER. Oh, no, it broke. Couple of years ago.

MOTHER. What broke? He had one of his light lunches and flopped into it.

ANN [*she laughs and turns back toward* JIM's *yard . . .*]. Oh, excuse me!

[JIM *has come to fence and is looking over it. He is smoking a cigar. As she cries out, he comes on around on stage.*]

JIM. How do you do. [*To* CHRIS.] She looks very intelligent!

CHRIS. Ann, this is Jim . . . Doctor Bayliss.

ANN [*shaking* JIM's *hand*]. Oh, sure, he writes a lot about you.

JIM. Don't you believe it. He likes everybody. In the Battalion he was known as Mother McKeller.

ANN. I can believe it . . . You know—? [*To* MOTHER.] It's so strange seeing him come out of that yard. [*To* CHRIS.] I guess I never grew up. It almost seems that Mom and Pop are in there now. And you and my brother doing algebra, and Larry trying to copy my home-work. Gosh, those dear dead days beyond recall.

JIM. Well, I hope that doesn't mean you want me to move out?

sue [*calling from offstage*]. Jim, come in here! Mr. Hubbard is on the phone!

jim. I told you I don't want . . .

sue. [*commandingly sweet*]. Please, dear! Please!

jim [*resigned*]. All right, Susie. [*Trailing off.*] All right, all right . . . [*To* ann.] I've only met you, Ann, but if I may offer you a piece of advice— When you marry, never—even in your mind—never count your husband's money.

sue [*from offstage*]. Jim?!

jim. At once! [*Turns and goes off.*] At once. [*He exits.*]

mother [ann *is looking at her. She speaks meaningfully*]. I told her to take up the guitar. It'd be a common interest for them. [*They laugh.*] Well, he loves the guitar!

ann [*as though to overcome* mother, *she becomes suddenly lively, crosses to* keller *on settee, sits on his lap*]. Let's eat at the shore tonight! Raise some hell around here, like we used to before Larry went!

mother [*emotionally*]. You think of him! You see? [*Triumphantly.*] She thinks of him!

ann [*with an uncomprehending smile*]. What do you mean, Kate?

mother. Nothing. Just that you . . . remember him, he's in your thoughts.

ann. That's a funny thing to say; how could I help remembering him?

mother [*it is drawing to a head the wrong way for her; she starts anew. She rises and comes to* ann]. Did you hang up your things?

ann. Yeah . . . [*To* chris.] Say, you've sure gone in for clothes. I could hardly find room in the closet.

mother. No, don't you remember? That's Larry's room.

ann. You mean . . . they're Larry's?

MOTHER. Didn't you recognize them?

ANN [*slowly rising, a little embarrassed*]. Well, it never occurred to me that you'd . . . I mean the shoes are all shined.

MOTHER. Yes, dear. [*Slight pause.* ANN *can't stop staring at her.* MOTHER *breaks it by speaking with the relish of gossip, putting her arm around* ANN *and walking with her.*] For so long I've been aching for a nice conversation with you, Annie. Tell me something.

ANN. What?

MOTHER. I don't know. Something nice.

CHRIS [*wryly*]. She means do you go out much?

MOTHER. Oh, shut up.

KELLER. And are any of them serious?

MOTHER [*laughing, sits in her chair*]. Why don't you both choke?

KELLER. Annie, you can't go into a restaurant with that woman any more. In five minutes thirty-nine strange people are sitting at the table telling her their life story.

MOTHER. If I can't ask Annie a personal question . . .

KELLER. Askin' is all right, but don't beat her over the head. You're beatin' her, you're beatin' her.

[*They are laughing.*]

ANN. [*to* MOTHER. *Takes pan of beans off stool, puts them on floor under chair and sits*]. Don't let them bulldoze you. Ask me anything you like. What do you want to know, Kate? Come on, let's gossip.

MOTHER [*to* CHRIS *and* KELLER]. She's the only one is got any sense. [*To* ANN.] Your mother . . . she's not getting a divorce, heh?

ANN. No, she's calmed down about it now. I think when he gets out they'll probably live together. In New York, of course.

MOTHER. That's fine. Because your father is still . . . I

mean he's a decent man after all is said and done.

ANN. I don't care. She can take him back if she likes.

MOTHER. And you? You . . . [*Shakes her head negatively.*] . . . go out much?

[*Slight pause.*]

ANN [*delicately*]. You mean am I still waiting for him?

MOTHER. Well, no, I don't expect you to wait for him but . . .

ANN [*kindly*]. But that's what you mean, isn't it?

MOTHER. . . . Well . . . yes.

ANN. Well, I'm not, Kate.

MOTHER [*faintly*]. You're not?

ANN. Isn't it ridiculous? You don't really imagine he's . . . ?

MOTHER. I know, dear, but don't say it's ridiculous, because the papers were full of it; I don't know about New York, but there was half a page about a man missing even longer than Larry, and he turned up from Burma.

CHRIS [*coming to* ANN]. He couldn't have wanted to come home very badly. Mom.

MOTHER. Don't be so smart.

CHRIS. You can have a helluva time in Burma.

ANN [*rises and swings around in back of* CHRIS]. So I've heard.

CHRIS. Mother, I'll bet you money that you're the only woman in the country who after three years is still . . .

MOTHER. You're sure?

CHRIS. Yes, I am.

MOTHER. Well, if you're sure then you're sure. [*She turns her head away an instant.*] They don't say it on the radio but I'm sure that in the dark at night they're still waiting for their sons.

CHRIS. Mother, you're absolutely—

MOTHER [*waving him off*]. Don't be so damned smart! Now stop it! [*Slight pause.*] There are just a few things you *don't* know. All of you. And I'll tell you one of them, Annie. Deep, deep in your heart you've always been waiting for him.

ANN [*resolutely*]. No, Kate.

MOTHER [*with increasing demand*]. But deep in your heart, Annie!

CHRIS. She ought to know, shouldn't she?

MOTHER. Don't let them tell you what to think. Listen to your heart. Only your heart.

ANN. Why does your heart tell you he's alive?

MOTHER. Because he has to be.

ANN. But why, Kate?

MOTHER [*going to her*]. Because certain things have to be, and certain things can never be. Like the sun has to rise, it has to be. That's why there's God. Otherwise anything could happen. But there's God, so certain things can never happen. I would know, Annie—just like I knew the day he [*Indicates* CHRIS.] went into that terrible battle. Did he write me? Was it in the papers? No, but that morning I couldn't raise my head off the pillow. Ask Joe. Suddenly, I knew. I knew! And he was nearly killed that day. Ann, you *know* I'm right!

ANN [*she stands there in silence, then turns trembling, going upstage*]. No, Kate.

MOTHER. I have to have some tea.

[FRANK *appears, carrying ladder.*]

FRANK. Annie! [*Coming down.*] How are you, gee whiz!

ANN [*taking his hand*]. Why, Frank, you're losing your hair.

KELLER. He's got responsibility.

FRANK. Gee whiz!

KELLER. Without Frank the stars wouldn't know when to come out.

FRANK [*laughs. To* ANN]. You look more womanly. You've matured. You . . .

KELLER. Take it easy, Frank, you're a married man.

ANN [*as they laugh*]. You still haberdashering?

FRANK. Why not? Maybe I too can get to be president. How's your brother? Got his degree, I hear.

ANN. Oh, George has his own office now!

FRANK. Don't say! [*Funereally.*] And your dad? Is he . . . ?

ANN [*abruptly*]. Fine. I'll be in to see Lydia.

FRANK [*sympathetically*]. How about it, does Dad expect a parole soon?

ANN [*with growing ill-ease*]. I really don't know, I . . .

FRANK [*staunchly defending her father for her sake*]. I mean because I feel, y'know, that if an intelligent man like your father is put in prison, there ought to be a law that says either you execute him, or let him go after a year.

CHRIS [*interrupting*]. Want a hand with that ladder, Frank?

FRANK [*taking cue*]. That's all right, I'll . . . [*Picks up ladder.*] I'll finish the horoscope tonight, Kate. [*Embarrassed.*] See you later, Ann, you look wonderful. [*He exits. They look at* ANN.]

ANN [*to* CHRIS, *sits slowly on stool*]. Haven't they stopped talking about Dad?

CHRIS [*comes down and sits on arm of chair*]. Nobody talks about him any more.

KELLER [*rises and comes to her*]. Gone and forgotten, kid.

ANN. Tell me. Because I don't want to meet anybody on the block if they're going to . . .

CHRIS. I don't want you to worry about it.

ANN [*to* KELLER]. Do they still remember the case, Joe?
Do they talk about you?

KELLER. The only one still talks about it is my wife.

MOTHER. That's because you keep on playing policeman with the kids. All their parents hear out of you
is jail, jail, jail.

KELLER. Actually what happened was that when I got
home from the penitentiary the kids got very interested in me. You know kids. I was [*Laughs.*] like the
expert on the jail situation. And as time passed they
got it confused and . . . I ended up a detective.
[*Laughs.*]

MOTHER. Except that *they* didn't get it confused. [*To*
ANN.] He hands out police badges from the Post
Toasties boxes. [*They laugh.*]

ANN [*looking wondrously at them, happily. She rises
and comes to* KELLER, *putting her arm around his
shoulder*]. Gosh, it's wonderful to hear you laughing
about it.

CHRIS. Why, what'd you expect?

ANN. The last thing I remember on this block was one
word—"Murderers!" Remember that, Kate? . . . Mrs.
Hammond standing in front of our house and yelling that word. . . . She's still around, I suppose?

MOTHER. They're all still around.

KELLER. Don't listen to her. Every Saturday night the
whole gang is playin' poker in this arbor. All the
ones who yelled murderer takin' my money now.

MOTHER. Don't, Joe; she's a sensitive girl, don't fool
her. [*To* ANN.] They still remember about Dad. It's
different with him— [*Indicates* JOE.] —he was exonerated, your father's still there. That's why I
wasn't so enthusiastic about your coming. Honestly,
I know how sensitive you are, and I told Chris, I
said . . .

KELLER. Listen, you do like I did and you'll be all right. The day I come home, I got out of my car;—but not in front of the house . . . on the corner. You should've been here, Annie, and you too, Chris; you'd-a seen something. Everybody knew I was getting out that day; the porches were loaded. Picture it now; none of them believed I was innocent. The story was, I pulled a fast one getting myself exonerated. So I get out of my car, and I walk down the street. But very slow. And with a smile. The beast! I was the beast; the guy who sold cracked cylinder heads to the Army Air Force; the guy who made twenty-one P-40's crash in Australia. Kid, walkin' down the street that day I was guilty as hell. Except I wasn't, and there was a court paper in my pocket to prove I wasn't, and I walked . . . past . . . the porches. Result? Fourteen months later I had one of the best shops in the state again, a respected man again; bigger than ever.

CHRIS [*with admiration*]. Joe McGuts.

KELLER [*now with great force*]. That's the only way you lick 'em is guts! [*To* ANN.] The worst thing you did was to move away from here. You made it tough for your father when he gets out. That's why I tell you, I like to see him move back right on this block.

MOTHER [*pained*]. How could they move back?

KELLER. It ain't gonna end *till* they move back! [*To* ANN.] Till people play cards with him again, and talk with him, and smile with him—you play cards with a man you know he can't be a murderer. And the next time you write him I like you to tell him just what I said. [ANN *simply stares at him.*] You hear me?

ANN [*surprised*]. Don't you hold anything against him?

KELLER. Annie, I never believed in crucifying people.

ANN [*mystified*]. But he was your partner, he dragged you through the mud. . . .

KELLER. Well, he ain't my sweetheart, but you gotta forgive, don't you?

ANN. You, either, Kate? Don't you feel any . . . ?

KELLER. [*to* ANN]. The next time you write Dad . . .

ANN. I don't write him.

KELLER [*struck*]. Well, every now and then you . . .

ANN [*a little shamed, but determined*]. No, I've *never* written to him. Neither has my brother. [*To* CHRIS.] Say, do you feel this way, too?

CHRIS. He murdered twenty-one pilots.

KELLER. What the hell kinda talk is that?

MOTHER. That's not a thing to say about a man.

ANN. What else can you say? When they took him away I followed him, went to him every visiting day. I was crying all the time. Until the news came about Larry. Then I realized. It's wrong to pity a man like that. Father or no father, there's only one way to look at him. He knowingly shipped out parts that would crash an airplane. And how do you know Larry wasn't one of t.em?

MOTHER. I was waiting for that. [*Going to her.*] As long as you're here, Annie, I want to ask you never to say that again.

ANN. You surprise me. I thought you'd be mad at him.

MOTHER. What your father did had nothing to do with Larry. Nothing.

ANN. But we can't know that.

MOTHER [*striving for control*]. As long as you're here!

ANN [*perplexed*]. But, Kate . . .

MOTHER. Put that out of your head!

KELLER. Because . . .

MOTHER [*quickly to* KELLER]. That's all, that's enough. [*Places her hand on her head.*] Come inside now, and have some tea with me. [*She turns and goes up steps.*]

KELLER [*to* ANN]. The one thing you . . .

MOTHER [*sharply*]. He's not dead, so there's no argument! Now come!

KELLER [*angrily*]. In a minute! [MOTHER *turns and goes into house.*] Now look, Annie . . .

CHRIS. All right, Dad, forget it.

KELLER. No, she doesn't feel that way. Annie . . .

CHRIS. I'm sick of the whole subject, now cut it out.

KELLER. You want her to go on like this? [*To* ANN.] Those cylinder heads went into P-40's only. What's the matter with you? You know Larry never flew a P-40.

CHRIS. So who flew those P-40's, pigs?

KELLER. The man was a fool, but don't make a murderer out of him. You got no sense? Look what it does to her! [*To* ANN.] Listen, you gotta appreciate what was doin' in that shop in the war. The both of you! It was a madhouse. Every half hour the Major callin' for cylinder heads, they were whippin' us with the telephone. The trucks were hauling them away hot, damn near. I mean just try to see it human, see it human. All of a sudden a batch comes out with a crack. That happens, that's the business. A fine, hairline crack. All right, so . . . so he's a little man, your father, always scared of loud voices. What'll the Major say?—Half a day's production shot. . . . What'll I say? You know what I mean? Human. [*He pauses.*] So he takes out his tools and he . . . covers over the cracks. All right . . . that's bad, it's wrong, but that's what a little man does. If I could have gone in that day I'd a told him—junk 'em, Herb, we can afford it. But alone he was afraid. But I know he meant no harm. He believed they'd hold up a hundred percent. That's a mistake, but it ain't murder. You understand me? It ain't right.

ANN [*she regards him a moment*]. Joe, let's forget it.

KELLER. Annie, the day the news came about Larry he was in the next cell to mine . . . Dad. And he cried, Annie . . . he cried half the night.

ANN [*touched*]. He shoulda cried all night.

[*Slight pause.*]

KELLER [*almost angered*]. Annie, I do not understand why you . . . !

CHRIS [*breaking in—with nervous urgency*]. Are you going to stop it?!

ANN. Don't yell at him. He just wants everybody happy.

KELLER [*clasps her around waist, smiling*]. That's my sentiments. Can you stand steak?

CHRIS. And champagne!

KELLER. Now you're operatin'! I'll call Swanson's for a table! Big time tonight, Annie!

ANN. Can't scare me.

KELLER [*to* CHRIS, *pointing at* ANN]. I like that girl. Wrap her up. [*They laugh. Goes up porch.*] You got nice legs, Annie! . . . I want to see everybody drunk tonight. [*Pointing to* CHRIS.] Look at him, he's blushin'! [*He exits, laughing, into house.*]

CHRIS [*calling after him*]. Drink your tea, Casanova. [*He turns to* ANN.] Isn't he a great guy?

ANN. You're the only one I know who loves his parents.

CHRIS. I know. It went out of style, didn't it?

ANN [*with a sudden touch of sadness*]. It's all right. It's a good thing. [*She looks about.*] You know? It's lovely here. The air is sweet.

CHRIS [*hopefully*]. You're not sorry you came?

ANN. Not sorry, no. But I'm . . . not going to stay. . . .

CHRIS. Why?

ANN. In the first place, your mother as much as told me to go.

CHRIS. Well . . .

ANN. You saw that . . . and then you . . . you've been kind of . . .

CHRIS. What?

ANN. Well . . . kind of embarrassed ever since I got here.

CHRIS. The trouble is I planned on kind of sneaking up on you over a period of a week or so. But they take it for granted that we're all set.

ANN. I knew they would. Your mother anyway.

CHRIS. How did you know?

ANN. From *her* point of view, why else would I come?

CHRIS. Well . . . would you want to? [ANN *still studies him.*] I guess you know this is why I asked you to come.

ANN. I guess this is why I came.

CHRIS. Ann, I love you. I love you a great deal. [*Finally.*] I love you. [*Pause. She waits.*] I have no imagination . . . that's all I know to tell you. [ANN, *waiting, ready.*] I'm embarrassing you. I didn't want to tell it to you here. I wanted some place we'd never been; a place where we'd be brand new to each other. . . . You feel it's wrong here, don't you? This yard, this chair? I want you to be ready for me. I don't want to win you away from anything.

ANN [*putting her arms around him*]. Oh, Chris, I've been ready a long, long time!

CHRIS. Then he's gone forever. You're sure.

ANN. I almost got married two years ago.

CHRIS. . . . why didn't you?

ANN. You started to write to me. . . .

[*Slight pause.*]

CHRIS. You felt something that far back?

ANN. Every day since!

CHRIS. Ann, why didn't you let me know?

ANN. I was waiting for you, Chris. Till then you never wrote. And when you did, what did you say? You sure can be ambiguous, you know.

CHRIS [*he looks toward house, then at her, trembling*]. Give me a kiss, Ann. Give me a . . . [*They kiss.*] God, I kissed you, Annie, I kissed Annie. How long, how long I've been waiting to kiss you!

ANN. I'll never forgive you. Why did you wait all these years? All I've done is sit and wonder if I was crazy for thinking of you.

CHRIS. Annie, we're going to live now! I'm going to make you so happy. [*He kisses her, but without their bodies touching.*]

ANN [*a little embarrassed*]. Not like that you're not.

CHRIS. I kissed you. . . .

ANN. Like Larry's brother. Do it like you, Chris. [*He breaks away from her abruptly.*] What is it, Chris?

CHRIS. Let's drive some place . . . I want to be alone with you.

ANN. No . . . what is it, Chris, your mother?

CHRIS. No . . . nothing like that . . .

ANN. Then what's wrong? . . . Even in your letters, there was something ashamed.

CHRIS. Yes. I suppose I have been. But it's going from me.

ANN. You've got to tell me—

CHRIS. I don't know how to start. [*He takes her hand. He speaks quietly, factually at first.*]

ANN. It wouldn't work this way.

[*Slight pause.*]

CHRIS. It's all mixed up with so many other things. . . . You remember, overseas, I was in command of a company?

ANN. Yeah, sure.

CHRIS. Well, I lost them.

ANN. How many?

CHRIS. Just about all.

ANN. Oh, gee!

CHRIS. It takes a little time to toss that off. Because they weren't just men. For instance, one time it'd been raining several days and this kid came to me, and gave me his last pair of dry socks. Put them in my pocket. That's only a little thing . . . but . . . that's the kind of guys I had. They didn't die; they killed themselves for each other. I mean that exactly; a little more selfish and they'd've been here today. And I got an idea—watching them go down. Everything was being destroyed, see, but it seemed to me that one new thing was made. A kind of . . . responsibility. Man for man. You understand me? —To show that, to bring that on to the earth again like some kind of a monument and everyone would feel it standing there, behind him, and it would make a difference to him. [*Pause.*] And then I came home and it was incredible. I . . . there was no meaning in it here; the whole thing to them was a kind of a—bus accident. I went to work with Dad, and that rat-race again. I felt . . . what you said . . . ashamed somehow. Because nobody was changed at all. It seemed to make suckers out of a lot of guys. I felt wrong to be alive, to open the bank-book, to drive the new car, to see the new refrigerator. I mean you can take those things out of a war, but when you drive that car you've got to know that it came out of the love a man can have for a man, you've got to be a little better because of that. Otherwise what you have is really loot, and there's blood on it. I didn't want to take any of it. And I guess that included you.

ANN. And you still feel that way?

CHRIS. I want you now, Annie.

ANN. Because you mustn't feel that way any more. Because you have a right to whatever you have. Everything, Chris, understand that? To me, too ... And the money, there's nothing wrong in your money. Your father put hundreds of planes in the air, you should be proud. A man should be paid for that. ...

CHRIS. Oh Annie, Annie ... I'm going to make a fortune for you!

KELLER [*offstage*]. Hello ... Yes. Sure.

ANN [*laughing softly*]. What'll I do with a fortune ...? [*They kiss. KELLER enters from house.*]

KELLER [*thumbing toward house*]. Hey, Ann, your brother ... [*They step apart shyly. KELLER comes down, and wryly ...*] What is this, Labor Day?

CHRIS [*waving him away, knowing the kidding will be endless*]. All right, all right ...

ANN. You shouldn't burst out like that.

KELLER. Well, nobody told me it was Labor Day. [*Looks around.*] Where's the hot dogs?

CHRIS [*loving it*]. All right. You said it once.

KELLER. Well, as long as I know it's Labor Day from now on, I'll wear a bell around my neck.

ANN [*affectionately*]. He's so subtle!

CHRIS. George Bernard Shaw as an elephant.

KELLER. George!—hey, you kissed it out of my head— your brother's on the phone.

ANN [*surprised*]. My brother?

KELLER. Yeah, George. Long distance.

ANN. What's the matter, is anything wrong?

KELLER. I don't know, Kate's talking to him. Hurry up, she'll cost him five dollars.

ANN [*she takes a step upstage, then comes down toward CHRIS*]. I wonder if we ought to tell your mother yet? I mean I'm not very good in an argument.

CHRIS. We'll wait till tonight. After dinner. Now don't get tense, just leave it to me.

KELLER. What're you telling her?

CHRIS. Go ahead, Ann. [*With misgivings,* ANN *goes up and into house.*] We're getting married, Dad. [KELLER *nods indecisively.*] Well, don't you say anything?

KELLER [*distracted*]. I'm glad, Chris, I'm just ... George is calling from Columbus.

CHRIS. Columbus!

KELLER. Did Annie tell you he was going to see his father today?

CHRIS. No, I don't think she knew anything about it.

KELLER [*asking uncomfortably*]. Chris! You ... you think you know her pretty good?

CHRIS [*hurt and apprehensive*]. What kind of a question ... ?

KELLER. I'm just wondering. All these years George don't go to see his father. Suddenly he goes ... and she comes here.

CHRIS. Well, what about it?

KELLER. It's crazy, but it comes to my mind. She don't hold nothin' against me, does she?

CHRIS [*angry*]. I don't know what you're talking about.

KELLER [*a little more combatively*]. I'm just talkin'. To his last day in court the man blamed it all on me; and this is his daughter. I mean if she was sent here to find out something?

CHRIS [*angered*]. Why? What is there to find out?

ANN [*on phone, offstage*]. Why are you so excited, George? What happened there?

KELLER. I mean if they want to open up the case again, for the nuisance value, to hurt us?

CHRIS. Dad ... how could you think that of her?

ANN [*still on phone*]. But what did he say to you, for God's sake?

KELLER. It couldn't be, heh. You know.

CHRIS. Dad, you amaze me . . .

KELLER [*breaking in*]. All right, forget it, forget it. [*With great force, moving about.*] I want a clean start for you, Chris. I want a new sign over the plant—Christopher Keller, Incorporated.

CHRIS [*a little uneasily*]. J. O. Keller is good enough.

KELLER. We'll talk about it. I'm going to build you a house, stone, with a driveway from the road. I want you to spread out, Chris, I want you to use what I made for you . . . [*He is close to him now.*] . . . I mean, with joy, Chris, without shame . . . with joy.

CHRIS [*touched*]. I will, Dad.

KELLER [*with deep emotion*]. . . . Say it to me.

CHRIS. Why?

KELLER. Because sometimes I think you're . . . ashamed of the money.

CHRIS. No, don't feel that.

KELLER. Because it's good money, there's nothing wrong with that money.

CHRIS [*a little frightened*]. Dad, you don't have to tell me this.

KELLER [*with overriding affection and self-confidence now. He grips* CHRIS *by the back of the neck, and with laughter between his determined jaws*]. Look, Chris, I'll go to work on Mother for you. We'll get her so drunk tonight we'll all get married! [*Steps away, with a wide gesture of his arm.*] There's gonna be a wedding, kid, like there never was seen! Champagne, tuxedoes . . . ! [*He breaks off as* ANN's *voice comes out loud from the house where she is still talking on phone.*]

ANN. Simply because when you get excited you don't control yourself. . . . [MOTHER *comes out of house.*] Well, what did he tell you for God's sake? [*Pause.*] All right, come then. [*Pause.*] Yes, they'll all be here. Nobody's running away from you. And try to get hold of yourself, will you? [*Pause.*] All right, all right. Good-bye. [*There is a brief pause as* ANN *hangs up receiver, then comes out of kitchen.*]

CHRIS. Something happen?

KELLER. He's coming here?

ANN. On the seven o'clock. He's in Columbus. [*To* MOTHER.] I told him it would be all right.

KELLER. Sure, fine! Your father took sick?

ANN [*mystified*]. No, George didn't say he was sick. I ... [*Shaking it off.*] I don't know, I suppose it's something stupid, you know my brother. . . . [*She comes to* CHRIS.] Let's go for a drive, or something. . . .

CHRIS. Sure. Give me the keys, Dad.

MOTHER. Drive through the park. It's beautiful now.

CHRIS. Come on, Ann. [*To them.*] Be back right away.

ANN [*as she and* CHRIS *exit up driveway*]. See you.

[MOTHER *comes down toward* KELLER, *her eyes fixed on him.*]

KELLER. Take your time. [*To* MOTHER.] What does George want?

MOTHER. He's been in Columbus since this morning with Steve. He's gotta see Annie right away, he says.

KELLER. What for?

MOTHER. I don't know. [*She speaks with warning.*] He's a lawyer now, Joe. George is a lawyer. All these years he never even sent a postcard to Steve. Since he got back from the war, not a postcard.

KELLER. So what?

MOTHER [*her tension breaking out*]. Suddenly he takes an airplane from New York to see him. An airplane!

KELLER. Well? So?

MOTHER [*trembling*]. Why?

KELLER. I don't read minds. Do you?

MOTHER. Why, Joe? What has Steve suddenly got to tell him that he takes an airplane to see him?

KELLER. What do I care what Steve's got to tell him?

MOTHER. You're sure, Joe?

KELLER [*frightened, but angry*]. Yes, I'm sure.

MOTHER [*she sits stiffly in a chair*]. Be smart now, Joe. The boy is coming. Be smart.

KELLER [*desperately*]. Once and for all, did you hear what I said? I said I'm sure!

MOTHER [*she nods weakly*]. All right, Joe. [*He straightens up.*] Just . . . be smart.

[KELLER, *in hopeless fury, looks at her, turns around, goes up to porch and into house, slamming screen door violently behind him.* MOTHER *sits in chair downstage, stiffly, staring, seeing.*]

CURTAIN

Act two

As twilight falls, that evening.

On the rise, CHRIS *is discovered sawing the broken-off tree, leaving stump standing alone. He is dressed in good pants, white shoes, but without a shirt. He disappears with tree up the alley when* MOTHER *appears on porch. She comes down and stands watching him. She has on a dressing-gown, carries a tray of grape-juice drink in a pitcher, and glasses with sprigs of mint in them.*

MOTHER [*calling up alley*]. Did you have to put on good pants to do that? [*She comes downstage and puts tray on table in the arbor. Then looks around uneasily, then feels pitcher for coolness.* CHRIS *enters from alley, brushing off his hands.*] You notice there's more light with that thing gone?

CHRIS. Why aren't you dressing?

MOTHER. It's suffocating upstairs. I made a grape drink for Georgie. He always liked grape. Come and have some.

CHRIS [*impatiently*]. Well, come on, get dressed. And what's Dad sleeping so much for? [*He goes to table and pours a glass of juice.*]

MOTHER. He's worried. When he's worried he sleeps. [*Pauses. Looks into his eyes.*] We're dumb, Chris. Dad and I are stupid people. We don't know anything. You've got to protect us.

CHRIS. You're silly; what's there to be afraid of?

MOTHER. To his last day in court Steve never gave up the idea that Dad made him do it. If they're going to open the case again I won't live through it.

CHRIS. George is just a damn fool, Mother. How can you take him seriously?

MOTHER. That family hates us. Maybe even Annie . . .

CHRIS. Oh, now, Mother . . .

MOTHER. You think just because you like everybody, they like you!

CHRIS. All right, stop working yourself up. Just leave everything to me.

MOTHER. When George goes home tell her to go with him.

CHRIS [*noncommittally*]. Don't worry about Annie.

MOTHER. Steve is her father, too.

CHRIS. Are you going to cut it out? Now, come.

MOTHER [*going upstage with him*]. You don't realize how people can hate, Chris, they can hate so much they'll tear the world to pieces. . . .

[ANN, *dressed up, appears on porch.*]

CHRIS. Look! She's dressed already. [*As he and* MOTHER *mount porch.*] I've just got to put on a shirt.

ANN [*in a preoccupied way*]. Are you feeling well, Kate?

MOTHER. What's the difference, dear. There are certain people, y'know, the sicker they get the longer they live. [*She goes into house.*]

CHRIS. You look nice.

ANN. We're going to tell her tonight.

CHRIS. Absolutely, don't worry about it.

ANN. I wish we could tell her now. I can't stand scheming. My stomach gets hard.

CHRIS. It's not scheming, we'll just get her in a better mood.

MOTHER [*offstage, in the house*]. Joe, are you going to sleep all day!

ANN [*laughing*]. The only one who's relaxed is your father. He's fast asleep.

CHRIS. I'm relaxed.

ANN. Are you?

CHRIS. Look. [*He holds out his hand and makes it shake.*] Let me know when George gets here. [*He goes into the house.*]

[*She moves aimlessly, and then is drawn toward tree stump. She goes to it, hesitantly touches broken top in the hush of her thoughts. Offstage* LYDIA *calls, "Johnny! Come get your supper!"* SUE *enters, and halts, seeing* ANN.]

SUE. Is my husband . . . ?

ANN [*turns, startled*]. Oh!

SUE. I'm terribly sorry.

ANN. It's all right, I . . . I'm a little silly about the dark.

SUE [*looks about*]. It is getting dark.

ANN. Are you looking for your husband?

SUE. As usual. [*Laughs tiredly.*] He spends so much time here, they'll be charging him rent.

ANN. Nobody was dressed so he drove over to the depot to pick up my brother.

SUE. Oh, your brother's in?

ANN. Yeah, they ought to be here any minute now. Will you have a cold drink?

SUE. I will, thanks. [ANN *goes to table and pours.*] My husband. Too hot to drive me to beach.—Men are like little boys; for the neighbors they'll always cut the grass.

ANN. People like to do things for the Kellers. Been that way since I can remember.

SUE. It's amazing. I guess your brother's coming to give you away, heh?

ANN [*giving her drink*]. I don't know. I suppose.

SUE. You must be all nerved up.

ANN. It's always a problem getting yourself married, isn't it?

SUE. That depends on your shape, of course. I don't see why you should have had a problem.

ANN. I've had chances—

SUE. I'll bet. It's romantic . . . it's very unusual to me, marrying the brother of your sweetheart.

ANN. I don't know. I think it's mostly that whenever I need somebody to tell me the truth I've always thought of Chris. When he tells you something you know it's so. He relaxes me.

SUE. And he's got money. That's important, you know.

ANN. It wouldn't matter to me.

SUE. You'd be surprised. It makes all the difference. I married an interne. On my salary. And that was bad, because as soon as a woman supports a man he owes her something. You can never owe somebody without resenting them. [ANN *laughs.*] That's true, you know.

ANN. Underneath, I think the doctor is very devoted.

SUE. Oh, certainly. But it's bad when a man always sees the bars in front of him. Jim thinks he's in jail all the time.

ANN. Oh . . .

SUE. That's why I've been intending to ask you a small favor, Ann . . . it's something very important to me.

ANN. Certainly, if I can do it.

SUE. You can. When you take up housekeeping, try to find a place away from here.

ANN. Are you fooling?

SUE. I'm very serious. My husband is unhappy with Chris around.

ANN. How is that?

SUE. Jim's a successful doctor. But he's got an idea he'd like to do medical research. Discover things. You see?

ANN. Well, isn't that good?

SUE. Research pays twenty-five dollars a week minus laundering the hair shirt. You've got to give up your life to go into it.

ANN. How does Chris?

SUE. [*with growing feeling*]. Chris makes people want to be better than it's possible to be. He does that to people.

ANN. Is that bad?

SUE. My husband has a family, dear. Every time he has a session with Chris he feels as though he's compromising by not giving up everything for research. As though Chris or anybody else isn't compromising. It happens with Jim every couple of years. He meets a man and makes a statue out of him.

ANN. Maybe he's right. I don't mean that Chris is a statue, but . . .

SUE. Now darling, you know he's not right.

ANN. I don't agree with you. Chris . . .

SUE. Let's face it, dear. Chris is working with his father, isn't he? He's taking money out of that business every week in the year.

ANN. What of it?

SUE. You ask me what of it?

ANN. I certainly do. [*She seems about to burst out.*] You oughtn't cast aspersions like that, I'm surprised at you.

SUE. You're surprised at me!

ANN. He'd never take five cents out of that plant if there was anything wrong with it.

SUE. You know that.

ANN. I know it. I resent everything you've said.

SUE [*moving toward her*]. You know what I resent, dear?

ANN. Please, I don't want to argue.

SUE. I resent living next door to the Holy Family. It makes me look like a bum, you understand?

ANN. I can't do anything about that.

SUE. Who is he to ruin a man's life? Everybody knows Joe pulled a fast one to get out of jail.

ANN. That's not true!

SUE. Then why don't you go out and talk to people? Go on, talk to them. There's not a person on the block who doesn't know the truth.

ANN. That's a lie. People come here all the time for cards and . . .

SUE. So what? They give him credit for being smart. I do, too, I've got nothing against Joe. But if Chris wants people to put on the hair shirt let him take off his broadcloth. He's driving my husband crazy with that phony idealism of his, and I'm at the end of my rope on it! [CHRIS *enters on porch, wearing shirt and tie now. She turns quickly, hearing. With a smile.*] Hello, darling. How's Mother?

CHRIS. I thought George came.

SUE. No, it was just us.

CHRIS [*coming down to them*]. Susie, do me a favor, heh? Go up to Mother and see if you can calm her. She's all worked up.

SUE. She still doesn't know about you two?

CHRIS [*laughs a little*]. Well, she senses it, I guess. You know my mother.

SUE [*going up to porch*]. Oh, yeah, she's psychic.

CHRIS. Maybe there's something in the medicine chest.

SUE. I'll give her one of everything. [*On porch.*] Don't worry about Kate; couple of drinks, dance her around a little . . . she'll love Ann. [*To* ANN.] Because you're the female version of him. [CHRIS *laughs.*] Don't be alarmed, I said version. [*She goes into house.*]

CHRIS. Interesting woman, isn't she?

ANN. Yeah, she's very interesting.

CHRIS. She's a great nurse, you know, she . . .

ANN [*in tension, but trying to control it*]. Are you still doing that?

CHRIS [*sensing something wrong, but still smiling*]. Doing what?

ANN. As soon as you get to know somebody you find a distinction for them. How do you know she's a great nurse?

CHRIS. What's the matter, Ann?

ANN. The woman hates you. She despises you!

CHRIS. Hey . . . what's hit you?

ANN. Gee, Chris . . .

CHRIS. What happened here?

ANN. You never . . . Why didn't you tell me?

CHRIS. Tell you what?

ANN. She says they think Joe is guilty.

CHRIS. What difference does it make what they think?

ANN. I don't care what they think, I just don't understand why you took the trouble to deny it. You said it was all forgotten.

CHRIS. I didn't want you to feel there was anything wrong in you coming here, that's all. I know a lot of people think my father was guilty, and I assumed there might be some question in your mind.

ANN. But I never once said I suspected him.

CHRIS. Nobody says it.

ANN. Chris, I know how much you love him, but it could never . . .

CHRIS. Do you think I could forgive him if he'd done that thing?

ANN. I'm not here out of a blue sky, Chris. I turned my back on my father, if there's anything wrong here now . . .

CHRIS. I know that, Ann.

ANN. George is coming from Dad, and I don't think it's with a blessing.

CHRIS. He's welcome here. You've got nothing to fear from George.

ANN. Tell me that . . . just tell me that.

CHRIS. The man is innocent, Ann. Remember he was falsely accused once and it put him through hell. How would you behave if you were faced with the same thing again? Annie, believe me, there's nothing wrong for you here, believe me, kid.

ANN. All right, Chris, all right. [*They embrace as* KELLER *appears quietly on porch.* ANN *simply studies him.*]

KELLER. Every time I come out here it looks like Playland!

[*They break and laugh in embarrassment.*]

CHRIS. I thought you were going to shave?

KELLER [*sitting on bench*]. In a minute. I just woke up, I can't see nothin'.

ANN. You look shaved.

KELLER. Oh, no. [*Massages his jaw.*] Gotta be extra special tonight. Big night, Annie. So how's it feel to be a married woman?

ANN [*laughs*]. I don't know, yet.

KELLER [*to* CHRIS]. What's the matter, you slippin'?
[*He takes a little box of apples from under the bench as they talk.*]

CHRIS. The great roué!

KELLER. What is that, roué?

CHRIS. It's French.

KELLER. Don't talk dirty.

[*They laugh.*]

CHRIS [*to* ANN]. You ever meet a bigger ignoramus?

KELLER. Well, somebody's got to make a living.

ANN [*as they laugh*]. That's telling him.

KELLER. I don't know, everybody's gettin' so goddam educated in this country there'll be nobody to take away the garbage. [*They laugh.*] It's gettin' so the only dumb ones left are the bosses.

ANN. You're not so dumb, Joe.

KELLER. I know, but you go into our plant, for instance. I got so many lieutenants, majors and colonels that I'm ashamed to ask somebody to sweep the floor. I gotta be careful I'll insult somebody. No kiddin'. It's a tragedy: you stand on the street today and spit, you're gonna hit a college man.

CHRIS. Well, don't spit.

KELLER [*breaks apple in half, passing it to* ANN *and* CHRIS]. I mean to say, it's comin' to a pass. [*He takes a breath.*] I been thinkin', Annie . . . your brother, George. I been thinkin' about your brother George. When he comes I like you to *brooch* something to him.

CHRIS. Broach.

KELLER. What's the matter with brooch?

CHRIS [*smiling*]. It's not English.

KELLER. When I went to night school it was brooch.

ANN [*laughing*]. Well, in day school it's broach.

KELLER. Don't surround me, will you? Seriously, Ann
. . . You say he's not well. George, I been thinkin',
why should he knock himself out in New York with
that cut-throat competition, when I got so many
friends here; I'm very friendly with some big law-
yers in town. I could set George up here.

ANN. That's awfully nice of you, Joe.

KELLER. No, kid, it ain't nice of me. I want you to
understand me. I'm thinking of Chris. [*Slight pause.*]
See . . . this is what I mean. You get older, you want
to feel that you . . . accomplished something. My
only accomplishment is my son. I ain't brainy.
That's all I accomplished. Now, a year, eighteen
months, your father'll be a free man. Who is he
going to come to, Annie? His baby. You. He'll come,
old, mad, into your house.

ANN. That can't matter any more, Joe.

KELLER. I don't want that to come between us. [*Gestures between* CHRIS *and himself.*]

ANN. I can only tell you that that could never happen.

KELLER. You're in love now, Annie, but believe me,
I'm older than you and I know—a daughter is a
daughter, and a father is a father. And it could
happen. [*He pauses.*] I like you and George to go to
him in prison and tell him . . . "Dad, Joe wants to
bring you into the business when you get out."

ANN [*surprised, even shocked*]. You'd have him as a
partner?

KELLER. No, no partner. A good job. [*Pause. He sees
she is shocked, a little mystified. He gets up, speaks
more nervously.*] I want him to know, Annie . . .
while he's sitting there I want him to know that
when he gets out he's got a place waitin' for him.
It'll take his bitterness away. To know you got a
place . . . it sweetens you.

ANN. Joe, you owe him nothing.

KELLER. I owe him a good kick in the teeth, but he's your father. . . .

CHRIS. Then kick him in the teeth! I don't want him in the plant, so that's that! You understand? And besides, don't talk about him like that. People misunderstand you!

KELLER. And I don't understand why she has to crucify the man.

CHRIS. Well, it's her father, if she feels . . .

KELLER. No, no . . .

CHRIS [*almost angrily*]. What's it to you? Why . . . ?

KELLER [*a commanding outburst in high nervousness*]. A father is a father! [*As though the outburst had revealed him, he looks about, wanting to retract it. His hand goes to his cheek.*] I better . . . I better shave. [*He turns and a smile is on his face. To* ANN.] I didn't mean to yell at you, Annie.

ANN. Let's forget the whole thing, Joe.

KELLER. Right. [*To* CHRIS.] She's likeable.

CHRIS [*a little peeved at the man's stupidity*]. Shave, will you?

KELLER. Right again.

[*As he turns to porch* LYDIA *comes hurrying from her house.*]

LYDIA. I forgot all about it . . . [*Seeing* CHRIS *and* ANN.] Hya. [*To* JOE.] I promised to fix Kate's hair for tonight. Did she comb it yet?

KELLER. Always a smile, hey, Lydia?

LYDIA. Sure, why not?

KELLER [*going up on porch*]. Come on up and comb my Katie's hair. [LYDIA *goes up on porch.*] She's got a big night, make her beautiful.

LYDIA. I will.

KELLER [*he holds door open for her and she goes into*

kitchen. To CHRIS *and* ANN]. Hey, that could be a song. [*He sings softly.*]

"Come on up and comb my Katie's hair . . .
Oh, come on up, 'cause she's my lady fair—"
[*To* ANN.] How's that for one year of night school?
[*He continues singing as he goes into kitchen.*]

"Oh, come on up, come on up, and comb my lady's hair—"

[JIM BAYLISS *rounds corner of driveway, walking rapidly.* JIM *crosses to* CHRIS, *motions him and pulls him down excitedly.* KELLER *stands just inside kitchen door, watching them.*]

CHRIS. What's the matter? Where is he?

JIM. Where's your mother?

CHRIS. Upstairs, dressing.

ANN [*crossing to them rapidly*]. What happened to George?

JIM. I asked him to wait in the car. Listen to me now. Can you take some advice? [*They wait.*] Don't bring him in here.

ANN. Why?

JIM. Kate is in bad shape, you can't explode this in front of her.

ANN. Explode what?

JIM. You know why he's here, don't try to kid it away. There's blood in his eye; drive him somewhere and talk to him alone.

[ANN *turns to go up drive, takes a couple of steps, sees* KELLER *and stops. He goes quietly on into house.*]

CHRIS [*shaken, and therefore angered*]. Don't be an old lady.

JIM. He's come to take her home. What does that mean? [*To* ANN.]. You know what that means. Fight it out with him some place else.

ANN [*she comes back down toward* CHRIS]. I'll drive . . . him somewhere.

CHRIS [*goes to her*]. No.

JIM. Will you stop being an idiot?

CHRIS. Nobody's afraid of him here. Cut that out! [*He starts for driveway, but is brought up short by* GEORGE, *who enters there.* GEORGE IS CHRIS' *age, but a paler man, now on the edge of his self-restraint. He speaks quietly, as though afraid to find himself screaming. An instant's hesitation and* CHRIS *steps up to him, hand extended, smiling.*] Helluva way to do; what'er you sitting out there for?

GEORGE. Doctor said your mother isn't well, I . . .

CHRIS. So what? She'd want to see you, wouldn't she? We've been waiting for you all afternoon. [*He puts his hand on* GEORGE's *arm, but* GEORGE *pulls away, coming across toward* ANN.]

ANN [*touching his collar*]. This is filthy, didn't you bring another shirt?

[GEORGE *breaks away from her, and moves down, examining the yard. Door opens, and he turns rapidly, thinking it is* KATE, *but it's* SUE. *She looks at him, he turns away and moves to fence. He looks over it at his former home.* SUE *comes downstage.*]

SUE [*annoyed*]. How about the beach, Jim?

JIM. Oh, it's too hot to drive.

SUE. How'd you get to the station—Zeppelin?

CHRIS. This is Mrs. Bayliss, George. [*Calling, as* GEORGE *pays no attention, staring at house.*] George! [GEORGE *turns.*] Mrs. Bayliss.

SUE. How do you do.

GEORGE [*removing his hat*]. You're the people who bought our house, aren't you?

SUE. That's right. Come and see what we did with it before you leave.

GEORGE [*he walks down and away from her*]. I liked it the way it was.

SUE [*after a brief pause*]. He's frank, isn't he?

JIM [*pulling her off*]. See you later. . . . Take it easy, fella. [*They exit.*]

CHRIS [*calling after them*]. Thanks for driving him! [*Turning to* GEORGE.] How about some grape juice? Mother made it especially for you.

GEORGE [*with forced appreciation*]. Good old Kate, remembered my grape juice.

CHRIS. You drank enough of it in this house. How've you been, George?—Sit down.

GEORGE [*he keeps moving*]. It takes me a minute. [*Looking around.*] It seems impossible.

CHRIS. What?

GEORGE. I'm back here.

CHRIS. Say, you've gotten a little nervous, haven't you?

GEORGE. Yeah, toward the end of the day. What're you, big executive now?

CHRIS. Just kind of medium. How's the law?

GEORGE. I don't know. When I was studying in the hospital it seemed sensible, but outside there doesn't seem to be much of a law. The trees got thick, didn't they? [*Points to stump.*] What's that?

CHRIS. Blew down last night. We had it there for Larry. You know.

GEORGE. Why, afraid you'll forget him?

CHRIS [*starts for* GEORGE]. Kind of a remark is that?

ANN [*breaking in, putting a restraining hand on* CHRIS]. When did you start wearing a hat?

GEORGE [*discovers hat in his hand*]. Today. From now on I decided to look like a lawyer, anyway. [*He holds it up to her.*] Don't you recognize it?

ANN. Why? Where . . . ?

GEORGE. Your father's . . . he asked me to wear it.

ANN. . . . How is he?

GEORGE. He got smaller.

ANN. Smaller?

GEORGE. Yeah, little. [*Holds out his hand to measure.*]

He's a little man. That's what happens to suckers, you know. It's good I went to him in time—another year there'd be nothing left but his smell.

CHRIS. What's the matter, George, what's the trouble?

GEORGE. The trouble? The trouble is when you make suckers out of people once, you shouldn't try to do it twice.

CHRIS. What does that mean?

GEORGE [*to* ANN]. You're not married yet, are you?

ANN. George, will you sit down and stop—?

GEORGE. Are you married yet?

ANN. No, I'm not married yet.

GEORGE. You're not going to marry him.

ANN. Why am I not going to marry him?

GEORGE. Because his father destroyed your family.

CHRIS. Now look, George . . .

GEORGE. Cut it short, Chris. Tell her to come home with me. Let's not argue, you know what I've got to say.

CHRIS. George, you don't want to be the voice of God, do you?

GEORGE. I'm . . .

CHRIS. That's been your trouble all your life, George, you dive into things. What kind of a statement is that to make? You're a big boy now.

GEORGE. I'm a big boy now.

CHRIS. Don't come bulling in here. If you've got something to say, be civilized about it.

GEORGE. Don't civilize me!

ANN. Shhh!

CHRIS [*ready to hit him*]. Are you going to talk like a grown man or aren't you?

ANN [*quickly, to forestall an outburst*]. Sit down, dear. Don't be angry, what's the matter? [*He allows her to seat him, looking at her.*] Now what happened? You kissed me when I left, now you . . .

GEORGE [*breathlessly*]. My life turned upside down since then. I couldn't go back to work when you left. I wanted to go to Dad and tell him you were going to be married. It seemed impossible not to tell him. He loved you so much . . . [*He pauses.*] Annie . . . we did a terrible thing. We can never be forgiven. Not even to send him a card at Christmas. I didn't see him once since I got home from the war! Annie, you don't know what was done to that man. You don't know what happened.

ANN [*afraid*]. Of course I know.

GEORGE. You can't know, you wouldn't be here. Dad came to work that day. The night foreman came to him and showed him the cylinder heads . . . they were coming out of the process with defects. There was something wrong with the process. So Dad went directly to the phone and called here and told Joe to come down right away. But the morning passed. No sign of Joe. So Dad called again. By this time he had over a hundred defectives. The Army was screaming for stuff and Dad didn't have anything to ship. So Joe told him . . . on the phone he told him to weld, cover up the cracks in any way he could, and ship them out.

CHRIS. Are you through now?

GEORGE [*surging up at him*]. I'm not through now! [*Back to* ANN.] Dad was afraid. He wanted Joe there if he was going to do it. But Joe can't come down . . . he's sick. Sick! He suddenly gets the flu! Suddenly! But he promised to take responsibility. Do you understand what I'm saying? On the telephone you can't have responsibility! In a court you can always deny a phone call and that's exactly what he did. They knew he was a liar the first time, but in the appeal they believed that rotten lie and now Joe is a big shot and your father is the patsy. [*He gets up*.] Now what're you going to do? Eat his food, sleep in his bed? Answer me; what're you going to do?

CHRIS. What're you going to do, George?

GEORGE. He's too smart for me, I can't prove a phone call.

CHRIS. Then how dare you come in here with that rot?

ANN. George, the court . . .

GEORGE. The court didn't know your father! But you know him. You know in your heart Joe did it.

CHRIS [*whirling him around*]. Lower your voice or I'll throw you out of here!

GEORGE. She knows. She knows.

CHRIS [*to* ANN]. Get him out of here, Ann. Get him out of here.

ANN. George, I know everything you've said. Dad told that whole thing in court, and they . . .

GEORGE [*almost a scream*]. The court did not know him, Annie!

ANN. Shhh!—But he'll say anything, George. You know how quick he can lie.

GEORGE [*turning to* CHRIS, *with deliberation*]. I'll ask you something, and look me in the eye when you answer me.

CHRIS. I'll look you in the eye.

GEORGE. You know your father . . .

CHRIS. I know him well.

GEORGE. And he's the kind of boss to let a hundred and twenty-one cylinder heads be repaired and shipped out of his shop without even knowing about it?

CHRIS. He's that kind of boss.

GEORGE. And that's the same Joe Keller who never left his shop without first going around to see that all the lights were out.

CHRIS [*with growing anger*]. The same Joe Keller.

GEORGE. The same man who knows how many minutes a day his workers spend in the toilet.

CHRIS. The same man.

GEORGE. And my father, that frightened mouse who'd never buy a shirt without somebody along—that man would dare do such a thing on his own?

CHRIS. On his own. And because he's a frightened mouse this is another thing he'd do;—throw the blame on somebody else because he's not man enough to take it himself. He tried it in court but it didn't work, but with a fool like you it works!

GEORGE. Oh, Chris, you're a liar to yourself!

ANN [*deeply shaken*]. Don't talk like that!

CHRIS [*sits facing* GEORGE]. Tell me, George. What happened? The court record was good enough for you all these years, why isn't it good now? Why did you believe it all these years?

GEORGE [*after a slight pause*]. Because you believed it. . . . That's the truth, Chris. I believed everything, because I thought you did. But today I heard it from his mouth. From his mouth it's altogether different than the record. Anyone who knows him, and knows your father, will believe it from his mouth. Your Dad took everything we have. I can't beat that. But she's one item he's not going to grab. [*He turns to* ANN.] Get your things. Everything they have is covered with blood. You're not the kind of a girl who can live with that. Get your things.

CHRIS. Ann . . . you're not going to believe that, are you?

ANN [*she goes to him*]. You know it's not true, don't you?

GEORGE. How can he tell you? It's his father. [*To* CHRIS.] None of these things ever even cross your mind?

CHRIS. Yes, they crossed my mind. Anything can cross your mind!

GEORGE. *He knows,* Annie. He knows!

CHRIS. The Voice of God!

GEORGE. Then why isn't your name on the business? Explain that to her!

CHRIS. What the hell has that got to do with . . . ?

GEORGE. Annie, why isn't his name on it?

CHRIS. Even when I don't own it!

GEORGE. Who're you kidding? Who gets it when he dies? [*To* ANN.] Open your eyes, you know the both of them, isn't that the first thing they'd do, the way they love each other?—J. O. Keller & Son? [*Pause.* ANN *looks from him to* CHRIS.] I'll settle it. Do you want to settle it, or are you afraid to?

CHRIS. . . . What do you mean?

GEORGE. Let me go up and talk to your father. In ten minutes you'll have the answer. Or are you afraid of the answer?

CHRIS. I'm not afraid of the answer. I know the answer. But my mother isn't well and I don't want a fight here now.

GEORGE. Let me go to him.

CHRIS. You're not going to start a fight here now.

GEORGE [*to* ANN]. What more do you want!!!

[*There is a sound of footsteps in the house.*]

ANN [*turns her head suddenly toward house*]. Someone's coming.

CHRIS [*to* GEORGE, *quietly*]. You won't say anything now.

ANN. You'll go soon. I'll call a cab.

GEORGE. You're coming with me.

ANN. And don't mention marriage, because we haven't told her yet.

GEORGE. You're coming with me.

ANN. You understand? Don't . . . George, you're not

going to start anything now! [*She hears footsteps.*] Shsh!

[MOTHER *enters on porch. She is dressed almost formally, her hair is fixed. They are all turned toward her. On seeing* GEORGE *she raises both hands, comes down toward him.*]

MOTHER. Georgie, Georgie.

GEORGE [*he has always liked her*]. Hello, Kate.

MOTHER [*she cups his face in her hands*]. They made an old man out of you. [*Touches his hair.*] Look, you're gray.

GEORGE [*her pity, open and unabashed, reaches into him, and he smiles sadly*]. I know, I . . .

MOTHER. I told you when you went away, don't try for medals.

GEORGE [*he laughs, tiredly*]. I didn't try, Kate. They made it very easy for me.

MOTHER [*actually angry*]. Go on. You're all alike. [*To* ANN.] Look at him, why did you say he's fine? He looks like a ghost.

GEORGE [*relishing her solicitude*]. I feel all right.

MOTHER. I'm sick to look at you. What's the matter with your mother, why don't she feed you?

ANN. He just hasn't any appetite.

MOTHER. If he ate in my house he'd have an appetite. [*To* ANN.] I pity your husband! [*To* GEORGE.] Sit down. I'll make you a sandwich.

GEORGE [*sits with an embarrassed laugh*]. I'm really not hungry.

MOTHER. Honest to God, it breaks my heart to see what happened to all the children. How we worked and planned for you, and you end up no better than us.

GEORGE [*with deep feeling for her*]. You . . . you haven't changed at all, you know that, Kate?

MOTHER. None of us changed, Georgie. We all love you.

Joe was just talking about the day you were born and the water got shut off. People were carrying basins from a block away—a stranger would have thought the whole neighborhood was on fire! [*They laugh. She sees the juice. To* ANN.] Why didn't you give him some juice!

ANN [*defensively*]. I offered it to him.

MOTHER [*scoffingly*]. You offered it to him! [*Thrusting glass into* GEORGE's *hand.*] Give it to him! [*To* GEORGE, *who is laughing.*] And now you're going to sit here and drink some juice . . . and look like something!

GEORGE [*sitting*]. Kate, I feel hungry already.

CHRIS [*proudly*]. She could turn Mahatma Ghandi into a heavyweight!

MOTHER [*to* CHRIS, *with great energy*]. Listen, to hell with the restaurant! I got a ham in the icebox, and frozen strawberries, and avocados, and . . .

ANN. Swell, I'll help you!

GEORGE. The train leaves at eight-thirty, Ann.

MOTHER [*to* ANN]. You're leaving?

CHRIS. No, Mother, she's not . . .

ANN [*breaking through it, going to* GEORGE]. You hardly got here; give yourself a chance to get acquainted again.

CHRIS. Sure, you don't even know us any more.

MOTHER. Well, Chris, if they can't stay, don't . . .

CHRIS. No, it's just a question of George, Mother, he planned on . . .

GEORGE [*he gets up politely, nicely, for* KATE's *sake*]. Now wait a minute, Chris . . .

CHRIS [*smiling and full of command, cutting him off*]. If you want to go, I'll drive you to the station now, but if you're staying, no arguments while you're here.

MOTHER [*at last confessing the tension*]. Why should

he argue? [*She goes to him, and with desperation
and compassion, stroking his hair.*] Georgie and us
have no argument. How could we have an argument,
Georgie? We all got hit by the same lightning, how
can you . . . ? Did you see what happened to Larry's
tree, Georgie? [*She has taken his arm, and unwill-
ingly he moves across stage with her.*] Imagine?
While I was dreaming of him in the middle of the
night, the wind came along and . . .

[LYDIA *enters on porch. As soon as she sees him.*]

LYDIA. Hey, Georgie! Georgie! Georgie! Georgie!
Georgie! [*She comes down to him eagerly. She has
a flowered hat in her hand, which* KATE *takes from
her as she goes to* GEORGE.]

GEORGE [*they shake hands eagerly, warmly*]. Hello,
Laughy. What'd you do, grow?

LYDIA. I'm a big girl now.

MOTHER [*taking hat from her*]. Look what she can do
to a hat!

ANN [*to* LYDIA, *admiring the hat*]. Did you make
that?

MOTHER. In ten minutes! [*She puts it on.*]

LYDIA [*fixing it on her head*]. I only rearranged it.

GEORGE. You still make your own clothes?

CHRIS [*of* MOTHER]. Ain't she classy! All she needs now
is a Russian wolfhound.

MOTHER [*moving her head*]. It feels like somebody is
sitting on my head.

ANN. No, it's beautiful, Kate.

MOTHER [*kisses* LYDIA—*to* GEORGE]. She's a genius! You
should've married her. [*They laugh.*] This one can
feed you!

LYDIA [*strangely embarrassed*]. Oh, stop that, Kate.

GEORGE [*to* LYDIA]. Didn't I hear you had a baby?

MOTHER. You don't hear so good. She's got three babies.

GEORGE [*a little hurt by it—to* LYDIA]. No kidding, three?

LYDIA. Yeah, it was one, two, three— You've been away a long time, Georgie.

GEORGE. I'm beginning to realize.

MOTHER [*to* CHRIS *and* GEORGE]. The trouble with you kids is you *think* too much.

LYDIA. Well, we think, too.

MOTHER. Yes, but not all the time.

GEORGE [*with almost obvious envy*]. They never took Frank, heh?

LYDIA [*a little apologetically*]. No, he was always one year ahead of the draft.

MOTHER. It's amazing. When they were calling boys twenty-seven Frank was just twenty-eight, when they made it twenty-eight he was just twenty-nine. That's why he took up astrology. It's all in when you were born, it just goes to show.

CHRIS. What does it go to show?

MOTHER [*to* CHRIS]. Don't be so intelligent. Some superstitions are very nice! [*To* LYDIA.] Did he finish Larry's horoscope?

LYDIA. I'll ask him now, I'm going in. [*To* GEORGE, *a little sadly, almost embarrassed.*] Would you like to see my babies? Come on.

GEORGE. I don't think so, Lydia.

LYDIA [*understanding*]. All right. Good luck to you, George.

GEORGE. Thanks. And to you . . . And Frank.

[*She smiles at him, turns and goes off to her house.* GEORGE *stands staring after her.*]

LYDIA [*as she runs off*]. Oh, Frank!

MOTHER [*reading his thoughts*]. She got pretty, heh?

GEORGE [*sadly*]. Very pretty.

MOTHER [*as a reprimand*]. She's beautiful, you damned fool!

GEORGE [*looks around longingly; and softly, with a catch in his throat*]. She makes it seem so nice around here.

MOTHER [*shaking her finger at him*]. Look what happened to you because you wouldn't listen to me! I told you to marry that girl and stay out of the war!

GEORGE [*laughs at himself*]. She used to laugh too much.

MOTHER. And you didn't laugh enough. While you were getting mad about Fascism Frank was getting into her bed.

GEORGE [*to* CHRIS]. He won the war, Frank.

CHRIS. All the battles.

MOTHER [*in pursuit of this mood*]. The day they started the draft, Georgie, I told you you loved that girl.

CHRIS [*laughs*]. And truer love hath no man!

MOTHER. I'm smarter than any of you.

GEORGE [*laughing*]. She's wonderful!

MOTHER. And now you're going to listen to me, George. You had big principles, Eagle Scouts the three of you; so now I got a tree, and this one [*Indicating* CHRIS.] when the weather gets bad he can't stand on his feet; and that big dope [*Pointing to* LYDIA'S *house.*] next door who never reads anything but Andy Gump has three children and his house paid off. Stop being a philosopher, and look after yourself. Like Joe was just saying—you move back here, he'll help you get set, and I'll find you a girl and put a smile on your face.

GEORGE. Joe? Joe wants me here?

ANN [*eagerly*]. He asked me to tell you, and I think it's a good idea.

MOTHER. Certainly. Why must you make believe you hate us? Is that another principle?—that you have to hate us? You don't hate us, George, I know you, you can't fool me, I diapered you. [*Suddenly, to* ANN.] You remember Mr. Marcy's daughter?

ANN [*laughing, to* GEORGE]. She's got you hooked already!

[GEORGE *laughs, is excited.*]

MOTHER. You look her over, George; you'll see she's the most beautiful . . .

CHRIS. She's got warts, George.

MOTHER [*to* CHRIS]. She hasn't got warts! [*To* GEORGE]. So the girl has a little beauty mark on her chin . . .

CHRIS. And two on her nose.

MOTHER. You remember. Her father's the retired police inspector.

CHRIS. Sergeant, George.

MOTHER. He's a very kind man!

CHRIS. He looks like a gorilla.

MOTHER [*to* GEORGE]. He never shot anybody.

[*They all burst out laughing, as* KELLER *appears in doorway.* GEORGE *rises abruptly, stares at* KELLER, *who comes rapidly down to him.*]

KELLER [*the laughter stops. With strained joviality*]. Well! Look who's here! [*Extending his hand.*] Georgie, good to see ya.

GEORGE [*shakes hands—somberly*]. How're you, Joe?

KELLER. So-so. Gettin' old. You comin' out to dinner with us?

GEORGE. No, got to be back in New York.

ANN. I'll call a cab for you. [*She goes up into the house.*]

KELLER. Too bad you can't stay, George. Sit down. [*To* MOTHER.] He looks fine.

MOTHER. He looks terrible.

KELLER. That's what I said, you look terrible, George.

[*They laugh.*] I wear the pants and she beats me with the belt.

GEORGE. I saw your factory on the way from the station. It looks like General Motors.

KELLER. I wish it was General Motors, but it ain't. Sit down, George. Sit down. [*Takes a cigar out of his pocket.*] So you finally went to see your father, I hear?

GEORGE. Yes, this morning. What kind of stuff do you make now?

KELLER. Oh, a little of everything. Pressure cookers, an assembly for washing machines. Got a nice, flexible plant now. So how'd you find Dad? Feel all right?

GEORGE [*searching* KELLER, *he speaks indecisively*]. No, he's not well, Joe.

KELLER [*lighting his cigar*]. Not his heart again, is it?

GEORGE. It's everything, Joe. It's his soul.

KELLER [*blowing out smoke*]. Uh huh—

CHRIS. How about seeing what they did with your house?

KELLER. Leave him be.

GEORGE [*to* CHRIS, *indicating* KELLER]. I'd like to talk to him.

KELLER. Sure, he just got here. That's the way they do, George. A little man makes a mistake and they hang him by the thumbs; the big ones become ambassadors. I wish you'd-a told me you were going to see Dad.

GEORGE [*studying him*]. I didn't know you were interested.

KELLER. In a way, I am. I would like him to know, George, that as far as I'm concerned, any time he wants, he's got a place with me. I would like him to know that.

GEORGE. He hates your guts, Joe. Don't you know that?

KELLER. I imagined it. But that can change, too.

MOTHER. Steve was never like that.

GEORGE. He's like that now. He'd like to take every man who made money in the war and put him up against a wall.

CHRIS. He'll need a lot of bullets.

GEORGE. And he'd better not get any.

KELLER. That's a sad thing to hear.

GEORGE [*with bitterness dominant*]. Why? What'd you expect him to think of you?

KELLER [*the force of his nature rising, but under control*]. I'm sad to see he hasn't changed. As long as I know him, twenty-five years, the man never learned how to take the blame. You know that, George.

GEORGE [*he does*]. Well, I . . .

KELLER. But you do know it. Because the way you come in here you don't look like you remember it. I mean like in 1937 when we had the shop on Flood Street. And he damn near blew us all up with that heater he left burning for two days without water. He wouldn't admit that was his fault, either. I had to fire a mechanic to save his face. You remember that.

GEORGE. Yes, but . . .

KELLER. I'm just mentioning it, George. Because this is just another one of a lot of things. Like when he gave Frank that money to invest in oil stock.

GEORGE [*distressed*]. I know that, I . . .

KELLER [*driving in, but restrained*]. But it's good to remember those things, kid. The way he cursed Frank because the stock went down. Was that Frank's fault? To listen to him Frank was a swindler. And all the man did was give him a bad tip.

GEORGE [*gets up, moves away*]. I know those things. . . .

KELLER. Then remember them, remember them. [ANN *comes out of house.*] There are certain men in the world who rather see everybody hung before they'll take blame. You understand me, George? [*They stand facing each other,* GEORGE *trying to judge him.*]

ANN [*coming downstage*]. The cab's on its way. Would you like to wash?

MOTHER [*with the thrust of hope*]. Why must he go? Make the midnight, George.

KELLER. Sure, you'll have dinner with us!

ANN. How about it? Why not? We're eating at the lake, we could have a swell time.

GEORGE [*long pause, as he looks at* ANN, CHRIS, KELLER, *then back to her*]. All right.

MOTHER. Now you're talking.

CHRIS. I've got a shirt that'll go right with that suit.

MOTHER. Size fifteen and a half, right, George?

GEORGE. Is Lydia . . . ? I mean—Frank and Lydia coming?

MOTHER. I'll get you a date that'll make her look like a . . . [*She starts upstage.*]

GEORGE [*laughs*]. No, I don't want a date.

CHRIS. I know somebody just for you! Charlotte Tanner! [*He starts for the house.*]

KELLER. Call Charlotte, that's right.

MOTHER. Sure, call her up.

[CHRIS *goes into house.*]

ANN. You go up and pick out a shirt and tie.

GEORGE [*he stops, looks around at them and the place*]. I never felt at home anywhere but here. I feel so . . . [*He nearly laughs, and turns away from them.*] Kate, you look so young, you know? You didn't change at all. It . . . rings an old bell. [*Turns to* KELLER.] You too, Joe, you're amazingly the same. The whole atmosphere is.

KELLER. Say, I ain't got time to get sick.

MOTHER. He hasn't been laid up in fifteen years. . . .

KELLER. Except my flu during the war.

MOTHER. Huhh?

KELLER. My flu, when I was sick during . . . the war.

MOTHER. Well, sure . . . [*To* GEORGE.] I mean except for that flu. [GEORGE *stands perfectly still.*] Well, it slipped my mind, don't look at me that way. He wanted to go to the shop but he couldn't lift himself off the bed. I thought he had pneumonia.

GEORGE. Why did you say he's never . . . ?

KELLER. I know how you feel, kid, I'll never forgive myself. If I could've gone in that day I'd never allow Dad to touch those heads.

GEORGE. She said you've never been sick.

MOTHER. I said he was sick, George.

GEORGE [*going to* ANN]. Ann, didn't you hear her say . . . ?

MOTHER. Do you remember every time you were sick?

GEORGE. I'd remember pneumonia. Especially if I got it just the day my partner was going to patch up cylinder heads. . . . What happened that day, Joe?

FRANK [*enters briskly from driveway, holding* LARRY'S *horoscope in his hand. He comes to* KATE]. Kate! Kate!

MOTHER. Frank, did you see George?

FRANK [*extending his hand*]. Lydia told me, I'm glad to . . . you'll have to pardon me. [*Pulling* MOTHER *over.*] I've got something amazing for you, Kate, I finished Larry's horoscope.

MOTHER. You'd be interested in this, George. It's wonderful the way he can understand the . . .

CHRIS [*entering from house*]. George, the girl's on the phone . . .

MOTHER [*desperately*]. He finished Larry's horoscope!

CHRIS. Frank, can't you pick a better time than this?

FRANK. The greatest men who ever lived believed in the stars!

CHRIS. Stop filling her head with that junk!

FRANK. Is it junk to feel that there's a greater power than ourselves? I've studied the stars of his life! I won't argue with you, I'm telling you. Somewhere in this world your brother is alive!

MOTHER [*instantly to* CHRIS]. Why isn't it possible?

CHRIS. Because it's insane.

FRANK. Just a minute now. I'll tell you something and you can do as you please. Just let me say it. He was supposed to have died on November twenty-fifth. But November twenty-fifth was his favorable day.

CHRIS. Mother!

MOTHER. Listen to him!

FRANK. It was a day when everything good was shining on him, the kind of day he should've married on. You can laugh at a lot of it, I can understand you laughing. But the odds are a million to one that a man won't die on his favorable day. That's known, that's known, Chris!

MOTHER. Why isn't it possible, why isn't it possible, Chris!

GEORGE [*to* ANN]. Don't you understand what she's saying? She just told you to go. What are you waiting for now?

CHRIS. Nobody can tell her to go.

[*A car horn is heard.*]

MOTHER [*to* FRANK]. Thank you, darling, for your trouble. Will you tell him to wait, Frank?

FRANK [*as he goes*]. Sure thing.

MOTHER [*calling out*]. They'll be right out, driver!

CHRIS. She's not leaving, Mother.

GEORGE. You heard her say it, he's never been sick!

MOTHER. He misunderstood me, Chris!

[CHRIS *looks at her, struck.*]

GEORGE [*to* ANN]. He simply told your father to kill pilots, and covered himself in bed!

CHRIS. You'd better answer him, Annie. Answer him.

MOTHER. I packed your bag, darling. . . .

CHRIS. What?

MOTHER. I packed your bag. All you've got to do is close it.

ANN. I'm not closing anything. He asked me here and I'm staying till he tells me to go. [*To* GEORGE.] Till Chris tells me!

CHRIS. That's all! Now get out of here, George!

MOTHER [*to* CHRIS]. But if that's how he feels . . .

CHRIS. That's all, nothing more till Christ comes, about the case or Larry as long as I'm here! [*To* ANN.] Now get out of here, George!

GEORGE [*to* ANN]. You tell me. I want to hear you tell me.

ANN. Go, George!

[*They disappear up the driveway,* ANN *saying "Don't take it that way, Georgie! Please don't take it that way."*]

CHRIS [*turns to his* MOTHER]. What do you mean, you packed her bag? How dare you pack her bag?

MOTHER. Chris . . .

CHRIS. How dare you back her bag?

MOTHER. She doesn't belong here.

CHRIS. Then I don't belong here.

MOTHER. She's Larry's girl.

CHRIS. And I'm his brother and he's dead, and I'm marrying his girl.

MOTHER. Never, never in this world!

KELLER. You lost your mind?

MOTHER. You have nothing to say!

KELLER [*cruelly*]. I got plenty to say. Three and a half years you been talking like a maniac—

MOTHER [*she smashes him across the face*]. Nothing. You have nothing to say. Now I say. He's coming back, and everybody has got to wait.

CHRIS. Mother, Mother . . .

MOTHER. Wait, wait . . .

CHRIS. How long? How long?

MOTHER [*rolling out of her*]. Till he comes; forever and ever till he comes!

CHRIS [*as an ultimatum*]. Mother, I'm going ahead with it.

MOTHER. Chris, I've never said no to you in my life, now I say no!

CHRIS. You'll never let him go till I do it.

MOTHER. I'll never let him go and you'll never let him go . . . !

CHRIS. I've let him go. I've let him go a long . . .

MOTHER [*with no less force, but turning from him*]. Then let your father go.

[*Pause.* CHRIS *stands transfixed.*]

KELLER. She's out of her mind.

MOTHER. Altogether! [*To* CHRIS, *but not facing them.*] Your brother's alive, darling, because if he's dead, your father killed him. Do you understand me now? As long as you live, that boy is alive. God does not let a son be killed by his father. Now you see, don't you? Now you see. [*Beyond control, she hurries up and into house.*]

KELLER [CHRIS *has not moved. He speaks insinuatingly, questioningly*]. She's out of her mind.

CHRIS [*a broken whisper*]. Then . . . you did it?

KELLER [*the beginning of plea in his voice*]. He never flew a P-40—

CHRIS [*struck. Deadly*]. But the others.

KELLER [*insistently*]. She's out of her mind. [*He takes a step toward* CHRIS, *pleadingly.*]

CHRIS [*unyielding*]. Dad . . . you did it?

KELLER. He never flew a P-40, what's the matter with you?

CHRIS [*still asking, and saying*]: Then you did it. To the others.

[*Both hold their voices down.*]

KELLER [*afraid of him, his deadly insistence*]. What's the matter with you? What the hell is the matter with you?

CHRIS [*quietly, incredibly*]. How could you do that? How?

KELLER. What's the matter with you!

CHRIS. Dad . . . Dad, you killed twenty-one men!

KELLER. What, killed?

CHRIS. You killed them, you murdered them.

KELLER [*as though throwing his whole nature open before* CHRIS]. How could I kill anybody?

CHRIS. Dad! Dad!

KELLER [*trying to hush him*]. I didn't kill anybody!

CHRIS. Then explain it to me. What did you do? Explain it to me or I'll tear you to pieces!

KELLER [*horrified at his overwhelming fury*]. Don't, Chris, don't. . . .

CHRIS. I want to know what you did, now what did you do? You had a hundred and twenty cracked engine-heads, now what did you do?

KELLER. If you're going to hang me then I . . .

CHRIS. I'm listening. God Almighty, I'm listening!

KELLER [*their movements now are those of subtle pursuit and escape.* KELLER *keeps a step out of* CHRIS' *range as he talks*]. You're a boy, what could I do! I'm in business, a man is in business; a hundred and twenty cracked, you're out of business; you got a process, the process don't work, you're out of business; you don't know how to operate, your stuff is no good; they close you up, they tear up your contracts, what the hell's it to them? You lay forty years into a business and they knock you out in five minutes, what could I do, let them take forty years, let them take my life away? [*His voice cracking.*] I never thought they'd install them. I swear to God.

I thought they'd stop 'em before anybody took off.

CHRIS. Then why'd you ship them out?

KELLER. By the time they could spot them I thought I'd have the process going again, and I could show them they needed me and they'd let it go by. But weeks passed and I got no kick-back, so I was going to tell them.

CHRIS. Then why didn't you tell them?

KELLER. It was too late. The paper, it was all over the front page, twenty-one went down, it was too late. They came with handcuffs into the shop, what could I do? [*He sits on bench.*] Chris . . . Chris, I did it for you, it was a chance and I took it for you. I'm sixty-one years old, when would I have another chance to make something for you? Sixty-one years old you don't get another chance, do ya?

CHRIS. You even knew they wouldn't hold up in the air.

KELLER. I didn't say that. . . .

CHRIS. But you were going to warn them not to use them. . . .

KELLER. But that don't mean . . .

CHRIS. It means you knew they'd crash.

KELLER. It don't mean that.

CHRIS. Then you *thought* they'd crash.

KELLER. I was afraid maybe. . . .

CHRIS. You were afraid maybe! God in heaven, what kind of a man are you? Kids were hanging in the air by those heads. You knew that!

KELLER. For you, a business for you!

CHRIS [*with burning fury*]. For me! Where do you live, where have you come from? For me!—I was dying every day and you were killing my boys and you did it for me? What the hell do you think I was thinking of, the goddam business? Is that as far as your mind can see, the business? What is that, the world—the business? What the hell do you mean, you did it for me? Don't you have a country? Don't you live in the world? What the hell are you? You're not even an animal, no animal kills his own, what are you? What must I do to you? I ought to tear the tongue out of your mouth, what must I do? [*With his fist he pounds down upon his father's shoulder. He stumbles away, covering his face as he weeps.*] What must I do, Jesus God, what must I do?

KELLER. Chris . . . My Chris . . .

CURTAIN

Act three

Two o'clock the following morning, MOTHER *is discovered on the rise, rocking ceaselessly in a chair, staring at her thoughts. It is an intense, slight sort of rocking. A light shows from upstairs bedroom, lower floor windows being dark. The moon is strong and casts its bluish light.*

Presently JIM, *dressed in jacket and hat, appears, and seeing her, goes up beside her.*

JIM. Any news?

MOTHER. No news.

JIM [*gently*]. You can't sit up all night, dear, why don't you go to bed?

MOTHER. I'm waiting for Chris. Don't worry about me, Jim, I'm perfectly all right.

JIM. But it's almost two o'clock.

MOTHER. I can't sleep. [*Slight pause.*] You had an emergency?

JIM [*tiredly*]. Somebody had a headache and thought he was dying. [*Slight pause.*] Half of my patients are quite mad. Nobody realizes how many people are walking around loose, and they're cracked as coconuts. Money. Money-money-money-money. You say it long enough it doesn't mean anything. [*She smiles, makes a silent laugh.*] Oh, how I'd love to be around when that happens!

MOTHER [*shakes her head*]. You're so childish, Jim! Sometimes you are.

JIM [*looks at her a moment*]. Kate. [*Pause.*] What happened?

KATE. I told you. He had an argument with Joe. Then he got in the car and drove away.

JIM. What kind of an argument?

MOTHER. An argument, Joe . . . he was crying like a child, before.

JIM. They argued about Ann?

MOTHER [*slight hesitation*]. No, not Ann. Imagine? [*Indicates lighted window above.*] She hasn't come out of that room since he left. All night in that room.

JIM [*looks at window, then at her*]. What'd Joe do, tell him?

MOTHER [*she stops rocking*]. Tell him what?

JIM. Don't be afraid, Kate, I know. I've always known.

MOTHER. How?

JIM. It occurred to me a long time ago.

MOTHER. I always had the feeling that in the back of his head, Chris . . . almost knew. I didn't think it would be such a shock.

JIM [*gets up*]. Chris would never know how to live with a thing like that. It takes a certain talent . . . for lying. You have it, and I do. But not him.

MOTHER. What do you mean . . . he's not coming back?

JIM. Oh, no, he'll come back. We all come back, Kate. These private little revolutions always die. The compromise is always made. In a peculiar way. Frank is right—every man does have a star. The star of one's honesty. And you spend your life groping for it, but once it's out it never lights again. I don't think he went very far. He probably just wanted to be alone to watch his star go out.

MOTHER. Just as long as he comes back.

JIM. I wish he wouldn't, Kate. One year I simply took off, went to New Orleans; for two months I lived on bananas and milk, and studied a certain disease. It was beautiful. And then she came, and she cried. And I went back home with her. And now I live in the usual darkness; I can't find myself; it's even hard sometimes to remember the kind of man I wanted to be. I'm a good husband; Chris is a good son—he'll come back.

[KELLER *comes out on porch in dressing-gown and slippers. He goes upstage—to alley.* JIM *goes to him.*]

JIM. I have a feeling he's in the park. I'll look around for him. Put her to bed, Joe; this is no good for what she's got. [JIM *exits up driveway.*]

KELLER [*coming down*]. What does he want here?

MOTHER. His friend is not home.

KELLER [*his voice is husky. Comes down to her*]. I don't like him mixing in so much.

MOTHER. It's too late, Joe. He knows.

KELLER [*apprehensively*]. How does he know?

MOTHER. He guessed a long time ago.

KELLER. I don't like that.

MOTHER [*laughs dangerously, quietly into the line*]. What you don't like . . .

KELLER. Yeah, what I don't like.

MOTHER. You can't bull yourself through this one, Joe, you better be smart now. This thing—this thing is not over yet.

KELLER [*indicating lighted window above*]. And what

is she doing up there? She don't come out of the room.

MOTHER. I don't know, what is she doing? Sit down, stop being mad. You want to live? You better figure out your life.

KELLER. She don't know, does she?

MOTHER. She saw Chris storming out of here. It's one and one—she knows how to add.

KELLER. Maybe I ought to talk to her?

MOTHER. Don't ask me, Joe.

KELLER [*almost an outburst*]. Then who do I ask? But I don't think she'll do anything about it.

MOTHER. You're asking me again.

KELLER. I'm askin' you. What am I, a stranger? I thought I had a family here. What happened to my family?

MOTHER. You've got a family. I'm simply telling you that I have no strength to think any more.

KELLER. You have no strength. The minute there's trouble you have no strength.

MOTHER. Joe, you're doing the same thing again; all your life whenever there's trouble you yell at me and you think that settles it.

KELLER. Then what do I do? Tell me, talk to me, what do I do?

MOTHER. Joe . . . I've been thinking this way. If he comes back . . .

KELLER. What do you mean "if"? . . . he's comin' back!

MOTHER. I think if you sit him down and you . . . explain yourself. I mean you ought to make it clear to him that you know you did a terrible thing. [*Not looking into his eyes.*] I mean if he saw that you realize what you did. You see?

KELLER. What ice does that cut?

MOTHER [*a little fearfully*]. I mean if you told him that you want to pay for what you did.

KELLER [*sensing . . . quietly*]. How can I pay?

MOTHER. Tell him . . . you're willing to go to prison. [*Pause.*]

KELLER [*struck, amazed*]. I'm willing to . . . ?

MOTHER [*quickly*]. You wouldn't go, he wouldn't ask you to go. But if you told him you wanted to, if he could feel that you wanted to pay, maybe he would forgive you.

KELLER. He would forgive me! For what?

MOTHER. Joe, you know what I mean.

KELLER. I don't know what you mean! You wanted money, so I made money. What must I be forgiven? You wanted money, didn't you?

MOTHER. I didn't want it that way.

KELLER. I didn't want it that way, either! What difference is it what you want? I spoiled the both of you. I should've put him out when he was ten like I was put out, and make him earn his keep. Then he'd know how a buck is made in this world. Forgiven! I could live on a quarter a day myself, but I got a family so I . . .

MOTHER. Joe, Joe . . . it don't excuse it that you did it for the family.

KELLER. It's got to excuse it!

MOTHER. There's something bigger than the family to him.

KELLER. Nothin' is bigger!

MOTHER. There is to him.

KELLER. There's nothin' he could do that I wouldn't forgive. Because he's my son. Because I'm his father and he's my son.

MOTHER. Joe, I tell you . . .

KELLER. Nothin's bigger than that. And you're goin' to tell him, you understand? I'm his father and he's my son, and if there's something bigger than that I'll put a bullet in my head!

MOTHER. You stop that!

KELLER. You heard me. Now you know what to tell him. [*Pause. He moves from her—halts.*] But he wouldn't put me away though . . . He wouldn't do that . . . Would he?

MOTHER. He loved you, Joe, you broke his heart.

KELLER. But to put me away . . .

MOTHER. I don't know. I'm beginning to think we don't really know him. They say in the war he was such a killer. Here he was always afraid of mice. I don't know him. I don't know what he'll do.

KELLER. Goddam, if Larry was alive he wouldn't act like this. He understood the way the world is made. He listened to me. To him the world had a forty-foot front, it ended at the building line. This one, everything bothers him. You make a deal, overcharge two cents, and his hair falls out. He don't understand money. Too easy, it came too easy. Yes, sir. Larry. That was a boy we lost. Larry. Larry. [*He slumps on chair in front of her.*] What am I gonna do, Kate. . . .

MOTHER. Joe, Joe, please . . . you'll be all right, nothing is going to happen. . . .

KELLER [*desperately, lost*]. For you, Kate, for both of you, that's all I ever lived for. . . .

MOTHER. I know, darling, I know. . . .

[ANN *enters from house. They say nothing, waiting for her to speak.*]

ANN. Why do you stay up? I'll tell you when he comes.

KELLER [*rises, goes to her*]. You didn't eat supper, did you? [*To* MOTHER.] Why don't you make her something?

MOTHER. Sure, I'll . . .

ANN. Never mind, Kate, I'm all right. [*They are unable to speak to each other.*] There's something I want to tell you. [*She starts then, halts.*] I'm not going to do anything about it. . . .

MOTHER. She's a good girl! [*To* KELLER.] You see? She's a . . .

ANN. I'll do nothing about Joe, but you're going to do something for me. [*Directly to* MOTHER.] You made Chris feel guilty with me. Whether you wanted to or not, you've crippled him in front of me. I'd like you to tell him that Larry is dead and that you know it. You understand me? I'm not going out of here alone. There's no life for me that way. I want you to set him free. And then I promise you, everything will end, and we'll go away, and that's all.

KELLER. You'll do that. You'll tell him.

ANN. I know what I'm asking, Kate. You had two sons. But you've only got one now.

KELLER. You'll tell him . . .

ANN. And you've got to say it to him so he knows you mean it.

MOTHER. My dear, if the boy was dead, it wouldn't depend on my words to make Chris know it. . . . The night he gets into your bed, his heart will dry up. Because he knows and you know. To his dying day he'll wait for his brother! No, my dear, no such thing. You're going in the morning, and you're going alone. That's your life, that's your lonely life. [*She goes to porch, and starts in.*]

ANN. Larry is dead, Kate.

MOTHER [*she stops*]. Don't speak to me.

ANN. I said he's dead. I know! He crashed off the coast of China November twenty-fifth! His engine didn't fail him. But he died. I know. . . .

MOTHER. How did he die? You're lying to me. If you know, how did he die?

ANN. I loved him. You know I loved him. Would I

have looked at anyone else if I wasn't sure? That's enough for you.

MOTHER [*moving on her*]. What's enough for me? What're you talking about? [*She grasps* ANN's *wrists.*]

ANN. You're hurting my wrists.

MOTHER. What are you talking about! [*Pause. She stares at* ANN *a moment then turns, and goes to* KELLER.]

ANN. Joe, go in the house. . . .

KELLER. Why should I. . . .

ANN. Please go.

KELLER. Lemme know when he comes. [KELLER *goes into house.*]

MOTHER [*sees* ANN *take a letter from her pocket*]. What's that?

ANN. Sit down . . . [MOTHER *moves left to chair, but does not sit.*] First you've got to understand. When I came, I didn't have any idea that Joe . . . I had nothing against him or you. I came to get married. I hoped . . . So I didn't bring this to hurt you. I thought I'd show it to you only if there was no other way to settle Larry in your mind.

MOTHER. Larry? [*Snatches letter from* ANN's *hand.*]

ANN. He wrote it to me just before he— [MOTHER *opens and begins to read letter.*] I'm not trying to hurt you, Kate. You're making me do this, now remember you're— Remember. I've been so lonely, Kate . . . I can't leave here alone again. [*A long, low moan comes from* MOTHER's *throat as she reads.*] You made me show it to you. You wouldn't believe me. I told you a hundred times, why wouldn't you believe me!

MOTHER. Oh, my God . . .

ANN [*with pity and fear*]. Kate, please, please . . .

MOTHER. My God, my God . . .

ANN. Kate, dear, I'm so sorry . . . I'm so sorry.

[CHRIS *enters from driveway. He seems exhausted.*]

CHRIS. What's the matter . . . ?

ANN. Where were you? . . . you're all perspired. [MOTHER *doesn't move.*] Where were you?

CHRIS. Just drove around a little. I thought you'd be gone.

ANN. Where do I go? I have nowhere to go.

CHRIS [*to* MOTHER]. Where's Dad?

ANN. Inside lying down.

CHRIS. Sit down, both of you. I'll say what there is to say.

MOTHER. I didn't hear the car. . . .

CHRIS. I left it in the garage.

MOTHER. Jim is out looking for you.

CHRIS. Mother . . . I'm going away. There are a couple of firms in Cleveland, I think I can get a place. I mean, I'm going away for good. [*To* ANN *alone.*] I know what you're thinking, Annie. It's true. I'm yellow. I was made yellow in this house because I suspected my father and I did nothing about it, but if I knew that night when I came home what I know now, he'd be in the district attorney's office by this time, and I'd have brought him there. Now if I look at him, all I'm able to do is cry.

MOTHER. What are you talking about? What else can you do?

CHRIS. I could jail him! I could jail him, if I were human any more. But I'm like everybody else now. I'm practical now. You made me practical.

MOTHER. But you have to be.

CHRIS. The cats in that alley are practical, the bums who ran away when we were fighting were practical. Only the dead ones weren't practical. But now I'm practical, and I spit on myself. I'm going away. I'm going now.

ANN [*goes up to him*]. I'm coming with you. . . .

CHRIS. No, Ann.

ANN. Chris, I don't ask you to do anything about Joe.

CHRIS. You do, you do . . .

ANN. I swear I never will.

CHRIS. In your heart you always will.

ANN. Then do what you have to do!

CHRIS. Do what? What is there to do? I've looked all night for a reason to make him suffer.

ANN. There's reason, there's reason!

CHRIS. What? Do I raise the dead when I put him behind bars? Then what'll I do it for? We used to shoot a man who acted like a dog, but honor was real there, you were protecting something. But here? This is the land of the great big dogs, you don't love a man here, you eat him! That's the principle; the only one we live by—it just happened to kill a few people this time, that's all. The world's that way, how can I take it out on him? What sense does that make? This is a zoo, a zoo!

ANN [*to* MOTHER]. You know what he's got to do! Tell him!

MOTHER. Let him go.

ANN. I won't let him go. You'll tell him what he's got to do. . . .

MOTHER. Annie!

ANN. Then I will!

[KELLER *enters from house.* CHRIS *sees him, goes down near arbor.*]

KELLER. What's the matter with you? I want to talk to you.

CHRIS. I've got nothing to say to you.

KELLER [*taking his arm*]. I want to talk to you!

CHRIS [*pulling violently away from him*]. Don't do that, Dad. I'm going to hurt you if you do that. There's nothing to say, so say it quick.

KELLER. Exactly what's the matter? What's the matter?
You got too much money? Is that what bothers you?

CHRIS [*with an edge of sarcasm*]. It bothers me.

KELLER. If you can't get used to it, then throw it away.
You hear me? Take every cent and give it to charity,
throw it in the sewer. Does that settle it? In the
sewer, that's all. You think I'm kidding? I'm tellin'
you what to do, if it's dirty then burn it. It's your
money, that's not my money. I'm a dead man, I'm an
old dead man, nothing's mine. Well, talk to me!—
what do you want to do!

CHRIS. It's not what I want to do. It's what you want to
do.

KELLER. What should I want to do? [CHRIS *is silent.*]
Jail? You want me to go to jail? If you want me to
go, say so! Is that where I belong?—then tell me so!
[*Slight pause.*] What's the matter, why can't you tell
me? [*Furiously.*] You say everything else to me, say
that! [*Slight pause.*] I'll tell you why you can't say
it. Because you know I don't belong there. Because
you know! [*With growing emphasis and passion,
and a persistent tone of desperation.*] Who worked
for nothin' in that war? When they work for nothin',
I'll work for nothin'. Did they ship a gun or a
truck outa Detroit before they got their price? Is
that clean? It's dollars and cents, nickels and dimes;
war and peace, it's nickels and dimes, what's clean?
Half the goddam country is gotta go if I go! That's
why you can't tell me.

CHRIS. That's exactly why.

KELLER. Then . . . why am *I* bad?

CHRIS. *I* know you're no worse than most men but I
thought you were better. I never saw you as a man.
I saw you as my father. [*Almost breaking.*] I can't
look at you this way, I can't look at myself! [*He
turns away unable to face* KELLER. ANN *goes quickly*

to MOTHER, *takes letter from her and starts for* CHRIS.
MOTHER *instantly rushes to intercept her.*]

MOTHER. Give me that!

ANN. He's going to read it! [*She thrusts letter into* CHRIS' *hand.*] Larry. He wrote it to me the day he died. . . .

KELLER. Larry!?

MOTHER. Chris, it's not for you. [*He starts to read.*] Joe . . . go away . . .

KELLER [*mystified, frightened*]. Why'd she say Larry, what . . . ?

MOTHER [*she desperately pushes him toward alley, glancing at* CHRIS]. Go to the street, Joe, go to the street! [*She comes down beside* KELLER.] Don't, Chris . . . [*Pleading from her whole soul.*] Don't tell him.

CHRIS [*quietly*]. Three and one half years . . . talking, talking. Now you tell me what you must do. . . . This is how he died, now tell me where you belong.

KELLER [*pleading*]. Chris, a man can't be a Jesus in this world!

CHRIS. I know all about the world. I know the whole crap story. Now listen to this, and tell me what a man's got to be! [*Reads.*] "My dear Ann: . . ." You listening? He wrote this the day he died. Listen, don't cry . . . listen! "My dear Ann: It is impossible to put down the things I feel. But I've got to tell you something. Yesterday they flew in a load of papers from the States and I read about Dad and your father being convicted. I can't express myself. I can't tell you how I feel—I can't bear to live any more. Last night I circled the base for twenty minutes before I could bring myself in. How could he have done that? Every day three or four men never come back and he sits back there doing business. . . . I don't know how to tell you what I feel . . .

I can't face anybody . . . I'm going out on a mission in a few minutes. They'll probably report me missing. If they do, I want you to know that you mustn't wait for me. I tell you, Ann, if I had him here now I could kill him—" [KELLER *grabs letter from* CHRIS' *hand and reads it. After a long pause.*] Now blame the world. Do you understand that letter?

KELLER [*he speaks almost inaudibly*]. I think I do. Get the car. I'll put on my jacket. [*He turns and starts slowly for the house.* MOTHER *rushes to intercept him.*]

MOTHER. Why are you going? You'll sleep, why are you going?

KELLER. I can't sleep here. I'll feel better if I go.

MOTHER. You're so foolish. Larry was your son too, wasn't he? You know he'd never tell you to do this.

KELLER [*looking at letter in his hand*]. Then what is this if it isn't telling me? Sure, he was my son. But I think to him they were all my sons. And I guess they were, I guess they were. I'll be right down. [*Exits into house.*]

MOTHER [*to* CHRIS, *with determination*]. You're not going to take him!

CHRIS. I'm taking him.

MOTHER. It's up to you, if you tell him to stay he'll stay. Go and tell him!

CHRIS. Nobody could stop him now.

MOTHER. You'll stop him! How long will he live in prison?—are you trying to kill him?

CHRIS [*holding out letter*]. I thought you read this!

MOTHER [*of Larry, the letter*]. The war is over! Didn't you hear?—it's over!

CHRIS. Then what was Larry to you? A stone that fell into the water? It's not enough for him to be sorry. Larry didn't kill himself to make you and Dad sorry.

MOTHER. What more can we be!

CHRIS. You can be better! Once and for all you can know there's a universe of people outside and you're responsible to it, and unless you know that, you threw away your son because that's why he died.

[*A shot is heard in the house. They stand frozen for a brief second.* CHRIS *starts for porch, pauses at step, turns to* ANN.]

CHRIS. Find Jim! [*He goes on into the house and* ANN *runs up driveway.* MOTHER *stands alone, transfixed.*]

MOTHER [*softly, almost moaning*]. Joe . . . Joe . . . Joe . . . Joe . . .

[CHRIS *comes out of house, down to* MOTHER's *arms.*]

CHRIS [*almost crying*]. Mother, I didn't mean to . . .

MOTHER. Don't dear. Don't take it on yourself. Forget now. Live. [CHRIS *stirs as if to answer.*] Shhh . . . [*She puts his arms down gently and moves toward porch.*] Shhh . . . [*As she reaches porch steps she begins sobbing, as*

THE CURTAIN FALLS

LOST IN THE STARS

by Maxwell Anderson

Based on the novel,
Cry, the Beloved Country, by Alan Paton,
as written to be set to music by Kurt Weill.

First production, October 30, 1949,
at the Music Box, New York,
with the following cast:

LEADER, *Frank Roane*
ANSWERER, *Joseph James*
NITA, *Elayne Richards*
GRACE KUMALO, *Gertrude Jeannette*
STEPHEN KUMALO, *Todd Duncan*
THE YOUNG MAN, *Lavern French*
THE YOUNG WOMAN, *Mabel Hart*
JAMES JARVIS, *Leslie Banks*
EDWARD JARVIS, *Judson Rees*
ARTHUR JARVIS, *John Morley*
JOHN KUMALO, *Warren Coleman*
PAULUS, *Charles McRae*
WILLIAM, *Roy Allen*
JARED, *William C. Smith*
ALEX, *Herbert Coleman*
FOREMAN, *Jerome Shaw*
MRS. MKIZE, *Georgette Harvey*
HLABENI, *William Marshall*
ELAND, *Charles Grunwell*
LINDA, *Sheila Guyse*
JOHANNES PAFURI, *Van Prince*
MATTHEW KUMALO, *William Greaves*
ABSALOM KUMALO, *Julian Mayfield*
ROSE, *Gloria Smith*
IRINA, *Inez Matthews*
POLICEMAN, *Robert Byrn*
WHITE WOMAN, *Biruta Ramoska*
WHITE MAN, *Mark Kramer*
THE GUARD, *Jerome Shaw*
BURTON, *John W. Stanley*
THE JUDGE, *Guy Spaull*
VILLAGER, *Robert McFerrin*
SINGERS

Act one

The curtain goes up in darkness and a picture of the Ixopo hills develops gradually in the background. From the orchestra pit a broad flight of steps leads up to the stage. A group of SINGERS *sits on these steps, so placed that they are not in the way of the action but can comment on it or ascend to take part in it at any time. The first scene is the tiny and cheap but clean sitting room in the home of* STEPHEN KUMALO, *near St. Mark's Church near Ndotsheni, Natal, South Africa. As the curtain rises, we see* SINGERS *entering from the pit onto the center stairs, and also from right and left stage to positions on the side steps. The* LEADER *takes his place center stage and sits on a basket which he carries on stage.*

LEADER [*sings*].
  There is a lovely road
  that runs from Ixopo into the hills.
  These hills
  are grass covered and rolling, and they are lovely
  beyond any singing of it.
  About you
  there is grass and bracken, and you may hear
  the forlorn crying of the titihoya bird.

The grass of the veld is rich and matted.
You cannot see the soil.
The grass holds the rain and mist,
and they seep into the ground, feeding
the streams in every clove.
The clove is cool and green and lovely beyond any
　　singing of it.

ANSWERER. But sing now about the lower hills.

LEADER.
Where you stand the grass is rich and matted—
but the rich green hills break down.
They fall to the valley below—
and, falling, change.
For they grow red and bare;
they cannot hold the rain and mist;
the streams run dry in the clove.
Too many cattle feed on the grass;
it is not kept or guarded or cared for.
It no longer keeps men, guards men, cares for men.
The titihoya cries here no more.

ANSWERER. Yes, wherever the hills have broken down
and the red clay shows through, there poor people
live and dig ever more desperately into the failing
earth.

LEADER [*sings*].
The great red hills stand desolate,
and the earth has torn away like flesh.
These are the valleys
of old men and old women,
of mothers and children.
The men are away.

The young men and the girls are away.
The soil cannot keep them any more.

[STEPHEN KUMALO *enters and sits on a chair behind the
table. As the last of the* SINGERS *go out the lights
come up on the sitting room.* GRACE KUMALO, *Stephen's wife, enters, and a small Zulu girl,* NITA, *runs
in with a letter and crosses to* STEPHEN.]

NITA [*handing the letter to* STEPHEN]. I bring a letter,
umfundisi.

STEPHEN. Where did you get it, my child?

NITA. From the store, umfundisi. The white man asked
me to bring it to you.

STEPHEN. That was good of you. Go well, small one.

[NITA *starts to go, but pauses.*]

GRACE. Perhaps you might be hungry, Nita.

NITA. Not—not very hungry.

STEPHEN. Perhaps a little hungry?

NITA. Yes, a little hungry, umfundisi.

GRACE. There is a little bowl on the kitchen table,
Nita. And a spoon beside it.

NITA. I thank you. [NITA *goes to the kitchen; Stephen
sits fingering his letter;* GRACE *crosses to him and
looks over his shoulder at the letter.*]

GRACE. From Johannesburg.

STEPHEN. Yes, August 9, 1949.

GRACE. "Reverend Stephen Kumalo, St. Mark's Church,
Ndotsheni, Natal." It is not from our son.

STEPHEN. No. It's a writing I haven't seen.

GRACE. It may bring news of him.

STEPHEN. Yes. Let me think. Our son Absalom is in
Johannesburg; my sister Gertrude is there—and my
brother John is there. But he has never written to
me. [*He picks up the knife from the table.*] Perhaps
the way to find out is to open it. [*He slits the flap*

with the knife and hands the letter to GRACE.] Read it, my helper. Your eyes are better than mine.

GRACE. It's from your brother John.

STEPHEN. Then this is truly an occasion. Read carefully, my helper.

GRACE. "Dear Stephen, you old faker in Christ. I don't know whether it was you who sent our dear sister Gertrude to Johannesburg or not, but if it was, for the love of your own Jesus send and fetch her back. She says she came looking for a husband who ran away from her. Maybe so. Anyway she's found plenty husbands, and the stories about the kind of house she keeps are not good for my business, because it's known here who she is. See to this soon, O brother in God, or I'll have the woman put away where she won't be so noticeable. Your affectionate brother, John." He's an evil man. [*She sits.*]

STEPHEN [*humorously*]. No, he honestly thinks that I am a faker. He thinks all men are fakers, perhaps because he's one. But I am not concerned about that. I am concerned about Gertrude—if she has taken to bad ways.

GRACE. What will you do?

STEPHEN. I don't know.

GRACE [*she has a plan*]. If you were in Johannesburg you could find Gertrude.

STEPHEN. It's many hundreds of miles. Where would I find the money to go to Johannesburg?

GRACE. There is the St. Chad's money.

STEPHEN. Absalom's money—the money we save for his school? You would have me use that?

GRACE. Should you not, Stephen? Absalom will never go now to St. Chad's.

STEPHEN. How can you say that? How can you say such a thing?

GRACE. He is in Johannesburg. When people go to Johannesburg they do not come back.

STEPHEN. But Absalom will! Absalom went to Johannesburg for one purpose—to earn money for his education! When he returns he will bring twelve pounds of his own to put with the twelve we have saved, and then he will have enough for a year at St. Chad's, and he will go there and learn quickly! I know him!

GRACE. It's nearly a year since we had a letter from him, Stephen. We do not know him now. He has been in the mines. No young man could work in the mines and not change. Absalom will not go to school. Take the money—use it!

STEPHEN. Do you know what you are saying? If I take his school money and use it to bring Gertrude back, then I have given up Absalom! I have said by this action that he will not make a place for himself, that we shall not see him nor be proud of him again, that he is only a drop in the great river of blacks that pours into the earth and is seen no more! I will not say this! I will not think it!

GRACE. I love him as much as you, but why has he not written to us? If there's nothing wrong he could have written.

STEPHEN. O mother of little faith! A letter can be lost so easily! We must not cease to believe in him. We must love him, and not doubt him. There's a great gulf between people, Grace, between husband and wife, between parents and child, between neighbor and neighbor. Even when you live in the same house it's deep and wide, except for the love between us. But when there is love, then distance doesn't matter at all—distance or silence or years.

[*He sings "Thousands of Miles."*]
How many miles
  To the heart of a child?
    Thousands of miles, thousands of miles.
When he lay on your breast
  He looked up and smiled
    Across tens of thousands,
    Thousands of miles.
Each lives alone
  In a world of dark,
Crossing the skies
  In a lonely arc,
Save when love leaps out like a leaping spark
  Over thousands, thousands of miles.

Not miles, or walls, or length of days,
  Nor the cold doubt of midnight can hold us apart,
For swifter than wings of the morning
  The pathways of the heart!
How many miles
  To the heart of a son?
    Thousands of miles, thousands of miles.
Farther off than the rails
  Or the roadways run
    Across tens of thousands,
    Thousands of miles
The wires and the ways,
  Reach far and thin
To the streets and days
  That close him in,
But there, as of old, he turns 'round to grin
  Over thousands—thousands of miles.

Not miles, or walls, or length of days,
  Nor the cold doubt of midnight can hold us apart,
For swifter than wings of the morning

The pathways of the heart!
Over tens of thousands of miles.

[NITA *enters from upstage door.*]

STEPHEN. Is the little bowl empty, Nita?

NITA. Yes, umfundisi. I thank you.

STEPHEN. Go well, my child.

NITA. Stay well, umfundisi. [*She skips out and off left.*]

GRACE. Stephen, please take the St. Chad's money. Go to Johannesburg.

STEPHEN. You're not thinking of Gertrude. You're thinking of Absalom.

GRACE. Yes. We have heard nothing from our son for a year—go to Johannesburg. Find him.

STEPHEN. If you wish it so much, it may be that I should go, my helper. I shall bring you word of Absalom. It will be good news, that I know. [*He crosses left and looks at the clock.*] I couldn't go today. The train goes at twelve, and it's past the hour. But I could go tomorrow.

GRACE [*her arms around him*]. You are my Stephen. [*The lights dim.*]

SCENE II

The station at Carrisbrooke, indicated only by a sema-phore. As the lights come up a white STATIONMASTER *announces the coming of the train and a group of* ZULUS *enters, singing a farewell to one of their number who has been called to work in the mines.*

STATIONMASTER. Attention! The train for Johannesburg will be here in five minutes! Have your baggage ready! Train for Johannesburg!

CHORUS.
> Johannesburg, Johannesburg.
> Johannesburg, Johannesburg.

LEADER.
> Train go now to Johannesburg,
> Farewell!

CHORUS.
> Farewell!

LEADER.
> Go well!

CHORUS.
> Go well!

LEADER.
> Train go now to Johannesburg,
> Farewell!

CHORUS.
> Farewell!

LEADER.
> Go well!

CHORUS.
> Go well!
> This boy we love, this brother,
> Go to Johannesburg!
> White man go to Johannesburg—
> He come back, he come back.
> Black man go to Johannesburg—
> Never come back, never come back!

YOUNG MAN [*speaking*]. I come back.
WOMAN. Please!
YOUNG MAN.
> All this they say—
> I fool them. I come back.

CHORUS [*sings*].
> Black man go to Johannesburg—
> Go, go, never come back

Go, go, never come back.
Train go now to Johannesburg—
Farewell, farewell,
Go well, go well!
This boy we love, this brother,
Go to Johannesburg.
White man go to Johannesburg,
He come back, he come back.
Black man go to Johannesburg,
Go, go, never come back—
Go, go, never come back, never come back
Never come back!

[JAMES JARVIS, *an Englishman of about fifty-five, enters, accompanied by his son,* ARTHUR, *and his grand-
son,* EDWARD. *They pause a minute to talk, the* ZULUS
diminish their singing to a pianissimo.]

ARTHUR. We're in plenty of time.

JARVIS. Yes—I can see the plume of smoke just over the
hill. The train will be here in three minutes.

EDWARD. I wonder who invented schools, and Latin
grammar.

ARTHUR. It's not only your school, son. I have to get
back to work, too.

EDWARD. Anyway, I'll always remember this is the
year I learned to ride horseback.

JARVIS. And I'll see that Danny gets his daily oats and
exercise till you're here again. Next vacation you
can wear longer stirrups and take a few jumps with
him.

EDWARD. Do you think he'll remember me?

JARVIS. I'm not sure just how much a horse remembers.
But he'll be here, and we'll all be here, waiting for
you. The old place gets pretty lonely with only
your grandmother and me.

EDWARD. It was the best mid-term I ever had.

JARVIS [*smiling*]. Thank you, Edward. [STEPHEN KU-
MALO *enters with his wife and crosses to center; he
is carrying a small black bag.*] It was among the best
I ever had. You have a book to read on the train?

EDWARD. I have my Latin grammar—but I'm planning
to look out the window a lot.

ARTHUR. There's Stephen Kumalo—and I haven't seen
him for a year. Forgive me. [*He starts toward* STE-
PHEN.]

JARVIS. Arthur!

ARTHUR. Yes?

JARVIS. I don't know what the customs are now in Johannesburg. They may have changed since I was
there. But in our village one does not go out of his
way to speak to a black.

ARTHUR. The customs have not changed in Johannesburg, Father. But I am not bound by these customs.
I have friends among the Zulus. And my friends are
my friends. [*He goes to* STEPHEN *and offers his hand.*]
Mr. Kumalo!

STEPHEN. Ah, Mr. Jarvis!

[*They shake hands.*]

ARTHUR. You're making a journey?

STEPHEN. To Johannesburg, sir. It is my first long journey. And a happy one—I go to see my son!

ARTHUR. Ah! And Mrs. Kumalo goes with you?

GRACE. No, sir. I stay with the house.

ARTHUR. I'm leaving today, too. I wish I'd had time to
see you while we were here.

STEPHEN. Sir, it is always a great pleasure to see you.
Perhaps when you come again—

ARTHUR. That's right—there's always a next time. And
I won't forget.

[ARTHUR *and* STEPHEN *shake hands again.*]

STEPHEN. I know you won't, sir.

[ARTHUR *returns to his father and son.*]

JARVIS. If you had struck me across the face you couldn't have hurt me more—or damaged me more, in the eyes of those who stand here. I suppose you know that?

ARTHUR. I don't believe that, Father. This is an old quarrel between us. We haven't time to settle it before the train goes. Perhaps we shall never settle it.

JARVIS. What you do in Johannesburg I can't alter! But here, where every eye is on us, where you are known as my son, you could avoid affronting me in such a fashion! Will you remember that in the future?

ARTHUR. Let's shake hands and agree to disagree, Father. The train is almost here.

JARVIS. You make no promises?

ARTHUR. I make no promises.

JARVIS. Then I'm not sure that I want you to come here again, Arthur!

ARTHUR. Father!

JARVIS. I'm sorry. Of course you'll come again.

ARTHUR. Not if it offends you, Father. But—my friends are my friends.

[ARTHUR *and* JARVIS *face each other. The* CHORUS *begins to imitate the approaching train.*]

EDWARD. Good-by, Grandfather.

JARVIS. Good-by, Edward.

ARTHUR. Good-by, sir. [*He puts out his hand.*]

JARVIS. Good-by, Arthur. [*He shakes hands with* ARTHUR. ARTHUR *and* EDWARD *go to the left.* STEPHEN *has started to go toward the train off-stage left, but steps back to let* ARTHUR *and* EDWARD *precede him. As* STEPHEN *and his wife go out the* ZULUS *shout to them.*]

LEADER. Go well, umfundisi.

STEPHEN. Stay well, you who dwell here.

[*The* CHORUS *and the* LEADER, *imitating the train, sing simultaneously.*]

LEADER.
  White man go to Johannesburg,
  He come back,
  He come back.
CHORUS.
  Clink, clink, clickety.
1ST VOICE [*imitating the whistle*].
  Whoo-oo-oo-oo!
CHORUS.
  Black man go to Johannesburg!
  Never come back, never come back!
  Clink, clink, clickety,
  clink, clink, clickety . . .

[*The lights fade.*]

SCENE III

JOHN KUMALO's *tobacco shop in Johannesburg. A counter with a small display of cigars, cigarettes, and tobacco.* JOHN *is conferring with some political lieutenants, all Zulus or Bantu.*

JOHN. Don't take it so hard, gentlemen, don't take it
  so hard. We won't get equal suffrage, we won't get
  social equality, we won't get any kind of equality—
  but those of us who are quick in the head will get
  along. That's the way it is everywhere, for whites
  and for Zulus. Use your head and you can live. Try
  to reform the world and somebody steals your meal-

ies. Now—suppose a Zulu says to you, "I demand equality; I want to vote and I want to be represented!" What do you say to him? You, Paulus?

PAULUS. I say to him, "Man, our Political League is out for just that; it's out for equality. We won't get it this year. We won't get it next year. But we'll get it!"

JOHN. What else do you say to him? William?

WILLIAM. I say to him, "We've got a doctor in our League, brother. Somebody gets sick he goes to your house first. You run out of mealies maybe and need some to tide you over. Come and see me. We got a barrel in the back room just for that."

JOHN. That's right. Long-term notes, like equality, make 'em big—we're never going to pay. Short-term notes, like a bite to eat, keep 'em small. We pay 'em on the dot. And in ten years, gentlemen, our League will own Johannesburg. [JARED, *a Zulu, enters.*] Yes, sir.

JARED. Some pipe tobacco, please.

JOHN. Native grown or imported?

JARED. Native grown. A quarter-pound. [*He gets his tobacco and goes out.*]

JOHN. And now, gentlemen, you're part of the biggest thing that's happening in this town!

[STEPHEN KUMALO *enters, holding a small Zulu boy,* ALEX, *by the hand.* JOHN *looks at* STEPHEN *without recognizing him.*]

JOHN. Yes, umfundisi?

STEPHEN. I've come to see you, John . . .

JOHN. It's Stephen. It's our old gospel bird, scratching 'round in the big city. You got my letter?

STEPHEN. Yes. This is Gertrude's son. Little Alex.

JOHN. Excuse me, gentlemen. My own brother, the son

of our mother, has come. [WILLIAM *and* PAULUS *go out.*] Well, any rain down your way this year?

STEPHEN. Less than we needed, John.

JOHN. You should pray, brother, you should pray. Now about Gertrude, she goes back with you to Ndotsheni?

STEPHEN. She allows the child to go with me. But she stays here.

JOHN. Brother, I want our sister out of this town. There's a limit to the number of bastard nephews a respectable tradesman can have.

STEPHEN. I asked her to come with me. She would not. And she said, "John won't put me away anywhere. He would have to find me first, and he won't find me."

JOHN. You have failed with her.

STEPHEN. Yes.

JOHN. Take her son, then, and go back to your hills and your sheet-iron chapel and your rusty god. I thought you might rid me of the woman. If you can't do that I have no further use for you.

STEPHEN. Honest and straightforward, aren't you, John? I'll go, but first there are two things I must ask. I have no room to stay in—

JOHN. There's no room here.

STEPHEN. Don't be afraid. I can pay for a room.

JOHN. Perhaps I can find you one, then. What else?

STEPHEN. My son Absalom. Did you see him while he was here?

JOHN. How much have you heard from Absalom?

STEPHEN. Four letters—from the mines—nearly a year ago. He was well, and working hard.

JOHN. I see. Well—your son left the mines and went about with my son Matthew for a while. They both stayed here. But your Absalom was not a good influence on Matthew.

STEPHEN. John!

JOHN. I had to tell them to get out.

STEPHEN. You sent them away?

JOHN. Yes.

STEPHEN. Do you know—where they went?

JOHN. Yes, I've written it somewhere.

STEPHEN. I hoped you would know. That makes it all easy. Now I thank my God—I thank my *Tixo*—

JOHN. You can leave your God out of it. He's not interested. 14 Krause Street, Doornfontein Textiles Company.

STEPHEN. Doornfontein Textiles Company, 14 Krause Street.

JOHN. That's it. And now you want a place to stay. [*He writes an address.*] You think I am a hard man.

STEPHEN. Brother, you have helped me. We do what we can.

JOHN. Brother, you're right. We do what we can. I hope you know what you do. You're the white man's dog, trained to bark and keep us in order. You know that.

STEPHEN. No, brother, I do not know it.

JOHN. They pile up mountains of gold, and they pay our sons three shillings a day, and out of this wage take a heavy tax. Is that fair?

STEPHEN. No, brother, it is not fair.

JOHN. Then why do you wear their Anglican clothes and read their Testament?

STEPHEN. Because all men do evil, I among them—and I wish all men to do better, I among them.

JOHN [*giving* STEPHEN *the address*]. Yes, blessed are the chicken-hearted. This will give you a place to sleep. It's expensive and it's in Shanty Town and it's not pleasant. Such are the customs of our city.

STEPHEN. I shan't mind. Good-by, John. [*He puts out his hand.*]

JOHN [*taking it*]. Good-by. You old faker in Christ.
STEPHEN. The same John! [*He starts out.*] 14 Krause
    Street. . . .
[*The lights dim and go out.*]

SCENE IV

The lights come up on the CHORUS *on the orchestra pit
steps.*

CHORUS [*sings*].
    14 Krause Street
      Textiles Company
    14 Krause Street
      Textiles Company
    14 Krause Street
      Textiles Company.

STEPHEN [*alone on the street*].
    Not miles, or walls, or length of days,
      Nor the cold doubt of midnight can hold us apart,
    For swifter than wings of the morning
      The pathways of the heart!

CHORUS [*sings*].
    14 Krause Street
      Textiles Company
    14 Krause Street
      Textiles Company.

[STEPHEN *is now seen speaking with a factory* FOREMAN
    *who stands behind a cashier's cage. He is looking
    up a record in a large volume.*]
FOREMAN. Yes, they did work here. Absalom Kumalo

and Matthew Kumalo. But they left us some months ago.

STEPHEN. Sir, did they work well?

FOREMAN. Why, I think so. I rather liked Absalom. A good lad.

STEPHEN. Thank you, sir. He's my son, you know. Could you tell me where they went?

FOREMAN. They had a house address when they were here. They lived with Mrs. Mkize, 77 Twenty-third Avenue, Alexandra.

STEPHEN. Thank you, sir.

[*The lights dim.*]

CHORUS [*sings*].
  Seventy-seven, Twenty-third Avenue—
    Mrs. Mkize—Twenty-third Avenue.

[STEPHEN *is now seen at a doorway.* MRS. MKIZE *appears in it as the lights come up.*]

STEPHEN. How long ago, Mrs. Mkize?

MRS. MKIZE. These many months.

STEPHEN. Do you know where he is now?

CHORUS [*sings*].
  Make no doubt
  It is fear that you see in her eyes!
  It is fear!

MRS. MKIZE. No, I do not know.

STEPHEN. Are you afraid of me?

MRS. MKIZE. No, I'm not afraid.

STEPHEN. But you tremble when I speak of him.

MRS. MKIZE. I don't know you. I don't know why you ask.

STEPHEN. I am his father. I wish him well—and you well.

MRS. MKIZE. His father? Then it would be better if you followed him no further.

STEPHEN. Why?

MRS. MKIZE. Umfundisi, they were friendly with a taxi driver named Hlabeni who lives near the stand in this same street. At number 25.

STEPHEN. Why should I look no further?

MRS. MKIZE. Lest you be hurt by it.

STEPHEN. What did he do?

MRS. MKIZE. In the middle of the night they brought things here, umfundisi. Clothes and watches and money. They left in haste. I think they were near to being discovered. Oh, follow him no further!

STEPHEN. Hlabeni, at 25 on this street?

MRS. MKIZE. Yes.

[*The lights dim.*]

CHORUS [*sings*].
 A taxi driver, known as Hlabeni,
  Taxi stand, in Twenty-third Avenue,
 What you must find is always a number,
  A number and a name.
 Though it sear the mind, say it over and over,
  Over and over,
  A boding song,
  Searing like flame.

LEADER [*sings*].
 Be there, my one son, be well there—

[STEPHEN *is now at* HLABENI'S *doorway.*]

HLABENI. I can tell you this much; they were picked up for something they'd done, and one of them went to jail for a while.

STEPHEN. What—had they done?

HLABENI. Oh, some wild trick like boys do.

STEPHEN. Which one went to prison?

HLABENI. Absalom. I don't know why Matthew didn't go, but he got out of it somehow. And Absalom's out now. He's on parole. Or that's what I heard.

STEPHEN. Where would he be?

HLABENI. You could ask the parole officer at the government building. He might know.

STEPHEN. Is it near?

HLABENI. Four or five miles.

STEPHEN. Could I find it tonight?

HLABENI. I'll tell you what I'll do. I'll draw you a map. That might help.

[*The lights dim.*]

CHORUS [*sings*].
What you must find is always a number,
    A number and a name,
In prison cells they give you a number,
    Tag your clothes with it,
    Print your shame!

LEADER [*sings*].
Be there, my one son, be well there—

VOICE [*speaking*]. But how could he be well there? How could he be well?

[*The lights come up on* STEPHEN *standing before* MARK ELAND, *the parole officer, a young white man.*]

ELAND. Yes, he's been paroled, umfundisi. We made an exception in his case, partly because of his good behavior, partly because of his age, but mainly because there was a girl who was pregnant by him.

STEPHEN. He is married, then?

ELAND. No, umfundisi. But the girl seemed fond of

him, so with all these things in mind—and with his
solemn undertaking that he would work hard to
support the child and its mother—we let him go.
He's living with the girl in Pimville.

STEPHEN. Is it far?

ELAND. It's some miles. It's among the shacks there,
and at night the streets are—well, pretty hard to get
about in. I think I'd have to take you.

STEPHEN. Could—could you go tonight, sir?

ELAND. Tonight I can't. But if you could come here
early tomorrow—

STEPHEN. Yes, sir. Thank you.

[*The lights dim out.*]

SCENE V

The lights come up as we see STEPHEN *striking a match
and lighting a candle in a tiny, squalid room.* ALEX
is with him.

ALEX. Uncle Stephen?

STEPHEN. Yes, Alex.

ALEX. The room is very small here, and not clean.

STEPHEN. Yes, it's the best they had.

ALEX. I hope we won't live here.

STEPHEN. No, no, Alex; you'll live in Ndotsheni. In
the country. In my home.

ALEX. Is it like this there?

STEPHEN. No, not at all like this. There are hills and
valleys, and trees growing on the hills and streams
running in the valleys.

ALEX. What will our house be like?

STEPHEN. It's a little grey house.

ALEX. Will there be grass in front of it?

STEPHEN. Yes, and flowers growing in the grass.

ALEX. Do you have a wife there?

STEPHEN. Yes.

ALEX. I don't like my mother. She hits me. And I hit her, too. Only she hits me harder!

STEPHEN. Nobody will hit you in my house.

ALEX. Tell me about the house. Why is it grey?

STEPHEN. Because it has not been painted.

ALEX. Is the water good when it comes from the tap, or do you have to boil it?

STEPHEN. There's no tap at all, boy. We get water from the spring. There's a tree that my son liked to climb. He built himself a place to sleep in it, like a nest. You will climb that tree.

ALEX. Is the nest still there?

STEPHEN. Yes, it's there.

ALEX. I see. I'm thinking about it. [*He looks out, imagining.*]

CHORUS [*sings*].
> What are you thinking,
>> Old man among the broken boxes
>>> Of Shanty Town?

> What do you see,
>> Child with the shining eyes,
>>> Among the broken hopes
>>>> Of Shanty Town?

STEPHEN [*sings "The Little Grey House"*].
> There's a little grey house
>> In a one-street town,
> And the door stands open,
>> And the steps run down;

And you prop up the window
  With a stick on the sill,
And you carry spring water
  From the bottom of the hill:
And the white star-of-Bethlehem
  Grows in the yard,
And I can't really describe it
  But I'm trying hard;
It's not much to tell about,
It's not much to picture out,
  And the only thing special is
    It's home.

CHORUS.

It's not much to sing about,
It's not much to picture out,
  And the only thing special is
    It's home.

STEPHEN.

It's a long road, God knows,
The long and turning iron road that leads to Ndot-
  sheni.
How I came, God knows, by what ridges, streams,
  and valleys,
And how we shall return is in God's keeping.
Many bright days, many dark nights, we must ride
  on iron
Before I see that house again!

There's a lamp in the room,
  And it lights the face
Of the one who waits there
  In her quiet place,
With her hands always busy

Over needle and thread,
Or the fire in the kitchen
   To bake tomorrow's bread.
And she always has love enough
   To take you in,
And her house will rest you
   Wherever you've been!

CHORUS.

It's not much to tell about,
It's not much to picture out,
   And the only thing special is
      It's home!

STEPHEN.

It's not much to tell about,
It's not much to picture out,
   And the only thing special is
      It's home!

[STEPHEN *carries* ALEX *up to the cot and covers him
with a blanket. He blows out the candle. The lights
dim out.*]

SCENE VI

*A dive in Shanty Town. Some strange harmonies have
crept into the last few bars and now we discover that
they were indications of another song that begins to
come from another part of the stage, still in darkness.
It's sung in the manner of a night-club entertainer.
The voice is a girl's. As the lights come up we see*
LINDA, *the singer,* MATTHEW KUMALO, JOHANNES PAFURI,
and ROSE *and* SUTTY, *two girls who came with the*

young men. ABSALOM KUMALO *sits alone and moody.*
Two DANCERS, *a man and a girl, dance to* LINDA's
singing.

LINDA [*sings "Who'll Buy"*].
 Who'll buy
 My juicy rutabagas?
 Who'll buy
 My yellow corn?
 Who'll buy asparagus or carrots or potatoes?
 Who wants my peppers and my ginger and tomatoes,
 The best you bit into
 Since you were born?
 If you want to make a supper dish fit for a king
 Look over what I offer, I offer everything!
 So try my, buy my
 Black-eyed peas;
 The garden of Eden
 Had nothing like these!
 You'll feel like flying, like a bird on the wing;
 You'll stay up there like a kite on a string:
 They're satisfactory, and they got a sting!
 So try my,
 Buy my
 Asparagus, yellow corn, black-eyed peas, tomatoes,
     potatoes, beans, and rutabagas—
 Who'll buy
 My oranges and melons?
 Who'll buy
 My prickly pears?
 Who'll pay shillings for my lemons and persimmons,
 Who wants apricots and nectarines and trimmin's,
 The best you laid lip to
 The last ten years?
 I haven't got a license, so I can undersell,

I haven't got a license, so I treat you well!
So try my, buy my
Pure veld honey!
In the garden of Eden
They never use money!
You'll feel like flying, like a bat out of hell,
You'll own high heaven and a landing field as well!
The apples of Paradise, they always jell!
So try my—

MATTHEW *and* JOHANNES.

Try my—

LINDA.

Buy my—

OTHERS.

Buy my—

LINDA.

Oranges, prickly pears, apricots, nectarines, tangerines, apples, groundnuts, bananas—

Buy my—

OTHERS.

Buy my—

LINDA.

Oh my—

OTHERS.

Oh my—

LINDA.

Oh my—

OTHERS.

Oh my—

LINDA.

Buy my—oh my—oh my—

JOHANNES. I'll take 'em! I'll take 'em all! You're off the market!

LINDA [*falling into* JOHANNES' *arms*]. Sold!

MATTHEW. Just one little technical problem here if you don't mind, lady. You said you had no license?

LINDA. That's right. No license. Just Johannes' little wild honey, that's all.

MATTHEW. Officer, arrest that woman and bring her before the court. [JOHANNES *brings* LINDA *down front as if to face the judge.*] In the first place, what is a —h'm—rutabaga?

LINDA. It's a vegetable, Your Lordship.

MATTHEW. You don't give that impression.

LINDA. What impression do I give, Your Lordship?

MATTHEW. Are you trying to corrupt this court?

LINDA. Yes, sir.

MATTHEW. Twenty years, hard!

JOHANNES. Your Lordship, your wig is dirty, your logic is full of holes, and your monocle don't fit you!

MATTHEW. I find you in contempt—hic! Damn that whisky and soda.

JOHANNES. What's the trouble, Your Monocle?

MATTHEW. Young man, did you address me as Your Monocle?

JOHANNES. Yes, Your Monocle.

MATTHEW. Forty years, hard!

JOHANNES. You got a little mixed here, Your Whisky and Soda! You're supposed to be trying this young lady!

MATTHEW. That's right. [*To* ROSE, *who is sitting on table.*] Make a note the young man's right. Hic. Put in that hic. That was a British hic. Put it in.

ROSE [*imaginary writing of notes*]. Yes, sir!

MATTHEW. Where's the persecution? Young man, will you persecute this young lady?

JOHANNES. I'd love to, Your Rutabaga. When do I begin?

MATTHEW. Woman, have you got anything to say?

LINDA. I throw myself on the mercy of the court. [*She throws herself into* JOHANNES' *arms.*]

MATTHEW. I'm the court, see! Throw yourself on me—not him!

ROSE. I throw myself on the mercy of the court! [ROSE *throws herself into* MATTHEW'S *arms.*]

JOHANNES. I demand justice!

MATTHEW. Remove that woman out of your pocket! And somebody scrape the court stenographer from the Judge's vest! Young man, you got justice, we all got justice! Justice is when the black man digs and the white man carries the brief case! Justice is when the black woman cooks and the white woman has breakfast in bed! If you want anything extra—you pay for it!

JOHANNES. Your Honor, would you accept a little money?

MATTHEW. What! Me, sir? A judge, sir? Take money, sir?—Yes, sir! All right, scrape her off your vest, Johannes! And get out of here, all of you! We'll be with you in a minute! Wait for us.

LINDA. Where are we going to wait?

MATTHEW. Outside!

LINDA. Matthew!

MATTHEW. Outside, I said! [*They go, leaving* JOHANNES, ABSALOM, *and* MATTHEW.] Wake up, Absalom! Now to begin with—how do we get in?

JOHANNES. You don't have to break into the house, I tell you; he never locks his doors, day or night.

MATTHEW. Why not?

JOHANNES. I don't know. He's got some theory. He says, "If anybody wants what I've got he can come in and take it."

ABSALOM. Then why would we need a gun when we go there?

MATTHEW. Because nobody ever knows when he's going to need a gun! And you've got a gun—and we might as well have it along!

ABSALOM. But Johannes says there won't be anybody there! The white man went for a trip somewhere and the servant gets home late every night.

MATTHEW. That's the way we think it's going to be, but if somebody happens to come in we don't want to take chances.

LINDA [*off stage*]. Matthew!

MATTHEW [*calling*]. We'll be right with you, pretty! [*To* ABSALOM.] So don't come without it. We might need it. What do you say?

ABSALOM. I think it's better without the gun.

MATTHEW. Well, I don't, see? And if you don't bring it you're not in on this at all. Look, I'm going to get to those new gold fields! And I'm going on my own. Now, if you want to help us raise the money to get there, you're in; you come along! But if you're scared to carry that cheap revolver of yours you're no use to us. So bring it or stay home.

LINDA [*off stage*]. Matthew!

MATTHEW [*to* JOHANNES]. We'll get rid of the girls. Think it over, country boy.

[JOHANNES *and* MATTHEW *go out to the right.* IRINA, *a young and pretty Zulu girl, enters from the left. She sees* ABSALOM *and crosses to him.*]

IRINA [*timidly*]. Absalom?

ABSALOM. Irina? What do you want?

IRINA. I came to tell you something.

ABSALOM. Yes?

IRINA. Something about the parole officer.

ABSALOM. What happened?

IRINA. He came to the cabin asking for you. And I lied. I had to lie. I told you were at work and things were going well. But he'll be at the factory tomorrow—and if you're not there—

ABSALOM. I don't think I will be there.

IRINA. What will happen to you, Absalom?

ABSALOM. I won't be there. I won't be anywhere where he can find me. Ever again.

IRINA. What will happen to us? You and me?

ABSALOM. We'll live in a better place than Shanty Town.

IRINA. When?

ABSALOM. When I come back.

IRINA. Are you going away?

ABSALOM. Yes, but not from you! To get something for you and me! Look, Irina, suppose I went home with you now and went to work tomorrow. What kind of life would we have?

IRINA. Like others.

ABSALOM. Yes, like the others. Shanty Town. Crawling with boarders and bugs and children. You'd have your baby, and I'd keep on at the factory, and you'd have another baby, and we'd live in the same shack and pay our taxes and our rent and pretty soon we're sleeping four in a room. Ten in a room. Filth. Nothing. And that's our fun. That's our life forever. That's what we get. Isn't it?

IRINA. I'll keep our place clean, Absalom.

ABSALOM. Nobody can keep those places clean! And I can't stand it. I don't want it that way—I love you, Irina. I want you to have something better than that.

IRINA. What could we have?

ABSALOM. I've never been able to bring you a gift, Irina. We've always had—not quite enough to live on. Even the way we live. I want to come back with

enough so we can set up a little shop, and be free
of work gangs, and keep our own house—

IRINA. Where could you get money for this?

ABSALOM. In the new gold fields. There's a new rich
strike, Irina. If you go there as a free man, not in
a labor gang, you can sometimes get ahead and save
something—

IRINA [*her arms about him*]. I'm afraid for you. Come
home with me.

ABSALOM. Wait for me, Irina. I'll come home when I
have something—when I am something.

IRINA. Where will you get money to go to the mines?

ABSALOM. We'll get it.

IRINA. You won't steal again?

ABSALOM. We'll get it.

IRINA. Oh, Absalom, Absalom, if you were caught once
more they could keep you from me a whole lifetime!
Come home with me, Absalom, come home with me!

ABSALOM. Oh, God damn this world! [*He kisses her.*]
Yes, I'll come with you.

[*They start out as* MATTHEW, *followed by* JOHANNES,
re-enters.]

MATTHEW. Where are you going, Absalom? [*He sees
Irina.*] It's his cook! It's his little cookie!

ABSALOM. I'm out of it.

MATTHEW. She gives the orders, huh? . . . You could be
rich, you know—

ABSALOM. I'm on parole. You're not.

MATTHEW. One more black boy loose in a gold field,
they'd never locate you.

ABSALOM. But even if we make money in the gold fields,
we still have to come back here. And they'll get me.

MATTHEW. Why would they? You'll change your name,
you'll be wearing new clothes, you'll have cash in
your pocket, you can walk up and buy a shack of
your own. There won't be any Absalom Kumalo.

There'll be a new man! A man—not somebody's
dumb ox!

ABSALOM. He's right, Irina—wait for me. It'll take a
little time, but wait for me.

IRINA. Please—

ABSALOM. Go now, Irina. I'll be back.

IRINA. Oh, Absalom—

ABSALOM. Go, Irina!

IRINA. Yes, I'll go. [*She goes out.*]

MATTHEW. That's more like it!

JOHANNES. You know what I heard? I heard there's
sometimes loose gold you can pan out of a river if
you get there before the land's all fenced.

MATTHEW. Some places you can take just a kitchen
pan and wash the dirt around in it and there's gold
at the bottom.

JOHANNES. It's that way beyond Rigval clove.

MATTHEW. And then, by God, we'll live like men! Johannes, you bring along that machinery you talked
about?

JOHANNES. I've got it where I can pick it up quick.

MATTHEW. Then pick it up, and pick up your feet!
This is the best time.

[*The lights dim as they go out.*]

SCENE VII

IRINA's *hut in Shanty Town. We see the interior of
the hut and the city behind it.* ELAND *enters, followed
by* STEPHEN. ELAND *knocks at the door.*

ELAND [*at the door*]. Irina!

IRINA [*going to the door*]. Come in, sir.

[ELAND *and* STEPHEN *enter her room.*]

ELAND. Thank you, Irina. This is the Reverend Stephen Kumalo, Irina, Absalom's father. I have told him about you, and he wishes to see you and to see Absalom. We'll go on from here to the factory. Absalom's there, of course?

IRINA. No, sir.

ELAND. But—when I was here—two days ago—

IRINA. Yes, sir. I lied to you.

ELAND. Where is he?

IRINA. I do not know. He's gone, I don't know where.

ELAND. This is another of my failures, then. They're like water. They live together, they get a child, they engage to marry, and the next day both have forgotten.

STEPHEN. Could I be alone with her a moment?

ELAND. I'll wait. [*He goes out.*]

STEPHEN. Irina?

IRINA. Yes—umfundisi.

STEPHEN. Perhaps my son never spoke of me to you. We love him very much, his mother and I—and I have come to Johannesburg thinking I might find him. Would you help me to find him?

IRINA. Yes, umfundisi.

STEPHEN. He has lived here with you for some time?

IRINA. Yes.

STEPHEN. You were not married in the church?

IRINA. No, umfundisi.

STEPHEN. And you are to have a child?

IRINA. Yes.

STEPHEN. Why has he left you?

IRINA. I—do not know.

STEPHEN. You distrust me?

IRINA. No, umfundisi.

STEPHEN. Do you have a family?

IRINA. I have no one.

STEPHEN. But you lived somewhere—before you met Absalom.

IRINA. I lived in Sophiatown.

STEPHEN. Alone?

IRINA [*picking nervously at the back of a chair*]. Nobody lives alone in Sophiatown.

STEPHEN. You lived with your first—husband?

IRINA. Yes. With my first.

STEPHEN. How many have there been?

IRINA. Three.

STEPHEN. Three. And now you will seek a fourth.

IRINA. No. I wait for Absalom.

STEPHEN. I think you would do anything! You would go to anyone! I am an old man, Absalom's father, but you would come to me if I asked you! Anything!

IRINA. No. I would not.

STEPHEN. You think an umfundisi is not a man? What if I desired you—with my whole body? What if I desire you now?

IRINA. You?

STEPHEN. Yes. I.

IRINA. It would not be right.

STEPHEN. Was it right before? With the others?

IRINA. No. It was not right.

STEPHEN. Then why would you not be willing with me?

IRINA. I do not know.

STEPHEN. Then you would be willing? [*She is silent.*] Would you be willing?

IRINA. No, I do not know. [*She twists her hands, looks away.*]

STEPHEN [*savagely*]. Speak! Tell me!

IRINA. I could be willing.

STEPHEN. Yes, you are a woman who would go to anyone.

IRINA. Why did you come here? How would I know

what you think—or what you want? I don't know
what power you have—or what you will do! I'm
alone here. I'm to have a child, and Absalom is
gone— [*She sits on the chair in a passion of crying.*]
and I love him! I want only Absalom. He brought
me only trouble—but I love him!

STEPHEN [*after a pause*]. Yes, I was wrong. I should not
have put you to such a test. Will you forgive me?
We all do what we must do. Not what we wish but
what we can. [*He crosses closer to her.*] Do you forgive me?

IRINA. Yes, umfundisi.

STEPHEN. I will go now, Irina, but I will come again.
I'm searching for my son. If I find him I will come
to tell you. My address is on this paper. [*He hands
her a slip of paper.*] If he comes back to you, please
let me know.

IRINA. Yes, umfundisi.

[*He goes out.*]

IRINA [*sings "Trouble Man"*].
   Since you came first to me,
      Dear one, glad one,
   You bring all the worst to me,
      Near one, sad one;
   There's trouble in your coming,
      Trouble in your laughter,
   There's trouble in your going,
      And trouble after.

   Since you were near to me,
      Lost one, mad one,
   No other is dear to me,
      Loved one, bad one;
   I love your dark silence,

Love your bright laughter
I love the trouble you bring me,
The crying after!

Trouble man, trouble man,
Since you've been gone,
Somehow I manage
Living here alone;
All day long
You don't catch me weeping
But, oh, God help me
When it comes time for sleeping,
When it comes time for sleeping here alone!

Trouble man, trouble man, walking out there,
Maybe in a strange place, God knows where,
Maybe in a strange town, hurrying and walking,
Listen to my blood and my bones here talking,
Listen to the blood in my hands and feet,
Finding you out on a far, strange street;
Finding the footprints out where you ran,
Asking, "Aren't you coming home, trouble man?
Trouble man! Trouble man! Trouble man! Trouble
    man!"
Saying, "All day long you don't catch me weeping,
But, oh, God help me when it comes time for sleep-
    ing,
When it comes time for sleeping here alone!"
    Trouble man! Trouble man!

[*The lights dim.*]

SCENE VIII

Kitchen in ARTHUR JARVIS' *home. As the lights come up we see a* SERVANT *placing dishes on the pantry shelves. We then see* JOHANNES, ABSALOM, *and* MATTHEW *entering from the left, handkerchiefs tied over their faces.* JOHANNES *is carrying an iron bar,* ABSALOM *carries a revolver.*

SERVANT [*turning as he hears the noise of their entrance*]. What do you want?

JOHANNES. We want money and clothes!

SERVANT. It's Johannes! I know you! You cannot do such a thing!

JOHANNES. Do you want to die?

SERVANT [*running to the door and opening it*]. Master! Master!

[JOHANNES *strikes the* SERVANT *over the head with the iron bar; the* SERVANT *falls.* ARTHUR JARVIS *comes into the doorway,* ABSALOM *fires the revolver.* ARTHUR JARVIS *falls to the floor.*]

MATTHEW. Quick! Get out!

[*The three run to the left, stop in panic, turn and run off to the right. The lights go out.*]

CHORUS [*sings "Murder in Parkwold"*].
  Murder in Parkwold!

WOMAN [*speaking*].
  He was shot at night!

CHORUS.
  Murder in Parkwold!

WOMAN [*speaking*].

Nobody knows why or by whom!

WHITES.

Murder in Parkwold!

MAN [*speaking*].

There was one shot only!

CHORUS.

Murder in Parkwold!

WOMAN [*speaking*].

He went to help the servant!

CHORUS.

Murder in Parkwold!

MAN [*speaking*].

The servant had called out!

WHITES.

Murder in Parkwold!

CHORUS.

Murder in Parkwold!

ALL.

In Parkwold, among the great houses,

Among the lighted streets and the wide gardens.

WOMAN [*speaking*].

There are not enough police!

[*The lights dim. The* CHORUS *goes out. From off-stage right comes a man's voice singing.*]

MAN.

Murder in Parkwold!

ANOTHER [*off-stage left*].

Murder in Parkwold!

[*The lights come up immediately on the next scene.*]

SCENE IX

ARTHUR JARVIS' *library. As the lights come up we see* JAMES JARVIS *seated in a chair by a desk, motionless and alone.* ELAND *knocks and then enters.*

ELAND. Mr. Jarvis? Mr. Jarvis?

JARVIS [*looking up*]. Yes, Eland.

ELAND. I could come later if I disturb you.

JARVIS. No—no. Come in.

ELAND. I have seen the police. They have arrested Pafuri, the one who used to work in your son's house —and he has been identified.

JARVIS. By whom?

ELAND. By the servant who was struck.

JARVIS. I think I remember the name. Pafuri. Johannes Pafuri. Yes, he was houseboy here. I suppose he could be guilty—not that it would help to fix the guilt. Our son is dead. Arthur is dead and punishment will not bring him back.

ELAND. The boy denies being involved, but he looks very guilty.

JARVIS. One thing I hope the police will remember; no man is to be punished unless guilty.

ELAND. They'll make very certain before they act, Mr. Jarvis. They assured me of that.

JARVIS. I differed sharply with my son concerning our policy toward the blacks, but in this I want what he would have wanted—that the guilty feel the penalty —no man else. I had quarreled with my son, I suppose you know that. I wish we'd had a chance to patch up that quarrel.

ELAND. I'm sure it wasn't serious.

JARVIS. Yes. It was serious. Over Negro equality. [*He rises.*] And the irony of it, that an advocate of Negro equality should have been killed by a Negro. There's only one course with them—a strong hand and a firm policy. They understand nothing but discipline, respect nothing else.

ELAND. There are good and bad among them.

JARVIS. Are there? At this moment I wonder.

ELAND. We can know them only by their actions. There was a man who came into this house with a pistol, came with intent to steal, and ended by committing murder. Let us find this one man and see that he is punished. Let us not blame the whole race.

JARVIS. You think he will be found?

ELAND. He will be found.

JARVIS. May he suffer as we suffer. As my wife suffers now.

ELAND. There's something I wanted to ask you, Mr. Jarvis. If you'd rather not stay in this house—

JARVIS. I want to stay here. This is where he worked. He was here when he heard the cry from the kitchen and ran to help.

ELAND. He will be a great loss to us. To our country and to me personally. As a parole officer—well, many times I'd have given up in despair except for him.

JARVIS. And yet they killed him. What would he have said about a crime like this?

ELAND. He would have said, "They live in such poverty and fear. They see no way out of their poverty or their fear and they grow desperate."

JARVIS. Yes. [*He sits.*] It sounds like him.

ELAND. You wish to be here alone?

JARVIS. Yes—I wish to be here alone.

[*The lights dim.* ELAND *goes out. Off-stage we hear again the cries repeated.*]

MAN [*sings, off-stage right*].
  Murder in Parkwold!
ANOTHER [*sings, off-stage left.*]
  Murder in Parkwold!

SCENE X

A street in Shanty Town. As the lights come up the street is empty. A MAN *and a* WOMAN *run through, knocking at doors. The* ZULUS *come out of their houses and gather in groups around three newspapers, reading intently. There is a whistle from off right— the street empties, and the houses go dark. A* POLICE-MAN *passes through, disappears. The people emerge from the houses, cluster again around the papers. A* WHITE MAN *and* WOMAN *enter from the right.*

WOMAN. These streets are full of evil; I'm afraid!
MAN. It's all right, take my arm. This is a shabby neighborhood.
WOMAN. Hush! [*The* POLICEMAN *re-enters from left and meets the couple center-stage. The* WOMAN *speaks with relief.*] Good evening, officer.
[*The* POLICEMAN *and the* WHITE COUPLE *go out left. The* NEGRO CHORUS *sings.*]

1ST MAN.
  It is fear!
2ND MAN.
  It is fear!

1ST WOMAN.
It is fear!
3RD MAN.
It is fear!
2ND MAN.
Who can enjoy the lovely land,
The seventy years,
The sun that pours down on the earth,
When there is fear in the heart?

[*A group of* WHITE SINGERS *enters.*]

WHITE MAN.
Who can walk quietly in the dusk
When behind the dusk there are whispers
And reckless hands?
WHITE CHORUS.
Yes, we fear them.
For they are many and we are few!
NEGRO QUARTET.
Who can be content
When he dares not raise his voice?
WHITE CHORUS.
It is fear!
NEGRO QUARTET.
For fear of the whip, the guard, the loss of his
house?
WHITE CHORUS.
It is fear!
NEGRO CHORUS.
For fear of the mines,
And the prison,
And the cell from which there is no return?
Yes, we fear them,
Though we are many and they are few!

WHITE.

Who can lie peacefully abed

When the dark without window is troubled

By those who hate you for what you are and what
you do?

NEGRO.

You think you know what it is to fear or to hate?

What is there you have not taken from us except
hate and fear?

Yes, we fear them, though we are many and they
are few!

WHITE.

Men are not safe in the streets,

Not safe in their houses.

NEGRO.

It is fear!

WHITE.

There are brutal murders.

NEGRO.

It is fear!

WHITE.

Robberies!

NEGRO.

It is fear!

WHITE.

Tonight again a man lies dead!

NEGRO.

Yes, it is fear!

WHITE.

Yes, it is fear!

NEGRO.

Fear of the few for the many!

WHITE.

Fear of the few for the many!

NEGRO.
It is fear!

WHITE.
It is fear!

NEGRO.
It is fear!

WHITE.
It is fear!

ALL.
Fear of the few for the many,
Fear of the many for the few!

[*The lights go out.*]

SCENE XI

The lights come up on ELAND, *who is pacing up and down.* STEPHEN *enters from the right, crosses to* ELAND.

STEPHEN. I came as soon as I could, sir. You say—my son is here? Absalom is here?

ELAND. Yes.

STEPHEN. Why is he here?

ELAND. It's not proved, of course—but the charge is that he killed Arthur Jarvis.

STEPHEN. He killed—

ELAND. It could not be worse. For me or you or him. Forgive me. What I feel is nothing—I know that. Only it's my life work to help. And this may destroy it all.

STEPHEN. Absalom is accused of killing Arthur Jarvis?

ELAND. Remember, it's not proved about Absalom, and I don't believe it! It cannot be true.

STEPHEN. Let me speak to Absalom. [*The lights come up on center stage; we see* ABSALOM *sitting on a stool in a cell, facing away from the entrance.*] My child, my child!

ABSALOM [*turning*]. My father!

STEPHEN. At last I have found you.

ABSALOM. Yes, my father.

STEPHEN. I have searched in every place for you—and I find you here. Why have they charged you with this terrible crime? [*There is no answer.*] Answer me, my child.

[ABSALOM *is still silent.*]

ELAND. You should rise when your father speaks to you, Absalom.

ABSALOM. Yes, sir. Oh, my father, my father! [*He reaches through the bars to his father.*]

STEPHEN. My son, my son, if I had only come sooner! But we shall make it all well yet, Absalom; for the courts are just, and when they have found that you did not kill it will be only a light punishment. [AB-SALOM *drops his father's hands.*] And when it ends you will come back to Ndotsheni and be content in our quietness. For you were a boy without guile and without anger, at home where there are hills and trees, not in these streets where men must live by their wits and without scruple. The hills are as beautiful as ever, Absalom. You will be happy there again.

ABSALOM. My father—

STEPHEN. Yes? [*Silence.*] Yes?

ABSALOM. I cannot say it.

STEPHEN. I know you so well, Absalom, that I know you could not be guilty of this crime, and so you need not fear what the judge will say. You will live again at Ndotsheni.

ABSALOM. I shall never come home.

STEPHEN. Why, my son?

ABSALOM. Because I am guilty.

STEPHEN. Of what, my son?

ABSALOM [*after a pause*]. I killed the white man.

STEPHEN. But—this cannot be true. He was shot—in his house.

ABSALOM. Yes.

ELAND. There are three men accused in this murder, Absalom. Do you try to shield someone?

ABSALOM. No, sir. There were three of us, Matthew Kumalo and Johannes Pafuri and I. It was Johannes who struck the servant, but it was I who carried the revolver, and—

STEPHEN. And—you killed this man?

ABSALOM. I did not mean to kill him. We thought he would not be there. Then suddenly he was there, and I was frightened—and—

[*A* GUARD *comes into the shadow from the right.*]

ELAND. It is time for us to go.

STEPHEN. My son, I stand here, and see you, and a kind of dizziness has come over me, so that I am not sure what is real, or whether this is a true place or in a dream. Did you tell me, you, my son Absalom, that you had—had killed—a man?

ABSALOM. Yes, my father, it is true.

GUARD. I'm sorry, umfundisi, it's time for you to go.

STEPHEN. May I come again?

GUARD. Yes, umfundisi. At certain hours on certain days. The hours are ended for this day.

STEPHEN. Absalom—

ABSALOM. Yes, my father.

STEPHEN. Stay well, my child.

ABSALOM. Go well, my father.

[STEPHEN *turns to go. The lights fade.*]

SCENE XII

The lights come up on STEPHEN *in his Shanty Town lodging, where he sits at a table trying to write.* ALEX, *in the cot near him, wakes and speaks.*

ALEX. Uncle Stephen?

STEPHEN. Yes, Alex.

ALEX. Is it very late?

STEPHEN. Yes, very late.

ALEX. But you are not asleep.

STEPHEN. No. I must write a letter.

ALEX. Do you know the best thing that ever happened to me?

STEPHEN. No.

ALEX. These shoes you bought me, with the brass toes and the brass heels. Would it be all right if I kept them in bed with me?

STEPHEN. If they're clean.

ALEX. I cleaned them on the quilt. I can see my face in the brass. I could walk all the way to Ndotsheni wearing these shoes!

STEPHEN. Please, Alex, lie and sleep. Or be silent. This is a hard letter.

ALEX. Who do you write to, Uncle Stephen?

STEPHEN. I write to my wife in Ndotsheni. To the mother at home. O *Tixo, Tixo!* O God of all lost people and of those who go toward death, tell me what to say to her! How can I say this to the mother, O my *Tixo?* That he has done this thing! That I cannot bring him home! That he will perhaps never, never come home!

ALEX. Uncle Stephen—who will not come home?

STEPHEN. My son Absalom.

ALEX. But Uncle Stephen, you are an umfundisi, and you can ask God to help you, and he will surely help you.

STEPHEN. I don't know, Alex.

[*He sings "Lost in the Stars."*]

Before Lord God made the sea and the land
He held all the stars in the palm of his hand,
And they ran through his fingers like grains of sand,
   And one little star fell alone.

Then the Lord God hunted through the wide night air
For the little dark star on the wind down there—
And he stated and promised he'd take special care
   So it wouldn't get lost again.

Now a man don't mind if the stars grow dim
And the clouds blow over and darken him,
So long as the Lord God's watching over them,
   Keeping track how it all goes on.

But I've been walking through the night and the day
Till my eyes get weary and my head turns grey,
And sometimes it seems maybe God's gone away,
Forgetting the promise that we heard him say—
And we're lost out here in the stars—
Little stars, big stars,
Blowing through the night,
And we're lost out here in the stars.

STEPHEN *and* CHORUS.

Little stars,

Big stars,
Blowing through the night,
And we're lost out here in the stars.

CURTAIN

Act two

SCENE I

The curtain goes up on a dark and bare stage. The CHORUS *enters in the dark. The lights come up after the music has begun.*

LEADER *and* CHORUS [*singing "The Wild Justice"*].
Have you fished for a fixed star
    With the lines of its light?
Have you dipped the moon from the sea
    With the cup of night?
Have you caught the rain's bow in a pool
    And shut it in?
Go hunt the wild justice down
    To walk with men.

Have you plotted the high cold course of a heron's
    flying,
Or the thought of an old man dying,
Or the covered labyrinth of
Why you love where you love?
Or, if one love you,
Why your love is true?
Only for a little, then,
Tease the wild justice down to dwell with men.

When the first judge sat in his place
And the murderer held his breath
With fear of death in his face,
Fear of death for death,
And all that could be said, for and against, was said,
And the books were balanced, and two, not one, were
    dead,
Was justice caught in this net?
Not yet, no, not quite yet, not yet.

No, tug first at the fixed star
    On the lines of its light,
Sieve the moon up out of the sea
    With the black seine of night,
Snare first the rain's bow in a pool
    And close it in.
The wild justice is not found
    In the haunts of men.
The wild justice is not found in the haunts of men!

[*The lights come up on* JOHN's *tobacco shop.* JOHN
stands behind the counter, STEPHEN *sits before him.*]

JOHN. When you go before a judge you have to have a
lawyer. Now a lawyer's paid to lie and make it sound
like the truth. I'm getting a good lawyer. A white
man's lawyer. And he'll do all he can for all three.
There's no use trying to defend one alone—they all
have to stick together in this. If they do that there's
a good chance, because the fact is there's not much
evidence against them.

STEPHEN. There's an identification, by the servant.

JOHN. Well, when our lawyer gets through with that,
maybe not. You see, the only one the servant says he
identified is Johannes Pafuri. He says he knew him
because of his eyes. He's got a peculiar twitch over
his eye, and the servant could see his eyes, even with

the mask on—so he says he's sure it was Johannes.
On the other hand, suppose it was somebody else
with a twitch over his eye? With the rest of his face
covered it would be hard to be sure it was Johannes,
wouldn't it? Well, the lawyer will bring that up.
And that'll shake the identification. And there's no
other evidence against them, positively none.

STEPHEN. Except that—they were there. They will have
to say that they were there.

JOHN. Why?

STEPHEN. Because it is the truth.

JOHN. The truth! Why would they tell the truth in a
court? Do they want to get themselves hanged? No,
if they all say they know nothing about it, they'll
get off, as sure as God's got whiskers.

STEPHEN. But in a court there is a plea—guilty or not
guilty.

JOHN. Yes. They'll plead not guilty. Everybody does.

STEPHEN. But Absalom says he will plead guilty.

JOHN. Good God! Why?

STEPHEN. Because he is guilty.

JOHN. Look, Stephen, if they don't all tell the same
story, anything can happen to them. Surely you see
that. Let them prove the boys guilty if they can. It's
not up to the defense to hand 'em their case on a
platter.

STEPHEN. I haven't told Absalom what to say. But he
says he will not lie again. That he's done his last
evil, and from now on he won't tell a lie or do any
wrong. And so he will tell them that he was there.
And that he shot Arthur Jarvis.

JOHN. Will he tell them Matthew was there—and
Johannes?

STEPHEN. Yes.

JOHN. Well—that changes everything. You better fix

that, brother, and fix it fast, or I give you my word
we'll fix Absalom. Talk to him, brother.

STEPHEN. I have. He will plead guilty.

JOHN. A man who pleads guilty to murder receives the
punishment of the first degree—and that's hanging
by your neck with a sack over your head. They don't
fool about that.

STEPHEN. He has already made a confession. He has admitted the whole charge.

JOHN. He can deny that. He can say he was out of his
mind—anything.

STEPHEN. And Matthew and Johannes will plead not
guilty?

JOHN. Of course they will. That's part of the game.
This is what happens in a court, Stephen. The defendant may be guilty as hell but he goes in and
pleads not guilty and his lawyer tries to make the
evidence look as if he's not guilty. The prosecution
may be weak as hell but it goes in and tries to make
things look as if the defendant's guilty as a hyena.
Each one tries to foul up the witnesses on the other
side and make his own witnesses look good. If the
defense piles up the most points, why fine, the old
sheep-face of a judge says he's not guilty. If the
prosecution piles up the most points, why old sheep-
face says hang him up. It's a game. Truth has nothing to do with it. Now if Absalom pleads guilty it
would make it look bad for all three—but don't let
him do it, brother, because I'm going to get Matthew
out of this, and anything Absalom says is going to be
used against him. By me, if necessary. So talk to
him, Stephen, talk to him as you never talked to
anybody before. He doesn't want to die—and you
don't want him to die. If you want him to live, tell
him to plead not guilty.

[*The lights dim.* JOHN *goes out.* STEPHEN *is left musing alone.*]

STEPHEN [*sings "The Soliloquy"*].
What have I come to here,
At this crossing of paths?
Must he tell a lie and live—
Or speak truth and die?
And, if this is so,
What can I say to my son?
O *Tixo, Tixo,* help me!

Often when he was young
    I have come to him and said,
"Speak truly, evade nothing, what you have done
    Let it be on your head."

And he heeded me not at all,
    Like rain he ran through my hands,
Concealing, as a boy will, taking what was not his,
    Evading commands.

For he seemed to hear none of my words;
    Turning, shifting, he ran
Through a tangle of nights and days,
Till he was lost to my sight, and ran far into evil—
And evil ways,
And he was stricken—
And struck back,
And he loved, and he was desperate with love and
    fear and anger,
And at last he came
To this—
O God of the humble and the broken—

O God of those who have nothing, nothing,
    nothing—
To this—
To the death of a man!
To the death of a man!

A man he had given to death.
    Then my words came back to him,
And he said, "I shall do no more evil, tell no more
    untruth;
    I shall keep my father's ways, and remember
    them."

And can I go to him now
    And say, "My son, take care,
Tell no truth in this court, lest it go ill with you
    here;
    Keep to the rules, beware"?

And yet if I say again,
    "It shall not profit a man
If he gain the whole world and lose his own soul,"
    I shall lose Absalom then.
    I shall lose Absalom then.
[*He speaks.*]
    I must find some other way—
Some other hope.
My son did not mean to kill his son,
Did not mean to kill.
[*He sings.*]
    O *Tixo, Tixo,* help me!
[*He speaks.*]
    To whom can I appeal?
[*He sings.*]

O *Tixo, Tixo,* help me!

[*He speaks.*]

Where can I turn now?

[*He sings.*]

O *Tixo, Tixo,* help me!

[*The lights dim out, and come up on the door of a well-kept residence in Johannesburg.* STEPHEN *goes to the door, knocks, gets no answer, and starts to go.* JAMES JARVIS *opens the door.*]

JARVIS. Yes? Did you knock?

STEPHEN. I—I'm sorry, sir. I—expected a servant to answer—I—

JARVIS. There are no servants here today, umfundisi. Did you wish to see one of them?

STEPHEN. No, umfundisi. I wished to see you.

JARVIS. Yes?

STEPHEN. I— [*His body fails him. His cane clatters to the ground and he sits on the step.* JARVIS *comes down to him.*] Forgive me, umnumzana— [*His hat lies beside him, he reaches for it, leaves it.*]

JARVIS. Are you ill, umfundisi?

[STEPHEN *doesn't answer, he is trembling, looking at the ground; finally he looks up and speaks.*]

STEPHEN. Forgive me—I—shall recover.

JARVIS. Do you wish water? Or food, perhaps? Are you hungry?

[STEPHEN *reaches for his cane, with another effort gets to his feet.* JARVIS *stands watching him, finally picks up his battered old hat and hands it to him.*]

STEPHEN. Thank you, sir. I am sorry. I shall go now.

JARVIS. But you said you wished to see me.

STEPHEN. Yes, sir.

JARVIS. Well, then—?

STEPHEN. I have no words to say it.

JARVIS. You are in fear of me. I do not know why.

STEPHEN. I cannot tell it, umnumzana.

JARVIS. I wish to help whenever I can. Is it so heavy a thing?

STEPHEN. It is the heaviest thing of all my years.

JARVIS. You need not be afraid. I try to be just.

STEPHEN. Umnumzana—this thing that is the heaviest thing of all my years—it is also the heaviest thing of all your years.

JARVIS. You can mean only one thing. But I still do not understand.

STEPHEN [*slowly*]. It was my son that killed your son.

[JARVIS *turns and walks away—then comes back to* STEPHEN.]

JARVIS. Why did you come?

STEPHEN. There were three who went to rob the house, umnumzana. Two of them have lied and said they were not there. My son has told truth, that he was there, that he fired the revolver that killed your son. He will die for this truthtelling, the lawyer thinks.

JARVIS. Not for his truthtelling.

STEPHEN. Umnumzana, could you intercede for him?

JARVIS. One does not seek to influence a court.

STEPHEN. He did not mean to kill. And he tells truth. Is there not a core of good in him who tells truth?

JARVIS. My son left his doors always open. He trusted his fellow men. And for this your son killed him.

STEPHEN. He never meant to kill. But the revolver was in his hand and he heard someone coming and was frightened.

JARVIS. Have you thought what it is for me that my son is dead?

STEPHEN. I have tried. I have thought of—my son—

JARVIS. Have you thought what it is for his mother? His mother will die of this. It's in her face.

STEPHEN. I know. I can see the face of my son's mother.
Forgive me, umnumzana—I know what this is to you.
But—if he were only to live—even shut up—even far
from us.

JARVIS. I try to be just. I know what it is to lose a son.
But—I say again—one does not try to influence a
court. And even if the judge were merciful, mercy
can be pitiless. If your son went free ten thousand
others might be misled into the death he escaped.
Better that one be punished where punishment is
deserved—and the ten thousand be warned.

STEPHEN. I think he did not mean evil, umnumzana.
And to die—when he is loved—

JARVIS. I know about death.

STEPHEN. If I could take him back to his home, umnumzana! Away from Johannesburg. He grew up in
Ndotsheni. Among the hills. There was no evil in
him then. From our house we could see up through
the clove to your great house. You were kind to the
folk who worked the little farms. Be kind again. A
terrible thing has befallen my people. We are lost.
Not many have found their way to the Christ, and
those who have not are lost. My son was lost. This
would not have happened if there were not the gold
mines, and the great city your people have built, and
the little hope we have.

JARVIS. Umfundisi, there are two races in South Africa.
One is capable of mastery and self-control—the other
is not. One is born to govern, the other to be gov-
erned. One is capable of culture and the arts of civilization—the other is not. The difference between us
is greater than that I live on a hill and you live in
the valley. If my son had killed your son I would
not have come to you for mercy. Nor to the judge.
Whether it were my son or yours, I would have said,
let him answer the law!

STEPHEN. You—you could save him—

JARVIS. You have neither heard nor understood me! There is only a handful of whites in South Africa to control the great tide of blacks—and the blacks have no control of their own! They have no mind to it— and no mind for it! It's their way to run and evade and lie and strike down in the dark! Those who will not keep order must be kept in order! Those who lift their hands to kill must know that the penalty for death is death!

STEPHEN [*humbly*]. Umnumzana—I read my Testament carefully. Jesus has not said this.

JARVIS. No, he has not, but where there is government it's true. Have you more to say to me?

STEPHEN. No, umnumzana.

[JARVIS *turns to go in. The lights dim.*]

SCENE II

The lights come up on IRINA'S *hut. We see* IRINA *hanging some clothes on a clothesline.*

IRINA [*sings "Stay Well"*].
　If I tell truth to you,
　　My love, my own,
　Grief is your gift to me,
　　Grief alone,
　Wild passion at midnight,
　　Wild anger at dawn,
　Yet when you're absent
　　I weep you gone.

　Stay well, O keeper of my love,
　Go well, throughout all your days,

Your star be my luckiest star above,
Your ways the luckiest ways.
Since unto you my one love is given,
And since with you it will remain,
Though you bring fear of hell, despair of heaven,
Stay well, come well to my door again.

[STEPHEN *enters from the left, knocks and then calls.*]

STEPHEN. Irina?

IRINA. Yes?

STEPHEN. The trial will begin tomorrow. Do you wish
to be there?

IRINA. Could I see him?

STEPHEN. Yes. All those in the court will see him.

IRINA. Then I wish to go. Umfundisi—is anything sure?

STEPHEN. Nothing is sure. He will be tried. It's not
known what will come of it.

IRINA. He might go free?

STEPHEN. I wish I could say yes. He says he will plead
guilty. He says he will speak the truth. If he does I
think he will stay in the prison. For a long time.

IRINA. For a long time.

STEPHEN. For a very long time.

IRINA. So that I will never see him?

STEPHEN. It may be many years.

IRINA. Many years.

STEPHEN. Would you wait for him—if it were so long?

IRINA. Yes, umfundisi. I would wait.

STEPHEN. He has asked me—would you wish to marry
him in the prison—so that your child will have his
name?

IRINA. Yes.

STEPHEN. He wishes it.

IRINA [*running to him*]. Umfundisi—

STEPHEN. Yes?

IRINA. Will they kill him?

STEPHEN. It's not known yet.

IRINA. I want him to live! I want him to come back to me!

STEPHEN. Even if it's many years?

IRINA. Yes.

STEPHEN. And you will wait?

IRINA. Yes.

STEPHEN. Even if he does not come back at all?

IRINA. I will still wait.

STEPHEN. And when the desire is on you?

IRINA. I desire only him.

STEPHEN [*stroking her hair*]. I will come tomorrow for you. And I will tell him that you wish the marriage. Stay well, Irina.

IRINA. Go well, my father.

[STEPHEN *goes out.* IRINA *sings* "Stay Well."]

When you have fled from me,
   My love, my own,
I've waited quietly,
   Here alone.
Some come back at midnight,
   Or come back at dawn,
Now that you're absent
   I weep you gone.

Go well, though wild the road and far
Stay well through darkening days,
Your star be still my luckiest star,
Your ways the luckiest ways,
Though into storm your lone bark be driven,
Though my eyes ache for you in vain,
Though you bring fear at dawn, despair at even,

Stay well, come well to my door again.

[*The lights dim.*]

SCENE III

A courtroom. The JUDGE's *bench is at the left; the* JUDGE *is seated.* ABSALOM *and* MATTHEW *are in the prisoner's dock. In the courtroom are all those we have seen who are concerned with this case or related to the prisoners:* IRINA, LINDA, JOHN, STEPHEN, *the* SERVANT, *and many* ZULU SPECTATORS. JAMES JARVIS, ELAND, *and a number of* WHITES *sit on the opposite side of the courtroom. As the lights come up* JOHANNES PAFURI *is in the witness box, center, and* BURTON, *the defense lawyer, is questioning him.*

BURTON. Johannes, you have been identified as one of three masked men who entered the kitchen of Arthur Jarvis on October eighth, between eleven and twelve. Were you there at that time?

JOHANNES. No, sir.

BURTON. Where were you?

JOHANNES. At Mrs. Ndela's house, in End Street.

BURTON. How do you know you were there at eleven?

JOHANNES. Because we had been dancing at a place in High Street till nearly eleven, and at eleven we were at Mrs. Ndela's.

BURTON. Who else was there?

JOHANNES. Matthew Kumalo was there, and the girls Linda and Rose.

BURTON. The witness is excused. Will Matthew Kumalo take the stand? [MATTHEW KUMALO *comes down into witness box.*] Matthew Kumalo, you are accused of being one of three masked men who entered the kitchen of Arthur Jarvis on October eighth, between eleven and twelve. Were you there at that time?

MATTHEW. No, sir.

BURTON. Where were you?

MATTHEW. At Mrs. Ndela's, in End Street.

BURTON. You are sure of the time?

MATTHEW. Yes, sir. We had been dancing at the place in High Street, and when we came to Mrs. Ndela's she said, "You are late, but come in," and we saw that it was near eleven.

BURTON. Do you know Absalom Kumalo?

MATTHEW. Yes, sir. He is the son of my father's brother.

BURTON. Was he with you on this evening?

MATTHEW. No, sir.

BURTON. Do you know where he was?

MATTHEW. No, sir.

BURTON. The witness is excused for the moment. [MAT-THEW *steps back to the bench and sits.* BURTON *crosses to the* JUDGE.] Your Honor, I am about to call the third defendant, Absalom Kumalo. Before I do so I wish to explain that his plea of guilty is his own choice, and that I have not attempted to influence him in any way.

JUDGE. I understand, sir. You may proceed.

BURTON. Absalom Kumalo, will take the stand. [ABSA-LOM *does so.*] Absalom Kumalo, you are accused of being one of three masked men who entered the kitchen of Arthur Jarvis on October eighth, be-tween eleven and twelve in the evening. Were you there at that time?

ABSALOM. Yes, sir.

BURTON. Who were the two masked men with you?

ABSALOM. Matthew Kumalo and Johannes Pafuri.

BURTON. What was your purpose in going there?

ABSALOM. To steal something from the house.

BURTON. Why did you choose this day?

ABSALOM. Because Johannes said the house would be empty at that time.

BURTON. The same Johannes Pafuri here?

ABSALOM. Yes, sir.

BURTON. When did you three go to this house?

ABSALOM. It was after eleven at night.

BURTON. Did you go there disguised?

ABSALOM. We tied handkerchiefs over our mouths.

BURTON. And then?

ABSALOM. We went into the kitchen and there was a servant there.

BURTON. This man?

ABSALOM. Yes, that is the man.

BURTON. Tell the court what happened then.

ABSALOM. This man was afraid. He saw my revolver. He said, "What do you want?" Johannes said, "We want money and clothes." This man said, "You cannot do such a thing." Johannes said, "Do you want to die?" Then this man called out, "Master! Master!" and Johannes struck him over the head with the iron bar.

BURTON. Did he call again?

ABSALOM. He made no sound.

BURTON. What did you do?

ABSALOM. No, we were silent—and listened.

BURTON. Where was your revolver?

ABSALOM. In my hand.

BURTON. And then?

ABSALOM. Then a white man came into the doorway.

BURTON. And then?

ABSALOM. I was frightened. I fired the revolver.

BURTON. And then?

ABSALOM. The white man fell.

BURTON. And then?

ABSALOM. Matthew said, "We must go." So we all went quickly.

BURTON. Where did you go?

ABSALOM. I wandered about. I wanted to find a place to hide.

JUDGE. I have a question to ask, Mr. Burton.

BURTON. Yes, Your Honor.

JUDGE. Why did you carry a revolver?

ABSALOM. It was to frighten the servant of the house.

JUDGE. Where did you get this revolver?

ABSALOM. I bought it from a man.

JUDGE. Was this revolver loaded when you bought it?

ABSALOM. It had two bullets in it.

JUDGE. How many bullets were in it when you went to this house?

ABSALOM. One.

JUDGE. What happened to the other?

ABSALOM. I took the revolver out into the hills and fired it.

JUDGE. What did you fire at?

ABSALOM. I fired at a tree.

JUDGE. Did you hit this tree?

ABSALOM. Yes, I hit it.

JUDGE. Then you thought, "Now I can fire this revolver"?

ABSALOM. Yes, that is so.

JUDGE. And when Matthew Kumalo and Johannes Pafuri say they were not with you at the time of the murder they are lying?

ABSALOM. Yes, they are lying.

JUDGE. Do you know where they went after the crime?

ABSALOM. No, I do not know.

JUDGE. Where did you go?

ABSALOM. I went to a plantation and buried the revolver.

JUDGE. And what did you do next?

ABSALOM. I prayed there.

JUDGE. What did you pray there?

ABSALOM. I prayed for forgiveness.

JUDGE. How did the police find you?

ABSALOM. Johannes Pafuri brought them to where I was.

JUDGE. And what did you tell them?

ABSALOM. I told them it was not Johannes who had killed the white man, it was I myself.

JUDGE. And how was the revolver found?

ABSALOM. No, I told the police where to find it.

JUDGE. And every word you have said is true?

ABSALOM. Every word is true.

JUDGE. There is no lie in it?

ABSALOM. There is no lie in it, for I said to myself, I shall not lie any more, all the rest of my days, nor do anything more that is evil.

JUDGE. In fact, you repented.

ABSALOM. Yes, I repented.

JUDGE. Because you were in trouble?

ABSALOM. Yes, because I was in trouble.

JUDGE. Did you have any other reason for repenting?

ABSALOM. No, I had no other reason.

JUDGE. I have no further questions, Mr. Burton.

BURTON. The witness is dismissed.

[*The lights dim on the courtroom, and the* CHORUS *comes forward.*]

CHORUS [*sings*].
 And here again, in this place,
 A man who has killed takes breath
 With the fear of death in his face,

Fear of death for death,
And are the terms of justice clearly met?
Not yet, no, not quite yet.

[*The courtroom lights come up again. The* SPECTATORS
are standing; the JUDGE *sits; they all sit except the*
three BOYS *who are awaiting sentence.*]

JUDGE. The evidence in this case is in many ways in-
conclusive, unsatisfactory, and fragmentary. Some
of the witnesses are or could be interested parties.
Some of the accused appear to have testified in col-
lusion with each other or other witnesses. There are
many points not clear, some of which, perhaps, will
now never be clear. It seems quite possible that
Matthew Kumalo and Johannes Pafuri are guilty
with Absalom Kumalo of the murder of Arthur
Jarvis. It was the identification of Pafuri by the
servant who was struck that led to Pafuri's arrest.
It was the arrest of Pafuri that led the police to arrest Absalom and later Matthew. The alibis offered
by Matthew and Johannes are obviously doubtful.
No reason has come to light why Absalom should
involve in the robbery and murder two men who
were not with him at the time and not guilty. And
yet, after long and thoughtful consideration, my
assessors and I have come to the conclusion that the
guilt of Matthew and Johannes is not sufficiently
established. [MATTHEW *and* JOHANNES *look at each*
other, puzzled.] There remains the case against Absalom Kumalo. Except for his plea and his confession the case against him remains substantially that
against Johannes and Matthew. His guilt is not established in the testimony alone, but that testimony,
taken together with his confession, leads us inescap-
ably to the conclusion that he is guilty. No reason

has been offered why he should confess to a deed he did not commit, and his own insistence that he had no intention to kill operates to validate the confession itself. Matthew Kumalo and Johannes Pafuri, you are discharged and may step down. [*They do so, move over right quietly;* LINDA *and* ROSE *rise and join them.*] Absalom Kumalo, have you anything to say before I pronounce sentence?

ABSALOM. I have only this to say, that I killed this man, but I did not mean to kill him, only I was afraid.

JUDGE. Absalom Kumalo, [*The* SPECTATORS *lean toward the* JUDGE, *who puts a little black cap on his head.*] I sentence you to be returned to custody, and to be hanged by the neck until you are dead. And may the Lord have mercy on your soul.

[IRINA *rises, then* STEPHEN. JARVIS *gets up and crosses the courtroom. As he does so he is met by* STEPHEN. JARVIS *steps back to let* STEPHEN *pass. He goes to* ABSALOM, *who stands stunned and motionless.*]

SCENE IV

The prison cell. The lights come up on the CHORUS.

CHORUS [*sings "Cry, the Beloved Country"*].
  Cry, the beloved country,
  Cry, the beloved land,
  the wasted childhood,
  the wasted youth,
  the wasted man!
  Cry, the broken tribes, and the broken hills,
  and the right and wrong forsaken,
  the greed that destroys us,

the birds that cry no more!
Cry, the beloved country,
Cry, the lost tribe, the lost son.

[*The* CHORUS *parts, revealing the prison cell.* ABSALOM
is in the cell, IRINA *near him.* STEPHEN *is reading
the marriage service.*]

STEPHEN. —to live together after God's ordinance in
the holy estate of Matrimony? Wilt thou obey him,
and serve him, love, honour, and keep him, and for-
saking all others, keep thee only unto him, so long
as ye both shall live?

IRINA. I will.

WOMAN [*sings*].
Cry, the unborn son,
the inheritor of our fear,
let him not laugh too gladly in the water of the
clove,
nor stand too silent
when the setting sun makes the veld red with fire.

STEPHEN. And now you are man and wife, my son, and
my daughter. Irina will come with me to Ndotsheni,
Absalom.

ABSALOM. I am glad, my father.

STEPHEN. We shall care for your child as if it were our
own.

ABSALOM. I thank you, my father.

STEPHEN. Will you wish to say good-by to Irina?

ABSALOM. There is no way to say good-by. My father, I
must go to—Pretoria.

STEPHEN. There will be an appeal.

ABSALOM. But it will not help. I am afraid. I am afraid
of the hanging.

STEPHEN. Be of courage, my son.

ABSALOM. It's no help to be of courage! O *Tixo, Tixo,*
I am afraid of the rope and the hanging!

[IRINA *kneels.*]

GUARD. You must go now.

ABSALOM. Where I go there will be no wife or child or
father or mother! There is no food taken or given!
And no marriage! Where I go! O *Tixo, Tixo!*

CHORUS [*sings*].
Cry, the unborn son,
fatherless,
let him not be moved by the song of the bird,
nor give his heart to a mountain
nor to a valley!

Cry, the beloved country!
Cry, the lost son,
the lost tribe—
the lost—
The great red hills stand desolate,
and the earth has torn away like flesh.
These are the valleys
of old men and old women,
of mothers and children.

WOMAN [*sings*].
Cry, the beloved land.

[*The lights dim.*]

SCENE V

As the lights come up we see ALEX *playing with a little*
Negro BOY *and* GIRL. *There is a small handmade toy*

between them. We can see the interior of the chapel,
center stage.

ALEX [*sings "Big Mole"*].
  Big Mole was a digger of the fastest kind;
  He'd dig in the earth like you think in your mind;
  When Big Mole came to the side of a hill
  Instead of going over he'd start in to drill.
  He promised his mother a well in the town
  And he brought boiling water from a thousand feet
    down!

  Down, down, down, down,
  Three mile, four mile, five mile down;
  He can go through rock, he can go through coal;
  Whenever you come to an oversize hole
  Down at the bottom is Big Black Mole!
  Big Black Mole, Big Black Mole!

  When Mole was a younker they showed him a mine;
  He said, "I like the idea fine,
  Let me have that hose, let me have that drill."
  If they hadn't shut it off he'd be boring still!
  And down at the bottom he chunked all around
  Till he chunked out a city six mile in the ground!

  Down, down, down, down,
  Three mile, four mile, five mile down;
  You can bet your pants, you can bet your soul,
  Whenever you come to a main-size hole
  Down at the bottom is Big Black Mole!
  Big Black Mole! Big Black Mole!

  Big Mole had a girl who was small and sweet;
  He promised her diamonds for her hands and feet;
  He dug so deep and he dug so well,

He broke right into the ceiling of hell,
And he looked the old devil spang in the eye,
And he said, "I'm not coming back here till I die!"

[EDWARD JARVIS *enters and stands listening.*]

ALEX [*sings*].
Down, down, down, down,
Three mile, four mile, five mile down;
He can go through rock, he can go through coal;
Whenever you come to a sure-enough hole,
Down at the bottom is Big Black Mole!
Big Black Mole, Big Black Mole, Big Black Mole!

EDWARD. Hi, there!

ALEX. Hi.

[*The other two* CHILDREN *get up and run off to the right.*]

EDWARD. You know, there's one thing I have to say for your voice—it's loud. It reminds me of Jericho.

ALEX. Jericho?

EDWARD. Yes, the man that knocked the town over with music.

ALEX. It was Joshua that broke the walls of the city with music. Jericho was the name of the city he destroyed.

EDWARD. How do you know that?

ALEX. My uncle read it to me out of the Old Testament.

EDWARD. Well, don't sing as loud as you can around here, or some of these walls might go down. [ED-WARD *laughs,* ALEX *joins him, they both laugh.*]

ALEX. I'll be very careful, sir.

EDWARD. I'm waiting for my grandfather now. We live up there in the hills.

ALEX. I know. I've seen you riding around up there. On a bicycle.

EDWARD. Sometimes I ride a bicycle, sometimes a horse. I can fall off both just fine. [*They laugh again.*] What have you got there?

ALEX. A digging machine.

EDWARD. Does it work?

ALEX. Not much. I made it myself.

EDWARD. What's your name?

ALEX. Alex.

EDWARD. Mine's Edward. I guess your uncle's the um-fundisi here.

ALEX. Yes, he is.

EDWARD. I know a lot of Zulu words. My father taught them to me. *Ingeli* is English.

ALEX. That's right.

EDWARD. What's the word for water?

ALEX. *Amanzi.*

EDWARD. And how do you say to die?

ALEX. *Siyafa.*

EDWARD. The young *Ingeli siyafa* for *amanzi*—is that right?

ALEX. You mean the English boy is dying for water?

EDWARD. Uh-huh. I am, too. Only I'd rather have milk, out of the fridge.

ALEX. The fridge?

EDWARD. You know, the refrigerator.

ALEX. My uncle doesn't have one.

EDWARD. How do you keep the milk cold?

ALEX. We have no milk. Nobody has milk in Ndot-sheni.

EDWARD. No milk!

ALEX. No. Can I get you some water?

EDWARD. Never mind. [*To himself.*] No milk . . . You know, you've got a real idea here; if you had something heavy on that string, and it had a point on it, and it kept dropping on the ground, it would really dig.

ALEX. Like a nail?

[JAMES JARVIS *enters from the left.*]

JARVIS. We're going now, Edward.

EDWARD. Yes, Grandfather. [*He rises.* ALEX *rises.*]

JARVIS. The car's at the market.

ALEX [*afraid of* JARVIS]. I have to go. [*He runs to the right.*]

EDWARD. Good-by, Alex!

ALEX [*stopping*]. Good-by—Edward! [*He runs off behind the chapel, waves to* EDWARD, *who also waves farewell.*]

JARVIS. Edward, when you are a man, you will live your own life. You will live as you please to live. But while you live with me, never let me see this again.

EDWARD. You mean talking with this boy?

JARVIS. I mean that.

EDWARD. But I like him. He's bright and he's nice.

JARVIS. There are not many rules in my house. I am lax in many ways, and not easily angered. [*He sits —his head in his hands.* EDWARD *sits beside him.*] I have lost so much that I don't know why I go on living, or what's worth saving. I don't know any more why any man should do his tasks or work for gain or love his child. I don't know why any child should obey—or whether good will come of it or evil. But I do know this; there are some things that I cannot bear to look on.

[*We hear organ music. The lights come up in the chapel.* PARISHIONERS *come in from the right and take their places in the chapel.* STEPHEN *and* GRACE *enter.* STEPHEN *stands before the pulpit.* JARVIS *still sits on the step.*]

STEPHEN [*speaking from the pulpit*]. I will say first the hardest thing I have to say. I am resigning from my pastorate at Ndotsheni. I shall be your umfundisi no more. It had been my hope to end my years here, but—I cannot now.

EDWARD. Aren't we going, Grandfather?

JARVIS. We'll wait a moment.

STEPHEN. My son Absalom will die tomorrow morning on the scaffold for a murder to which he confessed, and of which he was guilty. You all know of this. The man he killed was known to you, too. He was Arthur Jarvis. He was born in the hills above our little town. There was a brightness upon him even as a child. As a man he was a friend of our race, a friend of all men, a man all men could be proud of. And my son—killed him. And the mother of Arthur Jarvis is dead of grief for her son. My people, if I stay here now I become a hindrance to you, and not a help. I must go.

PARISHIONERS. You cannot go, umfundisi! You cannot go! No, umfundisi!

STEPHEN. This is a poor village, Ndotsheni, and it grows poorer. In the past when our little church was in desperate need we have sometimes turned to Arthur Jarvis, and he has helped us. He will not help here again. And no one will help you while I remain here, for the man who slew him was my son. I must go for still another reason, my dear people. When I began to serve my God and my church I had a sure faith that the God of our world ordered things well for men. I had a sure faith that though there was good and evil I knew which was good, and God knew it—and that men were better in their hearts for choosing good and not evil. Something has shaken this in me. I am not sure of my faith. I am lost. I am not sure now. I am not sure that we are not all lost. And a leader should not be lost. He should know the way, and so I resign my place.

MCRAE. Umfundisi, if you have lost your faith, I too have lost my faith.

PARISHIONERS. Yes.

MCRAE. Where does a man go, and what does he do when his faith is gone?

STEPHEN. I don't know.

PARISHIONERS. Oh, Stephen, you have always helped us. Please stay!

STEPHEN. If I keep my place, and this black thing has happened to my son and is said, little by little the few who still worship here will shrink away, the rusty roof will leak more, the floor will break till there is none, the windows will go—they will be thrown at and broken and will go—and the unpainted sides of this chapel I have loved will stand empty, roofless—and I shall live in despair beside it, knowing that I have done this thing to you and to my church by remaining. [STEPHEN *starts to go— they all reach out to him and he pauses.*]

VILLAGER [*sings "A Bird of Passage"*].
Lord of the heart, look down upon
    Our earthly pilgrimage,
Look down upon us where we walk
    From bright dawn to old age,
Give light not shed by any sun.
PARISHIONERS.
Lord of the heart!
MAN.
Not read on any page.
CHORUS.
Lord of the heart!

A bird of passage out of night
   Flies in at a lighted door,
Flies through and on in its darkened flight
   And then is seen no more.

[STEPHEN *stands for a moment at the pulpit, then turns and goes out.*]

This is the life of men on earth:
Out of darkness we come at birth
Into a lamplit room, and then—

EDWARD [*speaking through the music*]. What is it, Grandfather?
CHORUS [*sings*].
   Go forward into dark again,
   Go forward into dark again.

[*The lights dim.*]

SCENE VI

It is before daylight the next morning and STEPHEN *is sitting on a chair in front of the table in the room where we saw him in the first scene of the play. There is an extra chair upstage center added to this scene. Stephen sits watching the clock on the shelf. The* CHORUS *sings as the lights come up.*

CHORUS.
   Four o'clock, it will soon be four.

IRINA [*coming in*]. Umfundisi.

STEPHEN. Yes, Irina?

IRINA. She has fallen asleep. She meant to sit and watch
with you at this hour, and she has been awake till
only now—but now she sleeps.

STEPHEN. We won't wake her, Irina. If she sleeps and
the hour goes past, then at least it will be past.

IRINA. Even in her sleep she reaches for my hand.

STEPHEN. Sit beside her, Irina, if you can.

IRINA. Yes, I can. [*She starts to go.* STEPHEN *stops her.*]

STEPHEN. My daughter, I'm glad he found you and not
some other.

IRINA. I'm glad he found me, my father. [*She goes back
into the kitchen.*]

CHORUS [*sings*].
  Four o'clock, it will soon be four.

LEADER [*sings*].
  Why do they choose the morning,
  the morning, when men sleep sound?

CHORUS [*sings*].
  Four o'clock,
  it will soon be four.

STEPHEN [*speaks*].
  If they would kill me instead
  Absalom would make a good man.
  But it will never be.
  He is waiting now.
  Sleep, O mother. Sleep sound.
  Soon Absalom will sleep.

[JARVIS *enters from left, crosses to door, knocks.* STE-
PHEN, *almost unaware of what he is doing, answers.*]

STEPHEN. Yes—

JARVIS [*in the doorway*]. I hope you will forgive me
for coming at this hour, umfundisi.

STEPHEN [*rising*]. Why are you here?

JARVIS. May I come in?

STEPHEN. You—you wish to come into my house?

JARVIS. Yes.

STEPHEN. Come in, sir.

JARVIS [*entering*]. I stood outside your church yesterday and heard what you said to your people, and what they said to you. I want you to know that I will help you with the roof and with the painting—and whatever must be done. I will do whatever my son would have done.

STEPHEN. I—thank you, sir. The church will thank you.

JARVIS. Whatever you need.

STEPHEN. Mr. Jarvis. [*He looks at the clock.*] It's hard for me to think of the church or of—in a quarter of an hour my son is to die.

JARVIS. I know. I couldn't sleep—thinking of it.

STEPHEN. I think this does not touch you.

JARVIS. Yes. It does.

STEPHEN. I don't know how. I think it might be better if I sat here alone.

JARVIS. I know my presence pains you. I know I am the last man in the world you wish to see. And yet—may I stay for a moment?

STEPHEN. If you wish.

JARVIS. Stephen Kumalo, my wife is dead. My son is dead. I live in a house with a child who knows me only as an old man. I have thought many times I would be better dead. I thought myself alone in this desolation that used to be my home. But when I heard you yesterday I knew that your grief and mine were the same. I know now that of all the men who live near this great valley you are the one I would want for a friend. And—I have been walking about

—and came and knocked here now—because I wanted to sit with you in this hour—

STEPHEN. You want to sit with me?

JARVIS. Yes, if I may.

STEPHEN. Mr. Jarvis, you know that you can give me only charity. If you were seen to touch my hand, this town, this whole valley, would turn against you.

JARVIS. I've finished with that. I haven't come here lightly. I shall take your hand wherever I like, before whom I like. I shall come and worship in your church if I wish to worship. May I sit here with you?

STEPHEN. Yes, umnumzana. [JARVIS *starts to sit.*] This is not a good chair. [*He brings another chair and places it.* JARVIS *sits.*] It's almost the hour. O God— O *Tixo*—it is almost now.

JARVIS. But there will be a tomorrow, Stephen. Edward will come tomorrow to see Alex. He wants to come and play.

STEPHEN. I shall be gone. I shall never see this place again. Nor the path where Absalom ran to meet me—nor the hills where he played and came late to supper—nor the room where he slept—never, never again.

JARVIS. You must stay in Ndotsheni.

STEPHEN. If I stayed, do you know what I would preach here? That good can come from evil, and evil from good! That no man knows surely what is evil or what is good! That if there is a God He is hidden and has not spoken to men! That we are all lost here, black and white, rich and poor, the fools and the wise! Lost and hopeless and condemned on this rock that goes 'round the sun without meaning!

JARVIS. Not hopeless, Stephen, and not without meaning. For even out of the horror of this crime some things have come that are gain and not loss. My son's words to me and my understanding of my son. And your words in the chapel, and my understanding of those words—and your son's face in the courtroom when he said he would not lie any more or do any evil. I shall never forget that.

STEPHEN. You think well of my son?

JARVIS. I tried not to. But you and I have never had to face what Absalom faced there. A man can hardly do better than he did when he stood before the judge. Stay in Ndotsheni, Stephen, stay with those who cried out to you in the chapel. You have something to give them that nobody else can give them. And you can be proud of Absalom.

STEPHEN. And he is forgiven, and I am forgiven?

JARVIS. Let us forgive each other.

STEPHEN. Umnumzana—umnumzana!

JARVIS. Let us be neighbors. Let us be friends.

STEPHEN. Umnumzana—before the clock strikes—I shall stay in Ndotsheni. You are welcome in this house. I have a friend.

JARVIS. I have a friend.

[*The clock strikes four.* STEPHEN *sits and buries his head in his hands.* JARVIS *goes to him, puts an arm around him.*]

CHORUS [*sings*].
  Each lives alone in a world of dark,
  Crossing the skies in a lonely arc,
  Save when love leaps out like a leaping spark
  Over thousands, thousands of miles!

CURTAIN

THE MEMBER
OF THE WEDDING

by Carson McCullers

First production, January 5, 1950,
at the Empire Theatre, New York,
with the following cast:

BERENICE SADIE BROWN, *Ethel Waters*
FRANKIE ADDAMS, *Julie Harris*
JOHN HENRY WEST, *Brandon de Wilde*
JARVIS, *James Holden*
JANICE, *Janet de Gore*
MR. ADDAMS, *William Hansen*
MRS. WEST, *Margaret Barker*
HELEN FLETCHER, *Mitzie Blake*
DORIS, *Joan Shepard*
SIS LAURA, *Phyllis Walker*
T. T. WILLIAMS, *Harry Bolden*
HONEY CAMDEN BROWN, *Henry Scott*
BARNEY MACKEAN, *Jimmy Dutton*

ACT ONE
A late afternoon in August.
ACT TWO
Afternoon of the next day.
ACT THREE
Scene I *The Wedding Day*
 —afternoon of the next day following Act Two.
Scene II *4 a.m. the following morning.*
Scene III *Late afternoon, in the following November.*

Time: August, 1945
Place: A small Southern town

Act one

A part of a Southern back yard and kitchen. At stage left there is a scuppernong arbor. A sheet, used as a stage curtain, hangs raggedly at one side of the arbor. There is an elm tree in the yard. The kitchen has in the center a table with chairs. The walls are drawn with child drawings. There is a stove to the right and a small coal heating stove with coal scuttle in rear center of kitchen. The kitchen opens on the left into the yard. At the interior right a door leads to a small inner room. A door at the left leads into the front hall. The lights go on dimly, with a dreamlike effect, gradually revealing the family in the yard and BERENICE SADIE BROWN *in the kitchen.* BERENICE, *the cook, is a stout, motherly Negro woman with an air of great capability and devoted protection. She is about forty-five years old. She has a quiet, flat face and one of her eyes is made of blue glass. Sometimes when her socket bothers her, she dispenses with the false eye and wears a black patch. When we first see her she is wearing the patch and is dressed in a simple print work dress and apron.*

FRANKIE, *a gangling girl of twelve with blond hair cut like a boy's, is wearing shorts and a sombrero and is standing in the arbor gazing adoringly at her brother* JARVIS *and his fiancée* JANICE. *She is a dreamy, restless girl, and periods of energetic activity alternate with a rapt attention to her inward world of fantasy. She is thin and awkward and very much aware of being too tall.* JARVIS, *a good-looking boy of twenty-one, wearing an army uniform, stands by* JANICE. *He is awkward when he first appears because this is his betrothal visit.* JANICE, *a young, pretty, fresh-looking girl of eighteen or nineteen, is charming but rather ordinary, with brown hair done up in a small knot. She is dressed in her best clothes and is anxious to be liked by her new family.* MR. ADDAMS, FRANKIE's *father, is a deliberate and absent-minded man of about forty-five. A widower of many years, he has become set in his habits. He is dressed conservatively, and there is about him an old-fashioned look and manner.* JOHN HENRY, FRANKIE's *small cousin, aged seven, picks and eats any scuppernongs he can reach. He is a delicate, active boy and wears gold-rimmed spectacles which give him an oddly judicious look. He is blond and sunburned and when we first see him he is wearing a sun-suit and is barefooted.*

[BERENICE SADIE BROWN *is busy in the kitchen.*]

JARVIS. Seems to me like this old arbor has shrunk. I remember when I was a child it used to seem enormous. When I was Frankie's age, I had a vine swing here. Remember, Papa?

FRANKIE. It don't seem so absolutely enormous to me, because I am so tall.

JARVIS. I never saw a human grow so fast in all my life. I think maybe we ought to tie a brick to your head.

FRANKIE [*hunching down in obvious distress*]. Oh, Jarvis! Don't.

JANICE. Don't tease your little sister. I don't think Frankie is too tall. She probably won't grow much more. I had the biggest portion of my growth by the time I was thirteen.

FRANKIE. But I'm just twelve. When I think of all the growing years ahead of me, I get scared.

[JANICE *goes to* FRANKIE *and puts her arms around her comfortingly.* FRANKIE *stands rigid, embarrassed and blissful.*]

JANICE. I wouldn't worry.

[BERENICE *comes from the kitchen with a tray of drinks.* FRANKIE *rushes eagerly to help her serve them.*]

FRANKIE. Let me help.

BERENICE. Them two drinks is lemonade for you and John Henry. The others got liquor in them.

FRANKIE. Janice, come sit down on the arbor seat. Jarvis, you sit down too.

[JARVIS *and* JANICE *sit close together on the wicker bench in the arbor.* FRANKIE *hands the drinks around, then perches on the ground before* JANICE *and* JARVIS *and stares adoringly at them.*]

FRANKIE. It was such a surprise when Jarvis wrote home you are going to be married.

JANICE. I hope it wasn't a bad surprise.

FRANKIE. Oh, Heavens no! [*With great feeling.*] As a matter of fact . . . [*She strokes* JANICE's *shoes tenderly and* JARVIS' *army boot.*] If only you knew how I feel.

MR. ADDAMS. Frankie's been bending my ears ever since your letter came, Jarvis. Going on about weddings, brides, grooms, etc.

JANICE. It's lovely that we can be married at Jarvis' home.

MR. ADDAMS. That's the way to feel, Janice. Marriage is a sacred institution.

FRANKIE. Oh, it will be beautiful.

JARVIS. Pretty soon we'd better be shoving off for Winter Hill. I have to be back in barracks tonight.

FRANKIE. Winter Hill is such a lovely, cold name. It reminds me of ice and snow.

JANICE. You know it's just a hundred miles away, darling.

JARVIS. Ice and snow indeed! Yesterday the temperature on the parade ground reached 102.

[FRANKIE *takes a palmetto fan from the table and fans first* JANICE, *then* JARVIS.]

JANICE. That feels so good, darling. Thanks.

FRANKIE. I wrote you so many letters, Jarvis, and you never, never would answer me. When you were stationed in Alaska, I wanted so much to hear about Alaska. I sent you so many boxes of home-made candy, but you never answered me.

JARVIS. Oh, Frankie. You know how it is . . .

FRANKIE [*sipping her drink*]. You know this lemonade tastes funny. Kind of sharp and hot. I believe I got the drinks mixed up.

JARVIS. I was thinking my drink tasted mighty sissy. Just plain lemonade—no liquor at all.

[FRANKIE *and* JARVIS *exchange their drinks*. JARVIS *sips his*.]

JARVIS. This is better.

FRANKIE. I drank a lot. I wonder if I'm drunk. It makes me feel like I had four legs instead of two. I think I'm drunk. [*She gets up and begins to stagger around in imitation of drunkenness*.] See! I'm drunk! Look, Papa, how drunk I am! [*Suddenly she turns a handspring; then there is a blare of music from the club house gramophone off to the right*.]

JANICE. Where does the music come from? It sounds so close.

FRANKIE. It is. Right over there. They have club meetings and parties with boys on Friday nights. I watch
them here from the yard.

JANICE. It must be nice having your club house so
near.

FRANKIE. I'm not a member now. But they are holding
an election this afternoon, and maybe I'll be elected.

JOHN HENRY. Here comes Mama.

[MRS. WEST, JOHN HENRY's *mother, crosses the yard
from the right. She is a vivacious, blond woman of
about thirty-three. She is dressed in sleazy, rather
dowdy summer clothes.*]

MR. ADDAMS. Hello, Pet. Just in time to meet our new
family member.

MRS. WEST. I saw you out here from the window.

JARVIS [*rising, with* JANICE]. Hi, Aunt Pet. How is
Uncle Eustace?

MRS. WEST. He's at the office.

JANICE [*offering her hand with the engagement ring
on it*]. Look, Aunt Pet. May I call you Aunt Pet?

MRS. WEST [*hugging her*]. Of course, Janice. What a
gorgeous ring!

JANICE. Jarvis just gave it to me this morning. He
wanted to consult his father and get it from his store,
naturally.

MRS. WEST. How lovely.

MR. ADDAMS. A quarter carat—not too flashy but a good
stone.

MRS. WEST [*to* BERENICE, *who is gathering up the empty
glasses*]. Berenice, what have you and Frankie been
doing to my John Henry? He sticks over here in
your kitchen morning, noon and night.

BERENICE. We enjoys him and Candy seems to like it
over here.

MRS. WEST. What on earth do you do to him?

BERENICE. We just talks and passes the time of day. Occasionally plays cards.

MRS. WEST. Well, if he gets in your way just shoo him home.

BERENICE. Candy don't bother nobody.

JOHN HENRY [*walking around barefooted in the arbor*]. These grapes are so squelchy when I step on them.

MRS. WEST. Run home, darling, and wash your feet and put on your sandals.

JOHN HENRY. I like to squelch on the grapes.

[BERENICE *goes back to the kitchen.*]

JANICE. That looks like a stage curtain. Jarvis told me how you used to write plays and act in them out here in the arbor. What kind of shows do you have?

FRANKIE. Oh, crook shows and cowboy shows. This summer I've had some cold shows—about Esquimos and explorers—on account of the hot weather.

JANICE. Do you ever have romances?

FRANKIE. Naw . . . [*With bravado.*] I had crook shows for the most part. You see I never believed in love until now. [*Her look lingers on* JANICE *and* JARVIS. *She hugs* JANICE *and* JARVIS, *bending over them from back of the bench.*]

MRS. WEST. Frankie and this little friend of hers gave a performance of "The Vagabond King" out here last spring.

[JOHN HENRY *spreads out his arms and imitates the heroine of the play from memory, singing in his high childish voice.*]

JOHN HENRY. Never hope to bind me. Never hope to know. [*Speaking.*] Frankie was the king-boy. I sold the tickets.

MRS. WEST. Yes, I have always said that Frankie has talent.

FRANKIE. Aw, I'm afraid I don't have much talent.

JOHN HENRY. Frankie can laugh and kill people good. She can die, too.

FRANKIE [*with some pride*]. Yeah, I guess I die all right.

MR. ADDAMS. Frankie rounds up John Henry and those smaller children, but by the time she dresses them in the costumes, they're worn out and won't act in the show.

JARVIS [*looking at his watch*]. Well, it's time we shove off for Winter Hill—Frankie's land of icebergs and snow—where the temperature goes up to 102. [*JARVIS takes JANICE's hand. He gets up and gazes fondly around the yard and the arbor. He pulls her up and stands with his arm around her, gazing around him at the arbor and yard.*]

JARVIS. It carries me back—this smell of mashed grapes and dust. I remember all the endless summer afternoons of my childhood. It does carry me back.

FRANKIE. Me too. It carries me back, too.

MR. ADDAMS [*putting one arm around JANICE and shaking JARVIS' hand*]. Merciful Heavens! It seems I have two Methuselahs in my family! Does it carry you back to your childhood too, John Henry?

JOHN HENRY. Yes, Uncle Royal.

MR. ADDAMS. Son, this visit was a real pleasure. Janice, I'm mighty pleased to see my boy has such lucky judgment in choosing a wife.

FRANKIE. I hate to think you have to go. I'm just now realizing you're here.

JARVIS. We'll be back in two days. The wedding is Sunday.

[*The FAMILY move around the house toward the street. JOHN HENRY enters the kitchen through the back door. There are the sounds of "good-byes" from the front yard.*]

JOHN HENRY. Frankie was drunk. She drank a liquor drink.

BERENICE. She just made out like she was drunk—pretended.

JOHN HENRY. She said, "Look, Papa, how drunk I am," and she couldn't walk.

FRANKIE'S VOICE. Good-bye, Jarvis. Good-bye, Janice.

JARVIS' VOICE. See you Sunday.

MR. ADDAMS' VOICE. Drive carefully, son. Good-bye, Janice.

JANICE'S VOICE. Good-bye and thanks, Mr. Addams. Good-bye, Frankie darling.

ALL THE VOICES. Good-bye! Good-bye!

JOHN HENRY. They are going now to Winter Hill.

[*There is the sound of the front door opening, then of steps in the hall.* FRANKIE *enters through the hall.*]

FRANKIE. Oh, I can't understand it! The way it all just suddenly happened.

BERENICE. Happened? Happened?

FRANKIE. I have never been so puzzled.

BERENICE. Puzzled about what?

FRANKIE. The whole thing. They are so beautiful.

BERENICE [*after a pause*]. I believe the sun done fried your brains.

JOHN HENRY [*whispering*]. Me too.

BERENICE. Look here at me. You jealous.

FRANKIE. Jealous?

BERENICE. Jealous because your brother's going to be married.

FRANKIE [*slowly*]. No. I just never saw any two like them. When they walked in the house today it was so queer.

BERENICE. You jealous. Go and behold yourself in the mirror. I can see from the color of your eyes.

[FRANKIE *goes to the mirror and stares. She draws up*

her left shoulder, shakes her head, and turns away.]

FRANKIE [*with feeling*]. Oh! They were the two prettiest people I ever saw. I just can't understand how it happened.

BERENICE. Whatever ails you?—actin' so queer.

FRANKIE. I don't know. I bet they have a good time every minute of the day.

JOHN HENRY. Less us have a good time.

FRANKIE. Us have a good time? Us? [*She rises and walks around the table.*]

BERENICE. Come on. Less have a game of three-handed bridge.

[*They sit down at the table, shuffle the cards, deal, and play a game.*]

FRANKIE. Oregon, Alaska, Winter Hill, the wedding. It's all so queer.

BERENICE. I can't bid, never have a hand these days.

FRANKIE. A spade.

JOHN HENRY. I want to bid spades. That's what I was going to bid.

FRANKIE. Well, that's your tough luck. I bid them first.

JOHN HENRY. Oh, you fool jackass! It's not fair!

BERENICE. Hush quarreling, you two. [*She looks at both their hands.*] To tell the truth, I don't think either of you got such a grand hand to fight over the bid about. Where is the cards? I haven't had no kind of a hand all week.

FRANKIE. I don't give a durn about it. It is immaterial with me. [*There is a long pause. She sits with her head propped on her hand, her legs wound around each other.*] Let's talk about them—and the wedding.

BERENICE. What you want to talk about?

FRANKIE. My heart feels them going away—going farther and farther away—while I am stuck here by myself.

BERENICE. You ain't here by yourself. By the way, where's your Pa?

FRANKIE. He went to the store. I think about them, but I remembered them more as a feeling than as a picture.

BERENICE. A feeling?

FRANKIE. They were the two prettiest people I ever saw. Yet it was like I couldn't see all of them I wanted to see. My brains couldn't gather together quick enough to take it all in. And then they were gone.

BERENICE. Well, stop commenting about it. You don't have your mind on the game.

FRANKIE [*playing her cards, followed by* JOHN HENRY]. Spades are trumps and you got a spade. I have some of my mind on the game.

[JOHN HENRY *puts his donkey necklace in his mouth and looks away.*]

FRANKIE. Go on, cheater.

BERENICE. Make haste.

JOHN HENRY. I can't. It's a king. The only spade I got is a king, and I don't want to play my king under Frankie's ace. And I'm not going to do it either.

FRANKIE [*throwing her cards down on the table*]. See, Berenice, he cheats!

BERENICE. Play your king, John Henry. You have to follow the rules of the game.

JOHN HENRY. My king. It isn't fair.

FRANKIE. Even with this trick, I can't win.

BERENICE. Where is the cards? For three days I haven't had a decent hand. I'm beginning to suspicion something. Come on less count these old cards.

FRANKIE. We've worn these old cards out. If you would eat these old cards, they would taste like a combination of all the dinners of this summer together with a sweaty-handed, nasty taste. Why, the jacks and the queens are missing.

BERENICE. John Henry, how come you do a thing like that? So that's why you asked for the scissors and stole off quiet behind the arbor. Now, Candy, how come you took our playing cards and cut out the pictures?

JOHN HENRY. Because I wanted them. They're cute.

FRANKIE. See? He's nothing but a child. It's hopeless. Hopeless!

BERENICE. Maybe so.

FRANKIE. We'll just have to put him out of the game. He's entirely too young. [JOHN HENRY *whimpers*.]

BERENICE. Well, we can't put Candy out of the game. We gotta have a third to play. Besides, by the last count he owes me close to three million dollars.

FRANKIE. Oh, I am sick unto death. [*She sweeps the cards from the table, then gets up and begins walking around the kitchen.* JOHN HENRY *leaves the table and picks up a large blond doll on the chair in the corner.*] I wish they'd taken me with them to Winter Hill this afternoon. I wish tomorrow was Sunday instead of Saturday.

BERENICE. Sunday will come.

FRANKIE. I doubt it. I wish I was going somewhere for good. I wish I had a hundred dollars and could just light out and never see this town again.

BERENICE. It seems like you wish for a lot of things.

FRANKIE. I wish I was somebody else except me.

JOHN HENRY [*holding the doll*]. You serious when you gave me the doll a while ago?

FRANKIE. It gives me a pain just to think about them.

BERENICE. It is a known truth that gray-eyed people are jealous.

[*There are sounds of* CHILDREN *playing in the neighboring yard.*]

JOHN HENRY. Let's go out and play with the children.

FRANKIE. I don't want to.

JOHN HENRY. There's a big crowd, and they sound like they having a mighty good time. Less go.

FRANKIE. You got ears. You heard me.

JOHN HENRY. I think maybe I better go home.

FRANKIE. Why, you said you were going to spend the night. You just can't eat dinner and then go off in the afternoon like that.

JOHN HENRY. I know it.

BERENICE. Candy, Lamb, you can go home if you want to.

JOHN HENRY. But less go out, Frankie. They sound like they having a lot of fun.

FRANKIE. No, they're not. Just a crowd of ugly, silly children. Running and hollering and running and hollering. Nothing to it.

JOHN HENRY. Less go!

FRANKIE. Well, then I'll entertain you. What do you want to do? Would you like for me to read to you out of "The Book of Knowledge," or would you rather do something else?

JOHN HENRY. I rather do something else. [*He goes to the back door, and looks into the yard. Several young* GIRLS *of thirteen or fourteen, dressed in clean print frocks, file slowly across the back yard.*] Look. Those big girls.

FRANKIE [*running out into the yard*]. Hey, there. I'm mighty glad to see you. Come on in.

HELEN. We can't. We were just passing through to notify our new member.

FRANKIE [*overjoyed*]. Am I the new member?

DORIS. No, you're not the one the club elected.

FRANKIE. Not elected?

HELEN. Every ballot was unanimous for Mary Little-john.

FRANKIE. Mary Littlejohn! You mean that girl who just moved in next door? That pasty fat girl with those tacky pigtails? The one who plays the piano all day long?

DORIS. Yes. The club unanimously elected Mary.

FRANKIE. Why, she's not even cute.

HELEN. She is too; and, furthermore, she's talented.

FRANKIE. I think it's sissy to sit around the house all day playing classical music.

DORIS. Why, Mary is training for a concert career.

FRANKIE. Well, I wish to Jesus she would train some-where else.

DORIS. You don't have enough sense to appreciate a tal-ented girl like Mary.

FRANKIE. What are you doing in my yard? You're never to set foot on my Papa's property again. [FRANKIE *shakes* HELEN.] Son-of-a-bitches. I could shoot you with my Papa's pistol.

JOHN HENRY [*shaking his fists*]. Son-of-a-bitches.

FRANKIE. Why didn't you elect me? [*She goes back into the house.*] Why can't I be a member?

JOHN HENRY. Maybe they'll change their mind and in-vite you.

BERENICE. I wouldn't pay them no mind. All my life I've been wantin' things that I ain't been gettin'. Anyhow those club girls is fully two years older than you.

FRANKIE. I think they have been spreading it all over town that I smell bad. When I had those boils and had to use that black bitter-smelling ointment, old Helen Fletcher asked me what was that funny smell I had. Oh, I could shoot every one of them with a pistol.

[FRANKIE *sits with her head on the table.* JOHN HENRY

approaches and pats the back of FRANKIE's *neck.*]

JOHN HENRY. I don't think you smell so bad. You smell sweet, like a hundred flowers.

FRANKIE. The son-of-a-bitches. And there was something else. They were telling nasty lies about married people. When I think of Aunt Pet and Uncle Eustace! And my own father! The nasty lies! I don't know what kind of fool they take me for.

BERENICE. That's what I tell you. They too old for you.

[JOHN HENRY *raises his head, expands his nostrils and sniffs at himself. Then* FRANKIE *goes into the interior bedroom and returns with a bottle of perfume.*]

FRANKIE. Boy! I bet I use more perfume than anybody else in town. Want some on you, John Henry? You want some, Berenice? [*She sprinkles perfume.*]

JOHN HENRY. Like a thousand flowers.

BERENICE. Frankie, the whole idea of a club is that there are members who are included and the non-members who are not included. Now what you ought to do is to round you up a club of your own. And you could be the president yourself.

[*There is a pause.*]

FRANKIE. Who would I get?

BERENICE. Why, those little children you hear playing in the neighborhood.

FRANKIE. I don't want to be the president of all those little young left-over people.

BERENICE. Well, then enjoy your misery. That perfume smells so strong it kind of makes me sick.

[JOHN HENRY *plays with the doll at the kitchen table and* FRANKIE *watches.*]

FRANKIE. Look here at me, John Henry. Take off those glasses. [JOHN HENRY *takes off his glasses.*] I bet you don't need those glasses. [*She points to the coal scuttle.*] What is this?

JOHN HENRY. The coal scuttle.

FRANKIE [*taking a shell from the kitchen shelf*]. And this?

JOHN HENRY. The shell we got at Saint Peter's Bay last summer.

FRANKIE. What is that little thing crawling around on the floor?

JOHN HENRY. Where?

FRANKIE. That little thing crawling around near your feet.

JOHN HENRY. Oh. [*He squats down.*] Why, it's an ant. How did that get in here?

FRANKIE. If I were you I'd just throw those glasses away. You can see good as anybody.

BERENICE. Now quit picking with John Henry.

FRANKIE. They don't look becoming. [JOHN HENRY *wipes his glasses and puts them back on.*] He can suit himself. I was only telling him for his own good. [*She walks restlessly around the kitchen.*] I bet Janice and Jarvis are members of a lot of clubs. In fact, the army is kind of like a club.

[JOHN HENRY *searches through* BERENICE's *pocketbook.*]

BERENICE. Don't root through my pocketbook like that, Candy. Ain't a wise policy to search folks' pocketbooks. They might think you trying to steal their money.

JOHN HENRY. I'm looking for your new glass eye. Here it is. [*He hands* BERENICE *the glass eye.*] You got two nickels and a dime.

[BERENICE *takes off her patch, turns away and inserts the glass eye.*]

BERENICE. I ain't used to it yet. The socket bothers me. Maybe it don't fit properly.

JOHN HENRY. The blue glass eye looks very cute.

FRANKIE. I don't see why you had to get that eye. It has a wrong expression—let alone being blue.

BERENICE. Ain't anybody ask your judgment, wise-mouth.

JOHN HENRY. Which one of your eyes do you see out of best?

BERENICE. The left eye, of course. The glass eye don't do me no seeing good at all.

JOHN HENRY. I like the glass eye better. It is so bright and shiny—a real pretty eye. Frankie, you serious when you gave me this doll a while ago?

FRANKIE. Janice and Jarvis. It gives me this pain just to think about them.

BERENICE. It is a known truth that gray-eyed people are jealous.

FRANKIE. I told you I wasn't jealous. I couldn't be jealous of one of them without being jealous of them both. I 'sociate the two of them together. Somehow they're just so different from us.

BERENICE. Well, I were jealous when my foster-brother, Honey, married Clorina. I sent a warning I could tear the ears off her head. But you see I didn't. Clorina's got ears just like anybody else. And now I love her.

FRANKIE [*stopping her walking suddenly*]. J.A.—Janice and Jarvis. Isn't that the strangest thing?

BERENICE. What?

FRANKIE. J.A.—Both their names begin with "J.A."

BERENICE. And? What about it?

FRANKIE [*walking around the kitchen table*]. If only my name was Jane. Jane or Jasmine.

BERENICE. I don't follow your frame of mind.

FRANKIE. Jarvis and Janice and Jasmine. See?

BERENICE. No. I don't see.

FRANKIE. I wonder if it's against the law to change your name. Or add to it.

BERENICE. Naturally. It's against the law.

FRANKIE [*impetuously*]. Well, I don't care. F. Jasmine Addams.

JOHN HENRY [*approaching with the doll*]. You serious when you give me this? [*He pulls up the doll's dress and pats her.*] I will name her Belle.

FRANKIE. I don't know what went on in Jarvis' mind when he brought me that doll. Imagine bringing me a doll! I had counted on Jarvis bringing me something from Alaska.

BERENICE. Your face when you unwrapped that package was a study.

FRANKIE. John Henry, quit pickin' at the doll's eyes. It makes me so nervous. You hear me! [*He sits the doll up.*] In fact, take the doll somewhere out of my sight.

JOHN HENRY. Her name is Lily Belle. [*JOHN HENRY goes out and props the doll up on the back steps. There is the sound of an unseen NEGRO singing from the neighboring yard.*]

FRANKIE [*going to the mirror*]. The big mistake I made was to get this close crew cut. For the wedding, I ought to have long brunette hair. Don't you think so?

BERENICE. I don't see how come brunette hair is necessary. But I warned you about getting your head shaved off like that before you did it. But nothing would do but you shave it like that.

FRANKIE [*stepping back from the mirror and slumping her shoulders*]. Oh, I am so worried about being so tall. I'm twelve and five-sixths years old and already five feet five and three-fourths inches tall. If I keep on growing like this until I'm twenty-one, I figure I will be nearly ten feet tall.

JOHN HENRY [*re-entering the kitchen*]. Lily Belle is taking a nap on the back steps. Don't talk so loud, Frankie.

FRANKIE [*after a pause*]. I doubt if they ever get married or go to a wedding. Those freaks.

BERENICE. Freaks. What freaks you talking about?

FRANKIE. At the fair. The ones we saw there last October.

JOHN HENRY. Oh, the freaks at the fair! [*He holds out an imaginary skirt and begins to skip around the room with one finger resting on the top of his head.*] Oh, she was the cutest little girl I ever saw. I never saw anything so cute in my whole life. Did you, Frankie?

FRANKIE. No. I don't think she was cute.

BERENICE. Who is that he's talking about?

FRANKIE. That little old pin-head at the fair. A head no bigger than an orange. With the hair shaved off and a big pink bow at the top. Bow was bigger than the head.

JOHN HENRY. Shoo! She was too cute.

BERENICE. That little old squeezed-looking midget in them little trick evening clothes. And that giant with the hang-jaw face and them huge loose hands. And that morphidite! Half man—half woman. With that tiger skin on one side and that spangled skirt on the other.

JOHN HENRY. But that little-headed girl was cute.

FRANKIE. And that wild colored man they said came from a savage island and ate those real live rats? Do you think they make a very big salary?

BERENICE. How would I know? In fact, all them freak folks down at the fair every October just gives me the creeps.

FRANKIE [*after a pause, and slowly*]. Do I give you the creeps?

BERENICE. You?

FRANKIE. Do you think I will grow into a freak?

BERENICE. You? Why certainly not, I trust Jesus!

FRANKIE [*going over to the mirror, and looking at herself*]. Well, do you think I will be pretty?

BERENICE. Maybe. If you file down them horns a inch or two.

FRANKIE [*turning to face* BERENICE, *and shuffling one bare foot on the floor*]. Seriously.

BERENICE. Seriously, I think when you fill out you will do very well. If you behave.

FRANKIE. But by Sunday, I want to do something to improve myself before the wedding.

BERENICE. Get clean for a change. Scrub your elbows and fix yourself nice. You will do very well.

JOHN HENRY. You will be all right if you file down them horns.

FRANKIE [*raising her right shoulder and turning from the mirror*]. I don't know what to do. I just wish I would die.

BERENICE. Well, die then!

JOHN HENRY. Die.

FRANKIE [*suddenly exasperated*]. Go home! [*There is a pause.*] You heard me! [*She makes a face at him and threatens him with the fly swatter. They run twice around the table.*] Go home! I'm sick and tired of you, you little midget.

[JOHN HENRY *goes out, taking the doll with him.*]

BERENICE. Now what makes you act like that? You are too mean to live.

FRANKIE. I know it. [*She takes a carving knife from the table drawer.*] Something about John Henry just gets on my nerves these days. [*She puts her left ankle over her right knee and begins to pick with the knife at a splinter in her foot.*] I've got a splinter in my foot.

BERENICE. That knife ain't the proper thing for a splinter.

FRANKIE. It seems to me that before this summer I used always to have such a good time. Remember this spring when Evelyn Owen and me used to dress up in costumes and go down town and shop at the five-and-dime? And how every Friday night we'd spend the night with each other either at her house or here? And then Evelyn Owen had to go and move away to Florida. And now she won't even write to me.

BERENICE. Honey, you are not crying, is you? Don't that hurt you none?

FRANKIE. It would hurt anybody else except me. And how the wisteria in town was so blue and pretty in April but somehow it was so pretty it made me sad. And how Evelyn and me put on that show the Glee Club did at the High School Auditorium? [*She raises her head and beats time with the knife and her fist on the table, singing loudly with sudden energy.*] "Sons of toil and danger! Will you serve a stranger! And bow down to Burgundy!" [BERENICE *joins in on* "Burgundy." FRANKIE *pauses, then begins to pick her foot again, humming the tune sadly.*]

BERENICE. That was a nice show you children copied in the arbor. You will meet another girl friend you like as well as Evelyn Owen. Or maybe Mr. Owen will move back into town. [*There is a pause.*] Frankie, what you need is a needle.

FRANKIE. I don't care anything about my feet. [*She stomps her foot on the floor and lays down the knife on the table.*] It was just so queer the way it happened this afternoon. The minute I laid eyes on the pair of them I had this funny feeling. [*She goes over and picks up a saucer of milk near the cat-hole in back of the door and pours the milk in the sink.]* How old were you, Berenice, when you married your first husband?

BERENICE. I were thirteen years old.

FRANKIE. What made you get married so young for?

BERENICE. Because I wanted to.

FRANKIE. You never loved any of your four husbands but Ludie.

BERENICE. Ludie Maxwell Freeman was my only true husband. The other ones were just scraps.

FRANKIE. Did you marry with a veil every time?

BERENICE. Three times with a veil.

FRANKIE [*pouring milk into the saucer and returning the saucer to the cat-hole*]. If only I just knew where he is gone. Ps, ps, ps . . . Charles, Charles.

BERENICE. Quit worrying yourself about that old alley cat. He's gone off to hunt a friend.

FRANKIE. To hunt a friend?

BERENICE. Why certainly. He roamed off to find himself a lady friend.

FRANKIE. Well, why don't he bring his friend home with him? He ought to know I would be only too glad to have a whole family of cats.

BERENICE. You done seen the last of that old alley cat.

FRANKIE [*crossing the room*]. I ought to notify the police force. They will find Charles.

BERENICE. I wouldn't do that.

FRANKIE [*at the telephone*]. I want the police force, please . . . Police force? . . . I am notifying you about my cat . . . Cat! He's lost. He is almost pure Persian.

BERENICE. As Persian as I is.

FRANKIE. But with short hair. A lovely color of gray with a little white spot on his throat. He answers to the name of Charles, but if he don't answer to that, he might come if you call "Charlina." . . . My name is Miss F. Jasmine Addams and the address is 124 Grove Street.

BERENICE [*giggling as* FRANKIE *re-enters*]. Gal, they going to send around here and tie you up and drag you off to Milledgeville. Just picture them fat blue police chasing tomcats around alleys and hollering, "Oh Charles! Oh come here, Charlina!" Merciful Heavens.

FRANKIE. Aw, shut up!

[*Outside a voice is heard calling in a drawn-out chant, the words almost indistinguishable: "Lot of okra, peas, fresh butter beans . . ."*]

BERENICE. The trouble with you is that you don't have no sense of humor no more.

FRANKIE [*disconsolately*]. Maybe I'd be better off in jail.

[*The chanting voice continues and an ancient* NEGRO WOMAN, *dressed in a clean print dress with several petticoats, the ruffle of one of which shows, crosses the yard. She stops and leans on a gnarled stick.*]

FRANKIE. Here comes the old vegetable lady.

BERENICE. Sis Laura is getting mighty feeble to peddle this hot weather.

FRANKIE. She is about ninety. Other old folks lose their faculties, but she found some faculty. She reads futures, too.

BERENICE. Hi, Sis Laura. How is your folks getting on?

SIS LAURA. We ain't much, and I feels my age these days. Want any peas today? [*She shuffles across the yard.*]

BERENICE. I'm sorry, I still have some left over from yesterday. Good-bye, Sis Laura.

SIS LAURA. Good-bye. [*She goes off behind the house to the right, continuing her chant.*]

[*When the old* WOMAN *is gone* FRANKIE *begins walking around the kitchen.*]

FRANKIE. I expect Janice and Jarvis are almost to Winter Hill by now.

BERENICE. Sit down. You make me nervous.

FRANKIE. Jarvis talked about Granny. He remembers her very good. But when I try to remember Granny, it is like her face is changing—like a face seen under water. Jarvis remembers Mother too, and I don't remember her at all.

BERENICE. Naturally! Your mother died the day that you were born.

FRANKIE [*standing with one foot on the seat of the chair, leaning over the chair back and laughing*]. Did you hear what Jarvis said?

BERENICE. What?

FRANKIE [*after laughing more*]. They were talking about whether to vote for C. P. MacDonald. And Jarvis said, "Why I wouldn't vote for that scoundrel if he was running to be dogcatcher." I never heard anything so witty in my life. [*There is a silence during which* BERENICE *watches* FRANKIE, *but does not smile.*] And you know what Janice remarked. When Jarvis mentioned about how much I've grown, she said she didn't think I looked so terribly big. She said she got the major portion of her growth before she was thirteen. She said I was the right height and had acting talent and ought to go to Hollywood. She did, Berenice.

BERENICE. O.K. All right! She did!

FRANKIE. She said she thought I was a lovely size and would probably not grow any taller. She said all fashion models and movie stars . . .

BERENICE. She did not. I heard her from the window. She only remarked that you probably had already got your growth. But she didn't go on and on like that or mention Hollywood.

FRANKIE. She said to me . . .

BERENICE. She said to you! This is a serious fault with you, Frankie. Somebody just makes a loose remark and then you cozen it in your mind until nobody would recognize it. Your Aunt Pet happened to mention to Clorina that you had sweet manners and Clorina passed it on to you. For what it was worth. Then next thing I know you are going all around and bragging how Mrs. West thought you had the finest manners in town and ought to go to Hollywood, and I don't know what-all you didn't say. And that is a serious fault.

FRANKIE. Aw, quit preaching at me.

BERENICE. I ain't preaching. It's the solemn truth and you know it.

FRANKIE. I admit it a little. [*She sits down at the table and puts her forehead on the palms of her hands. There is a pause, and then she speaks softly.*] What I need to know is this. Do you think I made a good impression?

BERENICE. Impression?

FRANKIE. Yes.

BERENICE. Well, how would I know?

FRANKIE. I mean, how did I act? What did I do?

BERENICE. Why, you didn't do anything to speak of.

FRANKIE. Nothing?

BERENICE. No. You just watched the pair of them like they was ghosts. Then, when they talked about the wedding, them ears of yours stiffened out the size of cabbage leaves . . .

FRANKIE [*raising her hand to her ears*]. They didn't!

BERENICE. They did.

FRANKIE. Some day you going to look down and find that big fat tongue of yours pulled out by the roots and laying there before you on the table.

BERENICE. Quit talking so rude.

FRANKIE [*after a pause*]. I'm so scared I didn't make a good impression.

BERENICE. What of it? I got a date with T. T. and he's supposed to pick me up here. I wish him and Honey would come on. You make me nervous.

[FRANKIE *sits miserably, her shoulders hunched. Then with a sudden gesture she bangs her forehead on the table. Her fists are clenched and she is sobbing.*]

BERENICE. Come on. Don't act like that.

FRANKIE [*her voice muffled*]. They were so pretty. They must have such a good time. And they went away and left me.

BERENICE. Sit up. Behave yourself.

FRANKIE. They came and went away, and left me with this feeling.

BERENICE. Hosee! I bet I know something. [*She begins tapping with her heel: one, two, three—bang! After a pause, in which the rhythm is established, she begins singing.*] Frankie's got a crush! Frankie's got a crush! Frankie's got a crush on the *wedding!*

FRANKIE. Quit!

BERENICE. Frankie's got a crush! Frankie's got a crush!

FRANKIE. You better quit! [*She rises suddenly and snatches up the carving knife.*]

BERENICE. You lay down that knife.

FRANKIE. Make me. [*She bends the blade slowly.*]

BERENICE. Lay it down, *Devil*. [*There is a silence.*] Just throw it! You just!

[*After a pause* FRANKIE *aims the knife carefully at the closed door leading to the bedroom and throws it. The knife does not stick in the wall.*]

FRANKIE. I used to be the best knife thrower in this town.

BERENICE. Frances Addams, you goin' to try that stunt once too often.

FRANKIE. I warned you to quit pickin' with me.

BERENICE. You are not fit to live in a house.

FRANKIE. I won't be living in this one much longer; I'm going to run away from home.

BERENICE. And a good riddance to a big old bag of rubbage.

FRANKIE. You wait and see. I'm leavin' town.

BERENICE. And where do you think you are going?

FRANKIE [*gazing around the walls*]. I don't know.

BERENICE. You're going crazy. That's where you going.

FRANKIE. No. [*Solemnly.*] This coming Sunday after the wedding, I'm leaving town. And I swear to Jesus by my two eyes I'm never coming back here any more.

BERENICE [*going to* FRANKIE *and pushing her damp bangs back from her forehead*]. Sugar? You serious?

FRANKIE [*exasperated*]. Of course! Do you think I would stand here and say that swear and tell a story? Sometimes, Berenice, I think it takes you longer to realize a fact than it does anybody who ever lived.

BERENICE. But you say you don't know where you going. You going, but you don't know where. That don't make no sense to me.

FRANKIE [*after a long pause in which she again gazes around the walls of the room*]. I feel just exactly like somebody has peeled all the skin off me. I wish I had some good cold peach ice cream. [BERENICE *takes her by the shoulders.*]

[*During the last speech,* T. T. WILLIAMS *and* HONEY CAMDEN BROWN *have been approaching through the back yard.* T. T. *is a large and pompous-looking Negro man of about fifty. He is dressed like a church deacon, in a black suit with a red emblem in the lapel. His manner is timid and over-polite.* HONEY *is a slender, limber Negro boy of about twenty. He is quite light in color and he wears loud-colored, snappy clothes. He is brusque and there is about him an odd mixture of hostility and playfulness. He is very high-strung and volatile. They are trailed by* JOHN HENRY. JOHN HENRY *is dressed for afternoon in a clean white linen suit, white shoes and socks.* HONEY *carries a horn. They cross the back yard and knock at the back door.* HONEY *holds his hand to his head.*]

FRANKIE. But every word I told you was the solemn truth. I'm leaving here after the wedding.

BERENICE [*taking her hands from* FRANKIE's *shoulders and answering the door*]. Hello, Honey and T. T. I didn't hear you coming.

T. T. You and Frankie too busy discussing something. Well, your foster-brother, Honey, got into a ruckus standing on the sidewalk in front of the Blue Moon Café. Police cracked him on the haid.

BERENICE [*turning on the kitchen light*]. What! [*She examines* HONEY's *head.*] Why, it's a welt the size of a small egg.

HONEY. Times like this I feel like I got to bust loose or die.

BERENICE. What were you doing?

HONEY. Nothing. I was just passing along the street minding my own business when this drunk soldier came out of the Blue Moon Café and ran into me. I looked at him and he gave me a push. I pushed him back and he raised a ruckus. This white M.P. came up and slammed me with his stick.

T. T. It was one of those accidents can happen to any colored person.

JOHN HENRY [*reaching for the horn*]. Toot some on your horn, Honey.

FRANKIE. Please blow.

HONEY [*to* JOHN HENRY, *who has taken the horn*]. Now, don't bother my horn, Butch.

JOHN HENRY. I want to toot it some.

[JOHN HENRY *takes the horn, tries to blow it, but only succeeds in slobbering in it. He holds the horn away from his mouth and sings: "Too-ty-toot, too-ty-toot."* HONEY *snatches the horn away from him and puts it on the sewing table.*]

HONEY. I told you not to touch my horn. You got it full of slopper inside and out. It's ruined! [*He loses his temper, grabs* JOHN HENRY *by the shoulders and shakes him hard.*]

BERENICE [*slapping* HONEY]. Satan! Don't you dare touch that little boy! I'm going to stomp out your brains!

HONEY. You ain't mad because John Henry is a little boy. It's because he's a white boy. John Henry knows he needs a good shake. Don't you, Butch?

BERENICE. Ornery—no good!

[HONEY *lifts* JOHN HENRY *and swings him, then reaches in his pocket and brings out some coins.*]

HONEY. John Henry, which would you rather have—the nigger money or the white money?

JOHN HENRY. I rather have the dime. [*He takes it.*] Much obliged. [*He goes out and crosses the yard to his house.*]

BERENICE. You troubled and beat down and try to take it out on a little boy. You and Frankie just alike. The club girls don't elect her and she turns on John Henry too. When folks are lonesome and left out, they turn so mean. T. T., do you wish a small little quickie before we start?

T. T. [*looking at* FRANKIE *and pointing toward her*]. Frankie ain't no tattle-tale. Is you?

[BERENICE *pours a drink for* T. T.]

FRANKIE [*disdaining his question*]. That sure is a cute suit you got on, Honey. Today I heard somebody speak of you as Lightfoot Brown. I think that's such a grand nickname. It's on account of your travelling —to Harlem, and all the different places where you have run away, and your dancing. Lightfoot! I wish somebody would call me Lightfoot Addams.

BERENICE. It would suit me better if Honey Camden had brick feets. As it is, he keeps me so anxious-worried. C'mon, Honey and T. T. Let's go!

[HONEY *and* T. T. *go out.*]

FRANKIE. I'll go out into the yard.

[FRANKIE, *feeling excluded, goes out into the yard. Throughout the act the light in the yard has been darkening steadily. Now the light in the kitchen is throwing a yellow rectangle in the yard.*]

BERENICE. Now, Frankie, you forget all that foolishness we were discussing. And if Mr. Addams don't come home by good dark, you go over to the Wests'. Go play with John Henry.

HONEY *and* T. T. [*from outside*]. So long!

FRANKIE. So long, you all. Since when have I been scared of the dark? I'll invite John Henry to spend the night with me.

BERENICE. I thought you were sick and tired of him.

FRANKIE. I am.

BERENICE [*kissing* FRANKIE]. Good night, Sugar!

FRANKIE. Seems like everybody goes off and leaves me. [*She walks toward the Wests' yard, calling, with cupped hands.*] John Henry. John Henry.

JOHN HENRY'S VOICE. What do you want, Frankie?

FRANKIE. Come over and spend the night with me.

JOHN HENRY'S VOICE. I can't.

FRANKIE. Why?

JOHN HENRY. Just because.

FRANKIE. Because why? [JOHN HENRY *does not answer.*] I thought maybe me and you could put up my Indian tepee and sleep out here in the yard. And have a good time. [*There is still no answer.*] Sure enough. Why don't you stay and spend the night?

JOHN HENRY [*quite loudly*]. Because, Frankie. I don't want to.

FRANKIE [*angrily*]. Fool Jackass! Suit yourself! I only asked you because you looked so ugly and so lonesome.

JOHN HENRY [*skipping toward the arbor*]. Why, I'm not a bit lonesome.

FRANKIE [*looking at the house*]. I wonder when that Papa of mine is coming home. He always comes home by dark. I don't want to go into that empty, ugly house all by myself.

JOHN HENRY. Me neither.

FRANKIE [*standing with outstretched arms, and looking around her*]. I think something is wrong. It is too quiet. I have a peculiar warning in my bones. I bet you a hundred dollars it's going to storm.

JOHN HENRY. I don't want to spend the night with you.

FRANKIE. A terrible, terrible dog-day storm. Or maybe even a cyclone.

JOHN HENRY. Huh.

FRANKIE. •I bet Jarvis and Janice are now at Winter Hill. I see them just plain as I see you. Plainer. Something is wrong. It is too quiet.

[*A clear horn begins to play a blues tune in the distance.*]

JOHN HENRY. Frankie?

FRANKIE. Hush! It sounds like Honey.

[*The horn music becomes jazzy and spangling, then the first blues tune is repeated. Suddenly, while still unfinished, the music stops.* FRANKIE *waits tensely.*]

FRANKIE. He has stopped to bang the spit out of his horn. In a second he will finish. [*After a wait.*] Please, Honey, go on finish!

JOHN HENRY [*softly*]. He done quit now.

FRANKIE [*moving restlessly*]. I told Berenice that I was leavin' town for good and she did not believe me. Sometimes I honestly think she is the biggest fool that ever drew breath. You try to impress something on a big fool like that, and it's just like talking to a block of cement. I kept on telling and telling and telling her. I told her I had to leave this town for good because it is inevitable. Inevitable.

[MR. ADDAMS *enters the kitchen from the house, calling: "Frankie, Frankie."*]

MR. ADDAMS [*calling from the kitchen door*]. Frankie, Frankie.

FRANKIE. Yes, Papa.

MR. ADDAMS [*opening the back door*]. You had supper?

FRANKIE. I'm not hungry.

MR. ADDAMS. Was a little later than I intended, fixing a timepiece for a railroad man. [*He goes back through the kitchen and into the hall, calling: "Don't leave the yard!"*]

JOHN HENRY. You want me to get the weekend bag?

FRANKIE. Don't bother me, John Henry. I'm thinking.

JOHN HENRY. What you thinking about?

FRANKIE. About the wedding. About my brother and the bride. Everything's been so sudden today. I never believed before about the fact that the earth turns at the rate of about a thousand miles a day. I didn't understand why it was that if you jumped up in the air you wouldn't land in Selma or Fairview or somewhere else instead of the same back yard. But now it seems to me I feel the world going around very fast. [FRANKIE *begins turning around in circles with arms outstretched.* JOHN HENRY *copies her. They both turn.*] I feel it turning and it makes me dizzy.

JOHN HENRY. I'll stay and spend the night with you.

FRANKIE [*suddenly stopping her turning*]. No. I just now thought of something.

JOHN HENRY. You just a little while ago was begging me.

FRANKIE. I know where I'm going.

[*There are sounds of* CHILDREN *playing in the distance.*]

JOHN HENRY. Let's go play with the children, Frankie.

FRANKIE. I tell you I know where I'm going. It's like I've known it all my life. Tomorrow I will tell everybody.

JOHN HENRY. Where?

FRANKIE [*dreamily*]. After the wedding I'm going with them to Winter Hill. I'm going off with them after the wedding.

JOHN HENRY. You serious?

FRANKIE. Shush, just now I realized something. The trouble with me is that for a long time I have been just an "I" person. All other people can say "we." When Berenice says "we" she means her lodge and church and colored people. Soldiers can say "we" and mean the army. All people belong to a "we" except me.

JOHN HENRY. What are we going to do?

FRANKIE. Not to belong to a "we" makes you too lonesome. Until this afternoon I didn't have a "we," but now after seeing Janice and Jarvis I suddenly realize something.

JOHN HENRY. What?

FRANKIE. I know that the bride and my brother are the "we" of me. So I'm going with them, and joining with the wedding. This coming Sunday when my brother and the bride leave this town, I'm going with the two of them to Winter Hill. And after that to whatever place that they will ever go. [*There is a pause.*] I love the two of them so much and we belong to be together. I love the two of them so much because they are the *we* of me.

THE CURTAIN FALLS.

Act two

The scene is the same: the kitchen of the Addams home. BERENICE *is cooking.* JOHN HENRY *sits on the stool, blowing soap bubbles with a spool. It is the afternoon of the next day.*

[*The front door slams and* FRANKIE *enters from the hall.*]

BERENICE. I been phoning all over town trying to locate you. Where on earth have you been?

FRANKIE. Everywhere. All over town.

BERENICE. I been so worried I got a good mind to be seriously mad with you. Your Papa came home to dinner today. He was mad when you didn't show up. He's taking a nap now in his room.

FRANKIE. I walked up and down Main Street and stopped in almost every store. Bought my wedding dress and silver shoes. Went around by the mills.

Went all over the complete town and talked to nearly everybody in it.

BERENICE. What for, pray tell me?

FRANKIE. I was telling everybody about the wedding and my plans. [*She takes off her dress and remains barefooted in her slip.*]

BERENICE. You mean just people on the street? [*She is creaming butter and sugar for cookies.*]

FRANKIE. Everybody. Storekeepers. Monkey and monkey-man. A soldier. Everybody. And you know the soldier wanted to join with me and asked me for a date this evening. I wonder what you do on dates.

BERENICE. Frankie, I honestly believe you have turned crazy on us. Walking all over town and telling total strangers this big tale. You know in your soul this mania of yours is pure foolishness.

FRANKIE. Please call me F. Jasmine. I don't wish to have to remind you any more. Everything good of mine has got to be washed and ironed so I can pack them in the suitcase. [*She brings in a suitcase and opens it.*] Everybody in town believes that I'm going. All except Papa. He's stubborn as an old mule. No use arguing with people like that.

BERENICE. Me and Mr. Addams has some sense.

FRANKIE. Papa was bent over working on a watch when I went by the store. I asked him could I buy the wedding clothes and he said charge them at MacDougal's. But he wouldn't listen to any of my plans. Just sat there with his nose to the grindstone and answered with—kind of grunts. He never listens to what I say. [*There is a pause.*] Sometimes I wonder if Papa loves me or not.

BERENICE. Course he loves you. He is just a busy widow-man—set in his ways.

FRANKIE. Now I wonder if I can find some tissue paper to line this suitcase.

BERENICE. Truly, Frankie, what makes you think they want you taggin' along with them? Two is company and three is a crowd. And that's the main thing about a wedding. Two is company and three is a crowd.

FRANKIE. You wait and see.

BERENICE. Remember back to the time of the flood. Remember Noah and the Ark.

FRANKIE. And what has that got to do with it?

BERENICE. Remember the way he admitted them creatures.

FRANKIE. Oh, shut up your big old mouth!

BERENICE. Two by two. He admitted them creatures two by two.

FRANKIE [*after a pause*]. That's all right. But you wait and see. They will take me.

BERENICE. And if they don't?

FRANKIE [*turning suddenly from washing her hands at the sink*]. If they don't, I will kill myself.

BERENICE. Kill yourself, how?

FRANKIE. I will shoot myself in the side of the head with the pistol that Papa keeps under his handkerchiefs with Mother's picture in the bureau drawer.

BERENICE. You heard what Mr. Addams said about playing with that pistol. I'll just put this cookie dough in the icebox. Set the table and your dinner is ready. Set John Henry a plate and one for me. [BERENICE *puts the dough in the icebox.* FRANKIE *hurriedly sets the table.* BERENICE *takes dishes from the stove and ties a napkin around* JOHN HENRY's *neck.*] I have heard of many a peculiar thing. I have knew men to fall in love with girls so ugly that you wonder if their eyes is straight.

JOHN HENRY. Who?

BERENICE. I have knew women to love veritable satans and thank Jesus when they put their split hooves over the threshold. I have knew boys to take it into their heads to fall in love with other boys. You know Lily Mae Jenkins?

FRANKIE. I'm not sure. I know a lot of people.

BERENICE. Well, you either know him or you don't know him. He prisses around in a girl's blouse with one arm akimbo. Now this Lily Mae Jenkins fell in love with a man named Juney Jones. A man, mind you. And Lily Mae turned into a girl. He changed his nature and his sex and turned into a girl.

FRANKIE. What?

BERENICE. He did. To all intents and purposes. [BERE-NICE *is sitting in the center chair at the table. She says grace.*] Lord, make us thankful for what we are about to receive to nourish our bodies. Amen.

FRANKIE. It's funny I can't think who you are talking about. I used to think I knew so many people.

BERENICE. Well, you don't need to know Lily Mae Jenkins. You can live without knowing him.

FRANKIE. Anyway, I don't believe you.

BERENICE. I ain't arguing with you. What was we speaking about?

FRANKIE. About peculiar things.

BERENICE. Oh, yes. As I was just now telling you I have seen many a peculiar thing in my day. But one thing I never knew and never heard tell about. No, siree. I never in all my days heard of anybody falling in love with a wedding. [*There is a pause.*] And thinking it all over I have come to a conclusion.

JOHN HENRY. How? How did that boy change into a girl? Did he kiss his elbow? [*He tries to kiss his elbow.*]

BERENICE. It was just one of them things, Candy Lamb.

Yep, I have come to the conclusion that what you
ought to be thinking about is a beau. A nice little
white boy beau.

FRANKIE. I don't want any beau. What would I do with
one? Do you mean something like a soldier who
would maybe take me to the Idle Hour?

BERENICE. Who's talking about soldiers? I'm talking
about a nice little white boy beau your own age.
How 'bout that little old Barney next door?

FRANKIE. Barney MacKean! That nasty Barney!

BERENICE. Certainly! You could make out with him until somebody better comes along. He would do.

FRANKIE. You are the biggest crazy in this town.

BERENICE. The crazy calls the sane the crazy.

[BARNEY MACKEAN, *a boy of twelve, shirtless and
wearing shorts, and* HELEN FLETCHER, *a girl of twelve
or fourteen, cross the yard from the left, go through
the arbor and out on the right.* FRANKIE *and* JOHN
HENRY *watch them from the window.*]

FRANKIE. Yonder's Barney now with Helen Fletcher.
They are going to the alley behind the Wests' garage. They do something bad back there. I don't
know what it is.

BERENICE. If you don't know what it is, how come you
know it is bad?

FRANKIE. I just know it. I think maybe they look at
each other and peepee or something. They don't let
anybody watch them.

JOHN HENRY. I watched them once.

FRANKIE. What do they do?

JOHN HENRY. I saw. They don't peepee.

FRANKIE. Then what do they do?

JOHN HENRY. I don't know what it was. But I watched
them. How many of them did you catch, Berenice?
Them beaus?

BERENICE. How many? Candy Lamb, how many hairs is

in this plait? You're talking to Miss Berenice Sadie Brown.

FRANKIE. I think you ought to quit worrying about beaus and be content with T. T. I bet you are forty years old.

BERENICE. Wise-mouth. How do you know so much? I got as much right as anybody else to continue to have a good time as long as I can. And as far as that goes, I'm not so old as some peoples would try and make me. I ain't changed life yet.

JOHN HENRY. Did they all treat you to the picture show, them beaus?

BERENICE. To the show, or one thing or another. Wipe off your mouth.

[*There is the sound of piano tuning.*]

JOHN HENRY. The piano tuning man.

BERENICE. Ye Gods, I seriously believe this will be the last straw.

JOHN HENRY. Me too.

FRANKIE. It makes me sad. And jittery too. [*She walks around the room.*] They tell me that when they want to punish the crazy people in Milledgeville, they tie them up and make them listen to piano tuning. [*She puts the empty coal scuttle on her head and walks around the table.*]

BERENICE. We could turn on the radio and drown him out.

FRANKIE. I don't want the radio on. [*She goes into the interior room and takes off her dress, speaking from inside.*] But I advise you to keep the radio on after I leave. Some day you will very likely hear us speak over the radio.

BERENICE. Speak about what, pray tell me?

FRANKIE. I don't know exactly what about. But probably some eye witness account about something. We will be asked to speak.

BERENICE. I don't follow you. What are we going to eye witness? And who will ask you to speak?

JOHN HENRY [*excitedly*]. What, Frankie? Who is speaking on the radio?

FRANKIE. When I said *we*, you thought I meant you and me and John Henry West. To speak over the world radio. I have never heard of anything so funny since I was born.

JOHN HENRY [*climbing up to kneel on the seat of the chair*]. Who? What?

FRANKIE. Ha! Ha! Ho! Ho! Ho! Ho!

[FRANKIE *goes around punching things with her fist, and shadow boxing.* BERENICE *raises her right hand for peace. Then suddenly they all stop.* FRANKIE *goes to the window, and* JOHN HENRY *hurries there also and stands on tiptoe with his hands on the sill.* BERENICE *turns her head to see what has happened. The piano is still. Three young* GIRLS *in clean dresses are passing before the arbor.* FRANKIE *watches them silently at the window.*]

JOHN HENRY [*softly*]. The club of girls.

FRANKIE. What do you son-of-a-bitches mean crossing my yard? How many times must I tell you not to set foot on my Papa's property?

BERENICE. Just ignore them and make like you don't see them pass.

FRANKIE. Don't mention those crooks to me.

[T. T. *and* HONEY *approach by way of the back yard.* HONEY *is whistling a blues tune.*]

BERENICE. Why don't you show me the new dress? I'm anxious to see what you selected. [FRANKIE *goes into the interior room.* T. T. *knocks on the door. He and* HONEY *enter.*] Why T. T., what you doing around here this time of day?

T. T. Good afternoon, Miss Berenice. I'm here on a sad mission.

BERENICE [*startled*]. What's wrong?

T. T. It's about Sis Laura Thompson. She suddenly had a stroke and died.

BERENICE. What! Why she was by here just yesterday. We just ate her peas. They in my stomach right now, and her lyin' dead on the cooling board this minute. The Lord works in strange ways.

T. T. Passed away at dawn this morning.

FRANKIE [*putting her head in the doorway*]. Who is it that's dead?

BERENICE. Sis Laura, Sugar. That old vegetable lady.

FRANKIE [*unseen, from the interior room*]. Just to think —she passed by yesterday.

T. T. Miss Berenice, I'm going around to take up a donation for the funeral. The policy people say Sis Laura's claim has lapsed.

BERENICE. Well, here's fifty cents. The poor old soul.

T. T. She was brisk as a chipmunk to the last. The Lord had appointed the time for her. I hope I go that way.

FRANKIE [*from the interior room*]. I've got something to show you all. Shut your eyes and don't open them until I tell you. [*She enters the room dressed in an orange satin evening dress with silver shoes and stockings.*] These are the wedding clothes. [BERENICE, T. T. *and* JOHN HENRY *stare.*]

JOHN HENRY. Oh, how pretty!

FRANKIE. Now tell me your honest opinion. [*There is a pause.*] What's the matter? Don't you like it, Berenice?

BERENICE. No. It don't do.

FRANKIE. What do you mean? It don't do.

BERENICE. Exactly that. It just don't do. [*She shakes her head while* FRANKIE *looks at the dress.*]

FRANKIE. But I don't see what you mean. What is wrong?

BERENICE. Well, if you don't see it I can't explain it to you. Look there at your head, to begin with. [FRANKIE *goes to the mirror.*] You had all your hair shaved off like a convict and now you tie this ribbon around this head without any hair. Just looks peculiar.

FRANKIE. But I'm going to wash and try to stretch my hair tonight.

BERENICE. Stretch your hair! How you going to stretch your hair? And look at them elbows. Here you got on a grown woman's evening dress. And that brown crust on your elbows. The two things just don't mix. [FRANKIE, *embarrassed, covers her elbows with her hands.* BERENICE *is still shaking her head.*] Take it back down to the store.

T. T. The dress is too growny looking.

FRANKIE. But I can't take it back. It's bargain basement.

BERENICE. Very well then. Come here. Let me see what I can do.

FRANKIE [*going to* BERENICE, *who works with the dress*]. I think you're just not accustomed to seeing anybody dressed up.

BERENICE. I'm not accustomed to seein' a human Christmas tree in August.

JOHN HENRY. Frankie's dress looks like a Christmas tree.

FRANKIE. Two-faced Judas! You just now said it was pretty. Old double-faced Judas! [*The sounds of piano tuning are heard again.*] Oh, that piano tuner!

BERENICE. Step back a little now.

FRANKIE [*looking in the mirror*]. Don't you honestly think it's pretty? Give me your candy opinion.

BERENICE. I never knew anybody so unreasonable! You ask me my candy opinion, I give you my candy opinion. You ask me again, and I give it to you again. But what you want is not my honest opinion, but my good opinion of something I know is wrong.

FRANKIE. I only want to look pretty.

BERENICE. Pretty is as pretty does. Ain't that right, T. T.? You will look well enough for anybody's wedding. Excepting your own.

[MR. ADDAMS *enters through the hall door.*]

MR. ADDAMS. Hello, everybody. [*To* FRANKIE.] I don't want you roaming around the streets all morning and not coming home at dinner time. Looks like I'll have to tie you up in the back yard.

FRANKIE. I had business to tend to. Papa, look!

MR. ADDAMS. What is it, Miss Picklepriss?

FRANKIE. Sometimes I think you have turned stone blind. You never even noticed my new dress.

MR. ADDAMS. I thought it was a show costume.

FRANKIE. Show costume! Papa, why is it you don't ever notice what I have on or pay any serious mind to me? You just walk around like a mule with blinders on, not seeing or caring.

MR. ADDAMS. Never mind that now. [*To* T. T. *and* HONEY.] I need some help down at my store. My porter failed me again. I wonder if you or Honey could help me next week.

T. T. I will if I can, sir, Mr. Addams. What days would be convenient for you, sir?

MR. ADDAMS. Say Wednesday afternoon.

T. T. Now, Mr. Addams, that's one afternoon I promised to work for Mr. Finny, sir. I can't promise anything, Mr. Addams. But if Mr. Finny changes his mind about needing me, I'll work for you, sir.

MR. ADDAMS. How about you, Honey?

HONEY [*shortly*]. I ain't got the time.

MR. ADDAMS. I'll be so glad when the war is over and you biggety, worthless niggers get back to work. And, furthermore, you *sir* me! Hear me!

HONEY [*reluctantly*]. Yes—sir.

MR. ADDAMS. I better go back to the store now and get my nose down to the grindstone. You stay home, Frankie. [*He goes out through the hall door.*]

JOHN HENRY. Uncle Royal called Honey a nigger. Is Honey a nigger?

BERENICE. Be quiet now, John Henry. [*To Honey.*] Honey, I got a good mind to shake you till you spit. Not saying *sir* to Mr. Addams, and acting so impudent.

HONEY. T. T. said sir enough for a whole crowd of niggers. But for folks that calls me nigger, I got a real good nigger razor. [*He takes a razor from his pocket.* FRANKIE *and* JOHN HENRY *crowd close to look. When* JOHN HENRY *touches the razor,* HONEY *says:*] Don't touch it, Butch, it's sharp. Liable to hurt yourself.

BERENICE. Put up that razor, Satan! I worry myself sick over you. You going to die before your appointed span.

JOHN HENRY. Why is Honey a nigger?

BERENICE. Jesus knows.

HONEY. I'm so tensed up. My nerves been scraped with a razor. Berenice, loan me a dollar.

BERENICE. I ain't handing you no dollar, worthless, to get high on them reefer cigarettes.

HONEY. Gimme, Berenice, I'm so tensed up and miserable. The nigger hole. I'm sick of smothering in the nigger hole. I can't stand it no more.

[*Relenting,* BERENICE *gets her pocketbook from the shelf, opens it, and takes out some change.*]

BERENICE. Here's thirty cents. You can buy two beers.

HONEY. Well, thankful for tiny, infinitesimal favors. I better be dancing off now.

T. T. Same here. I still have to make a good deal of donation visits this afternoon.

[HONEY *and* T. T. *go to the door.*]

BERENICE. So long, T. T. I'm counting on you for to-morrow and you too, Honey.

FRANKIE *and* JOHN HENRY. So long.

T. T. Good-bye, you all. Good-bye. [*He goes out, crossing the yard.*]

BERENICE. Poor ole Sis Laura. I certainly hope that when my time comes I will have kept up my policy. I dread to think the church would ever have to bury me. When I die.

JOHN HENRY. Are you going to die, Berenice?

BERENICE. Why, Candy, everybody has to die.

JOHN HENRY. Everybody? Are you going to die, Frankie?

FRANKIE. I doubt it. I honestly don't think I'll ever die.

JOHN HENRY. What is "die"?

FRANKIE. It must be terrible to be nothing but black, black, black.

BERENICE. Yes, baby.

FRANKIE. How many dead people do you know? I know six dead people in all. I'm not counting my mother. There's William Boyd who was killed in Italy. I knew him by sight and name. An' that man who climbed poles for the telephone company. An' Lou Baker. The porter at Finny's place who was murdered in the alley back of Papa's store. Somebody drew a razor on him and the alley people said that his cut throat shivered like a mouth and spoke ghost words to the sun.

JOHN HENRY. Ludie Maxwell Freeman is dead.

FRANKIE. I didn't count Ludie; it wouldn't be fair. Because he died just before I was born. [*To Berenice.*] Do you think very frequently about Ludie?

BERENICE. You know I do. I think about the five years when me and Ludie was together, and about all the bad times I seen since. Sometimes I almost wish I had never knew Ludie at all. It leaves you too lonesome afterward. When you walk home in the evening on the way from work, it makes a little lonesome quinch come in you. And you take up with too many sorry men to try to get over the feeling.

FRANKIE. But T. T. is not sorry.

BERENICE. I wasn't referring to T. T. He is a fine upstanding colored gentleman, who has walked in a state of grace all his life.

FRANKIE. When are you going to marry with him?

BERENICE. I ain't going to marry with him.

FRANKIE. But you were just now saying . . .

BERENICE. I was saying how sincerely I respect T. T. and sincerely regard T. T. [*There is a pause.*] But he don't make me shiver none.

FRANKIE. Listen, Berenice, I have something queer to tell you. It's something that happened when I was walking around town today. Now I don't exactly know how to explain what I mean.

BERENICE. What is it?

FRANKIE [*now and then pulling her bangs or lower lip*]. I was walking along and I passed two stores with a alley in between. The sun was frying hot. And just as I passed this alley, I caught a *glimpse* of something in the corner of my left eye. A dark double shape. And this glimpse brought to my mind—so sudden and clear—my brother and the bride that I just stood there and couldn't hardly bear to look and see what it was. It was like they were there in that alley, although I knew that they are in Winter Hill almost a hundred miles away. [*There is a pause.*] Then I turn slowly and look. And you know what was there? [*There is a pause.*] It was just two colored boys. That was all. But it gave me such a queer feeling.

[BERENICE *has been listening attentively. She stares at*

FRANKIE, *then draws a package of cigarettes from her bosom and lights one.*]

BERENICE. Listen at me! Can you see through these bones in my forehead? [*She points to her forehead.*] Have you, Frankie Addams, been reading my mind? [*There is a pause.*] That's the most remarkable thing I ever heard of.

FRANKIE. What I mean is that . . .

BERENICE. I know what you mean. You mean right here in the corner of your eye. [*She points to her eye.*] You suddenly catch something there. And this cold shiver run all the way down you. And you whirl around. And you stand there facing Jesus knows what. But not Ludie, not who you want. And for a minute you feel like you been dropped down a well.

FRANKIE. Yes. That is it. [FRANKIE *reaches for a cigarette and lights it, coughing a bit.*]

BERENICE. Well, that is mighty remarkable. This is a thing been happening to me all my life. Yet just now is the first time I ever heard it put into words. [*There is a pause.*] Yes, that is the way it is when you are in love. A thing known and not spoken.

FRANKIE [*patting her foot*]. Yet I always maintained I never believed in love. I didn't admit it and never put any of it in my shows.

JOHN HENRY. I never believed in love.

BERENICE. Now I will tell you something. And it is to be a warning to you. You hear me, John Henry. You hear me, Frankie.

JOHN HENRY. Yes. [*He points his forefinger.*] Frankie is smoking.

BERENICE [*squaring her shoulders*]. Now I am here to tell you I was happy. There was no human woman in all the world more happy than I was in them days. And that includes everybody. You listening to me,

John Henry? It includes all queens and millionaires and first ladies of the land. And I mean it includes people of all color. You hear me, Frankie? No human woman in all the world was happier than Berenice Sadie Brown.

FRANKIE. The five years you were married to Ludie.

BERENICE. From that autumn morning when I first meet him on the road in front of Campbell's Filling Station until the very night he died, November, the year 1933.

FRANKIE. The very year and the very month I was born.

BERENICE. The coldest November I ever seen. Every morning there was frost and puddles were crusted with ice. The sunshine was pale yellow like it is in winter time. Sounds carried far away, and I remember a hound dog that used to howl toward sundown. And everything I seen come to me as a kind of sign.

FRANKIE. I think it is a kind of sign I was born the same year and the same month he died.

BERENICE. And it was a Thursday towards six o'clock. About this time of day. Only November. I remember I went to the passage and opened the front door. Dark was coming on; the old hound was howling far away. And I go back in the room and lay down on Ludie's bed. I lay myself down over Ludie with my arms spread out and my face on his face. And I pray that the Lord would contage my strength to him. And I ask the Lord to let it be anybody, but not let it be Ludie. And I lay there and pray for a long time. Until night.

JOHN HENRY. How? [*In a higher, wailing voice.*] How, Berenice?

BERENICE. That night he died. I tell you he died. Ludie! Ludie Freeman! Ludie Maxwell Freeman died! [*She hums.*]

FRANKIE [*after a pause*]. It seems to me I feel sadder

about Ludie than any other dead person. Although I never knew him. I know I ought to cry sometimes about my mother, or anyhow Granny. But it looks like I can't. But Ludie—maybe it was because I was born so soon after Ludie died. But you were starting out to tell some kind of a warning.

BERENICE [*looking puzzled for a moment*]. Warning? Oh, yes! I was going to tell you how this thing we was talking about applies to me. [*As* BERENICE *begins to talk* FRANKIE *goes to a shelf above the refrigerator and brings back a fig bar to the table.*] It was the April of the following year that I went one Sunday to the church where the congregation was strange to me. I had my forehead down on the top of the pew in front of me, and my eyes were open—not peeping around in secret, mind you, but just open. When suddenly this shiver ran all the way through me. I had caught sight of something from the corner of my eye. And I looked slowly to the left. There on the pew, just six inches from my eyes, was this *thumb*.

FRANKIE. What thumb?

BERENICE. Now I have to tell you. There was only one small portion of Ludie Freeman which was not pretty. Every other part about him was handsome and pretty as anyone would wish. All except this right thumb. This one thumb had a mashed, chewed appearance that was not pretty. You understand?

FRANKIE. You mean you suddenly saw Ludie's thumb when you were praying?

BERENICE. I mean I seen *this* thumb. And as I knelt there just staring at this thumb, I begun to pray in earnest. I prayed out loud! Lord, manifest! Lord, manifest!

FRANKIE. And did He—manifest?

BERENICE. Manifest, my foot! [*Spitting.*] You know who that thumb belonged to?

FRANKIE. Who?

BERENICE. Why, Jamie Beale. That big old no-good Jamie Beale. It was the first time I ever laid eyes on him.

FRANKIE. Is that why you married him? Because he had a mashed thumb like Ludie's?

BERENICE. Lord only knows. I don't. I guess I felt drawn to him on account of that thumb. And then one thing led to another. First thing I know I had married him.

FRANKIE. Well, I think that was silly. To marry him just because of that thumb.

BERENICE. I'm not trying to dispute with you. I'm just telling you what actually happened. And the very same thing occurred in the case of Henry Johnson.

FRANKIE. You mean to sit there and tell me Henry Johnson had one of those mashed thumbs too?

BERENICE. No. It was not the thumb this time. It was the coat. [FRANKIE *and* JOHN HENRY *look at each other in amazement. After a pause* BERENICE *continues.*] Now when Ludie died, them policy people cheated me out of fifty dollars so I pawned everything I could lay hands on, and I sold my coat and Ludie's coat. Because I couldn't let Ludie be put away cheap.

FRANKIE. Oh! Then you mean Henry Johnson bought Ludie's coat and you married him because of it?

BERENICE. Not exactly. I was walking down the street one evening when I suddenly seen this shape appear before me. Now the shape of this boy ahead of me was so similar to Ludie through the shoulders and the back of the head that I almost dropped dead there on the sidewalk. I followed and run behind

him. It was Henry Johnson. Since he lived in the
country and didn't come into town, he had chanced
to buy Ludie's coat and from the back view it looked
like he was Ludie's ghost or Ludie's twin. But how I
married him I don't exactly know, for, to begin
with, it was clear that he did not have his share of
sense. But you let a boy hang around you and you
get fond of him. Anyway, that's how I married
Henry Johnson.

FRANKIE. He was the one went crazy on you. Had eatin'
dreams and swallowed the corner of the sheet.
[*There is a pause.*] But I don't understand the point
of what you was telling. I don't see how that about
Jamie Beale and Henry Johnson applies to me.

BERENICE. Why, it applies to everybody and it is a warning.

FRANKIE. But how?

BERENICE. Why, Frankie, don't you see what I was
doing? I loved Ludie and he was the first man I
loved. Therefore I had to go and copy myself forever afterward. What I did was to marry off little
pieces of Ludie whenever I come across them. It was
just my misfortune they all turned out to be the
wrong pieces. My intention was to repeat me and
Ludie. Now don't you see?

FRANKIE. I see what you're driving at. But I don't see
how it is a warning applied to me.

BERENICE. You don't! Then I'll tell you. [FRANKIE *does
not nod or answer. The piano tuner plays an arpeg-
gio.*] You and that wedding tomorrow. That is what
I am warning about. I can see right through them
two gray eyes of yours like they was glass. And what
I see is the saddest piece of foolishness I ever knew.

JOHN HENRY [*in a low voice*]. Gray eyes is glass.

[FRANKIE *tenses her brows and looks steadily at* BERE-
NICE.]

BERENICE. I see what you have in mind. Don't think I
don't. You see something unheard of tomorrow, and
you right in the center. You think you going to
march to the preacher right in between your brother
and the bride. You think you going to break into
that wedding, and then Jesus knows what else.

FRANKIE. No. I don't see myself walking to the preacher
with them.

BERENICE. I see through them eyes. Don't argue with
me.

JOHN HENRY [*repeating softly*]. Gray eyes is glass.

BERENICE. But what I'm warning is this. If you start
out falling in love with some unheard-of thing like
that, what is going to happen to you? If you take a
mania like this, it won't be the last time and of that
you can be sure. So what will become of you? Will
you be trying to break into weddings the rest of your
days?

FRANKIE. It makes me sick to listen to people who don't
have any sense. [*She sticks her fingers in her ears and
hums.*]

BERENICE. You just settin' yourself this fancy trap to
catch yourself in trouble. And you know it.

FRANKIE. They will take me. You wait and see.

BERENICE. Well, I been trying to reason seriously. But
I see it is no use.

FRANKIE. You are just jealous. You are just trying to
deprive me of all the pleasure of leaving town.

BERENICE. I am just trying to head this off. But I still
see it is no use.

JOHN HENRY. Gray eyes is glass.

[*The piano is played to the seventh note of the scale
and this is repeated.*]

FRANKIE [*singing*]. Do, ray, mee, fa, sol, la, tee, do. Tee.
Tee. It could drive you wild. [*She crosses to the
screen door and slams it.*] You didn't say anything

about Willis Rhodes. Did he have a mashed thumb or a coat or something? [*She returns to the table and sits down.*]

BERENICE. Lord, now that really was something.

FRANKIE. I only know he stole your furniture and was so terrible you had to call the Law on him.

BERENICE. Well, imagine this! Imagine a cold bitter January night. And me laying all by myself in the big parlor bed. Alone in the house because everybody else had gone for the Saturday night. Me, mind you, who hates to sleep in a big empty bed all by myself at any time. Past twelve o'clock on this cold, bitter January night. Can you remember winter time, John Henry? [JOHN HENRY *nods.*] Imagine! Suddenly there comes a sloughing sound and a tap, tap, tap. So Miss Me . . . [*She laughs uproariously and stops suddenly, putting her hand over her mouth.*]

FRANKIE. What? [*Leaning closer across the table and looking intently at* BERENICE.] What happened?

[BERENICE *looks from one to the other, shaking her head slowly. Then she speaks in a changed voice.*]

BERENICE. Why, I wish you would look yonder. I wish you would look. [FRANKIE *glances quickly behind her, then turns back to* BERENICE.]

FRANKIE. What? What happened?

BERENICE. Look at them two little pitchers and them four big ears. [BERENICE *gets up suddenly from the table.*] Come on, chillin, less us roll out the dough for the cookies tomorrow. [BERENICE *clears the table and begins washing dishes at the sink.*]

FRANKIE. If it's anything I mortally despise, it's a person who starts out to tell something and works up people's interest, and then stops.

BERENICE [*still laughing*]. I admit it. And I am sorry.

But it was just one of them things I suddenly realized I couldn't tell you and John Henry.

[JOHN HENRY *skips up to the sink.*]

JOHN HENRY [*singing*]. Cookies! Cookies! Cookies!

FRANKIE. You could have sent him out of the room and told me. But don't think I care a particle about what happened. I just wish Willis Rhodes had come in about that time and slit your throat. [*She goes out into the hall.*]

BERENICE [*still chuckling*]. That is a ugly way to talk. You ought to be ashamed. Here, John Henry, I'll give you a scrap of dough to make a cookie man. [BERENICE *gives* JOHN HENRY *some dough. He climbs up on a chair and begins to work with it.* FRANKIE *enters with the evening newspaper. She stands in the doorway, then puts the newspaper on the table.*]

FRANKIE. I see in the paper where we dropped a new bomb—the biggest one dropped yet. They call it a atom bomb. I intend to take two baths tonight. One long soaking bath and scrub with a brush. I'm going to try to scrape this crust off my elbows. Then let out the dirty water and take a second bath.

BERENICE. Hooray, that's a good idea. I will be glad to see you clean.

JOHN HENRY. I will take two baths.

[BERENICE *has picked up the paper and is sitting in a chair against the pale white light of the window. She holds the newspaper open before her and her head is twisted down to one side as she strains to see what is printed there.*]

FRANKIE. Why is it against the law to change your name?

BERENICE. What is that on your neck? I thought it was a head you carried on that neck. Just think. Suppose I would suddenly up and call myself Mrs. Eleanor

Roosevelt. And you would begin naming yourself Joe Louis. And John Henry here tried to pawn himself off as Henry Ford.

FRANKIE. Don't talk childish; that is not the kind of changing I mean. I mean from a name that doesn't suit you to a name you prefer. Like I changed from Frankie to F. Jasmine.

BERENICE. But it would be a confusion. Suppose we all suddenly change to entirely different names. Nobody would ever know who anybody was talking about. The whole world would go crazy.

FRANKIE. I don't see what that has to do with it.

BERENICE. Because things accumulate around your name. You have a name and one thing after another happens to you and things have accumulated around the name.

FRANKIE. But what has accumulated around my old name? [BERENICE *does not reply.*] Nothing! See! My name just didn't mean anything. Nothing ever happened to me.

BERENICE. But it will. Things will happen.

FRANKIE. What?

BERENICE. You pin me down like that and I can't tell you truthfully. If I could, I wouldn't be sitting here in this kitchen right now, but making a fine living on Wall Street as a wizard. All I can say is that things will happen. Just what, I don't know.

FRANKIE. Until yesterday, nothing ever happened to me.

[JOHN HENRY *crosses to the door and puts on* BERENICE's *hat and shoes, takes her pocketbook and walks around the table twice.*]

BERENICE. John Henry, take off my hat and my shoes and put up my pocketbook. Thank you very much. [JOHN HENRY *does so.*]

FRANKIE. Listen, Berenice. Doesn't it strike you as strange that I am I and you are you? Like when you are walking down a street and you meet somebody. And you are you. And he is him. Yet when you look at each other, the eyes make a connection. Then you go off one way. And he goes off another way. You go off into different parts of town, and maybe you never see each other again. Not in your whole life. Do you see what I mean?

BERENICE. Not exactly.

FRANKIE. That's not what I meant to say anyway. There are all these people here in town I don't even know by sight or name. And we pass alongside each other and don't have any connection. And they don't know me and I don't know them. And now I'm leaving town and there are all these people I will never know.

BERENICE. But who do you want to know?

FRANKIE. Everybody. Everybody in the world.

BERENICE. Why, I wish you would listen to that. How about people like Willis Rhodes? How about them Germans? How about them Japanese?

[FRANKIE *knocks her head against the door jamb and looks up at the ceiling.*]

FRANKIE. That's not what I mean. That's not what I'm talking about.

BERENICE. Well, what *is* you talking about?

[*A* CHILD'S *voice is heard outside, calling:* "Batter up! Batter up!"]

JOHN HENRY [*in a low voice*]. Less play out, Frankie.

FRANKIE. No. You go. [*After a pause.*] This is what I mean.

[BERENICE *waits, and when* FRANKIE *does not speak again, says:*]

BERENICE. What on earth is wrong with you?

FRANKIE [*after a long pause, then suddenly, with hysteria*]. Boyoman! Manoboy! When we leave Winter Hill we're going to more places than you ever thought about or even knew existed. Just where we will go first I don't know, and it don't matter. Because after we go to that place we're going on to another. Alaska, China, Iceland, South America. Traveling on trains. Letting her rip on motorcycles. Flying around all over the world in airplanes. Here today and gone tomorrow. All over the world. It's the damn truth. Boyoman! [*She runs around the table.*]

BERENICE. Frankie!

FRANKIE. And talking of things happening. Things will happen so fast we won't hardly have time to realize them. Captain Jarvis Addams wins highest medals and is decorated by the President. Miss F. Jasmine Addams breaks all records. Mrs. Janice Addams elected Miss United Nations in beauty contest. One thing after another happening so fast we don't hardly notice them.

BERENICE. Hold still, fool.

FRANKIE [*her excitement growing more and more intense*]. And we will meet them. Everybody. We will just walk up to people and know them right away. We will be walking down a dark road and see a lighted house and knock on the door and strangers will rush to meet us and say: "Come in! Come in!" We will know decorated aviators and New York people and movie stars. We will have thousands and thousands of friends. And we will belong to so many clubs that we can't even keep track of all of them. We will be members of the whole world. Boyoman! Manoboy!

[FRANKIE *has been running round and round the table*

in wild excitement and when she passes the next time BERENICE *catches her slip so quickly that she is caught up with a jerk.*]

BERENICE. *Is* you gone raving wild? [*She pulls* FRANKIE *closer and puts her arm around her waist.*] Sit here in my lap and rest a minute. [FRANKIE *sits in* BERENICE'S *lap.* JOHN HENRY *comes close and jealously pinches* FRANKIE.] Leave Frankie alone. She ain't bothered you.

JOHN HENRY. I'm sick.

BERENICE. Now no, you ain't. Be quiet and don't grudge your cousin a little bit love.

JOHN HENRY [*hitting* FRANKIE]. Old mean bossy Frankie.

BERENICE. What she doing so mean right now? She just laying here wore out. [*They continue sitting.* FRANKIE *is relaxed now.*]

FRANKIE. Today I went to the Blue Moon—this place that all the soldiers are so fond of and I met a soldier—a red-headed boy.

BERENICE. What is all this talk about the Blue Moon and soldiers?

FRANKIE. Berenice, you treat me like a child. When I see all these soldiers milling around town I always wonder where they came from and where they are going.

BERENICE. They were born and they going to die.

FRANKIE. There are so many things about the world I do not understand.

BERENICE. If you did understand you would be God. Didn't you know that?

FRANKIE. Maybe so. [*She stares and stretches herself on* BERENICE'S *lap, her long legs sprawled out beneath the kitchen table.*] Anyway, after the wedding I won't have to worry about things any more.

BERENICE. You don't have to now. Nobody requires you to solve the riddles of the world.

FRANKIE [*looking at newspaper*]. The paper says this new atom bomb is worth twenty thousand tons of T.N.T.

BERENICE. Twenty thousand tons? And there ain't but two tons of coal in the coal house—all that coal.

FRANKIE. The paper says the bomb is a very important science discovery.

BERENICE. The figures these days have got too high for me. Read in the paper about ten million peoples killed. I can't crowd that many people in my mind's eye.

JOHN HENRY. Berenice, is the glass eye your mind's eye?

[JOHN HENRY *has climbed up on the back rungs of* BERENICE'S *chair and has been hugging her head. He is now holding her ears.*]

BERENICE. Don't yank my head back like that, Candy. Me and Frankie ain't going to float up through the ceiling and leave you.

FRANKIE. I wonder if you have ever thought about this? Here we are—right now. This very minute. Now. But while we're talking right now, this minute is passing. And it will never come again. Never in the world. When it is gone, it is gone. No power on earth could bring it back again.

JOHN HENRY [*beginning to sing*].
>   I sing because I'm happy,
>   I sing because I'm free,
>   For His eye is on the sparrow,
>   And I know He watches me.

BERENICE [*singing*].
>   Why should I feel discouraged?
>   Why should the shadows come?

Why should my heart be lonely,
Away from heaven and home?
For Jesus is my portion,
My constant friend is He,
For His eye is on the sparrow,
And I know He watches me.
So, I sing because I'm happy.

[JOHN HENRY *and* FRANKIE *join on the last three lines.*]

I sing because I'm happy,
I sing because I'm free,
For His eye is on the sparrow,
And I know He watches . . .

BERENICE. Frankie, you got the sharpest set of human bones I ever felt.

THE CURTAIN FALLS

Act three

SCENE I

The scene is the same: the kitchen. It is the day of the wedding. When the curtain rises BERENICE, *in her apron, and* T. T. WILLIAMS *in a white coat have just finished preparations for the wedding refreshments.* BERENICE *has been watching the ceremony through the half-open door leading into the hall. There are sounds of congratulations offstage, the wedding ceremony having just finished.*

BERENICE [*to* T. T. WILLIAMS]. Can't see much from this door. But I can see Frankie. And her face is a study.

And John Henry's chewing away at the bubble gum that Jarvis bought him. Well, sounds like it's all over. They crowding in now to kiss the bride. We better take this cloth off the sandwiches. Frankie said she would help you serve.

T. T. From the way she's been acting, I don't think we can count much on her.

BERENICE. I wish Honey was here. I'm so worried about him since what you told me. It's going to storm. It's a mercy they didn't decide to have the wedding in the back yard like they first planned.

T. T. I thought I'd better not minch the matter. Honey was in a bad way when I saw him this morning.

BERENICE. Honey Camden don't have too large a share of judgment as it is, but when he gets high on them reefers, he's got no more judgment than a four-year-old child. Remember that time he swung at the police and nearly got his eyes beat out?

T. T. Not to mention six months on the road.

BERENICE. I haven't been so anxious in all my life. I've got two people scouring Sugarville to find him. [*In a fervent voice.*] God, you took Ludie but please watch over my Honey Camden. He's all the family I got.

T. T. And Frankie behaving this way about the wedding. Poor little critter.

BERENICE. And the sorry part is that she's perfectly serious about all this foolishness. [FRANKIE *enters the kitchen through the hall door.*] Is it all over?

[T. T. *crosses to the icebox with sandwiches.*]

FRANKIE. Yes. And it was such a pretty wedding I wanted to cry.

BERENICE. You told them yet?

FRANKIE. About my plans—no, I haven't yet told them.

[JOHN HENRY *comes in and goes out.*]

BERENICE. Well, you better hurry up and do it, for they going to leave the house right after the refreshments.

FRANKIE. Oh, I know it. But something just seems to happen to my throat; every time I tried to tell them, different words came out.

BERENICE. What words?

FRANKIE. I asked Janice how come she didn't marry with a veil. [*With feeling.*] Oh, I'm so embarrassed. Here I am all dressed up in this tacky evening dress. Oh, why didn't I listen to you! I'm so ashamed.

[T. T. *goes out with a platter of sandwiches.*]

BERENICE. Don't take everything so strenuous like.

FRANKIE. I'm going in there and tell them now! [*She goes.*]

JOHN HENRY [*coming out of the interior bedroom, carrying several costumes*]. Frankie sure gave me a lot of presents when she was packing the suitcase. Berenice, she gave me all the beautiful show costumes.

BERENICE. Don't set so much store by all those presents. Come tomorrow morning and she'll be demanding them back again.

JOHN HENRY. And she even gave me the shell from the Bay. [*He puts the shell to his ear and listens.*]

BERENICE. I wonder what's going on up there. [*She goes to the door and opens it and looks through.*]

T. T. [*returning to the kitchen*]. They all complimenting the wedding cake. And drinking the wine punch.

BERENICE. What's Frankie doing? When she left the kitchen a minute ago she was going to tell them. I wonder how they'll take this total surprise. I have a feeling like you get just before a big thunder storm.

[FRANKIE *enters, holding a punch cup.*]

BERENICE. You told them yet?

FRANKIE. There are all the family around and I can't seem to tell them. I wish I had written it down on the typewriter beforehand. I try to tell them and the words just—die.

BERENICE. The words just die because the very idea is so silly.

FRANKIE. I love the two of them so much. Janice put her arms around me and said she had always wanted a little sister. And she kissed me. She asked me again what grade I was in school. That's the third time she's asked me. In fact, that's the main question I've been asked at the wedding.

[JOHN HENRY *comes in, wearing a fairy costume, and goes out.* BERENICE *notices* FRANKIE'S *punch and takes it from her.*]

FRANKIE. And Jarvis was out in the street seeing about this car he borrowed for the wedding. And I followed him out and tried to tell him. But while I was trying to reach the point, he suddenly grabbed me by the elbows and lifted me up and sort of swung me. He said: "Frankie, the lankie, the alaga fankie, the tee-legged, toe-legged, bow-legged Frankie." And he gave me a dollar bill.

BERENICE. That's nice.

FRANKIE. I just don't know what to do. I have to tell them and yet I don't know how to.

BERENICE. Maybe when they're settled, they will invite you to come and visit with them.

FRANKIE. Oh no! I'm going *with* them. [FRANKIE *goes back into the house. There are louder sounds of voices from the interior.* JOHN HENRY *comes in again.*]

JOHN HENRY. The bride and the groom are leaving. Uncle Royal is taking their suitcases out to the car.

[FRANKIE *runs to the interior room and returns with her suitcase. She kisses* BERENICE.]

FRANKIE. Good-bye, Berenice. Good-bye, John Henry. [*She stands a moment and looks around the kitchen.*] Farewell, old ugly kitchen. [*She runs out.*]

[*There are sounds of good-byes as the wedding party and the family guests move out of the house to the sidewalk. The voices get fainter in the distance. Then, from the front sidewalk there is the sound of disturbance.* FRANKIE's *voice is heard, diminished by distance, although she is speaking loudly.*]

FRANKIE'S VOICE. That's what I am telling you. [*Indistinct protesting voices are heard.*]

MR. ADDAMS' VOICE [*indistinctly*]. Now be reasonable, Frankie.

FRANKIE'S VOICE [*screaming*]. I have to go. Take me! Take me!

JOHN HENRY [*entering excitedly*]. Frankie is in the wedding car and they can't get her out. [*He runs out but soon returns.*] Uncle Royal and my Daddy are having to haul and drag old Frankie. She's holding onto the steering wheel.

MR. ADDAMS' VOICE. You march right along here. What in the world has come into you? [*He comes into the kitchen with* FRANKIE *who is sobbing.*] I never heard of such an exhibition in my life. Berenice, you take charge of her.

[FRANKIE *flings herself on the kitchen chair and sobs with her head in her arms on the kitchen table.*]

JOHN HENRY. They put old Frankie out of the wedding. They hauled her out of the wedding car.

MR. ADDAMS [*clearing his throat*]. That's sufficient, John Henry. Leave Frankie alone. [*He puts a caressing hand on* FRANKIE's *head.*] What makes you want to leave your old papa like this? You've got Janice and Jarvis all upset on their wedding day.

FRANKIE. I love them so!

BERENICE [*looking down the hall*]. Here they come. Now please be reasonable, Sugar.

[*The* BRIDE *and* GROOM *come in.* FRANKIE *keeps her face buried in her arms and does not look up. The* BRIDE *wears a blue suit with a white flower corsage pinned at the shoulder.*]

JARVIS. Frankie, we came to tell you good-bye. I'm sorry you're taking it like this.

JANICE. Darling, when we are settled we want you to come for a nice visit with us. But we don't yet have any place to live. [*She goes to* FRANKIE *and caresses her head.* FRANKIE *jerks.*] Won't you tell us good-bye now?

FRANKIE [*with passion*]. *We!* When you say *we*, you only mean you and Jarvis. And I am not included. [*She buries her head in her arms again and sobs.*]

JANICE. Please, darling, don't make us unhappy on our wedding day. You know we love you.

FRANKIE. See! *We*—when you say we, I am not included. It's not fair.

JANICE. When you come visit us you must write beautiful plays, and we'll all act in them. Come, Frankie, don't hide your sweet face from us. Sit up. [FRANKIE *raises her head slowly and stares with a look of wonder and misery.*] Good-bye, Frankie, darling.

JARVIS. So long, now, kiddo.

[*They go out and* FRANKIE *still stares at them as they go down the hall. She rises, crosses towards the door and falls on her knees.*]

FRANKIE. Take me! Take me!

[BERENICE *puts* FRANKIE *back on her chair.*]

JOHN HENRY. They put Frankie out of the wedding. They hauled her out of the wedding car.

BERENICE. Don't tease your cousin, John Henry.

FRANKIE. It was a frame-up all around.

BERENICE. Well, don't bother no more about it. It's over now. Now cheer up.

FRANKIE. I wish the whole world would die.

BERENICE. School will begin now in only three more weeks and you'll find another bosom friend like Evelyn Owens you so wild about.

JOHN HENRY [*seated below the sewing machine*]. I'm sick, Berenice. My head hurts.

BERENICE. No you're not. Be quiet, I don't have the patience to fool with you.

FRANKIE [*hugging her hunched shoulders*]. Oh, my heart feels so cheap!

BERENICE. Soon as you get started in school and have a chance to make these here friends, I think it would be a good idea to have a party.

FRANKIE. These baby promises rasp on my nerves.

BERENICE. You could call up the society editor of the *Evening Journal* and have the party written up in the paper. And that would make the fourth time your name has been published in the paper.

FRANKIE [*with a trace of interest*]. When my bike ran into that automobile, the paper called me Fankie Addams, F-A-N-K-I-E. [*She puts her head down again.*]

JOHN HENRY. Frankie, don't cry. This evening we can put up the tepee and have a good time.

FRANKIE. Oh, hush up your mouth.

BERENICE. Listen to me. Tell me what you would like and I will try to do it if it is in my power.

FRANKIE. All I wish in the world, is for no human being ever to speak to me as long as I live.

BERENICE. Bawl, then, misery.

[MR. ADDAMS *enters the kitchen, carrying* FRANKIE'S *suitcase, which he sets in the middle of the kitchen floor. He cracks his finger joints.* FRANKIE *stares at*

*him resentfully, then fastens her gaze on the suit-
case.*]

MR. ADDAMS. Well, it looks like the show is over and
the monkey's dead.

FRANKIE. You think it's over, but it's not.

MR. ADDAMS. You want to come down and help me at
the store tomorrow? Or polish some silver with the
shammy rag? You can even play with those old watch
springs.

FRANKIE [*still looking at her suitcase*]. That's my suitcase I packed. If you think it's all over, that only
shows how little you know. [T. T. *comes in.*] If I
can't go with the bride and my brother as I was
meant to leave this town, I'm going anyway. Somehow, anyhow, I'm leaving town. [FRANKIE *raises up
in her chair.*] I can't stand this existence—this
kitchen—this town—any longer! I will hop a train
and go to New York. Or hitch rides to Hollywood,
and get a job there. If worse comes to worse, I can
act in comedies. [*She rises.*] Or I could dress up like
a boy and join the Merchant Marines and run away
to sea. Somehow, anyhow, I'm running away.

BERENICE. Now, quiet down—

FRANKIE [*grabbing the suitcase and running into the
hall*]. Please, Papa, don't try to capture me.

[*Outside the wind starts to blow.*]

JOHN HENRY [*from the doorway*]. Uncle Royal,
Frankie's got your pistol in her suitcase.

[*There is the sound of running footsteps and of the
screen door slamming.*]

BERENICE. Run, catch her.

[T. T. *and* MR. ADDAMS *rush into the hall, followed by*
JOHN HENRY.]

MR. ADDAMS' VOICE. Frankie! Frankie! Frankie!

[BERENICE *is left alone in the kitchen. Outside the wind*

*is higher and the hall door is blown shut. There is
a rumble of thunder, then a loud clap. Thunder and
flashes of lightning continue.* BERENICE *is seated in
her chair, when* JOHN HENRY *comes in.*]

JOHN HENRY. Uncle Royal is going with my Daddy,
and they are chasing her in our car. [*There is a
thunder clap.*] The thunder scares me, Berenice.

BERENICE [*taking him in her lap*]. Ain't nothing going
to hurt you.

JOHN HENRY. You think they're going to catch her?

BERENICE [*putting her hand to her head*]. Certainly.
They'll be bringing her home directly. I've got such
a headache. Maybe my eye socket and all these troubles.

JOHN HENRY [*with his arms around* BERENICE]. I've got
a headache, too. I'm sick, Berenice.

BERENICE. No, you ain't. Run along, Candy. I ain't got
the patience to fool with you now.

[*Suddenly the lights go out in the kitchen, plunging
it in gloom. The sound of wind and storm continues
and the yard is a dark storm-green.*]

JOHN HENRY. Berenice!

BERENICE. Ain't nothing. Just the lights went out.

JOHN HENRY. I'm scared.

BERENICE. Stand still, I'll just light a candle. [*Muttering.*] I always keep one around, for such like emer-
gencies. [*She opens a drawer.*]

JOHN HENRY. What makes the lights go out so scarey
like this?

BERENICE. Just one of them things, Candy.

JOHN HENRY. I'm scared. Where's Honey?

BERENICE. Jesus knows. I'm scared, too. With Honey
snow-crazy and loose like this—and Frankie run off
with a suitcase and her Papa's pistol. I feel like every
nerve had been picked out of me.

JOHN HENRY [*holding out his seashell and stroking* BERENICE]. You want to listen to the ocean?

THE CURTAIN FALLS

SCENE II

The scene is the same. There are still signs in the kitchen of the wedding: punch glasses and the punch bowl on the drainboard. It is four o'clock in the morning. As the curtain rises, BERENICE *and* MR. ADDAMS *are alone in the kitchen. There is a crepuscular glow in the yard.*

MR. ADDAMS. I never was a believer in corporal punishment. Never spanked Frankie in my life, but when I lay my hands on her . . .

BERENICE. She'll show up soon—but I know how you feel. What with worrying about Honey Camden, John Henry's sickness and Frankie, I've never lived through such a anxious night. [*She looks through the window. It is dawning now.*]

MR. ADDAMS. I'd better go and find out the last news of John Henry, poor baby. [*He goes through the hall door.*]

[FRANKIE *comes into the yard and crosses to the arbor. She looks exhausted and almost beaten.* BERENICE *has seen her from the window, rushes into the yard and grabs her by the shoulders and shakes her.*]

BERENICE. Frankie Addams, you ought to be skinned alive. I been worried.

FRANKIE. I've been so worried too.

BERENICE. Where have you been this night? Tell me everything.

FRANKIE. I will, but quit shaking me.

BERENICE. Now tell me the A and the Z of this.

FRANKIE. When I was running around the dark scarey streets, I begun to realize that my plans for Hollywood and the Merchant Marines were child plans that would not work. I hid in the alley behind Papa's store, and it was dark and I was scared. I opened the suitcase and took out Papa's pistol. [*She sits down on her suitcase.*] I vowed I was going to shoot myself. I said I was going to count three and on three pull the trigger. I counted one—two—but I didn't count three—because at the last minute, I changed my mind.

BERENICE. You march right along with me. You going to bed.

FRANKIE. Oh, Honey Camden!

[HONEY CAMDEN BROWN, *who has been hiding behind the arbor, has suddenly appeared.*]

BERENICE. Oh, Honey, Honey. [*They embrace.*]

HONEY. Shush, don't make any noise; the law is after me.

BERENICE [*in a whisper*]. Tell me.

HONEY. Mr. Wilson wouldn't serve me so I drew a razor on him.

BERENICE. You kill him?

HONEY. Didn't have no time to find out. I been runnin' all night.

FRANKIE. Lightfoot, if you drew a razor on a white man, you'd better not let them catch you.

BERENICE. Here's six dolla's. If you can get to Fork Falls and then to Atlanta. But be careful slippin' through the white folks' section. They'll be combing the county looking for you.

HONEY [*with passion*]. Don't cry, Berenice.

BERENICE. Already I feel that rope.

HONEY. Don't you dare cry. I know now all my days have been leading up to this minute. No more "boy this—boy that"—no bowing, no scraping. For the first time, I'm free and it makes me happy. [*He begins to laugh hysterically.*]

BERENICE. When they catch you, they'll string you up.

HONEY [*beside himself, brutally*]. Let them hang me— I don't care. I tell you I'm glad. I tell you I'm happy. [*He goes out behind the arbor.*]

FRANKIE [*calling after him*]. Honey, remember you are Lightfoot. Nothing can stop you if you want to run away.

[MRS. WEST, *John Henry's mother, comes into the yard.*]

MRS. WEST. What was all that racket? John Henry is critically ill. He's got to have perfect quiet.

FRANKIE. John Henry's sick, Aunt Pet?

MRS. WEST. The doctors say he has meningitis. He must have perfect quiet.

BERENICE. I haven't had time to tell you yet. John Henry took sick sudden last night. Yesterday afternoon when I complained of my head, he said he had a headache too and thinking he copies me I said, "Run along, I don't have the patience to fool with you." Looks like a judgment on me. There won't be no more noise, Mrs. West.

MRS. WEST. Make sure of that. [*She goes away.*]

FRANKIE [*putting her arm around* BERENICE]. Oh, Berenice, what can we do?

BERENICE [*stroking* FRANKIE's *head*]. Ain't nothing we can do but wait.

FRANKIE. The wedding—Honey—John Henry—so much has happened that my brain can't hardly gather it in. Now for the first time I realize that the world is certainly—a sudden place.

BERENICE. Sometimes sudden, but when you are waiting, like this, it seems so slow.

THE CURTAIN FALLS

SCENE III

The scene is the same: the kitchen and arbor. It is months later, a November day, about sunset.

The arbor is brittle and withered. The elm tree is bare except for a few ragged leaves. The yard is tidy and the lemonade stand and sheet stage curtain are now missing. The kitchen is neat and bare and the furniture has been removed. BERENICE, *wearing a fox fur, is sitting in a chair with an old suitcase and doll at her feet.* FRANKIE *enters.*

FRANKIE. Oh, I am just mad about these Old Masters.

BERENICE. Humph!

FRANKIE. The house seems so hollow. Now that the furniture is packed. It gives me a creepy feeling in the front. That's why I came back here.

BERENICE. Is that the only reason why you came back here?

FRANKIE. Oh, Berenice, you know. I wish you hadn't given quit notice just because Papa and I are moving into a new house with Uncle Eustace and Aunt Pet out in Limewood.

BERENICE. I respect and admire Mrs. West but I'd never get used to working for her.

FRANKIE. Mary is just beginning this Rachmaninoff Concerto. She may play it for her debut when she is eighteen years old. Mary playing the piano and

the whole orchestra playing at one and the same
time, mind you. Awfully hard.

BERENICE. Ma-ry Littlejohn.

FRANKIE. I don't know why you always have to speak
her name in a tinged voice like that.

BERENICE. Have I ever said anything against her? All
I said was that she is too lumpy and marshmallow
white and it makes me nervous to see her just setting
there sucking them pigtails.

FRANKIE. Braids. Furthermore, it is no use our discussing a certain party. You could never possibly understand it. It's just not in you.

[BERENICE *looks at her sadly, with faded stillness, then
pats and strokes the fox fur.*]

BERENICE. Be that as it may. Less us not fuss and quarrel this last afternoon.

FRANKIE. I don't want to fuss either. Anyway, this is not
our last afternoon. I will come and see you often.

BERENICE. No, you won't, baby. You'll have other things
to do. Your road is already strange to me.

[FRANKIE *goes to* BERENICE, *pats her on the shoulder,
then takes her fox fur and examines it.*]

FRANKIE. You still have the fox fur that Ludie gave
you. Somehow this little fur looks so sad—so thin
and with a sad little fox-wise face.

BERENICE [*taking the fur back and continuing to stroke
it*]. Got every reason to be sad. With what has happened in these two last months. I just don't know
what I have done to deserve it. [*She sits, the fur
in her lap, bent over with her forearms on her knees
and her hands limply dangling.*] Honey gone and
John Henry, my little boy gone.

FRANKIE. You did all you could. You got poor Honey's
body and gave him a Christian funeral and nursed
John Henry.

BERENICE. It's the way Honey died and the fact that John Henry had to suffer so. Little soul!

FRANKIE. It's peculiar—the way it all happened so fast. First Honey caught and hanging himself in the jail. Then later in that same week, John Henry died and then I met Mary. As the irony of fate would have it, we first got to know each other in front of the lipstick and cosmetics counter at Woolworth's. And it was the week of the fair.

BERENICE. The most beautiful September I ever seen. Countless white and yellow butterflies flying around them autumn flowers—Honey dead and John Henry suffering like he did and daisies, golden weather, butterflies—such strange death weather.

FRANKIE. I never believed John Henry would die. [*There is a long pause. She looks out the window.*] Don't it seem quiet to you in here? [*There is another, longer pause.*] When I was a little child I believed that out under the arbor at night there would come three ghosts and one of the ghosts wore a silver ring. [*Whispering.*] Occasionally when it gets so quiet like this I have a strange feeling. It's like John Henry is hovering somewhere in this kitchen —solemn looking and ghost-gray.

A BOY'S VOICE [*from the neighboring yard*]. Frankie, Frankie.

FRANKIE [*calling to the* BOY]. Yes, Barney. [*To* BERENICE.] Clock stopped. [*She shakes the clock.*]

THE BOY'S VOICE. Is Mary there?

FRANKIE [*to* BERENICE]. It's Barney MacKean. [*To the* BOY, *in a sweet voice.*] Not yet. I'm meeting her at five. Come on in, Barney, won't you?

BARNEY. Just a minute.

FRANKIE [*to* BERENICE]. Barney puts me in mind of a Greek god.

BERENICE. What? Barney puts you in mind of a what?

FRANKIE. Of a Greek god. Mary remarked that Barney reminded her of a Greek god.

BERENICE. It looks like I can't understand a thing you say no more.

FRANKIE. You know, those old-timey Greeks worship those Greek gods.

BERENICE. But what has that got to do with Barney MacKean?

FRANKIE. On account of the figure.

[BARNEY MACKEAN, *a boy of thirteen, wearing a foot-ball suit, bright sweater and cleated shoes, runs up the back steps into the kitchen.*]

BERENICE. Hi, Greek god Barney. This afternoon I saw your initials chalked down on the front side-walk. M.L. loves B.M.

BARNEY. If I could find out who wrote it, I would rub it out with their faces. Did you do it, Frankie?

FRANKIE [*drawing herself up with sudden dignity*]. I wouldn't do a kid thing like that. I even resent you asking me. [*She repeats the phrase to herself in a pleased undertone.*] Resent you asking me.

BARNEY. Mary can't stand me anyhow.

FRANKIE. Yes she can stand you. I am her most intimate friend. I ought to know. As a matter of fact she's told me several lovely compliments about you. Mary and I are riding on the moving van to our new house. Would you like to go?

BARNEY. Sure.

FRANKIE. O.K. You will have to ride back with the furniture 'cause Mary and I are riding on the front seat with the driver. We had a letter from Jarvis and Janice this afternoon. Jarvis is with the Occupation Forces in Germany and they took a vacation trip to Luxembourg. [*She repeats in a pleased voice.*]

Luxembourg. Berenice, don't you think that's a lovely name?

BERENICE. It's kind of a pretty name, but it reminds me of soapy water.

FRANKIE. Mary and I will most likely pass through Luxembourg when we—are going around the world together.

[FRANKIE *goes out followed by* BARNEY *and* BERENICE *sits in the kitchen alone and motionless. She picks up the doll, looks at it and hums the first two lines of "I Sing Because I'm Happy." In the next house the piano is heard again, as the curtain falls.*]